LangChain in Action

Architecting multi-modal and context-aware agents

Deepak Kamboj

www.bpbonline.com

First Edition 2026

ISBN: 978-93-78544-200

LIMITS OF LIABILITY AND DISCLAIMER OF WARRANTY

To View Complete
BPB Publications Catalogue
Scan the QR Code:

www.bpbonline.com

Dedicated to

My beloved father,

Shri Nanak Chand Kamboj

You always believed that knowledge is the greatest gift one can leave behind for the world.

This book is my humble attempt to honour that belief.

About the Author

Deepak Kamboj is a senior software engineer and AI solution architect at Microsoft with over 25 years of experience in enterprise software, AI-powered automation, and developer productivity. He specializes in agentic workflows, **Model Context Protocol** (**MCP**) servers, multi-agent systems, and generative AI applications, delivering measurable organizational value.

At Microsoft, Deepak has helped multiple teams adopt modern Playwright-based test automation and has built AI-driven test generation and self-healing pipelines to improve engineering efficiency. He is a Copilot Champion, a Microsoft Hackathon participant and advisor, and a recognized accessibility champion.

Deepak holds a B.Tech. in computer science and engineering and is an active voice in the developer community through his LinkedIn newsletter AI Weekly, his GitHub projects, and speaking engagements focused on practical AI, automation at scale, and developer experience.

About the Reviewers

- **Krishnamoorthy Ramanath** is an agent engineering lead and data scientist at Gap Inc., specializing in the design and development of production-grade autonomous systems. With deep expertise across the machine learning lifecycle, he leverages modern AI frameworks to drive enterprise innovation and build scalable agents tailored to complex business needs.

  He brings extensive practical experience in predictive modeling, statistical analysis, and large-scale data architecture to deliver high-impact solutions.

  An alumnus of the **National Institute of Technology Karnataka** (**NITK**) Surathkal and the University of Minnesota's Carlson School of Management, Krishnamoorthy draws on his comprehensive background in both foundational machine learning and advanced agentic orchestration in his role as a technical reviewer for *LangChain in Action*.

- **Sachin Pawar** is an applied AI engineer and database specialist who builds production **retrieval-augmented generation** (**RAG**) applications using LangChain, Google ADK, and Anthropic APIs. With approximately 18 years of experience across Oracle, PostgreSQL, AlloyDB, and Spanner, he treats retrieval quality, vector index performance, and data freshness as first-class engineering problems rather than afterthoughts in LLM systems.

  Sachin has presented at Google Cloud Next and built database assessment and migration tooling adopted across enterprise engagements involving tens of thousands of databases. He writes and speaks on the intersection of databases and applied AI, and mentors engineers transitioning from traditional data infrastructure into LLM-powered systems.

  Sachin is particularly interested in evaluation frameworks, agentic workflows, and the production engineering practices that separate prototypes from reliable AI products. He believes the hardest problems in applied AI are usually data problems in disguise, and works at the intersection of these two worlds.

- **Anusha Dasarakothapalli** is a principal software engineer at Amazon, in the Applied AI services organization, specializing in distributed systems, large-scale data and streaming platforms, and AI-driven software infrastructure. She has over 10 years of experience designing and operating mission-critical cloud services and developer platforms used at a global scale. Her work focuses on building reliable, high-performance systems for data streaming, storage, and intelligent software development workflows. Throughout her career, Anusha has contributed to systems spanning real-time streaming platforms, large-scale storage services such as Amazon S3, Amazon S3 Glacier, Amazon Managed Streaming for Apache Kafka (MSK), and observability frameworks for modern AI-enabled software development. Her work currently focuses on developing next-generation agentic solutions for software development teams powered by artificial intelligence.

In addition to her engineering work, Anusha actively contributes to the broader technology community by participating in technical reviews, evaluating innovative research and engineering work, and supporting the advancement of emerging technologies in distributed systems and AI-driven software development.

Acknowledgement

There are a few people I want to thank for the continued and ongoing support they have given me during the writing of this book.

I would like to thank BPB Publications for their patience, guidance, and for giving this project the space it needed to become something I am truly proud of. It has been a pleasure to work with the BPB team from start to finish.

Thank you to the technical reviewers Krishnamoorthy Ramanath, Anusha Dasarakothapalli and Sachin Pawar for your detailed feedback to make this a much better book. You saw things I had stopped seeing, asked the right questions, and pushed the technical depth where it needed to go. Thanks for the time and care you took with each chapter.

I would like to thank Diya Kamboj for reviewing chapters and assisting with the diagrams throughout the book. Without your input I would not have been able to get the visuals as clear.

To my colleagues at Microsoft, and the broader LangChain and LangGraph open-source communities: the ideas in this book are based on real work, real conversations, and real problems. Thanks for the inspiration.

Books are written in the margins of everyday life, and this one was no different. The hours spent researching, coding, and writing were made possible by the patience and love of my family. Huge thanks to my wife Simmi and my children Diya and Uday for giving me the space to pursue this project and for reminding me, every day, what truly matters. This book belongs to you as much as it does to me.

I hope it helps you build something remarkable.

Preface

Artificial intelligence is no longer limited to text-based conversations or static workflows. Today's intelligent agents are expected to see, hear, speak, and feel; interpreting the world through multiple modalities while maintaining context and human sensitivity. LangChain in Action is written to help engineers and architects build systems that think, adapt, and respond naturally.

This book explores the architecture, design patterns, and implementation strategies that make multimodal intelligence practical. It connects research and real-world deployment, spanning the modern AI agent stack from contextual memory and embeddings to tool orchestration, emotional grounding, and multi-sensor reasoning. Through examples in telemedicine, emergency response, and customer engagement, it highlights both the technical depth and the responsibility involved in building context-aware AI.

Whether you are designing adaptive copilots, intelligent workflows, or large-scale agent systems, this book aims to provide the conceptual clarity and engineering discipline needed to build effective multimodal AI solutions.

The twelve chapters in this book move from fundamentals to production-grade architecture, with each chapter building on what came before:

Chapter 1: Building Your First LangChain Agent — This chapter sets up the mental model. You will learn how LangChain thinks about agents, tools, chains, and models, and why that structure matters.

Chapter 2: Designing Modular and Reusable LangChain Workflows — This chapter is about building things that last. Runnables, prompt templates, and compositional patterns keep your codebase from becoming a mess as requirements grow.

Chapter 3: LLM Reasoning and Agent Intelligence — This chapter covers how to choose the right model for the job, write prompts that work reliably, produce structured output, and keep costs under control.

Chapter 4: Building Multimodal LangChain Pipelines — This chapter is where images and audio enter the picture. You will build pipelines that treat multiple modalities as first-class inputs rather than afterthoughts.

Chapter 5: Building Vision-enabled Agents with Visual Intelligence — This chapter goes deeper into visual reasoning. GPT-4o, CLIP, OCR, and video keyframe extraction all make an appearance, grounded in a weather-themed use case that runs throughout the chapter.

Chapter 6: Building Conversational Agents with Voice Intelligence — This chapter adds a voice layer. Whisper and Azure Speech handle transcription, TTS gives your agent a voice, and by the end of the chapter you will have a working telemedicine assistant.

Chapter 7: Developing Context-aware Agents with Persistent Memory — This chapter tackles one of the harder problems in agent design: making your agent remember things. Short-term, long-term, and episodic memory patterns are all covered.

Chapter 8: Designing Emotion-aware Agents — Aware agents shows how to read emotional signals in text and audio, and how to use that information to make interactions feel more human and less robotic.

Chapter 9: Building Retrieval-enhanced Agents — This chapter covers RAG in depth, including vector stores, hybrid search, and the patterns that separate retrieval that works from retrieval that just looks like it works.

Chapter 10: Fusing Knowledge Networks for Advanced Reasoning — This chapter brings knowledge graphs into the mix and shows how combining them with LLM reasoning unlocks multi-hop inference that pure vector search cannot do.

Chapter 11: Creating Autonomous Agents that Perform Real-world Tasks — This chapter is where agents stop answering questions and start doing things. Tools, planning loops, and error recovery are the focus.

Chapter 12: Planning, Collaboration, and Evaluating Autonomous Agents — This chapter wraps up with multi-agent orchestration, LangGraph-based planning, and the evaluation frameworks you need before any of this goes to production.

Each chapter stands on its own and includes complete, runnable code. A consistent set of use cases runs throughout the book, including weather monitoring, telemedicine, and emergency response, so the examples feel connected rather than arbitrary.

You can read straight through or jump to the chapters most relevant to what you are building. *Chapter 4* is a natural starting point before *Chapters 5* and *6*. *Chapter 9* is easier to follow if you have read *Chapter 3* first. Everything else is largely independent.

Code Bundle and Coloured Images

Please follow the link to download the
Code Bundle and the ***Coloured Images*** of the book:

https://rebrand.ly/ju2x05g

The code bundle for the book is also hosted on GitHub at
https://github.com/bpbpublications/LangChain-in-Action.
In case there's an update to the code, it will be updated on the existing GitHub repository.

We have code bundles from our rich catalogue of books and videos available at https://github.com/bpbpublications. Check them out!

Errata

We take immense pride in our work at BPB Publications and follow best practices to ensure the accuracy of our content to provide an indulging reading experience to our subscribers. Our readers are our mirrors, and we use their inputs to reflect and improve upon human errors, if any, that may have occurred during the publishing processes involved. To let us maintain the quality and help us reach out to any readers who might be having difficulties due to any unforeseen errors, please write to us at: errata@bpbonline.com

Your support, suggestions and feedback are highly appreciated by the BPB Publications' Family.

Piracy

If you come across any illegal copies of our works in any form on the internet, we would be grateful if you would provide us with the location address or website name. Please contact us at business@bpbonline.com with a link to the material.

If you are interested in becoming an author

If there is a topic that you have expertise in, and you are interested in either writing or contributing to a book, please visit www.bpbonline.com. We have worked with thousands of developers and tech professionals, just like you, to help them share their insights with the global tech community. You can make a general application, apply for a specific hot topic that we are recruiting an author for, or submit your own idea.

Reviews

Please leave a review. Once you have read and used this book, why not leave a review on the site that you purchased it from? Potential readers can then see and use your unbiased opinion to make purchase decisions. We at BPB can understand what you think about our products, and our authors can see your feedback on their book. Thank you!

For more information about BPB, please visit www.bpbonline.com.

Join our Discord space

Join our Discord workspace for latest updates, offers, tech happenings around the world, new releases, and sessions with the authors:

https://discord.bpbonline.com

Table of Contents

Chapter 1
Building Your First LangChain Agent

Introduction

Every AI innovation begins with a simple question: *Can we design software that does not just execute commands but also makes intelligent decisions on its own?* In 2023, a Fortune 500 customer support team faced a serious challenge where their typical chatbot could answer only 40% of client queries, requiring human agents to deal with hundreds of repetitive questions every day. However, within three months of installing a LangChain-powered agent, that number went to 85%, saving the organization over ten thousand support hours monthly. This is not science fiction; this is the practical power of intelligent agents constructed with LangChain.

The change from traditional rule-based systems to autonomous **artificial intelligence** (**AI**) agents constitutes a significant transformation in software engineering. Traditional programs follow tight if-then logic, such as if a user asks about shipping, return the shipping policy. If they ask about returns, show the return form, but what happens when a consumer asks, *I ordered a blue jacket last week, but it has not arrived, and I need it for a wedding on Saturday - can you help?* Traditional systems break down, lacking the context, reasoning capacity, and tool access needed to handle real-world complexity.

LangChain agents completely changed the game. LangChain provides developers with a flexible, modular framework for building intelligent applications that are driven by **large language models** (**LLMs**). Unlike rigid chatbots that follow predetermined paths, agents are autonomous software entities that make decisions, employ tools dynamically, and reason through multi-step problems, all while maintaining the context and learnings from their interactions.

The results speak for themselves. A financial services organization deployed a LangChain agent that was able to cut down compliance document reviews from 6 hours to just 15 minutes. A healthcare business designed an assistant that sorts through patient questions, directs urgent cases to doctors, and answers routine health questions 24/7 with 98% accuracy. An e-commerce company created an agent that not only answers product questions but also proactively recommends things based on your browsing history, checks inventories across warehouses, and even negotiates bulk discounts, leading to a 34% rise in average order value.

These are not isolated examples; they signal a fundamental shift in how we develop software. This chapter begins your adventure into this new paradigm. You will learn to construct agents that combine reasoning with tool access, memory, and structured processes. You will understand the three-pillar LangChain ecosystem, which includes the framework for designing agents, LangGraph for orchestrating workflows, and LangSmith for monitoring. Most significantly, you will construct your first working agent. By the end of this chapter, you will have a functioning agent running on your machine and the foundation to develop increasingly advanced systems.

Note that agent development differs fundamentally from traditional programming. Instead of writing explicit logic for every scenario, you define goals, provide tools, and let the agent reason about how to achieve objectives. This requires a shift from deterministic thinking to probabilistic reasoning; embrace the ambiguity, and you will unlock tremendous capabilities.

Structure

This chapter covers the following topics:

- Understanding the platform for agent engineering
- LangChain's vision and design philosophy
- Learn LangChain fundamental components
- Setup your LangChain and API environment
- Build your first QA agent with LangChain
- Configure dev tools for efficient experimentation
- Debugging and testing LangChain agents
- Testing a complete QA agent pipeline
- Building a real-world LangChain agent

Objectives

By the end of this chapter, readers will gain a comprehensive understanding of the LangChain ecosystem and learn when to use the core components, such as the LangChain framework, LangGraph, and LangSmith, for different development needs. They will explore the evolution from traditional static chatbots to fully autonomous agents and understand the concept of the *Action Gap* that LangChain is designed to bridge. Readers will also learn how to set up a complete development environment that follows best practices for **application programming interface** (**API**) key management, dependency control, and overall security. The chapter will discuss the essential building blocks of LangChain, including prompts, chains, agents, tools, and memory systems, and show how these elements work together to create powerful AI-driven workflows. In addition, readers will build a fully functioning QA agent from scratch that can reason through problems, choose tools dynamically, and complete multi-step tasks.

They will gain hands-on experience with tracing, execution logs, and observability features to debug agent behavior and understand how it makes decisions. The chapter will also introduce testing strategies such as unit tests, mocking techniques, and validation methods to ensure that agents perform reliably in production environments. Finally, readers will learn to apply the ReAct reasoning pattern, allowing agents to think, act, and observe in iterative loops in order to solve complex problems clearly and effectively.

Understanding the platform for agent engineering

Before we start building agents, let us build an understanding of LangChain and why it has become the go-to platform for agent engineering. LangChain is not just another AI library but rather a complete platform that is designed to make building production-ready AI agents as simple as possible.

LangChain is a platform for agent engineering that provides the frameworks, tools, and services needed to build, deploy, and observe AI agents that can reason, use tools, and interact with external systems.

Three-pillar LangChain ecosystem

LangChain provides a whole ecosystem for building, orchestrating, and observing AI agents in production. Think of it as three specialized tools working together, as shown in the following figure:

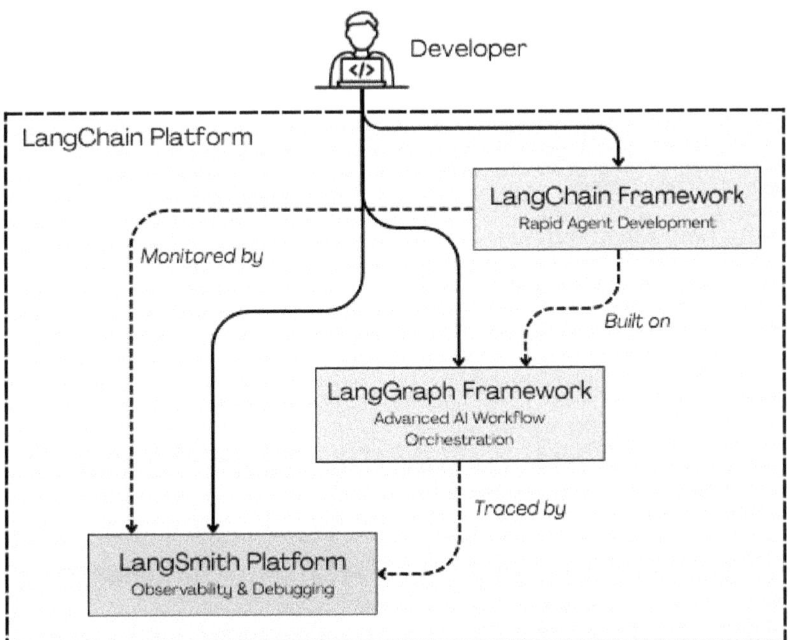

***Figure 1.1**: LangChain platform architecture with three specialized components*

Understanding each component

To make strong LangChain agents, you need to understand how each basic part of the ecosystem works. Each part, including prompts, chains, agents, tools, memory, and retrievers, has its own job and works with the others in a modular way. You can create processes that are both versatile and easy to keep up with if you know how these parts function together. This basic understanding gives you the power to make agents that can think, act, and change to handle difficult jobs. As you move on, you will discover how abstraction and composability make it easy to improve and expand your ideas for use in the real-world.

Rapid agent development with LangChain framework

Purpose: Transform an idea into a functional agent in a matter of minutes rather than days.

Your starting point for agent engineering is LangChain. It offers high-level abstractions that handle the intricacy of agent architecture, so you can focus on what your agent does instead of how it does it.

Core capabilities:

- **10-line agents**: Complete working agents with minimal code.
- **Model flexibility**: Swap seamlessly between OpenAI, Anthropic, Google, or any LLM provider.
- **Built-in patterns**: Leverage proven patterns like ReAct, Plan-Execute, etc.
- **Tool integration**: Create tools using decorator-based patterns.
- **Memory systems**: Automatic conversation tracking and context management.

When to use the LangChain framework:

- Building your first agent.
- Prototyping new ideas quickly.
- Standard conversational agents.
- Simple tool-calling workflows.
- Learning agent concepts.

LangGraph framework delivering precision control for complex workflows

Purpose: Build sophisticated, production-grade workflows with complete control over agent behavior.

LangGraph is a low-level framework for orchestrating complex agent workflows. It is built for scenarios where you need deterministic control, state management, and advanced patterns like **human-in-the-loop** (**HITL**).

Core capabilities:

- **Durable execution**: Agents pause, resume, and recover from failures.
- **State persistence**: Maintain context across long-running processes.
- **Human-in-the-loop**: Seamless human oversight and intervention.
- **Graph-based flows**: Define complex workflows as computational graphs.
- **Checkpoint systems**: Save and restore agent state at any point.

Note: **LangChain agents are built on top of LangGraph. When you use LangChain, you are already using LangGraph under the hood, but with simplified abstractions.**

When to use LangGraph:

- Multi-step workflows requiring precise control.
- Applications needing human approval steps.
- Long-running processes that must survive restarts.
- Complex branching logic and conditional flows.
- Advanced error recovery patterns.

LangSmith platform enabling production operations and observability

Purpose: Monitor, debug, evaluate, and optimize agents in production.

LangSmith provides the observability layer that helps transform experimental agents into production-ready systems. It is not about building the agents but rather about understanding, monitoring, and improving them.

Core capabilities:

- **Execution tracing**: See every step your agent takes.
- **Performance metrics**: Token usage, latency, cost tracking.
- **Error debugging**: Identify and diagnose failures quickly.
- **Quality evaluation**: Test agent performance systematically.
- **Deployment monitoring**: Track production agent behavior.

When to use LangSmith:

- Any production deployment (always use it).
- Debugging complex agent failures.
- Optimizing token usage and costs.
- Evaluating agent quality and reliability.
- Understanding agent decision-making processes.

Comparing LangChain, LangGraph and LangSmith

Each component serves a distinct purpose. Refer to the following table to build an understanding of when to use which tool, which is crucial for building effective AI agents:

Component	Best for	Code complexity	Control level	When to use
LangChain	Rapid agent development	Minimal (under 10 lines)	High-level abstractions	Quick prototypes, simple agents, getting started.
LangGraph	Complex workflows	Moderate to high	Fine-grained control	Multi-step workflows, HITL, state management.
LangSmith	Production monitoring	Configuration only	N/A (observability)	All production deployments, debugging, and evaluation.

***Table 1.1**: Comparison of LangChain ecosystem components by use case and complexity*

Note: **Start every project with LangChain. Move to LangGraph only when you need explicit control over agent execution flow, state persistence, or HITL patterns. Always use LangSmith in production.**

Purpose and solutions for agent engineering challenges

Before LangChain, building AI agents meant addressing the same infrastructure challenges repeatedly. Every project required specific solutions for model integration, agent architecture, memory management, and error handling. This caused tremendous friction and hindered progress.

The following table outlines how LangChain alters this landscape by providing standardized solutions:

Challenge	Without LangChain	With LangChain
Model integration	Custom API wrappers for each provider.	Standard interface for all models.
Agent architecture	Build reasoning loops from scratch.	Pre-built agent patterns (ReAct, Plan-Execute).
Memory management	Custom conversation tracking.	Built-in memory components.
Tool integration	Manual function calling setup.	Standardized tool interfaces.
Error handling	Custom retry and fallback logic.	Automatic error recovery.
Observability	Custom logging and monitoring.	Built-in tracing and metrics.
Deployment	Manual scaling and monitoring.	Platform-managed deployment.

***Table 1.2**: Standardized solutions for agent engineering challenges*

LangChain's advantage in composable agent engineering

LangChain's ultimate power stems from its composable architecture. Instead of constructing monolithic systems, you can construct agents from standardized components that interact with each other effortlessly. This is similar to how you might build with LEGO blocks. Each piece has a common interface, but you may combine them in endless ways to create exactly what you need.

The following figure gives a visual overview of how the LangChain framework integrates core components, such as prompt engineering, autonomous agents, tools, memory, and data connections, with advanced orchestration and observability platforms like LangGraph, LangFlow, and LangSmith. This modular design highlights how huge language models interact with multiple workflow aspects, enabling developers to build scalable, maintainable, and production-ready AI agents.

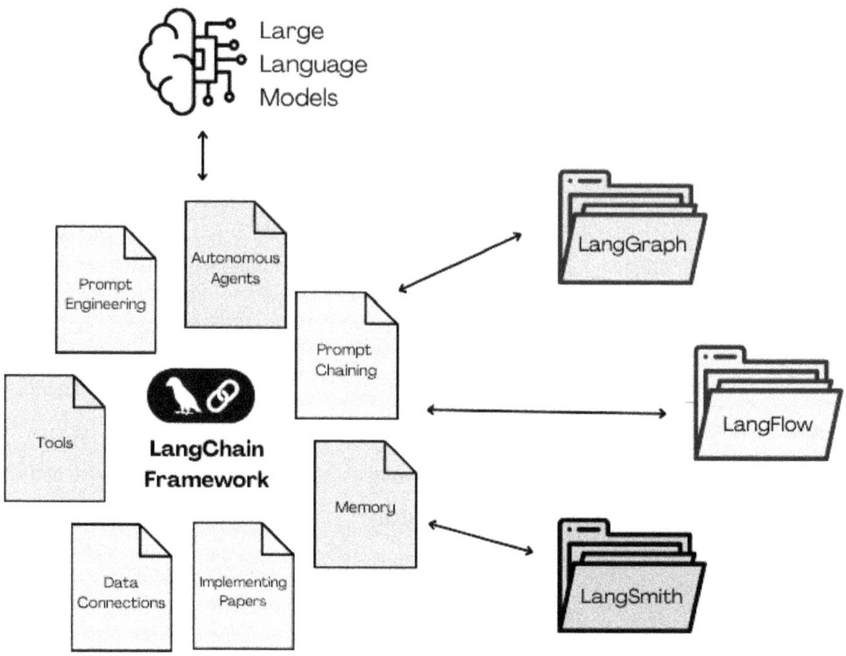

Figure 1.2: Components of the LangChain framework and its ecosystem

This composability means:

- **Reusability**: Write a tool once, utilize it across multiple agents.
- **Maintainability**: Update individual components without damaging the complete system.
- **Testability**: Test each component in isolation before integration.
- **Flexibility**: Swap components (like changing LLM providers) with minimal code changes.
- **Scalability**: Add new capabilities by adding new components, not rewriting systems.

Tip: **Start with LangChain for rapid prototyping, then use LangGraph when you need fine-grained control over agent behavior and execution flow.**

Understanding the LangChain package ecosystem

LangChain is not a single monolithic package; it is a modular ecosystem where you install only what you need. This helps keep your dependencies lightweight and your applications maintainable.

The following figure depicts the modular structure of the LangChain package ecosystem, illustrating how each core and extended package works together to allow agent creation. This visual guide helps clarify which components to install for different project needs, ensuring your process remains lightweight, maintainable, and matched to your application requirements.

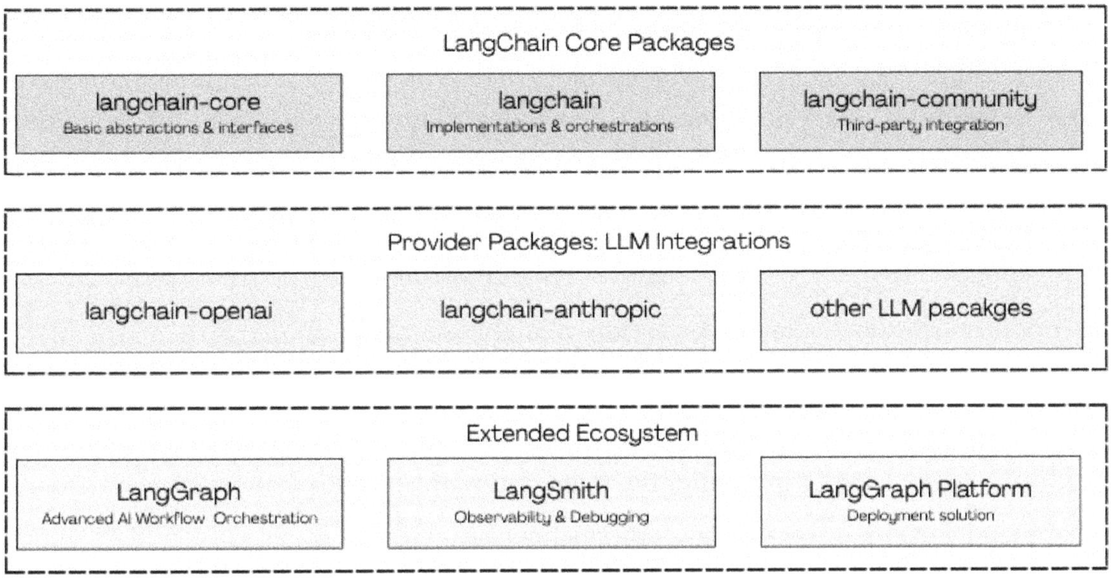

***Figure 1.3**: LangChain packages ecosystem*

The core packages are as follows:

- **langchain-core**: The foundation layer, including base classes and interfaces:
  - Automatically installed with any LangChain package.
  - Contains fundamental abstractions used across the ecosystem.
- **langchain**: The major framework package:
  - Agents, chains, memory systems, and utilities.
  - Your primary import for developing agents.
- **langchain-community**: Community-contributed integrations:
  - Tools, document loaders, vector storage.
  - Third-party service integrations.
  - Experimental features
- **Provider packages**: Separate packages for each LLM provider:
  - `langchain-openai` for OpenAI (GPT-4, GPT-3.5).
  - `langchain-anthropic` for Anthropic (Claude).
  - `langchain-google-genai` for Google (Gemini).
  - Keeps dependencies lightweight: install only what you use.

Extended packages include:

- **LangGraph**: An orchestration framework that allows you to build stateful agents and complex workflows with LLMs. It helps manage the flow of information between different components.
- **LangSmith**: A development and debugging platform that helps with monitoring, evaluating, and improving LLM applications. It provides visibility into what is happening inside your application.
- **LangGraph Platform**: A commercial deployment solution for turning LangGraph applications into production-ready APIs and assistants.

This modular structure means a typical project might only need:

```
pip install langchain langchain-openai python-dotenv
```

Note: **LangChain agents are built on top of LangGraph. When you use LangChain, you are already using LangGraph under the hood, but with simplified abstractions.**

Rather than installing dozens of unused dependencies. We will cover the complete setup in the upcoming sections.

Evolution of chatbots into intelligent agents and bridging the action gap

To understand why LangChain is revolutionary, refer to the following table to briefly trace how we arrived at modern agent engineering:

Era	Technology	Capabilities	Limitations
Rule-based (1960 to 2010)	Pattern matching, decision trees	Scripted responses	No learning, brittle
Statistical ML (2010 to 2019)	RNNs, early Transformers	Intent classification	Limited context
LLM revolution (2020 to 2023)	GPT-3/4, BERT	Natural understanding	No tool use
Agent engineering (2023 to Now)	LangChain, function calling	Tool use, planning, reasoning	Platform complexity
Production agents (Now)	LangChain Platform	Observable, scalable, reliable	Our focus in this book

***Table 1.3**: Milestones in conversational AI and agent evolution*

The following list outlines the three key shifts:

- **Rules | Learning (2010s)**: The approach to learning shifted. Systems began to learn from data, finding patterns on their own, instead of needing to have every possible situation programmed manually.
- **Narrow | General (2022)**: One LLM manages numerous tasks instead of distinct models per task.
- **Passive | Active (2023)**: Agents do real-world actions instead of only answering questions and responding.

Bridging the action gap

The change from the LLM revolution to the agent era is defined by solving what we call the action gap. Consider a typical LLM asked to do a complex, real-world task:

```
User: "Send an email to John about the project update."
LLM: "Here is a template for the email you should send: 'Dear John...'"
```

The LLM reasoned well, but the end outcome was text about the action, not the deed itself. The AI could not physically execute the command.

In contrast, an example agent constructed with LangChain:

```
User: "Send an email to John about the project update."
Agent: Calls email_tool → "Email successfully sent to John."
```

This capability, the power to reason, select a tool, execute the tool, and integrate the result, is what defines LangChain and the topic of this book.

LangChain's vision and design philosophy

LangChain's vision revolves around making intelligent agent creation accessible, scalable, and production-ready for everyone. Its design philosophy stresses modularity and composability, allowing developers to break down complex procedures into manageable, reusable components. By offering standardized interfaces for prompts, models, chains, memory, agents, and tools, LangChain enables flexibility and extensibility across developing AI systems. The framework's commitment to abstraction and composability, especially through the **LangChain Expression Language** (**LCEL**), empowers users to construct sophisticated workflows with minimal code. Ultimately, LangChain bridges the gap between prototypes and production systems, enabling developers to construct agents that reason, act, and connect with real-world data and tools efficiently.

Core problem of unifying LLM workflows

During the early days of the LLM revolution, developers faced a frustrating challenge, which was that every application required reinventing the same infrastructure. Managing conversation memory, chaining operations, and integrating tools, each project started from scratch with brittle, custom code.

LangChain was built to solve this very problem. Its founding insight was that the LLMs become truly powerful only when connected to external computation and data. So, the framework's mission is to democratize intelligent agents by eliminating the gap between prototypes and production.

Two pillars of design

LangChain's architecture is built on two primary technical priorities that help make it flexible, standardized, and ready for real-world complexity. The details are as follows:

- **Abstraction and composability**: The first pillar is focused on breaking down complex applications into manageable, reusable pieces and defining the workflow between them:
    - **Abstraction (Modularity)**: LangChain provides standard interfaces for every conceptual component required to build an application, which includes prompts, models, chains, memory, agents, and tools. This ensures that each piece is a distinct, modular block.
    - **Composability (via LCEL)**: These modular blocks are designed to be easily chained together. The LCEL provides a powerful, declarative syntax (using the pipe operator, `|`) to define complex workflows seamlessly. This shift moves the developer's focus from writing wiring code to designing the overall flow.

      Components combine like LEGO blocks:

      ```
      chain = prompt | llm | output_parser
      ```
- **Standardization and extensibility**: The second pillar ensures the framework remains relevant across evolving models and connects the LLM to the world outside its training data:
    - **Standardization (Model neutrality)**: LangChain provides a consistent API interface for calling any supported LLM, regardless of the provider (OpenAI, Anthropic, Google, etc.). This commitment to a universal standard is crucial for preventing **vendor lock-in**, allowing developers to swap models based on cost, performance, or availability without rewriting application logic.

All components use the same interface:

```
result = component.invoke(input)
results = component.batch([inputs])
stream = component.stream(input)
```

- **Extensibility**: The framework must allow the LLM to take *real-world actions*. This is achieved through *Tools*, which are standard interfaces for any external function or API (e.g., searching the web, querying a database, or sending an email). Tools effectively extend the model's capabilities beyond its original training data.

  Easy to add custom components:

```
from langchain.tools import BaseTool

class CustomTool(BaseTool):
    name = "my_tool"
    description = "What it does"

    def _run(self, query: str) -> str:
        return "result"
```

Design philosophy in practice

Theory is essential, but let us see how these design principles translate into actual code. The contrast between using LangChain and building from scratch illustrates why the framework matters.

Refer to the following code for building an agent without LangChain (~30 lines):

```
import openai

# Manual API key management
openai.api_key = os.getenv("OPENAI_API_KEY")

# Manual tool selection logic
def select_tool(llm_response):
    if "search" in llm_response.lower():
        return search_tool
    elif "calculate" in llm_response.lower():
        return calculator_tool
    return None

# Manual conversation history tracking
conversation_history = []
```

```
# Manual error handling
try:
    response = openai.ChatCompletion.create(
        model="gpt-4o-mini",
        messages=conversation_history
    )
    conversation_history.append(response)

    tool = select_tool(response)
    if tool:
        result = tool.run()
        # More manual response handling...
except Exception as e:
    # Manual error recovery...
    pass
```

This code works, but it is fragile. Every edge case requires custom handling. Testing is difficult because concerns are mixed together. Reusing this logic in another project means copying and modifying the entire block.

Refer to the following code for building a similar agent with LangChain (~8 lines):

```
from langchain.agents import initialize_agent
from langchain_openai import ChatOpenAI

agent = initialize_agent(
    tools=[search_tool, calculator_tool],
    llm=ChatOpenAI(model="gpt-4o-mini")
)

result = agent.run("What's the sum of 2 and 16?")
```

The LangChain version handles all the complexity we coded manually:

- API key management
- Tool selection logic
- Conversation history
- Error handling and retries
- Response parsing

More importantly, this code is testable, reusable, and maintainable. The design principles we discussed are not just philosophy; they translate directly into better code.

Learn LangChain's fundamental components

Before you start building intelligent agents, let us break down LangChain's core components, which include prompts, chains, agents, tools, memory, and retrievers. Each has a specific job. Chains define your workflow, agents make decisions, tools take actions, memory keeps track of context, and retrievers pull in knowledge your model does not have. Once you understand how these pieces fit together, you can build anything from a simple chatbot to an enterprise-scale reasoning system.

Setup

We need to import the essential libraries and dependencies to run the code successfully:

- Installs the core LangChain packages:
  - **langchain**: Major framework package
  - **langchain-openai**: Integration module for OpenAI models (ChatGPT, GPT-4, etc.).
  - **langchain-community**: It now contains connectors like retrievers, vectorstores, tools, etc. that used to be in LangChain.
- **`faiss-cpu`**; **Facebook AI Similarity Search** (**FAISS**), a vector database used for fast semantic search on CPU.
- Imports the `os` library to work with environment variables.
- Sets our OpenAI API key as an environment variable.
- Replace **`"your_api_key"`** with our actual key from OpenAI's dashboard

To begin constructing intelligent agents using LangChain, you first need to establish your environment and import the needed libraries. The following code snippet explains how to set your OpenAI API key, initialize the essential LangChain modules, including prompt templates, output parsers, memory, and agent utilities, and instantiate a language model using GPT-4o-mini. This basic configuration guarantees your agent is ready to answer user queries, manage context, and connect with tools for advanced reasoning and automation:

```
import os
os.environ["OPENAI_API_KEY"] = "your_api_key"

from langchain_openai import ChatOpenAI
from langchain_core.prompts import ChatPromptTemplate, PromptTemplate
from langchain_core.output_parsers import StrOutputParser
from langchain.memory import ConversationBufferMemory
from langchain.agents import load_tools, initialize_agent

llm = ChatOpenAI(model="gpt-4o-mini")
```

Note: **LangChain agents are built on top of LangGraph. When you use LangChain, you are already using LangGraph under the hood, but with simplified abstractions.**

The details are as follows:

- **Prompts**: Prompts are the instructions you give to the LLM. Instead of typing out the same thing repeatedly, LangChain gives you tools like **`PromptTemplate`** and **`ChatPromptTemplate`**. These let you create reusable templates where you just plug in different variables each time.

  This example demonstrates how to use LangChain's prompt templates to interact with a language model for translation tasks. By formatting the prompt and invoking the model, you can easily generate dynamic responses based on user input:

  ```
  prompt = ChatPromptTemplate.from_template(
      "Translate to French: {text}")

  final_prompt = prompt.format_messages(text="Hi!! my name is Geek.")

  response = llm.invoke(final_prompt)
  print(response.content)
  ```

- **Chains**: Chains are pipelines that connect prompts and models together. Instead of calling the LLM once, a chain lets us define a workflow (e.g., summarize text | then translate):

  ```
  prompt = PromptTemplate.from_template("Summarize in one line:\n\
  n{text}")
  parser = StrOutputParser()
  chain = prompt | llm | parser
  result = chain.invoke({"text": "LangChain simplifies building LLM
  applications."})
  print(result)
  ```

- **Memory**: LLMs are normally stateless (they forget past messages). Memory in LangChain solves this by storing conversation history:

  ```
  from langchain.chains import ConversationChain
  from langchain.memory import ConversationBufferMemory

  memory = ConversationBufferMemory()
  conversation = ConversationChain(llm=llm, memory=memory)

  print(conversation.predict(input="Hello, my name is Geek."))
  print(conversation.predict(input="Can you remind me what my name is?"))
  ```

- **Retrievers**: LLMs have a knowledge cutoff. Retrievers allow us to connect them with external knowledge bases like PDFs, docs, and databases. Vector stores like FAISS store embeddings for fast search:

```
from langchain_openai import OpenAIEmbeddings
from langchain_community.vectorstores import FAISS

embeddings = OpenAIEmbeddings()

docs = [
    "LangChain is a powerful LLM framework.",
    "It allows integration with external data and APIs.",
    "LangServe is used for deployment."
]

vectorstore = FAISS.from_texts(docs, embeddings)

query = "What is LangChain used for?"

retriever = vectorstore.as_retriever()
results = retriever.get_relevant_documents(query)

for r in results:
    print("Retrieved:", r.page_content)
```

- **Agents**: Agents can decide what action to take: call a tool (e.g., calculator, search) or just answer directly:

```
from langchain.agents import load_tools, initialize_agent

tools = load_tools(["llm-math"], llm=llm)

agent = initialize_agent(
    tools, llm, agent="zero-shot-react-description", verbose=True)

response = agent.run("What is 25 multiplied by 16?")
print(response)
```

- **Output parsers**: By default, LLMs return plain text. Output parsers help us force structured formats like **JavaScript Object Notation** (**JSON**), making the results easier to use in apps:

```
from langchain.output_parsers import StructuredOutputParser,
ResponseSchema

schemas = [
    ResponseSchema(name="language", description="Detected language"),
    ResponseSchema(name="sentiment", description="Sentiment (positive/
negative/neutral)")
]

parser = StructuredOutputParser.from_response_schemas(schemas)
format_instructions = parser.get_format_instructions()

template = """Analyze: {text}
{format_instructions}"""

prompt = PromptTemplate(
    template=template,
    input_variables=["text"],
    partial_variables={"format_instructions": format_instructions}
)

chain = prompt | llm | parser
result = chain.invoke({"text": "I love AI!"})
print(result)  # {'language': 'English', 'sentiment': 'positive'}
```

Setup your LangChain and API environment

Before writing a single line of code, it is crucial to create a stable, reproducible environment where your LangChain projects can thrive. In this section, you will set up your Python environment, configure your API keys, and check your installation, ensuring everything works smoothly before you begin experimenting.

Note: **Before getting started, make sure your system is ready for development. You will need Python 3.8 or higher installed and accessible from your system's PATH, along with pip, the Python package manager, to install required dependencies. Finally, make sure you have a valid OpenAI API key (or an API key from another supported LLM provider) so that your LangChain agent can securely connect to the model and process requests.**

The following steps are to set up your Python environment:

1. Create a virtual environment and install packages. Run the following commands in your project folder to create a virtual environment and install all the required packages:

```
# Create and activate virtual environment
python -m venv langchain_env
source langchain_env/bin/activate  # macOS/Linux
# langchain_env\Scripts\activate  # Windows

# Install packages
pip install langchain langchain-openai python-dotenv

# Create .env file
echo "OPENAI_API_KEY=sk-your-key-here" > .env

# Add to .gitignore
echo ".env" >> .gitignore
```

2. This creates a directory `langchain_env` containing an isolated Python environment. You can run the installs individually or combine them. The following is an example combined with a command:

```
pip install langchain langchain-openai python-dotenv
```

3. Alternatively, to pin dependencies, create a `requirements.txt`:

```
langchain
langchain-openai
python-dotenv
```

4. Then install with:

```
pip install -r requirements.txt
```

5. Create a file named `.env` in the project root and add your API key.

6. Verify the setup by using a quick test. Create a file **`test_setup.py`** with the following contents (this matches the imports used above):

```
# test_setup.py
from langchain_openai import ChatOpenAI
from dotenv import load_dotenv
import os

load_dotenv()  # reads .env into environment variables
```

```
# optional: show that the env var is present (don't print the secret)
if not os.getenv("OPENAI_API_KEY"):
    raise SystemExit("OPENAI_API_KEY not found in .env file.")

# instantiate the model (example: gpt-4o-mini as in your snippet)
llm = ChatOpenAI(model="gpt-4o-mini")

# call the model (API and wrapper behavior depends on installed
versions)
response = llm.invoke("Say 'Setup successful!")

# Print the textual content returned by the wrapper
print(response.content)
```

7. Run it:

```
python test_setup.py
```

8. Expected behavior; the script prints a short model response (for example: **`Setup successful!`**), indicating the environment and API access are working.

Note: **When dealing with your LangChain agent, ensure that your `OPENAI_API_KEY` is appropriately set in a `.env` file, with the precise key name, and that you have restarted your shell or reactivated your virtual environment if needed. If you encounter import issues, validate that the virtual environment is active and that `langchain` and `langchain-openai` are installed (pip list). For model call issues connected to permission or invoicing, check your OpenAI account and API key status on the provider dashboard. Be mindful that LangChain and provider wrappers may vary over time, so always consult the documentation for the right class and method signatures. Finally, never print your complete API key in logs or output to avoid exposing important information.**

Build your first QA agent with LangChain

Now that you can understand the environment, we should build your first agent. You will create a simple **question answering** (**QA**) agent that interprets user questions, reasons through them, and responds intelligently using just a few lines of code. This foundational exercise shows how LangChain transforms static text generation into interactive reasoning.

Understanding fundamental components of LangChain

Before creating a full agent, you must comprehend the atomic components that power it. Think of these pieces as the main inputs and procedures the agent employs to generate a coherent, action-oriented response.

Refer to the following table that discusses the purpose and analogy of each component:

SupervisorComponent	Purpose (role)	Analogy
Prompt template	The reusable blueprint for instructions.	A reusable instruction sheet
LLM	The foundational AI model that handles reasoning.	The brain (The actual processor)
Chain	A predefined sequence of steps or components.	The assembly line
Memory	The mechanism to recall previous turns in a conversation.	The conversation history
Tool	An external function or API that the Agent can call.	A calculator or screwdriver used when needed
Agent	The decision-making core chooses the correct Tool and logic path.	The conductor, manager or supervisor

***Table 1.4**: Roles and analogies of core LangChain components in agent workflows*

These components interact in sophisticated ways, often requiring the agent to reflect on its own thought process (a pattern known as **ReAct**, which we will explore in depth).

The following picture demonstrates how big language models and LangChain agents interact within a workflow, illustrating the modular structure and the relationships between prompts, chains, tools, memory, and retrievers:

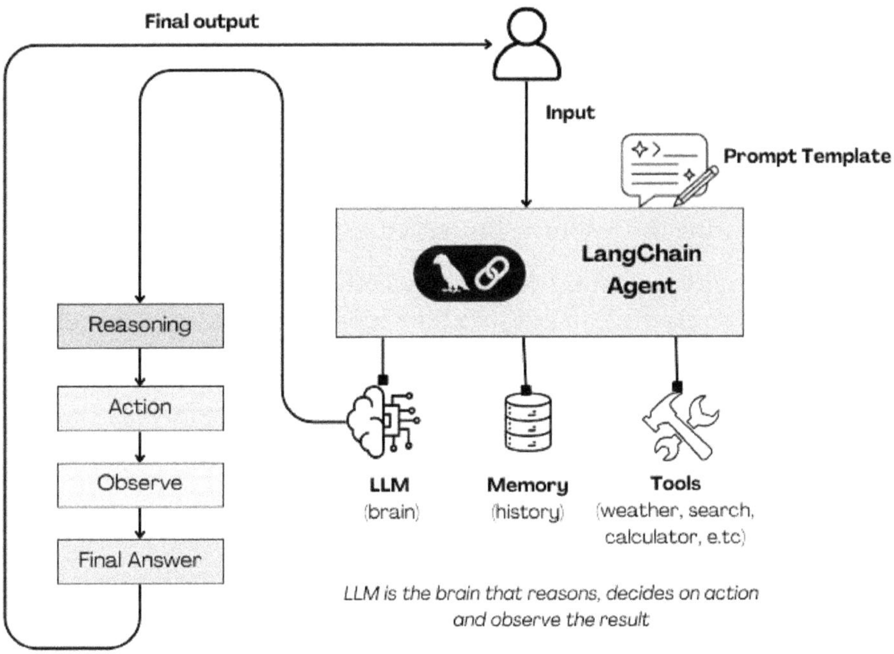

***Figure 1.4**: LLM and LangChain agent illustrations*

This picture helps understand how each component contributes to constructing intelligent, action-oriented agents that can reason, act, and adapt in real-world circumstances.

The following steps provide a practical guide to implementing modular LangChain workflows. By following this sequence, you will learn how to structure, extend, and validate agent components for scalable and maintainable AI solutions:

1. **Create a simple LLM chain with LCEL (simple_chain.py)**: Let us start simple and just a prompt + LLM chain using the following code:

```
from langchain_openai import ChatOpenAI
from langchain_core.prompts import ChatPromptTemplate
from langchain_core.output_parsers import StrOutputParser
from dotenv import load_dotenv

load_dotenv()

prompt = ChatPromptTemplate.from_template("Answer concisely:
{question}")
llm = ChatOpenAI(model="gpt-4o-mini", temperature=0)
parser = StrOutputParser()

chain = prompt | llm | parser

response = chain.invoke({"question": "What is LangChain?"})
print(response)
```

   - The **`Prompt Template`** serves as the blueprint for how the language model should reply, establishing the structure and tone of the output. Once the template is applied, the LLM, in this case, an OpenAI GPT model, processes the input question and creates a response based on the stated instructions. Finally, the **`OutputParser`** takes the raw output from the model and translates it into a clean, usable text format, ensuring the response fits with the desired structure.

2. **Add an agent with a custom tool (get_weather.py)**: You can add simple tools for specific tasks. For example, a **`get_weather`** tool that the agent can call when needed, as shown in the following code:

```
def get_weather(location: str) -> str:
    """Mock weather info."""
    weather_data = {
        "Seattle": "Rainy, 12°C",
        "San Francisco": "Cloudy, 18°C",
        "New York": "Sunny, 22°C"
    }
    return weather_data.get(location, "Weather data not available")
```

```
from langchain_openai import ChatOpenAI
from langchain.agents import initialize_agent, Tool, AgentType
from dotenv import load_dotenv

load_dotenv()

tools = [
    Tool(
        name="WeatherTool",
        func=get_weather,
        description="Get current weather for a city. Input: city name"
    )
]

llm = ChatOpenAI(model="gpt-4o-mini", temperature=0)
agent = initialize_agent(tools, llm, agent=AgentType.ZERO_SHOT_REACT_
DESCRIPTION, verbose=True)

question = "What's the weather like in Seattle?"
response = agent.run(question)
print(response)
```

- When the agent receives a question, it begins by reasoning through the problem, essentially *thinking* about the best approach to respond. Based on its internal logic and accessible tools, it decides to use the **Weather** tool to retrieve the necessary information. After collecting the result, the agent synthesizes the data and generates a final answer that fits the user's request.

3. **Adding a conversational memory to the agent (agent_with_memory.py)**: Let us make the agent remember the past interactions:

```
from langchain_openai import ChatOpenAI
from langchain.agents import initialize_agent, AgentType
from langchain.memory import ConversationBufferMemory
from dotenv import load_dotenv
from tools.get_weather import get_weather
from langchain.agents import Tool

load_dotenv()

tools = [
    Tool(
        name="WeatherTool",
```

```
            func=get_weather,
            description="Get current weather for a city. Input: city name"
        )
    ]

    memory = ConversationBufferMemory(
        memory_key="chat_history",
        return_messages=True
    )

    agent = initialize_agent(
        tools=tools,
        llm=ChatOpenAI(model="gpt-4o-mini"),
        agent=AgentType.CONVERSATIONAL_REACT_DESCRIPTION,
        memory=memory,
        verbose=True
    )

    question = "What's the weather like in Seattle?"
    response = agent.run(question)
    print(response)
```

The agent is meant to retain past inputs, allowing it to establish context over time. This capability enables the agent to maintain a coherent conversation rather than considering each question as an individual request. By remembering what was stated earlier, the agent may deliver more relevant and personalized responses, creating a smooth and dynamic experience for the user.

Configure dev tools for efficient experimentation

In this section, you will learn how to set up your development tools for efficient experimentation using **Visual Studio Code** (**VS Code**). A well-configured environment not only speeds up your workflow but also guarantees that your projects are replicable, organized, and easy to share with others. By the end, you will have a ready-to-use system that allows fast iteration, smooth tool integration, and consistent results, so you can focus more on building and testing your LangChain agents and less on troubleshooting your setup.

Note: **To get started quickly, first install VS Code and then add the recommended extensions to enhance your development experience. Next, create a project folder and include a `/.vscode` directory to store your workspace settings. Set up your preferred Python environment, whether it is venv, Conda, Poetry, or a Dev Container, and add a `requirements.txt` or `pyproject.toml` file to manage dependencies. Finally, configure your `tasks.json` and `launch.json` files for automation and debugging support. Once everything is in place, you are ready to start experimenting and building your LangChain agents efficiently.**

Tell VS Code to use the `.venv` interpreter (Command Palette | Python: Select Interpreter).

To provide a consistent and efficient coding experience for your entire team, it is crucial to design your workspace settings intelligently. The following steps will guide you in setting up shared workspace configurations in the **`.vscode`** folder and activating format-on-save, helping everyone preserve clean code throughout rapid development cycles:

1. **Configure VS Code workspace settings**: Create a **`.vscode/settings.json`** file to define workspace-specific configurations. This allows you to adjust editor settings, linting rules, formatting preferences, and other environment choices for your project without changing global VS Code settings, guaranteeing consistency throughout your team and experiments:

   `.vscode/settings.json`:

   ```
   {
     "python.pythonPath": "${workspaceFolder}/.venv/bin/python",
     "editor.formatOnSave": true,
     "editor.codeActionsOnSave": {
       "source.organizeImports": true
     },
     "files.exclude": {
       "**/__pycache__": true,
       ".venv": true
     },
     "python.analysis.typeCheckingMode": "basic"
   }
   ```

   a. Keep the workspace settings in `.vscode` folder so all teammates share the same defaults. Additionally, enable `formatOnSave` to keep code tidy during quick iterations.

   b. Install essential VS Code extensions to make coding and experimentation smoother:

      - **Python (ms-python.python)**: Core Python support.
      - **Pylance (ms-python.vscode-pylance)**: Type checking and autocomplete.
      - **Jupyter**: Run notebooks interactively.
      - **Prettier / Black**: Auto-format your JS/Python code.

- **ESLint**: Catch issues and enforce code quality in JavaScript/TypeScript.
- OpenAI's Codex-related tooling or extensions for code-oriented workflow

2. **Task automations**: Create a **`tasks.json`** file to define typical build and debugging tasks. This enables you to automate repetitive commands, such as executing scripts, tests, or environment setups, directly from VS Code, optimizing your workflow and saving time during development:

   `.vscode/tasks.json`:

```
{
  "version": "2.0.0",
  "tasks": [
    {
      "label": "Install deps",
      "type": "shell",
      "command": "pip install -r requirements.txt",
      "group": "build"
    },
    {
      "label": "Run current file (python)",
      "type": "shell",
      "command": "${config:python.pythonPath} -u ${file}",
      "presentation": { "reveal": "silent", "panel": "shared" }
    },
    {
      "label": "Run experiment 001",
      "type": "shell",
      "command": "${config:python.pythonPath} experiments/exp_001_quick_
test.py",
      "group": "test"
    }
  ]
}
```

   Run tasks with **`Terminal → Run Task`** or bind keys.

3. **Debug configuration**: Create a **`launch.json`** file to define standard debugging configurations. This allows you to easily execute and debug your code in VS Code without continuously setting up breakpoints or custom instructions, making your development workflow more efficient and consistent:

   `.vscode/launch.json`:

```
{
  "version": "0.2.0",
```

```
"configurations": [
  {
    "name": "Python: Current File (Integrated)",
    "type": "python",
    "request": "launch",
    "program": "${file}",
    "console": "integratedTerminal",
    "justMyCode": false
  },
  {
    "name": "Attach to Process",
    "type": "python",
    "request": "attach",
    "processId": "${command:pickProcess}"
  }
]
}
```

Note: **Use breakpoints + variable watches. | Use conditional breakpoints to skip repetitive steps. | Use `justMyCode=false` to step into dependencies if needed.**

Debugging and testing LangChain agents

As your projects grow in complexity, debugging and testing become critical. Intelligent agents do not just follow static logic; they think, make decisions, and interact with numerous tools, so understanding what happens behind the scenes is crucial to developing dependable systems. In this section, you will learn how to evaluate your agent's logic, trace its actions step-by-step, and determine when things go wrong. You will also cover best practices for structured logging, error management, and automated testing, helping you develop agents that are not only clever but also reliable and trustworthy in real-world circumstances.

Note: **Debugging is a vital skill when working with LangChain agents because they consist of many interconnected components, including prompts, chains, tools, memory, retrievers, and more. Each part contributes to how the agent reasons and performs tasks, so understanding their interactions is essential. Effective debugging allows you to trace how the agent chooses tools, pinpoint where reasoning or parsing might fail, and measure latency to uncover performance bottlenecks. Most importantly, it helps you handle exceptions gracefully, ensuring that your workflows remain stable and reliable even when unexpected issues arise.**

The following steps define fundamental debugging and exception-handling procedures for LangChain agents. By following this procedure, you will ensure your workflows stay stable, reliable, and resilient, even when unforeseen challenges happen:

1. **Enable debug mode**: LangChain provides a built-in debug mode that prints detailed reasoning traces to your console, which is perfect for understanding intermediate steps:

```
# debug_weather.py
from langchain.globals import set_debug

# Enable LangChain global debug output
set_debug(True)
from langchain_openai import ChatOpenAI
from langchain.agents import initialize_agent, Tool, AgentType

# Define the weather tool
def get_weather(location: str) -> str:
    """Mock weather data."""
    weather_data = {
        "Seattle": "Rainy, 12°C",
        "San Francisco": "Cloudy, 18°C",
        "New York": "Sunny, 22°C"
    }
    return weather_data.get(location, "Weather data not available")

# Wrap the tool for LangChain
tools = [
    Tool(
        name="WeatherTool",
        func=get_weather,
        description="Provides the current weather for a given city."
    )
]

# Initialize the LLM
llm = ChatOpenAI(model="gpt-4o-mini", temperature=0)

# Initialize the agent
agent = initialize_agent(
    tools=tools,
    llm=llm,
```

```
    agent=AgentType.ZERO_SHOT_REACT_DESCRIPTION
)

# Run the agent with a weather query
result = agent.run("What is the weather in Seattle?")
print(result)
```

Debug output shows reasoning steps like the following:

```
[DEBUG] Thought: I should use the WeatherTool.
[DEBUG] Action: WeatherTool
[DEBUG] Input: Seattle
[DEBUG] Observation: Rainy, 12°C
[DEBUG] Final Answer: The weather in Seattle is Rainy, 12°C.
```

2. **Add application-level logging**: LangChain's debug mode is great for reasoning traces. You should also add your own structured logs to monitor the app, especially when running multiple agents or long sessions:

```
# logging_setup_weather.py
import logging

# Configure logging once at app start
logging.basicConfig(
    level=logging.INFO,
    format="%(asctime)s [%(levelname)s] %(name)s - %(message)s",
)
logger = logging.getLogger(__name__)
logger.info("Starting agent...")

from langchain_openai import ChatOpenAI
from langchain.agents import initialize_agent, Tool, AgentType

# Define the weather tool
def get_weather(location: str) -> str:
    logger.debug(f"WeatherTool called with: {location}")
    weather_data = {
        "Seattle": "Rainy, 12°C",
        "San Francisco": "Cloudy, 18°C",
        "New York": "Sunny, 22°C"
```

```
    }
    result = weather_data.get(location, "Weather data not available")
    logger.info(f"WeatherTool result: {result}")
    return result

# Wrap the tool for LangChain
tools = [
    Tool(
        name="WeatherTool",
        func=get_weather,
        description="Provides the current weather for a given city."
    )
]

# Initialize the LLM
llm = ChatOpenAI(model="gpt-4o-mini", temperature=0)

# Initialize the agent
agent = initialize_agent(
    tools=tools,
    llm=llm,
    agent=AgentType.ZERO_SHOT_REACT_DESCRIPTION,
    verbose=True
)
logger.info("Agent initialized successfully.")

# Run the agent with a weather query
result = agent.run("What is the weather in San Francisco?")
logger.info(f"Final result: {result}")
```

You will see both LangChain reasoning traces and your application-level logs, clearly separated.

3. **Debug tool behavior and outputs**: When your tools depend on APIs or I/O (e.g., weather, DB, or file system), wrap them with debug logs and safeguards:

```
def get_weather(location: str) -> str:
    logger.info(f"Fetching weather for: {location}")
    try:
```

```
        # simulate a call
        if not location:
            raise ValueError("Location missing")
        result = f"Sunny 25°C in {location}"
        logger.debug(f"Weather result: {result}")
        return result
    except Exception as e:
        logger.error(f"Weather tool failed: {str(e)}")
        return f"Error fetching weather: {str(e)}"
```

   - Use `logger.debug()` for data traces, `logger.info()` for successful steps, and `logger.error()` for failures.

4. **Error handling for stable agents**: Agents often fail due to malformed outputs or tool exceptions. Wrap your tool logic with a try/except to keep experiments running instead of crashing:

```
def safe_tool(input_text: str) -> str:
    try:
        result = complex_calculation(input_text)
        return result
    except Exception as e:
        logger.error(f"Tool failed on input '{input_text}': {e}")
        return f"Error: {str(e)}"
```

   - You can even wrap tool execution in a retry decorator:

```
from tenacity import retry, stop_after_attempt, wait_fixed

@retry(stop=stop_after_attempt(3), wait=wait_fixed(1))
def reliable_tool(input_text):
    # your tool logic
    ...
```

5. **Inspect agent traces and intermediate steps**: LangChain agents record thought, action, observation, and final answer. When you set `verbose=True` on your agent or chain:

```
agent = initialize_agent(
    tools=tools,
    llm=llm,
    agent=AgentType.ZERO_SHOT_REACT_DESCRIPTION,
    verbose=True
)
```

   - You will see traces like:

```
> Entering new AgentExecutor chain...
```

```
Thought: I need to find the current weather for the requested city.
Action: WeatherTool
Action Input: Seattle
Observation: Rainy, 12°C
Thought: I now have the weather information.
Final Answer: The weather in Seattle is Rainy, 12°C.
```

- For complex pipelines, you can also inspect:

```
result = chain.invoke({"question": "What is LangChain?"},
config={"callbacks": [YourCustomHandler()]})
```

If you need detailed step data programmatically, attach a callback handler using `langchain_core.callbacks`.

Testing a complete QA agent pipeline

Once your first LangChain agent is up and running, the next step is to test the full pipeline to ensure everything works consistently from end to end. Testing is what turns a decent prototype into a dependable system; it confirms that your tools, logic, and agent behavior provide consistent and predictable outcomes. In this section, you will learn how to manually test your pipeline, write unit tests for individual components, and utilize mocking techniques to simulate real-world scenarios without relying on live APIs. By the end, you will have a robust framework for verifying your agents with confidence before deploying them in production.

Note: **Before you begin writing tests, make sure you have `pytest` installed, it is a lightweight and powerful testing framework that makes automation simple. You can install it using the following command (`pip install pytest`). Once installed, you will be able to run all your test files with a single command (`pytest -v`), making it easy to verify that your LangChain agent, tools, and logic are working exactly as expected.**

- **Manual testing**: You can quickly verify your QA agent works by running a simple script:

```
tests/run_agent.py
from agent.qa_agent_weather import agent

question = "What's the weather like in Seattle?"
response = agent.run(question)
print("Agent Response:", response)
```

  - **Run**:

```
python run_agent.py
```

  - **Expected output**:

```
Agent Response: The weather in Seattle is Rainy, 12°C.
```

This confirms that the agent correctly calls the **WeatherTool** and returns the expected result.

- **Automated testing with Pytest**: Automated tests help ensure your agent and tools behave consistently:

```
tests/test_agent.py

import pytest
from agent.qa_agent_weather import agent

def test_weather_tool_known_city():
    result = agent.run("What's the weather in Seattle?")
    assert "Rainy" in result or "12" in result

def test_weather_tool_unknown_city():
    result = agent.run("What's the weather in Mars?")
    assert "not available" in result.lower()
```

- **Mocking external tools (optional for real APIs)**: If your `get_weather` tool calls a real API, you can mock it to avoid hitting live endpoints.

  Example using **unittest.mock**:

```
from unittest.mock import patch
from agent.qa_agent_weather import agent

@patch("tools.get_weather.get_weather", return_value="Sunny, 25°C")
def test_weather_tool_mocked(mock_func):
    result = agent.run("What's the weather in Paris?")
    assert "25" in result
    mock_func.assert_called_once_with("Paris")
```

  Mocking is a powerful technique in testing because it eliminates external dependencies, allowing tests to run in isolation without relying on real services or APIs. This makes the tests fast and highly repeatable, ensuring consistent results across different environments. Additionally, mocking provides a safe approach for **continuous integration/continuous deployment** (**CI/CD**) pipelines, reducing the risk of failures caused by network issues or third-party service outages and enabling reliable automation throughout the development lifecycle.

- **Run all tests**: To run all tests in your suite, use the command **pytest -v**. This will execute every test and display detailed results, such as:

```
pytest -v
```

- **Expected output**:

```
tests/test_agent.py::test_weather_tool_known_city PASSED
tests/test_agent.py::test_weather_tool_unknown_city PASSED
tests/test_agent.py::test_weather_tool_mocked PASSED
```

Testing and assertions best practices

To ensure deterministic, reproducible results:

- Use *deterministic inputs* for predictable outputs.
- Write tests for *both known and unknown cases.*
- Combine *manual and automated tests* for robust validation.

This workflow ensures your QA agent reliably handles both expected and edge-case inputs while providing clear, reproducible results.

Building a real-world LangChain agent

Once you understand the basics of LangChain, the next step is to examine how these ideas work in practice by building a complete agent system. This section demonstrates how to create a multi-tool agent that can intelligently switch between different capabilities, performing mathematical calculations and retrieving information from a knowledge base. You will see how agents reason through complex queries that require multiple tools, making autonomous decisions about which tool to use and when.

This practical example will help you understand the core principles of agent behavior: breaking down problems, selecting appropriate tools, and combining results into coherent answers. By working through this implementation, you will gain the foundation needed to build more sophisticated agents that can handle diverse tasks in your own applications, whether in data analysis, customer service, research assistance, or any domain requiring intelligent task routing and execution.

Note: **To avoid package conflicts, always install your dependencies in a virtual environment. After activating it, install all required packages for your LangChain agent:`pip install langchain langchain-openai python-dotenv pytest`. This ensures your environment is isolated and your agent runs with the correct package versions.**

- **Calculator tool (tools/calculator.py)**: This tool evaluates mathematical expressions safely using Python's eval function and returns the calculated result:

```
def calculate(expression: str) -> str:
    """Evaluates a mathematical expression."""
    try:
        result = eval(expression)
```

```
        return f"The result is {result}"
    except Exception as e:
        return f"Error calculating: {str(e)}"
```

The function wraps eval in a try-except block to catch any invalid expressions and return meaningful error messages instead of crashing.

- **Database search tool (tools/search_tool.py)**: This tool simulates a knowledge base search by matching keywords in the query against a predefined dictionary of information:

```
def search_database(query: str) -> str:
    """Mock database search."""
    knowledge_base = {
        "langchain": "LangChain is a framework for building LLM 
applications.",
        "python": "Python is a high-level programming language.",
        "ai": "Artificial Intelligence is the simulation of human 
intelligence."
    }

   for key, value in knowledge_base.items():
        if key in query.lower():
            return value
    return "No information found in database."
```

The search iterates through the knowledge base and returns the first matching entry, or a not-found message if no matches exist.

- **Multi-tool agent configuration (agent/ agent/multi_tool_agent.py)**: This file initializes the agent with both calculator and search capabilities, allowing it to decide which tool to use based on the user's query:

```
from langchain_openai import ChatOpenAI
 from langchain.agents import initialize_agent, Tool, AgentType
 from tools.calculator import calculate
 from tools.search_tool import search_database
 from dotenv import load_dotenv

load_dotenv()

tools = [
    Tool(
        name="Calculator",
        func=calculate,
```

```
        description="Useful for mathematical calculations. Input: valid
Python expression."
    ),
    Tool(
        name="DatabaseSearch",
        func=search_database,
        description="Search for information in the knowledge base.
Input: search query."
    )
]

llm = ChatOpenAI(model="gpt-4o-mini", temperature=0)
agent = initialize_agent(
    tools=tools,
    llm=llm,
    agent=AgentType.ZERO_SHOT_REACT_DESCRIPTION,
    verbose=True
)
```

The agent uses the **ZERO_SHOT_REACT_DESCRIPTION** strategy, which enables it to reason about which tool to use without requiring examples.

- **Running the agent (run_agent.py)**: This script demonstrates three different query types: pure calculation, pure information retrieval, and a combined query requiring both tools:

```
from agent.multi_tool_agent import agent

# Mathematical query
print("Query 1: Calculate 156 multiplied by 23")
response1 = agent.run("What is 156 multiplied by 23?")
print("Response:", response1)

print("\n" + "="*50 + "\n")

# Information retrieval query
print("Query 2: What is LangChain?")
response2 = agent.run("What is LangChain?")
print("Response:", response2)

print("\n" + "="*50 + "\n")

# Combined query
print("Query 3: Combined calculation and information")
```

```
 response3 = agent.run("Calculate 50 plus 30, then tell me about
Python.")
 print("Response:", response3)
```

Each query tests a different capability, demonstrating how the agent automatically selects the appropriate tool without explicit instructions.

- **Agent reasoning process**: Here is how the agent thinks through a complex query that requires using both tools sequentially:

```
Query: "Calculate 156 times 23, then tell me about LangChain"

> Thought: I need to perform a calculation first.
 > Action: Calculator
 > Input: 156 * 23
 > Observation: The result is 3588
 > Thought: Now I need to find information about LangChain.
 > Action: DatabaseSearch
 > Input: langchain
 > Observation: LangChain is a framework for building LLM applications.
 > Final Answer: 156 multiplied by 23 equals 3588. LangChain is a
framework for building LLM applications.
```

The agent breaks down the complex request into steps, executing each tool in sequence and combining the results into a coherent final answer.

- **Testing the agent (tests/test_multi_tool_agent.py)**: These automated tests verify that each tool works correctly in isolation and that the agent can handle queries requiring multiple tools:

```
# tests/test_multi_tool_agent.py
 import pytest
 from agent.multi_tool_agent import agent

def test_calculator_tool():
     result = agent.run("What is 100 divided by 4?")
     assert "25" in result

def test_search_tool():
     result = agent.run("What is Python?")
     assert "programming language" in result.lower()

def test_combined_tools():
     result = agent.run("Calculate 10 plus 5, then tell me about AI.")
     assert "15" in result
     assert "intelligence" in result.lower()
```

The first test verifies the calculator, the second test checks information retrieval, and the third test ensures the agent can chain multiple tools together.

- **Running the tests**: Execute the test suite using `pytest` to validate all agent functionality:

```
pytest -v tests/test_multi_tool_agent.py
```

  This command runs all three tests and provides detailed output showing which tests passed or failed.

Conclusion

Building your first LangChain agent is the first step toward a new way of thinking about AI systems. In this chapter, you learned how to create a reasoning, tool-using agent and how the LangChain ecosystem (LangChain framework, LangGraph, and LangSmith) supports the path from development to production. The chapter connected theory and practice by taking you from simple LLM prompts to agents that can reason, choose tools, and act in real-world scenarios. More importantly, it showed that intelligent systems require a shift from static programming to composable, autonomous workflows. With LangChain, you are not just automating tasks, you are building systems that can reason and adapt.

In the next chapter, you will move beyond simple agents and learn how to design modular, reusable workflows that scale. You will explore how to structure core LangChain components, apply chain-based architecture, and build custom tools that can be reused across projects. The chapter also covers dynamic prompt templates, structured output parsers, and LCEL for flexible pipeline design. Through practical examples and design patterns, you will turn your code into cleaner, production-ready modules that are easier to extend and maintain. By the end, you will have a practical toolkit for building agents that are both manageable and future-ready.

CHAPTER 2
Designing Modular and Reusable LangChain Workflows

Introduction

Building intelligent agents that can scale from proof-of-concept to production requires more than just making a few **application programming interface** (**API**) calls. This chapter walks you through transforming your LangChain applications from simple prototypes into robust systems you can maintain, test, and confidently deploy. We will start by looking at why those big, monolithic code structures break down as your project grows and how **LangChain Expression Language** (**LCEL**) offers a smarter, more flexible approach through modular design.

We will cover three essential areas for building production-ready agents. First, we will cover the basics of modular design. You will learn how the runnable protocol and composable components let you adapt your system to new requirements without having to rebuild everything from scratch. Next, we get hands-on with implementation by building reusable prompt templates, creating custom tools, and setting up structured parsers that actually work together. Finally, we will explore advanced topics like error handling, testing strategies, and powerful patterns like router chains and **retrieval-augmented generation** (**RAG**) that help you solve tricky real-world problems.

Structure

This chapter covers the following topics:

- Need for modularity in scaling agents
- Mastering the building blocks for reusability
- Implementing flexible compositions with LCEL
- Chain-level error handling and fallbacks
- Design patterns for production-grade agents
- Building a production-grade modular weather agent

Objectives

This chapter aims to shift your perspective from writing scripts to designing systems. You will learn about why monolithic agents break down as they grow and how to build modular workflows using LCEL. With LCEL's pipe operators, you will compose components that automatically support streaming, async execution, and batch processing. You will then learn about the core building blocks: dynamic prompt templates that separate instructions from inputs, custom tools for external integrations, and structured output parsers that enforce data contracts. Using Pydantic schemas, you will create type-safe interfaces that catch errors early and integrate cleanly with other systems.

Next, we will cover production patterns like chaining components for complex workflows, running operations in parallel, and adding fallback mechanisms for resilience. You will also explore advanced designs, including Router Chains for intelligent routing, RAG for grounding responses in external knowledge, and MapReduce for processing large documents. Finally, you will learn testing strategies with unit and integration tests, debugging techniques using verbose mode and tracing, and how to organize code into reusable libraries. By the end, you will know how to build agent systems that evolve gracefully as requirements change.

Need for modularity in scaling agents

Going from a working prototype to a production-ready AI application usually comes down to one thing, i.e., modularity. An application is modular when its parts are designed to be independent and interchangeable. With LangChain, building using a modular approach is key for building agents that are scalable, maintainable, and future-proof.

Monolithic vs. modular agent design

When first experimenting with LangChain, it is common to write a single, long script that handles prompt formatting, **large language model** (**LLM**) invocation, and output processing. This approach is known as a monolithic agent. While simple for a **proof of concept** (**PoC**), it quickly becomes a barrier to scaling. If you need to swap the underlying model (e.g., from GPT-4 to a local open-source LLM) or change how the output is parsed, you are forced to rewrite large sections of code that were intertwined with other logic.

The solution is adopting a modular agent design, the philosophy at the heart of modern LangChain, and specifically the LCEL. A modular workflow treats every action, from prompt formatting to calling an external tool, as a small, independent unit. These units adhere to the runnable protocol, which means they all share a standard interface (**`.invoke()`**, **`.stream()`**, **`.ainvoke()`**, **`.batch()`**) and can be seamlessly connected using the pipe operator (**|**).

Note: **All LangChain components that implement the runnable protocol automatically gain support for streaming, async execution, batch processing, and observability. This is a core advantage of LCEL over legacy approaches.**

This component-based approach helps enhance maintainability and testability as you can validate each component individually.

The following table provides a comprehensive comparison of monolithic and modular workflows. We will look at how they handle composition, concurrency, streaming, and overall flexibility:

Feature	Monolithic workflow (Legacy)	Modular workflow (LCEL)
Composition	Nested object creation (`LLMChain(Prompt, LLM)`)	Declarative pipe operator (|)
Scaling/Concurrency	Manual threading/async handling	Automatic parallel execution (`RunnableParallel`)
Streaming	LLM-dependent, complex implementation	Built-in via `.stream()` method on any chain
Component Swap	Requires rewriting large code blocks	Simply replace a Runnable object in the chain

***Table 2.1**: Comparison of monolithic vs. modular workflow approaches*

Example code comparison for weather agent

Let us look at two ways to build the same weather agent to better understand the differences between these approaches:

- **Monolithic workflow (hard to modify)**: The monolithic approach tightly couples all components into a single function call. This makes it difficult to test or replace individual components of the program. Refer to the following code:

```
from langchain.agents import create_agent

def get_weather(city: str) -> str:
    """Get weather for a given city."""
    return f"It's always sunny in {city}!"

# The model, tools, and system prompt are locked
# into one single call, making them hard to swap.
agent = create_agent(
    model="gpt-4o-mini",
    tools=[get_weather],
```

```
        system_prompt="You are a helpful assistant",
)

# Run the agent
response = agent.invoke(
    {"messages": [{"role": "user", "content": "what is the weather in
sf"}]}
)
```

- **Modular workflow (easy to scale)**: The modular approach, on the other hand, breaks down everything into separate, independent components. This way, each component can be tested, modified, or replaced without touching the rest. Refer to the following code:

```
from langchain_core.prompts import ChatPromptTemplate
from langchain_openai import ChatOpenAI
from langchain_core.tools import tool

# Note: The create_agent function is replaced by explicit chaining
@tool
def get_weather(city: str) -> str:
    """Get weather for a given city."""
    return f"It's always sunny in {city}!"

# 1. Define independent components (Runnables)
prompt = ChatPromptTemplate.from_messages([
    ("system", "You are a helpful assistant"),
    ("user", "{input}"),
])
llm = ChatOpenAI(model="gpt-4o-mini", temperature=0)

# 2. Chain them with the pipe operator
modular_chain = prompt | llm
```

Tip: **When starting a new project, you should use the modular approach from the get-go. This is because refactoring monolithic code to LCEL later is much more time-consuming than simply building modularly from the start.**

Identifying essential LangChain workflow components

A complex agent workflow can simply be thought of as different combinations of a few core components. Understanding these building blocks and how they conform to the runnable protocol is essential for building modular systems. Any object that implements this protocol is called a Runnable, and Runnables can be chained together, as shown in the following figure:

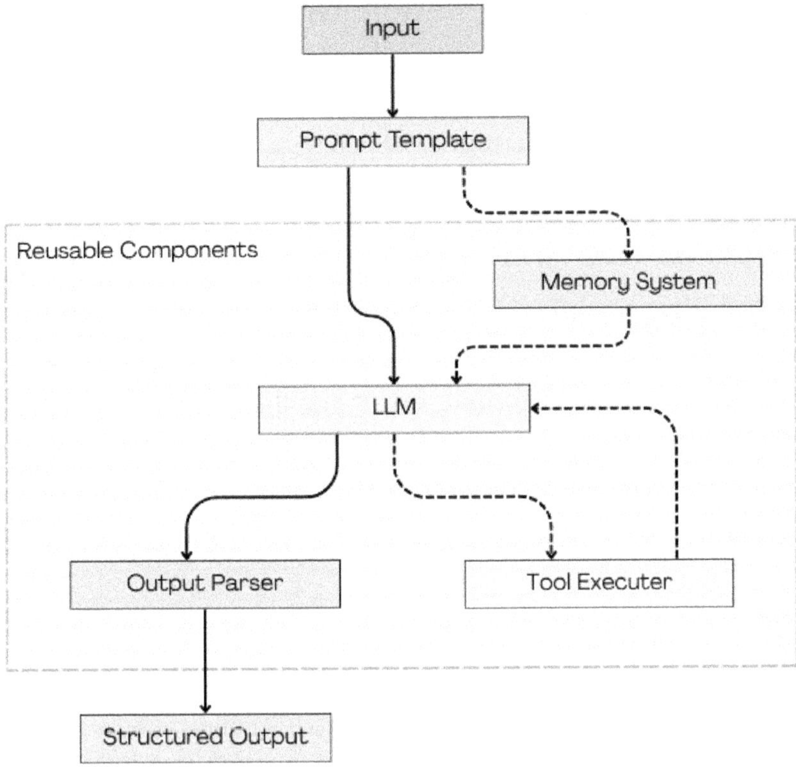

***Figure 2.1**: Basic LangChain component flow*

The following table is a breakdown of the four essential component types you will use in virtually every LangChain workflow:

Component	Responsibility	Example use
Prompt templates	Format inputs for models	Dynamic prompts with variables
LLMs	Generate text responses	GPT-4, Claude, Llama
Output parsers	Structure model outputs	JSON, CSV, custom formats
Memory	Store conversation context	Chat history, summaries
Tools	Perform specific actions	API calls, calculations
Chains	Orchestrate sequences	Multi-step workflows
Agents	Make tool decisions	ReAct, planning agents

***Table 2.2**: LangChain component types and responsibilities*

By treating each of these components as a distinct, reusable module, we move away from monolithic code and towards a flexible, scalable pipeline. In the following sections, we will go over how to use LCEL to connect these Runnables together.

Design principles for effective components

To build modular systems, it is important to understand some proven software engineering principles.

Single responsibility principle

The **single responsibility principle** (**SRP**) dictates that each component should have one, and only one, reason to change:

- A prompt template should format text; it should not invoke the LLM or parse the response.
- An output parser should structure data; it should not fetch data from external databases.

To make the principle concrete, the same idea can be restated in negative form by clarifying what each component must not do:

- A prompt template formats text, but it does not call the LLM or parse responses.
- An output parser structures data, but it does not fetch data from databases.

When a component violates SRP, it becomes a *god object* that knows and does too much. These complex components resist reuse because they carry unnecessary *baggage*. If your summarization component also handles API authentication details, you cannot easily reuse it in a context with a different authentication scheme. Keeping components focused on their core responsibility makes them predictable, testable, and inherently reusable.

> Note: **If you find yourself writing a component with more than one clear purpose, consider splitting it into multiple smaller components. This is a strong indicator that SRP is being violated.**

It is helpful to see how responsibilities move through a modular LangChain workflow in order to better comprehend how the single responsibility principle works in real-world situations. The following figure illustrates how each component avoids tightly coupled or overburdened responsibilities by concentrating on a single issue and communicating through clearly defined boundaries:

***Figure 2.2**: Single responsibility components in a modular LangChain workflow*

The following code demonstrates the correct application of SRP, where each component has a single, focused responsibility:

```
# Good: Separate concerns
prompt_template = ChatPromptTemplate.from_template("Summarize: {text}")
llm = ChatOpenAI()
parser = StrOutputParser()

# The chain is simple composition of three single-responsibility Runnables
chain = prompt_template | llm | parser
```

Composability through standard interfaces

Components should connect through well-defined, standardized interfaces. In LangChain, this standard is the runnable protocol, a contract defining how components receive input and produce output via methods like **`.invoke()`**, **`.stream()`**, and **`.ainvoke()`**.

When all components implement the same protocol, they compose naturally and seamlessly using the LCEL pipe operator (|). This composability allows you to build complex systems from simple, verified parts. You can create specialized chains for different domains (e.g., a **`FinanceChain`** and an **`HRChain`**), and then compose these chains into a powerful routing system.

Crucially, the pipe operator (|) is not just syntactic sugar; it creates a new Runnable that inherits all the benefits of the protocol. This means your final, complex composition automatically gains:

- Streaming support
- **Asynchronous** (**Async**) execution
- Batch processing
- Tracing and observability

You focus on business logic while LangChain handles the orchestration and complexity. It is useful to see how separate LangChain components are integrated into a single executable pipeline in order to comprehend how standardized interfaces facilitate seamless composition. The sequential composition of components implementing the runnable protocol is shown in *Figure 2.3*, which enables data to move through each step in a predictable and traceable way:

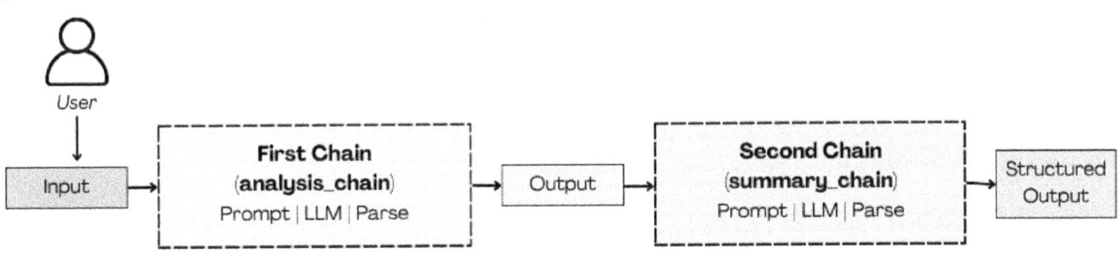

***Figure 2.3**: Sequential LangChain component flow*

The following example demonstrates how components implementing the runnable protocol can be seamlessly composed into increasingly complex pipelines:

```
# Components compose naturally through standard interfaces
analysis_chain = prompt | model | json_parser
summary_chain = summary_prompt | model | str_parser

# Compositions can themselves be composed into a larger pipeline
full_pipeline = analysis_chain | summary_chain
# The full_pipeline is also a Runnable and supports .stream()
```

Mastering the building blocks for reusability

Modular agent design is built upon the simple concept that all components are Runnables, objects with a standardized interface that can be connected using the pipe operator (|). To achieve maximum reusability, we must design these foundational components, prompts, tools, and parsers, to be self-contained and easily swappable.

Designing effective dynamic prompt templates

Prompts are the primary interface between your application and language models. A well-designed prompt produces consistent, high-quality responses. A poorly designed prompt yields unpredictable results, requiring extensive error handling and user frustration.

Static prompts, hardcoded strings with no variability, work for simple cases but quickly become limiting. Real applications need prompts that adapt to context, like incorporating user input, adjusting tone based on audience, including relevant examples, or switching between languages. This is where prompt templates become essential.

LangChain's prompt template system provides structured, maintainable ways to create dynamic prompts. Rather than concatenating strings (error-prone and hard to read), you define templates with clear variable placeholders. The template engine handles formatting, escaping, and validation while you focus on crafting effective instructions. The LangChain prompt template is a Python class used to create a specific prompt (on instruction) to send to an LLM. By using prompt templates, we can reproduce the same instruction while requiring minimal input from the user.

The prompt template is arguably the most crucial reusable component, as it dictates the LLM's persona, constraints, and overall behavior. For modern LangChain, we primarily use **`ChatPromptTemplate`**. This class explicitly separates the input into distinct roles, such as system, human, and AI, providing far more granular control and reliable instruction adherence than simple text prompts.

To maximize reusability, you should clearly separate your hard-coded system instructions (the agent's persona, rules, and constraints) from your dynamic input variables (like user questions, city names, or conversation history). This separation allows you to use the same system logic with different user inputs or vice versa.

Instead of repeating the question to LLM, you can create a template for that question as follows:

```
from langchain_core.prompts import PromptTemplate

# Simple template with variables
template = PromptTemplate(
    input_variables=["topic", "tone"],
    template="Write a {tone} article about {topic}."
)

# Format the prompt
prompt = template.format(topic="AI", tone="professional")
```

Now, you only need to give the topic and tone in the input box to run the prompt.

The following code demonstrates how to create a reusable weather prompt template that separates static persona definitions from dynamic city input:

```
from langchain_core.prompts import ChatPromptTemplate

# 1. System Prompt establishes persona and rules (reusable across many tasks)
system_template = (
    "You are a helpful weather information assistant. "
    "Your output must be clear, concise, and friendly."
)

# 2. Human Prompt defines the immediate task and dynamic input
# The {city} variable is the dynamic part provided at runtime.
human_template = "What's the weather like in {city}?"

# 3. Combine into a reusable template object
weather_prompt = ChatPromptTemplate.from_messages([
    ("system", system_template),
    ("human", human_template)
])

# The prompt is now a Runnable and ready to be chained:
# print(weather_prompt.invoke({"city": "San Francisco"}).to_string())
```

By defining the prompt template as a standalone **Runnable**, you can easily test its output or inject it into any complex chain without modifying the rest of the workflow.

Creating and registering reusable custom tools

Tools are the *eyes and hands* of your agent, allowing it to interact with the external world (databases, APIs, web searches). Any standard Python function can be converted into a Runnable tool using the **`@tool`** decorator from **`langchain_core`**.

The function's docstring is crucial, as it provides the natural language context the LLM uses for reasoning. The LLM relies on this description to decide *when* and *how* to call the tool. Therefore, the tool name and description must be unambiguous and action-oriented. We use Python type hints (e.g., **`city: str`**) to automatically define the tool's required input schema, which the LLM uses to correctly format its function call.

Note: **The quality of your tool's docstring directly impacts the LLM's ability to use it correctly. Always write clear, detailed docstrings that explain what the tool does, when to use it, and what inputs it expects.**

Here is an example of a properly structured custom tool with comprehensive documentation and type hints:

```
from langchain_core.tools import tool

@tool
def get_weather(city: str, unit: str = "fahrenheit") -> str:
    """
    Gets the current temperature for a given city.
    Use this tool when the user asks about temperature or weather conditions.
    Input: The city name (string) and temperature unit (optional:
'fahrenheit' or 'celsius').
    """
    # ... In a real application, this calls a weather API ...
    if city.lower() == "san francisco":
        return "72°F" if unit == "fahrenheit" else "22°C"
    return "75°F" if unit == "fahrenheit" else "24°C"

# The function is now a Runnable and ready to be passed to an agent.
# print(get_weather.invoke({"city": "San Francisco", "unit": "fahrenheit"}))
```

The modular design allows you to create a library of these **`@tool`** functions and dynamically select and register only the ones relevant to a specific agent's task, drastically improving both performance and safety.

Building custom tools with clear contracts

Let us examine how to build custom tools that agents can rely on. The key is to define a clear contract that specifies the inputs the tool accepts, the actions it performs, and the outputs it produces. LangChain uses Pydantic models to enforce these contracts at runtime, catching errors before they cause problems.

The following code demonstrates how to build a weather-related custom tool using the **BaseTool** class with explicit input validation and error handling:

```
from langchain.tools import BaseTool
 from pydantic import BaseModel, Field
 from typing import Type

class WeatherInput(BaseModel):
     """Input schema for weather tool."""
     city: str = Field(description="Name of the city to get weather for")
     unit: str = Field(default="celsius", description="Temperature unit:
'celsius' or 'fahrenheit'")

class WeatherTool(BaseTool):
     """Custom weather lookup tool."""
     name = "get_weather"
     description = "Get current weather for a city. Input: city name and
temperature unit"
     args_schema: Type[BaseModel] = WeatherInput

    def _run(self, city: str, unit: str = "celsius") -> str:
         """Execute the weather lookup."""
         try:
             # In production, this would call a real weather API
             temp = "22°C" if unit == "celsius" else "72°F"
             return f"Weather in {city}: {temp}, partly cloudy"
         except Exception as e:
             return f"Error fetching weather: {str(e)}"

    async def _arun(self, city: str, unit: str = "celsius") -> str:
         """Async version."""
         return self._run(city, unit)
```

Following best practices ensures your tools are reliable and maintainable in production environments. Clear descriptions help the LLM understand when and how to use each tool, preventing misuse and improving agent accuracy. Input validation through Pydantic schemas catches errors early, while proper error handling ensures graceful degradation when external APIs fail. Finally, maintaining single responsibility for each tool keeps your codebase modular and makes tools easy to test, debug, and reuse across different agents.

Production-ready tools require four key practices: **clear descriptions** that specify when to use the tool (e.g., "Calculate math expressions" vs. "calculator"), **input validation** using Pydantic schemas, **error handling** that returns useful messages rather than exceptions, and **single responsibility** where each tool performs one focused task. These practices improve LLM tool selection and ensure reliable execution.

Registering tools with agents

Once you have created custom tools, registering them with agents is straightforward. You instantiate your tools and pass them to the agent creation function. The agent automatically discovers tool capabilities by reading their names, descriptions, and input schemas. The LLM uses these descriptions to determine which tool to invoke based on the user's query.

The following example demonstrates how to register multiple weather-related tools with an agent and let the LLM automatically select the appropriate tool based on user queries:

```
from langchain.agents import create_agent
 from langchain_core.tools import tool

# Create custom weather tools
 @tool
 def get_current_weather(city: str) -> str:
     """Get current weather conditions for a city.
     Use this when users ask about current weather, temperature, or
conditions."""
     return f"Current weather in {city}: 72°F, partly cloudy"

# Register tools with agent - the agent uses tool descriptions to decide when
to invoke each tool
 agent = create_agent(
     model="gpt-4o-mini",
     tools=[get_current_weather],
     system_prompt="You are a helpful weather assistant with access to
current weather and forecast tools"
 )

# Agent automatically selects appropriate tool based on user query
 result = agent.invoke({
     "messages": [{"role": "user", "content": "What's the weather like in
Boston?"}]
 })
 # The agent will automatically call get_current_weather("Boston")
```

Tip: **Write detailed, specific tool descriptions that clearly explain when each tool should be used. The quality of these descriptions directly impacts the agent's ability to select the correct tool for each query.**

Parsing structured results using output parsers

Language models produce text. Your application needs structured data objects, dictionaries, lists, and typed values. This mismatch creates integration challenges. You could parse LLM output with regular expressions, string splitting, or manual parsing logic, but these approaches are fragile and error-prone.

While LLMs are excellent text generators, they can struggle to consistently produce reliable structured data (like JSON or XML) without strict guidance. Output parsers solve this critical issue by injecting specific formatting instructions into the prompt and then strictly validating the LLM's raw text response against a defined schema.

Output parsers bridge this gap systematically. They transform unstructured text into structured data using predefined schemas. More importantly, they can inject formatting instructions into your prompts, guiding the LLM to produce output that's easier to parse reliably.

We rely on the **`PydanticOutputParser`** as the industry standard. This parser leverages the Pydantic library to define a data model, ensuring the output is not just syntactically correct but also semantically valid. The process involves three steps:

1. **Define the schema**: Create a Pydantic BaseModel that specifies the exact structure, types, and descriptions of the desired output.
2. **Generate instructions**: The parser automatically generates a detailed, often complex, text string that describes the required JSON format and is injected into the prompt alongside the user's query.
3. **Validate/parse**: The parser attempts to convert the LLM's raw text output string into the Pydantic object, raising a clean, detectable error if the formatting fails.

String output parser for simple cases

The string parser is deceptively simple but useful. It strips whitespace, removes markdown code fences if present, and returns clean text. This normalization prevents issues caused by LLMs adding decorative formatting or leading/trailing spaces:

```
from langchain_core.output_parsers import StrOutputParser

parser = StrOutputParser()

chain = prompt | model | parser
 result = chain.invoke({"text": "Hello"})  # Returns clean string
```

JSON output parser with type safety

The following code demonstrates how to use **`JsonOutputParser`** to extract structured person information with automatic format instruction generation:

```
from langchain_core.output_parsers import JsonOutputParser
 from pydantic import BaseModel, Field

class Person(BaseModel):
     """Person information."""
     name: str = Field(description="Person's name")
     age: int = Field(description="Person's age")
     occupation: str = Field(description="Person's job")

# Create parser
 parser = JsonOutputParser(pydantic_object=Person)

# Add format instructions to prompt
 prompt = ChatPromptTemplate.from_template(
     """Extract person information from the text.

    {format_instructions}

    Text: {text}
     """
 )

# Inject format instructions
 chain = prompt.partial(format_instructions=parser.get_format_instructions())
| model | parser

# Get structured output
 result = chain.invoke({"text": "John Smith is a 30-year-old engineer"})
 # result = {"name": "John Smith", "age": 30, "occupation": "engineer"}
```

The following code demonstrates how to define a structured output schema using Pydantic and instantiate the corresponding parser:

```
from pydantic import BaseModel, Field
from langchain_core.output_parsers import PydanticOutputParser

# 1. Define the desired structured output
class WeatherForecast(BaseModel):
    city: str = Field(description="The name of the city.")
    temperature: str = Field(description="Current temperature with unit.")
    conditions: list[str] = Field(description="List of weather conditions
(e.g., sunny, cloudy).")

# 2. Instantiate the parser
```

```
parser = PydanticOutputParser(pydantic_object=WeatherForecast)

# 3. Get the formatting instructions to add to the prompt
# This text is added to the ChatPromptTemplate to guide the LLM's output.
# format_instructions = parser.get_format_instructions()
```

Tip: **Always test your Pydantic parsers with sample LLM outputs to ensure the schema is neither too strict (causing frequent failures) nor too loose (allowing invalid data through).**

By making the parser a dedicated Runnable, you enforce a strong contract for the data flowing out of the LLM, making downstream processing reliable and your application robust.

Defining runnable input and output schemas

While Pydantic Output Parsers (refer to *Parsing structured results using output parsers* section) define the structure of what the chain *returns*, it is equally important to define the structure of what the chain *accepts*. Every Runnable has an inherent input and output schema, which can be inspected using the **`.input_schema`** and **`.output_schema`** properties.

This visibility establishes a schema contract for the component, which is crucial for building robust integrations. You can ensure type safety for the entire chain input by using Pydantic to define a structured input model.

Using Pydantic for structured input

To define a formal, structured input for your chain, you can use a Pydantic model. This is especially useful when your chain requires multiple, distinct input fields (e.g., a city name and a specific date for a weather request).

The following is an example of defining a Pydantic model that enforces type safety for chain inputs:

```
# Code Block: Defining a Pydantic Model for Structured Input
from pydantic import BaseModel, Field

class WeatherRequest(BaseModel):
    """Structured input model for the weather report chain."""
    city: str = Field(description="The name of the city for the forecast.")
    date: str = Field(description="The specific date for the forecast (e.g.,
'tomorrow').")

# The chain must be adapted to accept this structured dictionary input.
# You can inspect the expected input:
# print(weather_report_chain.input_schema.schema())
```

Note: **Inspecting `.input_schema` and `.output_schema` is invaluable when debugging type mismatches or when integrating your chain with other systems. These schemas are automatically generated from your Pydantic models.**

By defining this model, you ensure that anyone using your reusable weather chain provides the correct, expected data structure, preventing runtime errors related to missing or malformed input arguments.

Implementing flexible compositions with LCEL

The transition from basic chains to production-ready, modular workflows is achieved through the LCEL. LCEL is not just a syntax; it is the definitive, modern standard for constructing agents in LangChain, ensuring automatic access to powerful features like streaming, concurrent execution, and tracing.

Introduction to LCEL

LCEL provides a declarative, fluent way to compose any object that implements the runnable protocol. A Runnable is any object that adheres to the standard interface (`.invoke()`, `.stream()`, `.ainvoke()`, `.batch()`), making its input and output predictable. By treating all components (prompts, models, parsers, tools) as Runnables, LCEL allows them to be seamlessly connected.

The core of LCEL is the pipe operator. This operator chains Runnables together, directing the output of the component on the left to be the input of the component on the right:

Syntax: `Runnable_A | Runnable_B | Runnable_C`

Note: **The pipe operator creates a new Runnable, not just a linear sequence of calls. This means the entire chain inherits all runnable protocol methods (`.invoke()`, `.stream()`, `.batch()`, etc.) automatically.**

Definition: **Runnable is a unit of work that can be invoked, batched, streamed, transformed and composed.**

It is useful to compare the high-level pipe-based syntax with the underlying execution contract it builds upon in order to comprehend how LCEL streamlines workflow construction. LCEL functions as a declarative layer on top of the Runnable interface, as shown in *Figure 2.4*, enabling developers to create readable pipelines while gaining access to robust, standardized execution capabilities:

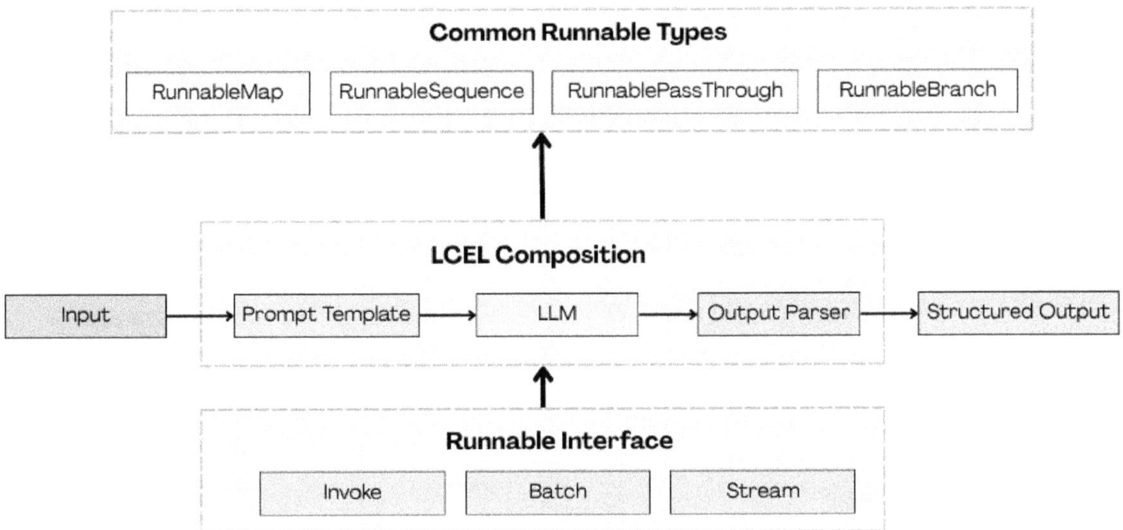

***Figure 2.4**: Basic LCEL composition and runnable interface*

Table 2.3 compares LCEL with the Runnable interface to make the distinction easier to understand. In simple terms, LCEL is the readable pipe-based syntax you write, while the Runnable interface is the common execution contract behind each step. This helps show how the declarative pipe syntax maps directly to the standardized capabilities that Runnables provide.

Concept	LCEL	Runnable interface
What it is	A high-level, declarative, pipe-based syntax for chaining steps.	A low-level, universal interface that all LCEL components are built on.
Core idea	Build pipelines using the pipe operator |, similar to Unix pipes, so data flows left-to-right through each step.	Treat every step as a Runnable object that can be composed, transformed, and executed in a uniform way.
Pipe operator	The | operator connects two Runnables; a | b means *run a, then feed its output to b.*	Uses operator overloading, so a | b returns a new **`RunnableSequence`** (or similar composite Runnable).
Syntax style	Short, expressive, chain-like syntax: prompt | model | parser.	More explicit and object-oriented. Construct and wire up **`RunnableSequence`**, **`RunnableMap`**, etc. directly.

Concept	LCEL	Runnable interface
Composition	Composition is primarily via `|`, plus helpers like **`.assign()`**, **`.map()`**, **`.pick()`**, **`branch()`**, and parallel helpers.	Same compositions expressed with concrete classes are **`RunnableSequence`**, **`RunnableMap`**, **`RunnableBranch`**, **`RunnableParallel`**, etc.
Execution	Any LCEL chain is itself a Runnable, so it supports **`.invoke()`**, **`.batch()`**, **`.stream()`**.	Runnable is the execution engine that every concrete Runnable exposes **`.invoke()`**, **`.batch()`**, **`.stream()`** and related methods.
Transforms	Transform helpers are **`.assign()`**, **`.map()`**, **`.pick()`** for branching, fan-out, and shaping inputs/outputs.	Same transforms via Runnable classes (**`RunnableMap`**, **`RunnableParallel`**, etc.).
Parallelism	**`RunnableParallel`** via LCEL helpers.	Directly instantiate **`RunnableParallel`**.
Conditionals	**`branch()`** in LCEL.	**`RunnableBranch`** manually.
Error handling	**`.with_retry()`**, **`.with_fallback()`** built in.	Same manually implemented

Table 2.3: Comparison of LangChain expression language and runnable interface

Concept: LCEL allows you to express your workflow as a simple, readable pipeline, minimizing the boilerplate code that was common in older LangChain versions.

The following example demonstrates a complete LCEL chain that processes weather queries through three connected components:

```
from langchain_openai import ChatOpenAI
from langchain_core.prompts import ChatPromptTemplate
from langchain_core.output_parsers import StrOutputParser

# 1. Instantiate Runnable components
model = ChatOpenAI(model="gpt-4o-mini", temperature=0)
prompt = ChatPromptTemplate.from_template("What's the weather like in
{city}?")
output_parser = StrOutputParser()

# 2. Chain them using the pipe operator
# The entire chain is now one single Runnable object
weather_chain = prompt | model | output_parser

# The LCEL chain automatically inherits streaming capabilities:
```

```
# for chunk in weather_chain.stream({"city": "Seattle"}):
#     print(chunk, end="", flush=True)
```

The following figure visualizes the data flow through this LCEL chain, showing how input is transformed at each stage:

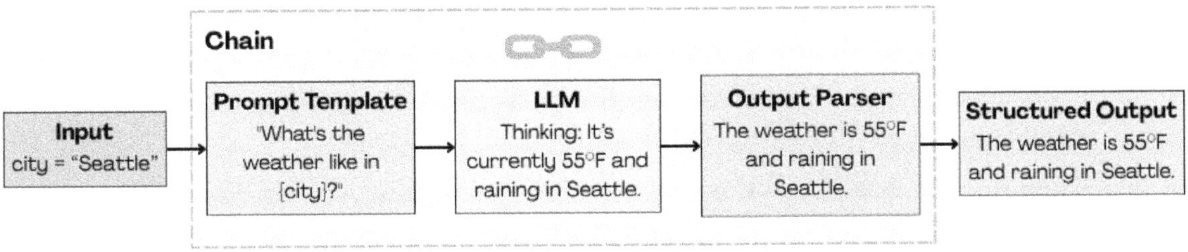

***Figure 2.5**: LCEL weather chain flow from prompt to model to output parser*

This structure is visually intuitive and easy to trace.

Applying modular design using LCEL chains

LCEL provides specialized Runnables that enable non-linear logic and advanced composition, greatly expanding modularity.

Parallel execution with RunnableParallel

The **`RunnableParallel`** construct is essential for latency reduction and concurrent execution. It accepts a dictionary of Runnables and runs all of them simultaneously. This is useful when multiple components, such as data retrieval from two different sources or the formatting of two separate inputs, do not depend on each other.

The dictionary keys become the keys in the output.

Tip: **Use `RunnableParallel` whenever you have independent operations that do not depend on each other's results. This can dramatically reduce latency, especially when calling multiple APIs or retrieving data from different sources.**

The following figure illustrates how **`RunnableParallel`** executes multiple operations concurrently and merges their outputs:

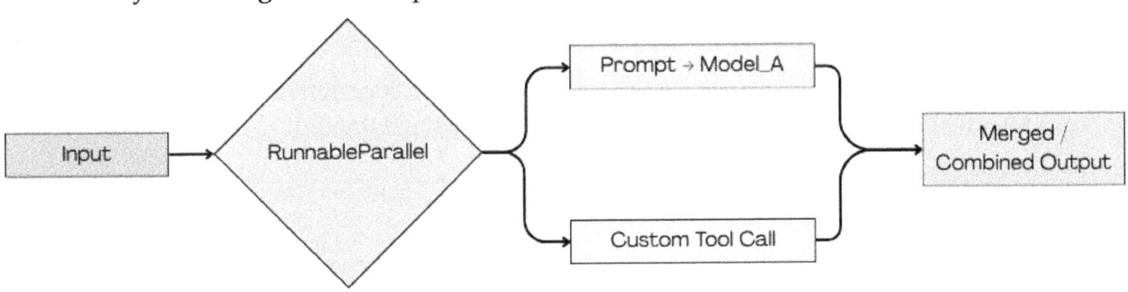

***Figure 2.6**: Parallel LCEL chain using RunnableParallel*

Input output transformation with RunnablePassthrough and RunnableLambda

To manage and transform data between steps, LCEL provides two simple yet powerful Runnables:

- **RunnablePassthrough**: The simplest Runnable; it just passes the input through unchanged. It is most commonly used with **RunnableParallel** to ensure the original input is preserved or made accessible to parallel branches.
- **RunnableLambda**: This wraps any standard Python function (lambda or full function) to easily implement intermediate data transformation, formatting, or custom business logic within the chain.

Refactoring LangChain agent with LCEL

The agent built in *Chapter 1, Building Your First LangChain Agent*, likely used older, verbose, and less scalable code (e.g., using **LLMChain**). Refactoring it to LCEL immediately demonstrates the modular benefits and aligns the code with production standards.

This table highlights the syntactic and functional improvements achieved by refactoring legacy LangChain code to LCEL:

Component	Legacy	LCEL refactor
Chain	`LLMChain(prompt=p, llm=m)`	`p | m | StrOutputParser()`
Input	`chain.run(city="Seattle")`	`chain.invoke({"city": "Seattle"})`
Streaming	Manual logic/callbacks	`for chunk in chain.stream(input): ...`

Table 2.4: Legacy vs. LCEL refactoring comparison

The primary improvement in the refactored code is using a dictionary within the LCEL chain. This dictionary creation is equivalent to **RunnableParallel** and is the mechanism for structuring the input for the next component.

This code example demonstrates a complete RAG chain refactored using LCEL, with parallel operations for context retrieval and input passthrough:

```
from langchain_core.runnables import RunnablePassthrough
from langchain_core.output_parsers import StrOutputParser

# Assume 'retriever' (a component that fetches context) and 'model' are
defined
# Assume 'RAG_prompt' is a ChatPromptTemplate expecting 'context' and
'question'
```

```
# The chain structure (dictionary) runs two operations in parallel:
# 1. "context": calls the retriever
# 2. "question": uses RunnablePassthrough to get the original input
refactored_chain = (
    {
        "context": retriever, # Retrieves data based on the full input
        "question": RunnablePassthrough() # Passes the original input query
    }
    | RAG_prompt # The prompt receives {'context': ..., 'question': ...}
    | model
    | StrOutputParser()
)

# This single chain is now a robust, modular RAG system.
```

By leveraging LCEL, you transform previously complex, tightly coupled code into a clear, decoupled sequence of modular Runnables, making your agent effortlessly maintainable and scalable.

Chain-level error handling and fallbacks

In production environments, external service failures (such as API timeouts, rate limits, or unexpected model errors) are inevitable. A core advantage of the LCEL is its native support for defining fault tolerance directly within the chain structure using the **`.with_fallbacks()`** method.

This method allows you to define one or more fallback Runnables that will automatically be executed if the primary component fails, ensuring service continuity without requiring complex **`try...except`** blocks around your entire workflow.

Implementing automatic recovery with .with_fallbacks()

The **`.with_fallbacks()`** method is highly modular, as it can be applied to any individual Runnable component, be it an LLM, a tool, or an entire nested chain. This enables granular control over recovery strategies.

Use case for model redundancy

The most common use case is ensuring that if a high-cost, high-performance model (e.g., **`gpt-4o`**) fails or hits a rate limit, the chain automatically switches to a more reliable, lower-cost alternative (e.g., **`gpt-4o-mini`**).

The following implementation shows how to create a resilient model configuration with automatic fallback from a premium to a standard model:

```
# Code Block: Implementing Model Fallback
from langchain_openai import ChatOpenAI
from langchain_core.prompts import ChatPromptTemplate
from langchain_core.output_parsers import StrOutputParser

# Define the primary (expensive/high-performance) model
primary_model = ChatOpenAI(model="gpt-4o", temperature=0)

# Define the fallback (reliable/cheap) model
fallback_model = ChatOpenAI(model="gpt-4o-mini", temperature=0)

# Apply the fallback using .with_fallbacks()
resilient_model = primary_model.with_fallbacks([fallback_model])

# Create a weather query chain with model resilience
prompt = ChatPromptTemplate.from_template("What's the weather like in
{city}?")
parser = StrOutputParser()

resilient_chain = prompt | resilient_model | parser

# This chain will use GPT-4o first, and then GPT-4o-mini if it fails
# result = resilient_chain.invoke({"city": "Seattle"})
```

Use case for tool and service fallbacks

The fallback mechanism is not limited to just models; it applies to any Runnable, including custom tools or complex sub-chains.

Imagine a critical task that first attempts to fetch weather data from a fast, premium weather API service, but if that fails, it should attempt a slower, free weather API instead.

This code demonstrates tool-level fallback implementation, where a premium weather API is backed by a reliable free alternative:

```
# Code Block: Implementing Tool Fallback
from langchain_core.tools import tool

@tool
def premium_weather_api(city: str) -> str:
    """Fast, accurate weather data from premium API service."""
    # Simulates a fast but potentially unreliable premium service
```

```
    return f"Premium weather data for {city}"

@tool
def free_weather_api(city: str) -> str:
    """Reliable but slower free weather API fallback."""
    # Simulates a slower but more reliable free service
    return f"Free weather data for {city}"

# Define the primary tool with a fallback to the slower tool
resilient_weather_tool = premium_weather_api.with_fallbacks([free_weather_
api])

# The agent's chain will try the premium API first, then the free API
# This ensures weather data is always retrieved even if the premium service
fails
```

The key takeaways for fallbacks are as follows:

- **Granularity**: Fallbacks can be defined on a single component, not just the entire workflow.
- **Automatic**: The recovery is handled automatically by the LCEL runtime; no manual error checking is needed.
- **Sequential**: Fallbacks are executed in the order they are listed until one succeeds or the list is exhausted.

Note: **Order your fallbacks from most specific/expensive to most general/cheap. For example, try a premium API before falling back to a free one, or attempt a specialized model before using a general-purpose one.**

Debugging modular workflows without LangSmith

Modular LCEL chains, particularly those involving fallbacks (refer to *Chain-level error handling and fallbacks* section) or parallel processing (**`RunnableParallel`**), can be difficult to debug using simple **`print()`** statements. Since we are focusing strictly on native LangChain capabilities, we rely on verbose logging and chain tracing context managers to monitor execution.

Verbose mode

The simplest way to see what is happening inside a chain is by setting the **`verbose=True`** flag during the initialization of the LLM or agent components. This outputs internal thoughts, prompts sent to the model, and tool calls to your console.

Here is how to enable verbose logging for a model to see detailed execution information:

```
# Code Block: Enabling Verbose Mode
# Set verbose=True on the model or the overall AgentExecutor
model = ChatOpenAI(temperature=0, verbose=True)

# This prints execution details for all components downstream of the model
```

Note: **Verbose mode can produce significant console output in complex chains. Consider using it selectively during development and disabling it in production environments.**

The native tracing context manager

For more granular control over complex Runnables, LangChain provides a built-in context manager for local tracing. This allows you to group related executions and see the hierarchy of calls within the chain.

You can use the **`trace_as_chain_group`** context manager from **`langchain_core.globals`** to define a logical group for tracing, making it easier to review the nested execution steps in your local logs.

The following example shows how to wrap chain execution in a tracing context for detailed inspection of intermediate steps:

```
# Code Block: Using Local Tracing Context
from langchain_core.globals import trace_as_chain_group

# Assuming 'weather_report_chain' is your compiled LCEL Runnable
input_data = {"city": "Boston"}

with trace_as_chain_group("Weather_Report_Execution", inputs=input_data) as
handler:
    # Run the chain within the context manager
    result = weather_report_chain.invoke(input_data)

# The handler object provides access to the trace structure locally,
# allowing programmatic inspection of intermediate steps (e.g., tool inputs/
outputs)
# if needed for complex debugging scenarios.
```

By leveraging these native features, you can still gain crucial visibility into the execution path of your LCEL Runnables, essential for diagnosing issues like prompt injection failures or unexpected tool outputs.

Design patterns for production-grade agents

Moving beyond functional prototypes requires adopting established design patterns and maintaining a structured codebase. These patterns simplify complex decision-making and ensure that your agent logic remains predictable, testable, and scalable, even as the application grows.

Applying design patterns to organize logic

To build truly robust applications, we move from simple linear chains to complex architectural patterns that manage how input is processed and routed.

Router chains pattern for a multi-chain approach

The router chain pattern addresses the challenge of creating a single agent that handles diverse requests. Instead of trying to make one general-purpose LLM handle all specialized logic (e.g., finance, HR, technical support), a primary LLM, acting as a router, first classifies the user's query and then delegates the task to a specialized sub-chain.

This is implemented using the **`RunnableBranch`** component. **`RunnableBranch`** takes a list of condition/runnable pairs, executing the runnable corresponding to the first condition that evaluates to **`True`**.

The following figure illustrates the router chain pattern where a classifier model routes queries to specialized sub-chains based on query type:

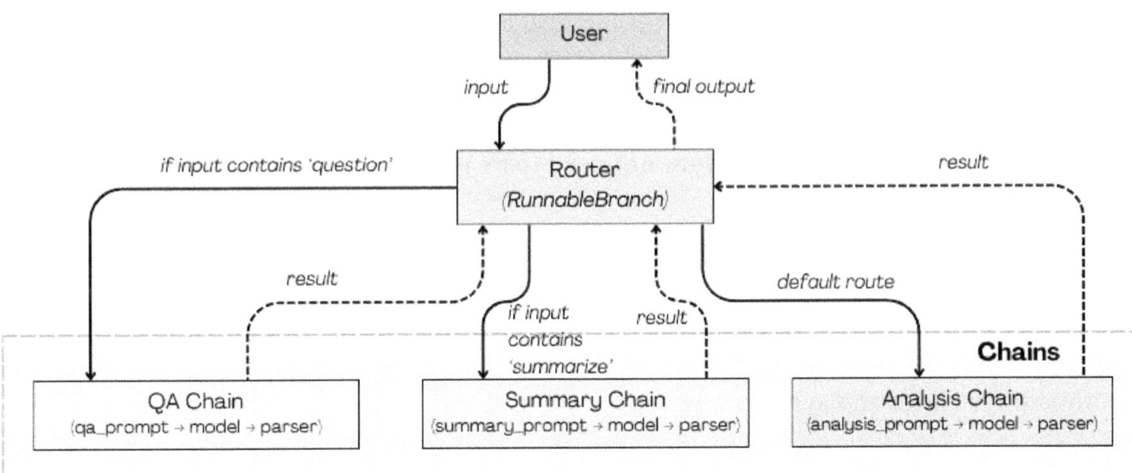

***Figure 2.7**: Router pattern for domain-specific handling with RunnableBranch*

LangChain offers the router chain pattern to manage various user intents within a single agent without forming a monolithic chain. This pattern ensures that each chain stays focused on a single responsibility while the overall agent remains flexible and scalable by evaluating user input in an initial decision step and dynamically routing it to a specialized sub-chain.

The following code demonstrates the router chain pattern to manage various user intents within a single agent:

```
from langchain_core.runnables import RunnableBranch

# Define specialized chains
 qa_chain = qa_prompt | model | parser
 summary_chain = summary_prompt | model | parser
 analysis_chain = analysis_prompt | model | parser

# Create router
 router = RunnableBranch(
     (lambda x: "question" in x["input"].lower(), qa_chain),
     (lambda x: "summarize" in x["input"].lower(), summary_chain),
     analysis_chain  # default
 )

result = router.invoke({"input": "What is AI?"})
```

This approach offers two key benefits:

- **Efficiency**: Specialized sub-chains can use smaller, cheaper LLMs or highly tuned prompts, saving cost and latency.
- **Accuracy**: The agent only uses the necessary tools and knowledge base for the specific task, reducing hallucinations and improving grounding.

Tip: **When implementing router chains, use a lightweight, fast model for the routing decision itself. The routing LLM does not need to be powerful, it just needs to classify the query correctly.**

Retrieval-augmented generation chain

The RAG pattern is the most prevalent and powerful technique for grounding LLM responses in external, proprietary data. It transforms the workflow from a simple Q&A system into an information retrieval and synthesis system.

The RAG chain uses a retriever component (e.g., a vector database search) to fetch relevant context from an external knowledge base *before* the prompt is sent to the LLM. The context is then injected directly into the prompt template, effectively giving the LLM the information it needs to answer the question accurately.

The following figure shows the chain structure (Implemented via LCEL):

***Figure 2.8**: Illustration of the chain via LCEL*

The following figure visualizes how RAG retrieves relevant context and integrates it into the prompt before LLM processing:

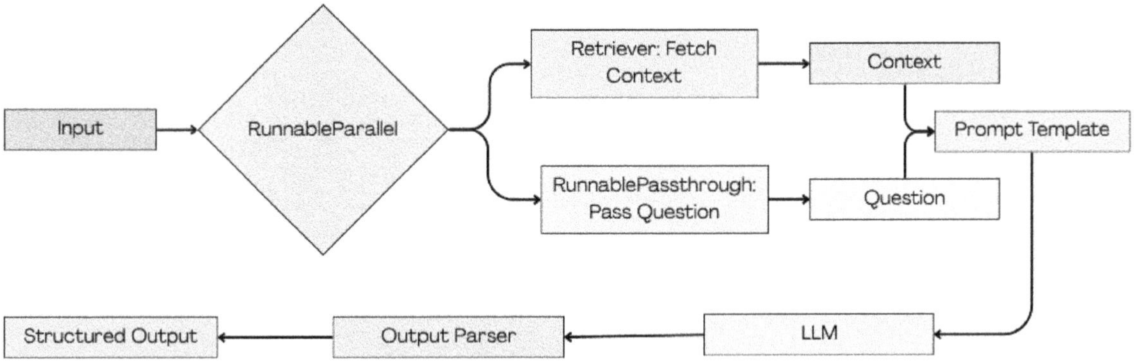

***Figure 2.9**: Illustration of the RAG chain*

This implementation demonstrates a complete RAG chain using LCEL with parallel retrieval and question passthrough:

```
from langchain_core.runnables import RunnablePassthrough, RunnableParallel
from langchain_core.output_parsers import StrOutputParser
from langchain_core.prompts import ChatPromptTemplate
from langchain_openai import ChatOpenAI
from langchain_community.vectorstores import FAISS
from langchain_openai import OpenAIEmbeddings

# 1. Create vector store with weather information
vectorstore = FAISS.from_texts(
    [
        "San Francisco typically has mild weather year-round with fog in summer.",
        "Seattle is known for rainy weather, especially in fall and winter.",
        "Boston experiences cold winters with snow and warm, humid summers."
    ],
    embedding=OpenAIEmbeddings()
)
```

```
# 2. Create retriever from vector store
 retriever = vectorstore.as_retriever(search_kwargs={"k": 2})

# 3. Define RAG prompt that expects both context and question
 rag_prompt = ChatPromptTemplate.from_template("""
 Use the following context to answer the question. If you cannot answer based
on the context, say so.

Context: {context}

Question: {question}

Answer:
 """)

# 4. Create model and parser
 model = ChatOpenAI(model="gpt-4o-mini", temperature=0)
 parser = StrOutputParser()

# 5. Build parallel retrieval component
 parallel_retrieval = RunnableParallel(
     context=retriever,  # Fetches relevant context from vector store
     question=RunnablePassthrough()  # Passes the user's question unchanged
 )

# 6. Assemble the complete RAG chain
 rag_chain = parallel_retrieval | rag_prompt | model | parser

# Usage example:
 # answer = rag_chain.invoke("What's the weather like in Seattle?")
 # The retriever fetches relevant context, which is then used by the LLM to
generate an informed answer
```

This RAG implementation leverages **`RunnableParallel`** (via dictionary syntax) to simultaneously retrieve context and preserve the original question, then combines them in the prompt for accurate, grounded responses.

The MapReduce pattern for summarization

When dealing with large volumes of text (e.g., hundreds of retrieved documents, a long meeting transcript, or a very large context from a RAG retrieval), fitting all the data into the LLM's context window becomes impossible. The MapReduce pattern is the standard solution for this challenge.

This pattern breaks down a massive task into many small, parallel tasks (the map phase) and then aggregates the results into a single final output (the reduce phase):

- **Map phase (parallel processing)**: The large input text is split into smaller, manageable chunks. Each chunk is passed independently to an LLM with a prompt asking for a partial summary. This is inherently parallel and highly efficient, perfect for implementation with `RunnableParallel` in LCEL.
- **Reduce phase (aggregation)**: The small, partial summaries are collected. They are then passed to a final LLM call with a prompt asking it to synthesize all partial summaries into one coherent, final response.

Use case: Summarizing a 50-page technical report by processing it in 10-page chunks.

Implementation note: **LangChain provides a built-in `load_summarize_chain` utility that simplifies creating MapReduce , but understanding the underlying LCEL composition is vital for customization. The MapReduce logic relies heavily on modularity. Refer to the Implementing flexible compositions with LCEL section.**

The following figure visualizes the MapReduce pattern, showing how large documents are split, processed in parallel, and then aggregated into a final summary:

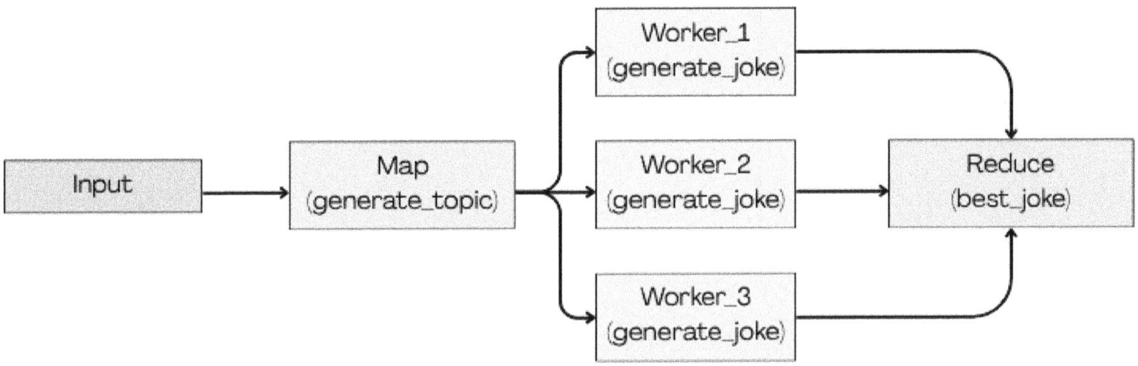

***Figure 2.10**: Illustration of the MapReduce pattern*

The *map* phase processes each chunk independently, producing intermediate results (summaries, extracted data, classifications). The *reduce* phase combines these intermediate results into a final output. This pattern is familiar from distributed computing but applies perfectly to LangChain workflows:

```
from langchain.chains import MapReduceDocumentsChain
from langchain.text_splitter import RecursiveCharacterTextSplitter

# Split documents
splitter = RecursiveCharacterTextSplitter(chunk_size=1000)
chunks = splitter.split_text(long_document)
```

```
# Map: Summarize each chunk
map_chain = prompt | model | parser
summaries = [map_chain.invoke({"text": chunk}) for chunk in chunks]

# Reduce: Combine summaries
reduce_prompt = ChatPromptTemplate.from_template(
    "Combine these summaries: {summaries}"
)
reduce_chain = reduce_prompt | model | parser
final_summary = reduce_chain.invoke({"summaries": "\n".join(summaries)})
```

This pattern is invaluable for long documents. The map phase handles chunks in parallel (if you implement parallel execution), making efficient use of resources. The reduce phase synthesizes results, creating coherent output from distributed processing, as shown in the following figure:

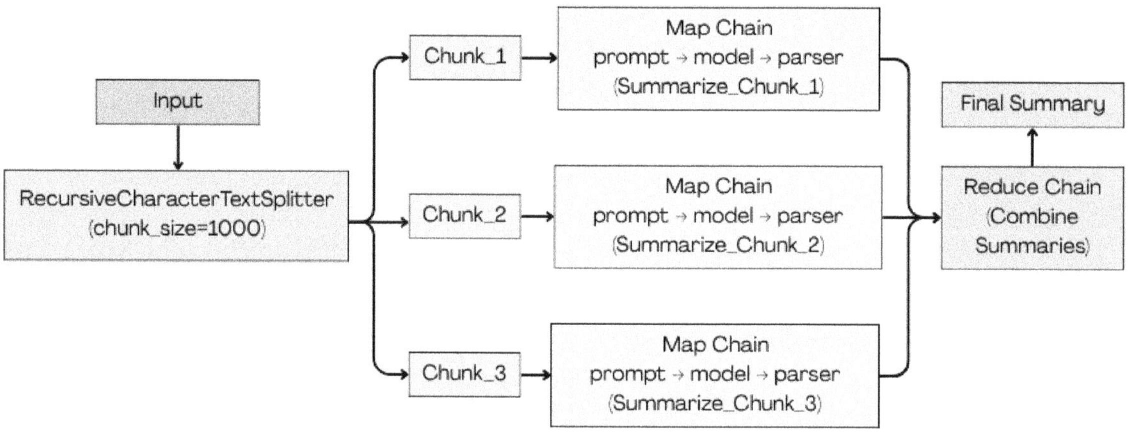

***Figure 2.11**: MapReduce pattern for summarization*

Building modular libraries for reusable agents

For large projects, code must be organized into logical modules that can be easily imported and reused. This enforces true reusability beyond simple component-level chaining.

Project structure guide

A standard, maintainable structure for a LangChain project separates components based on their function:

```
my_project/
├── src/
```

```
│   ├── agents/       # Top-level agent logic and complex chains (e.g.,
weather_agent.py)
│   ├── prompts/      # All ChatPromptTemplate definitions (e.g., weather_
prompts.py)
│   ├── tools/        # All custom functions decorated with @tool
│   └── schemas/      # All pydantic.BaseModel definitions for structured
output
└── main.py           # Entry point and configuration
```

Reusability via functions

The most modular practice is defining Python functions that accept configuration arguments (like a specific LLM or list of tools) and return a Runnable. This allows a chain to be configured dynamically and imported anywhere in the project, treating the chain itself as a factory object.

The following factory function demonstrates how to create configurable, reusable chains that can be instantiated with different components:

```
# Function defined in src/agents/weather_agent.py
def create_weather_chain(llm_model, weather_prompt, output_parser):
    """Returns a fully configured LCEL Runnable for weather queries."""
    # This function defines the chain structure but takes the components as
arguments
    return (
        weather_prompt
        | llm_model
        | output_parser # The chain is instantly ready for invoke/stream/
batch
    )
# In main.py: weather_agent = create_weather_chain(model_A, prompt_B,
parser_C)
```

Testing strategy for reusable components

Modular design is incomplete without a robust testing strategy. The primary benefit of breaking a workflow into small Runnables is that each piece can be tested in isolation, guaranteeing its behavior before it is composed into a complex chain. A production-grade component must be validated through two types of tests, i.e., unit tests and integration tests.

Tip: **Never skip unit tests in favor of only integration tests. Unit tests are faster, more reliable, and pinpoint exactly where failures occur. Integration tests are essential but should complement, not replace, unit testing.**

Unit tests for component isolation

Unit tests establish design discipline in addition to correctness. Uncertain responsibilities, hidden dependencies, and excessively coupled logic quickly come to light when components are tested separately. By promoting clearer boundaries and more straightforward interfaces, this feedback loop strengthens the single responsibility principle. Strong unit-test coverage eventually serves as both a design guide and a quality safeguard, guaranteeing that every LangChain component stays reusable, predictable, and focused as the system develops.

Unit tests focus on individual components, like the **`get_current_weather`** tool, without executing the full LCEL chain or making external LLM calls. The goal and method of unit tests are as follows:

- **Goal**: Verify the tool's input contract, internal logic, and predictable output structure (even though the output is simulated JSON).
- **Method**: Run the tool function directly and check its return value against known inputs.

The following unit tests demonstrate how to validate individual tool behavior without invoking the full chain or making external API calls:

```
# tests/test_weather_tool.py - Unit Test Example
import pytest
from your_module.tools import get_current_weather

# Simplified Unit Test Example
def test_weather_tool():
    """Test weather tool returns expected format."""
    result = get_current_weather.invoke("Boston")
    data = json.loads(result)
    assert "temp" in data
    assert "condition" in data
```

Integration tests for end-to-end validation

Integration tests verify that the composed components (tool, prompt, and LLM) work correctly together to produce a coherent, final result. For this, we must hit the live LLM API. The goal and method of integration tests are as follows:

- **Goal**: Verify the LLM successfully interpreted the raw tool output (JSON) and transformed it into the requested friendly, natural language report.
- **Method**: Invoke the full LCEL Runnable and check the output for correctness, context, and format.

This integration test validates the entire chain by executing it against a live LLM and verifying the end-to-end output quality:

```
# tests/test_weather_chain.py - Integration Test Example
@pytest.mark.integration
def test_weather_report_integration(weather_report_chain):
    """Integration test for the full weather report LCEL chain."""

    city = "Boston"
    # Run the full LCEL chain, hitting the live LLM
    report = weather_report_chain.invoke(city)

    # 1. Check for LLM interpretation and relevance
    assert len(report) > 30
    assert city in report

    # 2. Check for transformation: The report should NOT contain the raw tool
output structure
    # (i.e., the LLM correctly interpreted the JSON)
    assert 'temp' not in report.lower()
    assert 'condition' not in report.lower()

    # 3. Check for successful formatting (expected output of a good system
prompt)
    assert "report" in report.lower() or "forecast" in report.lower()
```

By enforcing this two-tiered testing strategy, you ensure the reliability of both the individual component's function (unit test) and the complete production workflow (integration test). This is the hallmark of a maintainable, modular system.

Building a production-grade modular weather agent

This section brings together all the modular design concepts introduced throughout this chapter into a single, cohesive example. By incrementally assembling a production-ready weather information agent, we demonstrate how prompts, tools, structured output parsers, and LCEL-based composition work together as a unified system. The focus is not on learning new syntax, but on applying sound architectural principles such as single responsibility, composability, fault tolerance, and testability to build an agent that is reliable, reusable, and easy to evolve as requirements change. We will construct an LCEL-based agent capable of retrieving weather information (using an external tool) and formatting the results in a structured format (using Pydantic):

- **Define structured output**: Create the **WeatherReport** Pydantic model.
- **Define tool**: Create a custom **get_weather_data** tool.
- **Define prompt**: Create the **ChatPromptTemplate** and inject the parser's format instructions.
- **Assemble the chain**: Use LCEL to combine the components into a single **RunnableSequence**.

The modular execution flow of the weather agent is summarized below, showing how data is transformed and enriched at each stage of the LCEL pipeline.

The agent begins with raw user input, retrieves weather data using a dedicated tool, injects the retrieved context into a prompt, invokes the language model, and finally parses the response into a validated Pydantic object.

The complete implementation ties together all concepts from this chapter into a single, production-ready weather information agent as follows:

```
# Final Code Block: Assembling the complete LCEL chain
from langchain_openai import ChatOpenAI
from langchain_core.prompts import ChatPromptTemplate
from langchain_core.runnables import RunnablePassthrough
from langchain_core.output_parsers import PydanticOutputParser
from .schemas import WeatherReport # Import Pydantic model

# 1. Define Components
model = ChatOpenAI(model="gpt-4o-mini", temperature=0)
tool = get_weather_data # Assuming this is defined as a Runnable Tool
parser = PydanticOutputParser(pydantic_object=WeatherReport)

# 2. Define Prompt with instructions
template = "Based on the weather data: {weather_data}. Format the weather
report. {format_instructions}"
prompt = ChatPromptTemplate.from_template(template).partial(
    format_instructions=parser.get_format_instructions()
)

# 3. Assemble the LCEL Chain
weather_chain = (
    # First, run the tool to get the weather data
    {"weather_data": tool, "city": RunnablePassthrough()}
    # Then, pass weather data and city to the prompt
    | prompt
    # Send formatted prompt to the LLM
```

```
        | model
        # Finally, parse the result into a structured object
        | parser
)

# Result: weather_report = weather_chain.invoke("San Francisco")
```

The resulting **`weather_chain`** is a single, robust **`Runnable`** that takes a city name and returns a validated **`WeatherReport`** object, embodying the power and reusability of modular LCEL design.

Conclusion

By learning modular design and the LCEL, this chapter gave us the skills we needed to move from simple scripts to production-grade agent operations. To make components that can be put together, including prompts, tools, and parsers, we used the SRP and the runnable protocol. We were able to use the pipe operator (|) to design strong chains, .with_fallbacks() to make them fault-tolerant, and sophisticated structures like the Router chain and the MapReduce pattern. We made sure that the reusable parts we made here are a solid, manageable base for all future AI applications by setting clear rules for testing and debugging with verbose logging.

In the next chapter, LLM Reasoning and Agent Intelligence goes deep into the agent's cognitive foundation, now that you know how to build in modules. We will talk about how to turn basic LLM calls into powerful problem-solving systems by using advanced reasoning frameworks. Using annotated code and visual diagrams, you will understand the pros and cons of **Reasoning + Acting** (**ReAct**), Plan-and-Execute, and **tree-of-thoughts** (**ToT**). We will also talk about important production problems, like how to choose and integrate models, how to use advanced prompt engineering to get better results, and how to make cost and performance more efficient. You will learn how to make smart, cost-effective agents for any complicated activity by looking at real-world benchmarks and using log analysis.

CHAPTER 3
LLM Reasoning and Agent Intelligence

Introduction

You have learned how to use the **LangChain Expression Language** (**LCEL**) to build modular, reusable parts of a program and put them together. You can now reliably design a multi-step workflow. A real AI agent is not just a set of processes; it is a system that can make decisions, plan, and fix itself on the go.

This chapter marks the transition from building chains to building agent systems. We move from how the parts fit together to how an agent produces useful behavior through the interaction of the **large language model** (**LLM**), prompts, context, tools, and control flow. Rather than treating the LLM as a standalone reasoning engine, it is more accurate to view it as a probabilistic pattern predictor whose outputs are heavily shaped by the instructions and information it receives. In practice, much of an agent's apparent reasoning emerges from the broader loop around the model: prompts that structure the task, tools that gather or transform information, and iterative cycles of thought, action, and observation that guide the system toward a result.

We will explain the basic reasoning frameworks that make this behavior possible by contrasting the simple **Reasoning and Acting** (**ReAct**) pattern with more complicated methods like plan-and-execute and the tree of thoughts.

However, an LLM rarely works alone in a production-grade agent. It is usually part of a broader system that supplies knowledge, maintains state, and coordinates actions. **Retrieval-augmented generation** (**RAG**) grounds the model in external documents and current data rather than relying only on its training parameters, which improves factuality and domain relevance. Memory preserves useful context across turns or steps, allowing the agent to remember prior interactions, intermediate results, or user preferences. Orchestration is the control layer that connects prompts, tools, retrieval, and execution logic so the agent can decide what to do next and carry out multi-step workflows reliably. Together, these surrounding systems turn a standalone LLM into an effective agent capable of grounded, stateful, and coordinated reasoning.

Structure

This chapter covers the following topics:

- Model integration and performance evaluation
- Prompt engineering for agent reasoning
- Implementing advanced agent reasoning frameworks
- Orchestrating and customizing agent executors
- Benchmarking and optimization

Objectives

The principles of agent intelligence and the abilities required to build, test, and improve a powerful reasoning engine will be clear to you by the end of this chapter. Using both cost-effective solutions like Claude 3 Haiku and high-performance models like GPT-4o, you will investigate how to incorporate multiple LLMs into a single agent workflow.

You will also discover why the most important element influencing agent behavior is model selection. Ultimately, you will develop a sound strategy to compare the accuracy, speed, and cost of various LLM backends, allowing you to decide which models are most appropriate for production deployment based on data.

Model integration and performance evaluation

The core of every intelligent agent is the LLM itself, which acts as the agent's central processing unit for reasoning and decision-making. In a production environment, you must be able to integrate and benchmark many models to guarantee you select the ideal balance of dependability, speed, and cost for the task.

Integrating various LLMs into agent workflows

LangChain's architecture concentrates on model agnosticism, a paradigm that allows developers to consider models from multiple suppliers (OpenAI, Anthropic, Google) as interchangeable components. This is achieved using the standardized **`BaseLanguageModel`** interface, which all model wrappers conform to.

Model swapping in LCEL

Swapping a model in a complex agent architecture is surprisingly straightforward, typically requiring only a change in the model object definition, confirming the effectiveness of modular LCEL design from *Chapter 2, Designing Modular and Reusable LangChain Workflows*.

The following code explains how to generate two similar chains with different LLMs, illustrating the model-agnostic design pattern in action:

```
# Code Block: Swapping LLMs in a Runnable
from langchain_openai import ChatOpenAI
from langchain_anthropic import ChatAnthropic
from langchain_core.prompts import ChatPromptTemplate
from langchain_core.output_parsers import StrOutputParser

# 1. Define LLM 1 (High-Performance)
llm_gpt4o = ChatOpenAI(model="gpt-4o", temperature=0)

# 2. Define LLM 2 (Cost-Effective)
llm_claude = ChatAnthropic(model="claude-3-haiku-20240307", temperature=0)

prompt = ChatPromptTemplate.from_template("What is the weather forecast for
{city}? Provide a brief summary.")

# Create the initial chain using GPT-4o
chain_gpt = prompt | llm_gpt4o | StrOutputParser()

# The same prompt can be reused immediately with Claude 3 Haiku
chain_claude = prompt | llm_claude | StrOutputParser()
```

The beauty of LCEL and the Runnable interface is that swapping models is as simple as replacing one Runnable LLM instance with another, provided their input/output schemas are compatible.

Quick overview of remote versus local LLMs

The world of LLMs offers a spectrum of choices, primarily categorized by where they run:

- **Remote LLMs (API-based)**:
  - **Examples**: OpenAI (GPT models), Anthropic (Claude), Google (Gemini), Cohere.
  - **Pros**: Generally, the highest performance, the largest models, easy to use (just an API key), and no local setup.
  - **Cons**: Cost per token, data privacy concerns (data sent to provider), reliance on external service, potential latency.
- **Local LLMs (self-hosted)**:
  - **Examples**: Llama 2, Mistral, Gemma, Phi-2 (run via tools like Ollama, LM Studio, vLLM).

- **Pros**: Zero ongoing cost after initial setup, full data privacy (data stays on your machine), no internet dependency (after model download), and greater control and customization.
- **Cons**: Requires powerful local hardware [**graphics processing unit** (**GPU**) often essential for larger models], initial setup can be more involved, performance might lag behind top-tier remote models.

LangChain provides seamless integrations for both, allowing you to build your LCEL pipelines with a clear separation of concerns.

Model trade-offs for agent reliability

When choosing an LLM for agentic workloads (where the model must decide on tools), the attention changes beyond simple response quality to structural reliability. The details are as follows:

- **Tool calling reliability**: The most crucial factor. Modern agents depend on the LLM generating syntactically valid, structured JSON or Pydantic calls for tools. Models with specialized tool-calling APIs (like GPT-4o and Claude 3 Opus) offer much higher dependability than those depending merely on prompt-based text processing.
- **Context window size**: Agents use the context window as a scratchpad (to store thoughts, actions, and observations). A bigger context window facilitates longer agent trajectories and complicated, multi-step reasoning before memory is discharged.

Benchmarking cost, speed, and accuracy

An agent that is brilliant but too slow or expensive is not production-ready. We must build a framework to systematically measure performance across different reasoning processes (which we shall discuss in the *Implementing advanced agent reasoning frameworks* section).

Defining agent benchmarks

We focus on three orthogonal indicators that provide a holistic view of agent performance. The following table presents the basic metrics used to evaluate agent systems, along with their measurement approaches and relative importance:

Metric	Definition	Measurement technique	Importance for agents
Accuracy	Percentage of tasks completed successfully (correct tool use, correct final answer).	Deterministic testing and LLM-as-a-Judge (evaluators).	Highest (If the agent fails the task, all other metrics are irrelevant).
Latency (speed)	End-to-end time (in seconds) from initial query to final output.	Python's **time** library, including LLM inference and external tool execution.	High (directly impacts user experience).
Cost	Total token usage (input and output) per query run.	**tiktoken** library, or tracking usage via model API response metadata.	Critical (agents generate high token usage due to iterative loops).

***Table 3.1**: Core agent benchmarking metrics and measurement approaches*

Implementing a benchmarking strategy in LangChain

To record cost and delay measurements exactly, we leverage the callback system provided by LangChain. A custom callback handler can collect the exact token consumption and timing for every LLM call throughout the agent's iterative loop.

The following code builds a custom callback handler that counts total execution time and token consumption across all LLM calls inside an agent run:

```
# Code Block: Implementing a Basic Timing and Token Callback
from langchain_core.callbacks import BaseCallbackHandler
import time

class BenchmarkCallback(BaseCallbackHandler):
    """Tracks cumulative time and token usage for an agent run."""
    def __init__(self):
        self.start_time = None
        self.total_tokens = 0
        self.total_cost = 0 # Requires cost mapping per model

    def on_llm_start(self, *args, **kwargs):
        if self.start_time is None:
            self.start_time = time.time()

    def on_llm_end(self, response, **kwargs):
        # Accumulate token usage from the LLM's metadata
```

```
        usage = response.llm_output.get('token_usage', {})
        self.total_tokens += usage.get('total_tokens', 0)
        # Note: Cost calculation would involve multiplying tokens by the
model's price per token

    def get_results(self):
        latency = time.time() - self.start_time
        return {"latency_seconds": latency, "total_tokens": self.total_
tokens}

# Usage: agent_executor.invoke(input, config={"callbacks":
[BenchmarkCallback()]})
```

Visualizing the swap and interoperability

The flexibility to shift models while preserving the complex agent loop is the essential takeaway of LangChain's modular design.

The following figure depicts how the **AgentExecutor** maintains a fixed orchestration loop while multiple LLM models can be smoothly changed in and out:

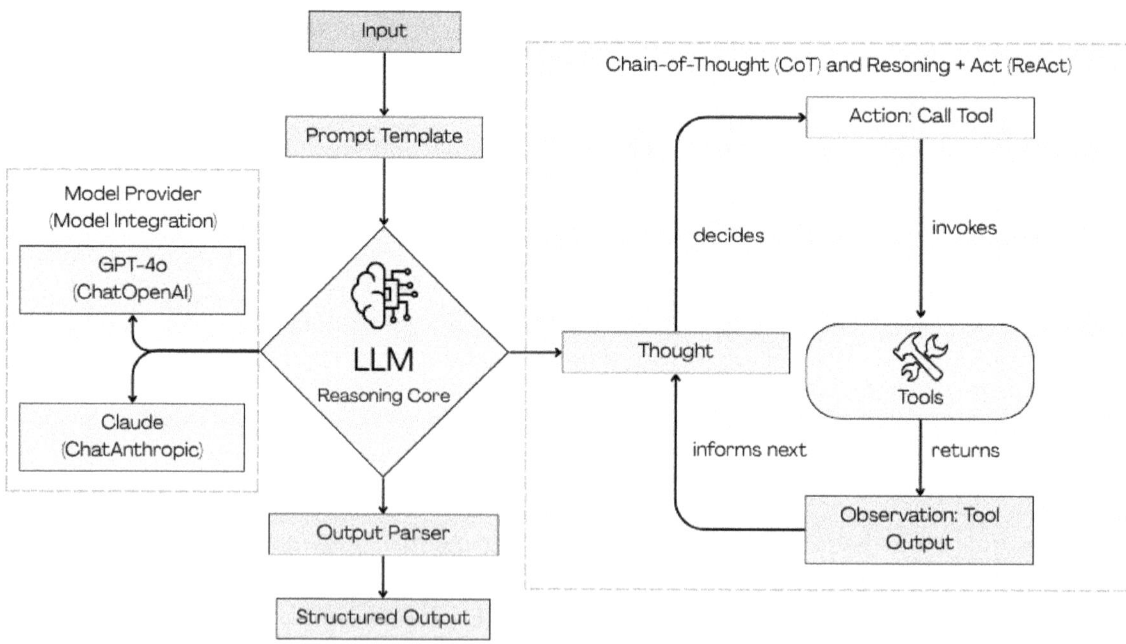

Figure 3.1: AgentExecuter, the core agent loop

This figure highlights how the **AgentExecutor** (the core loop) remains stable, but the specific LLM inside the Reasoning Core may be simply replaced, directly affecting the final benchmark scores without changing the business logic or tools.

Prompt engineering for agent reasoning

In the context of agent design, prompt engineering is not about eliciting a good answer; it is about designing the LLM's reasoning loop. The prompt must identify the agent's identification, clarify its limits, and specify the specific protocol it must follow when using tools. The quality of your prompt engineering immediately defines the agent's reliability and resilience.

Mastering prompt engineering for better outputs

Effective agent prompts must transform the LLM into a meticulous, step-by-step planner. This is achieved by rigid organization and explicit guidelines.

System prompt as the agent's constitution

The system prompt is the most significant portion of the agent's settings. It is the agent's immutable source of truth, sent at the beginning of every interaction:

- **Role and persona**: Define the agent's identification and tone (e.g., *You are a specialized data analyst agent*).
- **Tool use guidelines**: This is critical. You must specifically describe when the agent must utilize a tool versus when it must not. For example, *always utilize the* **`web_search`** *tool for any content dated after 2023. Do not answer questions regarding current events based on your internal understanding.*
- **Action protocol**: Specify the exact syntax the LLM must use to output an action (e.g., *Always format your tool call output using the JSON structure provided.*).

Example system prompt snippet

The following system prompt explains how to build unambiguous criteria for agent behavior, including role description, tool usage restrictions, and action protocols:

```
# Code Block: System Prompt Snippet for Agent Guidelines
SYSTEM: You are a professional, step-by-step reasoning agent.
Your primary goal is to answer the user's question using the tools available.

## RULES OF ENGAGEMENT
1.  **ALWAYS** begin your turn with a 'Thought' explaining your reasoning.
2.  **NEVER** generate a tool call (Action) without first having a 'Thought'.
3.  **DO NOT** answer the question directly unless all necessary information
     has been gathered.
4.  **TOOLS** must be called using the exact function signature provided.

## AVAILABLE TOOLS
[Tool descriptions generated by LangChain go here]
```

Fundamentals of few-shot and chain-of-thought

All sophisticated reasoning frameworks (ReAct, ToT, P&E) rely on the ideas of **chain-of-thought** (**CoT**), typically supplemented with **few-shot prompting** (**FSP**) to standardize the LLM's output.

Chain-of-thought prompting

CoT is the approach of commanding the LLM to output its intermediate reasoning processes before getting to the ultimate result. For agents, this is codified as the *thought* stage:

- **Mechanism**: Adding a simple directive like *think step by step* or, more formally, in the agent loop, demanding the thought field, requires the LLM to execute logical decomposition.
- **Benefits**: CoT boosts accuracy on complex tasks, provides transparency into the agent's logic (crucial for debugging), and converts the LLM into an active planner.

The following code explains how to implement chain-of-thought prompting for weather-related queries:

```
# Code Block: Chain-of-Thought Prompting Implementation
from langchain_openai import ChatOpenAI
from langchain_core.prompts import ChatPromptTemplate

# Create CoT prompt with explicit step-by-step instruction
cot_prompt = ChatPromptTemplate.from_messages([
    ("system", "You are a weather analysis assistant. Always think step by
step before providing your final answer."),
    ("human", "{question}\n\nLet's approach this step by step:")
])

llm = ChatOpenAI(model="gpt-4o-mini", temperature=0)
cot_chain = cot_prompt | llm

# Example usage
result = cot_chain.invoke({
    "question": "If it's 10°C in Paris and 5°C warmer in London, what's the
temperature in London in Fahrenheit?"
})
# Output will show step-by-step reasoning:
# Step 1: Paris is 10°C
# Step 2: London is 5°C warmer, so 10 + 5 = 15°C
# Step 3: Convert 15°C to Fahrenheit: (15 × 9/5) + 32 = 59°F
# Final Answer: 59°F
```

Few-shot prompting

FSP entails delivering entire, successful instances of problem-solving trajectories directly in the prompt context:

- **Application to agents**: FSP is crucial for training the agent on protocol adherence. You do not use FSP to teach the LLM general information; you use it to teach the LLM the correct format for a thought (e.g., always referencing the observation), the correct syntax and structure for a tool call (action), and when to appropriately stop the loop with a final answer.
- **LangChain implementation**: LangChain's **`FewShotPromptTemplate`** or **`FewShotChatMessagePromptTemplate`** is used to dynamically insert these high-quality examples into the prompt before the user's question.

The following code demonstrates a complete example trajectory utilizing a weather query that would be provided in the prompt to teach the agent correct protocol adherence:

```
# Code Block: Conceptual Few-Shot Example for Tool Use Logic
example = {
    "input": "What is the weather in Paris?",
    "agent_trajectory": [
        "Thought: I need to use the weather tool to get the current
forecast.",
        "Action: get_weather(city='Paris')",
        "Observation: {'temp': '10C', 'condition': 'rain'}",
        "Thought: The tool returned the data. I will now synthesize the final
answer.",
        "Final Answer: It is currently 10°C and raining in Paris."
    ]
}
# This complete trajectory (input, thoughts, actions, observation, final
answer)
# is placed in the prompt to guide the model's behavior.
```

The following code demonstrates a practical implementation of few-shot prompting using LangChain templates:

```
# Code Block: Few-Shot Prompting with LangChain
from langchain_openai import ChatOpenAI
from langchain_core.prompts import FewShotChatMessagePromptTemplate,
ChatPromptTemplate

# Define few-shot examples for weather agent protocol
examples = [
```

```
    {
        "input": "What's the weather in Tokyo?",
        "output": """Thought: I need to use the get_weather tool to retrieve
current conditions for Tokyo.
Action: get_weather
Action Input: {"city": "Tokyo"}
Observation: Temperature: 22°C, Condition: Sunny
Thought: I have the weather information. I can now provide the final answer.
Final Answer: The weather in Tokyo is currently 22°C and sunny."""
    },
    {
        "input": "Convert 20°C to Fahrenheit",
        "output": """Thought: I need to use the temperature converter tool
for this conversion.
Action: convert_temperature
Action Input: {"celsius": 20, "target_unit": "F"}
Observation: 68°F
Thought: The conversion is complete. I can provide the answer.
Final Answer: 20°C is equal to 68°F."""
    }
]
# Create example prompt template
example_prompt = ChatPromptTemplate.from_messages([
    ("human", "{input}"),
    ("ai", "{output}")
])

# Create few-shot prompt template
few_shot_prompt = FewShotChatMessagePromptTemplate(
    example_prompt=example_prompt,
    examples=examples
)

# Combine with system message and user input
final_prompt = ChatPromptTemplate.from_messages([
    ("system", "You are a weather agent. Follow the exact pattern shown in
the examples."),
    few_shot_prompt,
    ("human", "{input}")
])

llm = ChatOpenAI(model="gpt-4o-mini", temperature=0)
chain = final_prompt | llm
```

```
# Use the chain with few-shot examples
result = chain.invoke({"input": "What's the weather in Paris and convert it
to Fahrenheit?"})
```

For simpler use cases where you do not need the chat message structure, LangChain also provides the traditional **`FewShotPromptTemplate`**:

```
# Code Block: Alternative Few-Shot Pattern for Non-Chat Scenarios
from langchain_core.prompts import FewShotPromptTemplate, PromptTemplate

# Define few-shot examples
examples = [
    {
        "input": "What's the temperature in Tokyo?",
        "output": "I need to check the weather tool for Tokyo's current
temperature."
    },
    {
        "input": "Convert 25°C to Fahrenheit",
        "output": "Using the conversion formula: (25 × 9/5) + 32 = 77°F"
    }
]

# Create example template
example_template = PromptTemplate(
    input_variables=["input", "output"],
    template="Input: {input}\nOutput: {output}"
)
# Create few-shot prompt template
few_shot_template = FewShotPromptTemplate(
    examples=examples,
    example_prompt=example_template,
    prefix="You are a weather assistant. Here are some examples of how to
respond:",
    suffix="Input: {input}\nOutput:",
    input_variables=["input"]
)

# Generate prompt for new input
prompt = few_shot_template.format(input="What's the weather in London?")
# This injects the examples into the prompt before the new query
```

Zero-shot prompting

Zero-shot prompting is the simplest strategy where the agent receives only task instructions without any examples. The LLM relies totally on its pre-trained knowledge and the clarity of the instructions to perform the work correctly:

- **Mechanism**: The prompt gives explicit instructions about what the agent should do, what format to follow, and what tools are accessible, but provides no tangible instances of successful job completion.
- **Benefits**: Zero-shot prompting is token-efficient, fast to implement, and configurable. It works effectively with advanced models that have excellent instruction-following capabilities, and when the task corresponds with patterns the model has seen during training.

The following code demonstrates zero-shot prompting for a weather agent:

```
# Code Block: Zero-Shot Prompting for Agents
from langchain_openai import ChatOpenAI
from langchain_core.prompts import ChatPromptTemplate

# Zero-shot prompt with clear instructions but no examples
zero_shot_prompt = ChatPromptTemplate.from_messages([
    ("system", """You are a weather assistant.

Rules:
1. Always state your reasoning before taking action
2. Use available tools to get current information
3. Provide concise, accurate answers

Available tools:
- get_weather(city: str) - Get current weather for a city
- convert_temperature(celsius: float, target: str) - Convert temperatures"""),
    ("human", "{query}")
])

llm = ChatOpenAI(model="gpt-4o-mini", temperature=0)
chain = zero_shot_prompt | llm

# The model receives no examples, only instructions
result = chain.invoke({"query": "What's the weather in Tokyo?"})
```

Limitations: Zero-shot prompting may yield uneven formatting, struggle with sophisticated multi-step protocols, or misinterpret task requirements when instructions are confusing. This is especially difficult for agent tool calling, where correct formatting is crucial.

Comparing zero-shot versus few-shot prompting

Understanding when to utilize zero-shot versus few-shot prompting is critical for maximizing agent performance and development efficiency.

The following table compares zero-shot and few-shot prompting methodologies across important dimensions:

Characteristic	Zero-shot prompting	Few-shot prompting
Definition	Agent relies solely on instructions without examples.	Agent learns from concrete examples provided in the prompt.
Prompt complexity	Simple, minimal token usage.	More complex, higher token usage due to examples.
Setup time	Fast (just write instructions).	Slower (requires crafting quality examples).
Accuracy	Lower for complex or novel tasks.	Higher, especially for specific formats or protocols.
Token cost	Lower (no example overhead).	Higher (examples consume tokens on every call).
Model dependency	Works best with advanced models (GPT-4, Claude Opus).	Effective even with smaller models (GPT-3.5, Claude Haiku).
Protocol adherence	Moderate (may deviate from exact format).	High (examples enforce consistent structure).
Best for	Simple tasks, well-known patterns, exploratory queries.	Complex formatting, specific protocols, agent tool calls.
Maintenance	Easy (just update instructions).	Moderate (must keep examples relevant and correct).
Iteration speed	Fast (quick instruction changes).	Slower (updating examples requires careful review).

Table 3.2*: A comparison of zero-shot and few-shot prompting approaches*

Strategy selection for agent prompting

Choosing the correct prompting strategy is critical for balancing performance, cost, and reliability:

- **Utilize zero-shot prompting to:**
  - **Manage standard tasks**: Rely on the model's natural ability to handle well-defined, simple instructions.

    - **Explore new domains**: Use this when established example patterns do not yet exist for a specific problem.
    - **Minimize operational costs**: Reduce token consumption in budget-sensitive scenarios.
    - **Leverage advanced models**: Deploy on state-of-the-art models with superior instruction-following.
- **Utilize few-shot prompting to:**
    - **Enforce protocol adherence**: Ensure exact formatting for (Thought | Action | Observation) sequences.
    - **Guarantee structural accuracy**: Maintain complex outputs like JSON or specific templates.
    - **Train domain patterns**: Teach the model specific logic or industry-standard behaviors.
    - **Ensure consistency**: Stabilize behavior across multiple iterative agent runs.
    - **Optimize smaller models**: Enable high performance on less capable or smaller LLM backends.

The following code shows how to combine chain-of-thought with few-shot prompting for maximum agent reliability:

```
# Code Block: Combined CoT and Few-Shot Prompting
from langchain.agents import create_react_agent, AgentExecutor
from langchain_core.prompts import PromptTemplate
from langchain import hub

# Pull base ReAct prompt and customize with few-shot examples
base_prompt = hub.pull("hwchase17/react")

# Add few-shot examples to the prompt prefix
few_shot_prefix = """
Here are examples of correct agent behavior:

Example 1:
Question: What's the weather in London?
Thought: I should use the weather tool to get current conditions.
Action: get_weather
Action Input: {{"city": "London"}}
Observation: 15°C, Cloudy
Thought: I have the information needed.
```

```
Final Answer: The weather in London is 15°C and cloudy.

Example 2:
Question: Get weather for Berlin and convert to Fahrenheit
Thought: This requires two steps - get weather, then convert temperature.
Action: get_weather
Action Input: {{"city": "Berlin"}}
Observation: 18°C, Partly cloudy
Thought: Now I need to convert 18°C to Fahrenheit.
Action: convert_temperature
Action Input: {{"celsius": 18}}
Observation: 64.4°F
Thought: I have completed both steps.
Final Answer: Berlin's weather is 18°C (64.4°F) and partly cloudy.

Now handle the user's question following this exact pattern:
"""

# Create custom prompt with few-shot examples
custom_prompt = PromptTemplate(
    template=few_shot_prefix + base_prompt.template,
    input_variables=base_prompt.input_variables
)

# Create agent with enhanced prompt
tools = [get_weather, convert_temperature]
agent = create_react_agent(llm, tools, custom_prompt)

agent_executor = AgentExecutor(
    agent=agent,
    tools=tools,
    verbose=True,
    handle_parsing_errors=True
)
```

Understanding the CoT and ReAct structure

The following figure explains how CoT is the needed component for the ReAct loop's decision-making stage.

The figure depicts how the LLM's inference stage is directed by few-shot examples and driven to produce organized thoughts, enabling the whole ReAct protocol:

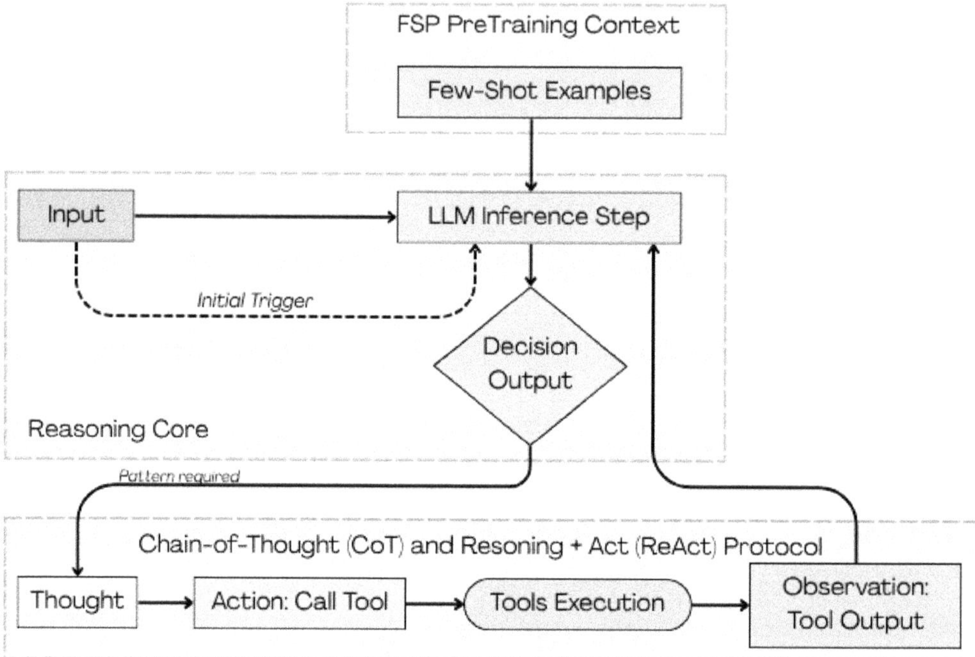

Figure 3.2: *Few-shot prompts guide agent reasoning*

The figure indicates that the LLM's inference (B) is driven by external few-shot examples (H) and is forced to produce a thought (D), which is the mechanism of CoT, making the full ReAct protocol possible.

Implementing advanced agent reasoning frameworks

While basic agents rely on simple prompt-and-response methods, advanced agents utilize precise reasoning frameworks that determine *how* the LLM processes information, plans, and performs actions. Choosing a suitable framework is the most essential architectural decision for agent performance, cost, and reliability.

Reasoning and acting

The ReAct framework is the most generally adopted design pattern for constructing dynamic, general-purpose agents. It effectively blends CoT reasoning with the capacity to execute external tools (action), allowing the agent to continuously alter its approach based on the environment's feedback.

ReAct cycle

The ReAct agent acts in an iterative, tight loop that simulates human problem-solving, alternating between thinking and doing:

- **Thought**: The LLM performs internal reasoning, analyzing the previous observation or the initial input, finding the next required action, and preparing the tool call arguments (this is the CoT component).
- **Action**: The LLM outputs a structured call to a registered tool, indicating the function name and necessary inputs (e.g., **`Search(query="current stock price of Google")`**).
- **Observation**: The agent executor performs the tool and sends the raw, structured result (e.g., the stock price) back to the LLM. The LLM processes this new information, and the cycle repeats until the goal is accomplished.

The following figure illustrates how the reasoning steps unfold within the agent, showing how structured thought processes guide each subsequent action:

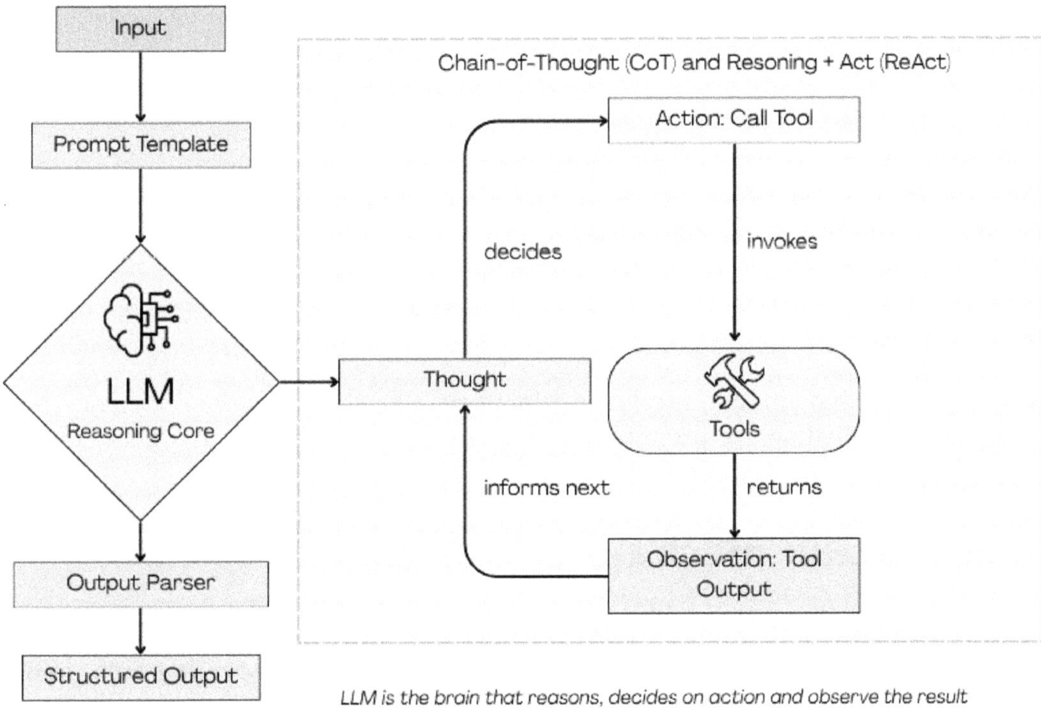

Figure 3.3: Chain-of-thought reasoning flow

LangChain implementation

LangChain simplifies this complex loop into the **`create_react_agent`** tool, which handles the prompt formatting (injecting the thought/action/observation structure) and the parsing logic.

The following code demonstrates how to set up a basic ReAct agent utilizing LangChain's standard implementation with weather-related utilities, including LLM configuration, prompt template loading, and executor setup:

```
# Code Block: Basic ReAct Agent Setup
from langchain.agents import create_react_agent, AgentExecutor
from langchain_openai import ChatOpenAI
from langchain_core.tools import tool # Assume tools are defined here

# 1. Define LLM and Tools (from Chapter 2)
llm = ChatOpenAI(model="gpt-4o", temperature=0)
# tools = [get_weather_tool, temperature_converter_tool]

# 2. Pull the standard ReAct prompt template from LangChain Hub
from langchain import hub
react_prompt = hub.pull("hwchase17/react")

# 3. Create the Agent Runnable
agent_runnable = create_react_agent(llm, tools, react_prompt)

# 4. Create the Executor to manage the loop (handles Thought->Action->Observation)
agent_executor = AgentExecutor(agent=agent_runnable, tools=tools, verbose=True, handle_parsing_errors=True)

# result = agent_executor.invoke({"input": "What is the current temperature in London in Fahrenheit?"})
```

Trade-offs: ReAct is dynamic and excels at exploratory tasks. Its weakness is efficiency; because the LLM must be called and re-prompted after *every* action, it is prone to higher latency and token cost for long, multi-step problems.

Self-correction mechanisms for handling LLM limitations

Agent resilience is its ability to detect, contain, and recover from failures that occur mid-loop. In practice, these failures extend beyond obvious parser exceptions and include hallucinated tool names or arguments, silent tool errors that return incomplete but plausible output, stale or conflicting context carried forward from earlier steps, and context drift where the agent gradually moves away from the user's goal. A production-ready agent must therefore validate actions before execution, inspect observations after execution, and periodically re-anchor itself to the original task:

- **Validation and explicit recovery paths**: The executor should not assume the LLM's proposed action is valid. Before running a tool, validate the tool name, required arguments, argument types, and business constraints. This catches common failure modes such as hallucinated tool inputs, malformed JSON, missing parameters, or impossible values. After execution, treat the tool result as untrusted input as well: if the response is empty, inconsistent with the schema, or clearly incomplete, convert that condition into an explicit observation for the LLM rather than silently continuing. For example, the observation might state: **`"Observation: Tool call failed validation because the argument city_code is not supported. Reformat the action using the documented schema."`**
- **Guardrails, verification, and re-anchoring**: To prevent compounding errors, the executor should combine loop limits with lightweight verification checkpoints. **`max_iterations`** and timeout budgets stop repeated failed actions, but they are not enough on their own. The agent should also detect silent errors by checking whether a tool observation actually answers the intended subtask, and it should mitigate context drift by restating the current objective, relevant constraints, and completed progress after several steps or after any failure. This re-anchoring step helps the model recover if it starts optimizing for the wrong subgoal, overfits to a noisy observation, or forgets the original user request.

Plan-and-Execute framework

The **Plan-and-Execute** (**P&E**) paradigm offers long-term stability by establishing a clear boundary between strategic thought and tactical execution. It is designed to counter ReAct's flaw of *short-term thinking*.

Plan-and-Execute architecture

Plan-and-Execute uses at least two discrete phases, commonly implemented with two different LLMs:

- **Planner (LLM call 1)**: Receives the initial difficult query and constructs a full, fixed, sequential plan (a to-do list) upfront. This phase uses the most capable (and potentially most expensive) model.
- **Executor (tool/agent loop)**: Runs one stage of the plan at a time. The executor is often a lighter-weight agent (often a stripped-down ReAct or a basic tool-calling model) that concentrates solely on completing the present task, not re-planning the entire sequence.

Without the use of a visual diagram, this sequence shows the agent's decision flow step-by-step. The model first generates an initial idea, then assesses what further information is required and chooses the best tool or course of action. Following receipt of the outcome, the agent reviews its progress and modifies its logic before moving on to the following phase.

Until the agent comes up with a final, trustworthy response, this iterative cycle of thinking, acting, and improving continues.

LangChain implementation conceptual walkthrough

To use P&E, you need to define what the planner's output is (using Pydantic to make sure a list of steps is returned) and then go through that list.

The following code shows how to set up P&E in theory, including the planner chain, executor function, and orchestration loop:

```
# Conceptual Code Block: LCEL Structure for Plan-and-Execute
from langchain_core.runnables import RunnableLambda
from langchain_openai import ChatOpenAI
# PlanOutput is a Pydantic model: list[str] of steps
from .schemas import PlanOutput

# 1. The Planner Chain (Strategic Decision-Maker)
planner_prompt = ChatPromptTemplate.from_template("Generate a precise,
numbered to-do list for this query: {query}")
planner_chain = planner_prompt | ChatOpenAI(model="gpt-4o") |
PydanticOutputParser(pydantic_object=PlanOutput)

# 2. The Executor Function (Tactical Tool-User)
# This Executor will be a specialized ReAct Agent (or simple LCEL chain)
def execute_step(step_context):
    """Function to run the current step using a simpler, cheaper LLM."""
    step = step_context["step"]
    # Internal logic uses a local executor agent to execute the step using
available tools
    executor_llm = ChatOpenAI(model="gpt-3.5-turbo")
    # ... executor logic here ...
    return f"Result of step '{step}': Success."

# 3. Looping the Plan (Orchestration - done outside core LCEL)
# The final composition involves a standard Python loop managing the
execution:
def plan_and_execute_workflow(query):
    plan_object = planner_chain.invoke({"query": query})
    all_results = []

    for step in plan_object.steps:
        result = RunnableLambda(execute_step).invoke({"step": step})
        all_results.append(result)
```

```
    # Final step: Synthesize the final answer from all_results
    return synthesize_final_answer(query, all_results)
```

The advantages and implementation details of LangChain are as follows:

- **Robustness**: The predetermined plan prevents the agent from being distracted by unanticipated observations or getting lost in the middle of a long trajectory.
- **Cost optimization**: You can use a powerful model (e.g., GPT-4o) only for the key planning stage and a cheaper model (e.g., GPT-3.5) for the many subsequent execution steps, substantially cutting overall cost.
- **LangChain implementation**: This pattern is commonly implemented by creating a Pydantic schema for the **`Plan`** (a list of strings) and utilizing an outer chain to feed this plan sequentially into a sub-agent (the executor).

Tree-of-thoughts framework

The **tree-of-thoughts** (**ToT**) architecture provides the most computationally intensive and advanced reasoning paradigm. It advances beyond a single linear path (ReAct or P&E) to enable strategic search by investigating numerous viable options concurrently.

Tree-of-thoughts concept

At any decision point, the agent undertakes three steps:

1. **Expand**: Generate numerous candidate *thoughts* or possible next actions (e.g., *A: Get current weather from API, B: Check historical weather patterns, C: Compare weather across nearby cities*).
2. **Score**: Use a secondary LLM or a special heuristic to evaluate the candidates based on how promising they are for accomplishing the objective.
3. **Prune**: Discard the low-scoring alternatives, preserving only the top k promising paths. The procedure then repeats, expanding on the remaining pathways, building a search tree.

Implementation note

Implementing a true ToT requires sophisticated orchestration using concepts like LangGraph (or complex LCEL with **`RunnableParallel`** and **`RunnableBranch`** from *Chapter 2, Designing Modular and Reusable LangChain Workflows*). The chapter focuses on the conceptual framework where the Expand phase leverages LCEL's **`RunnableParallel`** to conduct many initial LLM calls. The score/prune phase employs a specific LLM prompt and a structured output parser to pick the ideal thought path, enabling the agent to spend computing resources on the most promising reasoning pathways.

The following table presents a complete comparison of the three primary reasoning frameworks, showing their thinking styles, planning methodologies, and best use cases:

Characteristic	ReAct	Plan-and-Execute	Tree-of-thoughts
Thinking style	Reactive (Step-by-step improvisation).	Strategic (Fixed upfront plan).	Exploratory (Parallel search).
Long-term plan	Implicit, volatile.	Explicit, persistent.	Multiple, competing plans.
Best for	Dynamic, exploratory tasks (e.g., live customer support).	Critical, long, sequential tasks (e.g., complex data migration).	Strategic puzzles, multi-hypothesis research.
Token cost	Moderate (Call per step).	High (Longer plan and execution).	Very high (Multiple LLM calls per decision).
Latency	Medium	Slow (Due to initial planning overhead).	Slowest (Requires waiting for multiple parallel inference steps).

Table 3.3: Comprehensive comparison of agent reasoning frameworks

In practice, choose ReAct when the task is interactive, the next step depends on fresh observations, and low implementation complexity is more important than maximum efficiency. It is often the best default for user-facing agents and lightweight tool use, but its step-by-step loop can increase latency and token cost as the number of actions grows. Choose Plan-and-Execute when the task is longer, more structured, and can be decomposed into stable substeps ahead of time. This approach adds upfront planning overhead, but it usually improves reliability and makes costs easier to manage for complex sequential workflows. Choose tree-of-thoughts when the problem has multiple plausible solution paths, and quality depends on exploring alternatives rather than committing early to one route. The trade-off is that ToT is typically the most expensive and slowest option, so it is best reserved for high-value tasks where a deeper search justifies the extra compute.

Orchestrating and customizing agent executors

The agent executor is the runtime environment that powers the agent's intelligence. It serves as the ultimate orchestrator, responsible for controlling the iterative loop of the chosen reasoning framework (ReAct, P&E, etc). It takes the LLM's raw action output and safely runs the matching tool, giving the outcome back to the model as an observation.

Comparing and using different LangChain agents

LangChain provides many optimized base agent types, each pre-configured to handle varied LLM capabilities and specialized use cases. Choosing the correct base agent simplifies implementation and utilizes the model's innate strengths.

Zero-shot ReAct agent

Zero-shot agents work without specific examples, relying on the LLM's pre-trained knowledge and generic directions. The **`zero-shot-react-description`** agent type employs tool descriptions to decide which actions to take, making it adaptable for general-purpose jobs.

The following points summarize how this generalpurpose agent operates:

- **Mechanism**: This is the most general-purpose agent. It relies totally on prompt engineering (Thought | Action | Observation) to steer the LLM's output into a parsable text format.
- **Use cases**: Simple question-answering, information retrieval, basic job automation, where tool selection is straightforward based on descriptions alone. Highly versatile and interoperable with practically any LLM (even older or open-source models) where the LLM does not allow native function calling APIs.

The following code depicts a basic zero-shot ReAct agent setup:

```
# Code Block: Zero-Shot ReAct Agent
from langchain.agents import create_react_agent, AgentExecutor

# Create Zero-Shot ReAct agent
tools = [get_weather, convert_temperature]
agent = create_react_agent(llm, tools, prompt)

agent_executor = AgentExecutor(
    agent=agent,
    tools=tools,
    verbose=True,
    handle_parsing_errors=True
)
```

Conversational ReAct agent

Conversational agents expand zero-shot capabilities with memory, enabling them to maintain context across several exchanges. The **`conversational-react-description`** agent type recalls earlier encounters, making conversations more coherent and individualized.

- **Mechanism**: Builds upon the ReAct framework but includes a conversation buffer that preserves the full history of user interactions and agent answers during a session.
- **Use cases**: Chatbots, customer support systems, and personal assistants requiring multi-turn interaction and context awareness. Essential for applications where understanding conversation history is critical to generating suitable responses.

The following code demonstrates a conversational ReAct agent with memory:

```
# Code Block: Conversational ReAct Agent
from langchain.agents import create_react_agent, AgentExecutor
from langchain.memory import ConversationBufferMemory

# Create conversational agent with memory
memory = ConversationBufferMemory(memory_key="chat_history", return_
messages=True)
tools = [get_weather, convert_temperature]
agent = create_react_agent(llm, tools, prompt)

agent_executor = AgentExecutor(
    agent=agent,
    tools=tools,
    memory=memory,
    verbose=True,
    handle_parsing_errors=True
)
```

The following table provides a concise comparison of the key elements discussed in this section, helping readers understand how each component contributes to the overall agent workflow:

Feature	Zero-shot ReAct	Conversational ReAct
Uses memory/chat history	No	Yes
Context carried between turns	No	Yes
Best for	Single-turn tasks	Multi-turn chat agents
Needs a conversational prompt	Optional	Required
Tool usage format	ReAct	ReAct and memory awareness

***Table 3.4**: Key difference between zero-shot vs. conversational ReAct*

Structured tool agent

When tools demand complicated, structured inputs (such as JSON objects or specified parameter kinds), structured tool agents flourish. The **`structured-chat-zero-shot-react-description`** agent type handles tools with complicated input schemas successfully.

- **Mechanism**: Optimized for models developed for structured outputs. This agent shines in conversational scenarios where the ultimate output is not merely a text string, but typically a structured JSON response meant for external system consumption (e.g., refreshing a UI or calling another internal microservice).

- **Use cases**: API integrations with complex parameters, database activities requiring structured queries, and multi-parameter function calls. Ideal when tools have extensive input schemas that demand accurate parameter formatting.

The following code demonstrates a structured tool agent for complex schemas:

```
# Code Block: Structured Tool Agent
from langchain.agents import create_structured_chat_agent, AgentExecutor

# Create structured tool agent
tools = [weather_tool]  # Tool with Pydantic schema
agent = create_structured_chat_agent(llm, tools, prompt)

agent_executor = AgentExecutor(
    agent=agent,
    tools=tools,
    verbose=True,
    handle_parsing_errors=True
)
```

OpenAI function-calling agent

Modern LangChain applications increasingly employ OpenAI's native function-calling capabilities, which allow more reliable tool selection and parameter extraction compared to text-based parsing.

- **Mechanism**: The modern standard. This agent is meant for models that have native function/tool calling APIs (e.g., GPT-4o, Claude 3, Gemini). The LLM's output is a structured JSON object specifying the function call, which the executor reads directly.
- **Advantage**: This solution is substantially faster and significantly more reliable than relying on the executor to parse and evaluate tool calls from unstructured text.
- **Use cases**: Production systems needing the greatest reliability, applications using GPT-3.5-Turbo or GPT-4, and circumstances where structured outputs are critical.

The following code exhibits an OpenAI function-calling agent:

```
# Code Block: OpenAI Function-Calling Agent
from langchain.agents import create_openai_functions_agent, AgentExecutor

# Create OpenAI functions agent
tools = [get_current_weather, get_weather_forecast]
agent = create_openai_functions_agent(llm, tools, prompt)

agent_executor = AgentExecutor(
```

```
    agent=agent,
    tools=tools,
    verbose=True,
    handle_parsing_errors=True
)
```

Note: **For new projects utilizing OpenAI models, favor function-calling agents (`create_openai_functions_agent`) over text-based ReAct agents. Function calling delivers improved dependability, cleaner tool parameter extraction, and lower token consumption.**

LLM providers and model selection

Choosing the best LLM provider and model entails balancing capabilities, cost, latency, and operational constraints. Chat completion models are often selected for agents due to their greater task completion, reasoning, and planning skills compared to base completion models.

OpenAI industry standard

OpenAI's GPT models have become the de facto standard for production AI agents. The OpenAI API **software development kit** (**SDK**) paradigm is now extensively used across different providers, giving a consistent integration experience.

The key models are as follows:

- **GPT-4**: Highest capability for complex reasoning, planning, and tool use. Best for production systems when quality is paramount.
- **GPT-3.5-Turbo**: Faster and more cost-effective, appropriate for simpler jobs and high-volume applications.
- **GPT-4-Turbo**: Balanced performance between GPT-4's capability and better speed/cost efficiency.

Integration pattern: The following code explains how to integrate OpenAI models into your agent workflow using the standard ChatOpenAI interface:

```
from langchain_openai import ChatOpenAI

llm = ChatOpenAI(
    model="gpt-4",
    temperature=0,  # Deterministic for agent reasoning
    api_key=os.environ["OPENAI_API_KEY"]
)
```

Anthropic safety-focused alternative

Anthropic's Claude models stress responsible AI techniques, with great performance on reasoning tests and excellent instruction-following capabilities.

The key models are as follows:

- **Claude 3 Opus**: Highest capability, vying with GPT-4.
- **Claude 3 Sonnet**: Balanced performance and cost.
- **Claude 3 Haiku**: Fast, cost-effective for simple tasks.

Integration pattern: The following code shows how to integrate Anthropic's Claude models using the **ChatAnthropic** wrapper with the same interface patterns:

```
from langchain_anthropic import ChatAnthropic

llm = ChatAnthropic(
    model="claude-3-opus-20240229",
    temperature=0,
    api_key=os.environ["ANTHROPIC_API_KEY"]
)
```

Open-source privacy and cost control

Open-source LLMs via platforms like LM Studio, Ollama, or vLLM provide privacy and cost control but may require greater infrastructure investment.

Some popular models are as follows:

- **Llama 2/3**: Meta's open models with great generic capabilities.
- **Mistral**: Efficient models with good reasoning performance.
- **Phi-3**: Microsoft's small yet capable models.

The advantages and disadvantages are mentioned as follows:

- **Advantages**: No per-token costs, data privacy, and customizable flexibility.
- **Disadvantages**: Infrastructure overhead, maybe worse quality, and demands GPU resources.

Note: **Use commercial models (OpenAI, Anthropic) for important thinking problems and complicated agent behaviors. Deploy open-source models for high-volume, simpler activities when cost management and privacy outweigh the need for maximal capacity.**

Creating custom AgentExecutors for complex orchestration

While the default **AgentExecutor** handles the main ReAct loop, sophisticated applications sometimes require custom business logic to be inserted into the execution cycle.

Basic implementation of the first ReAct agent

Let us start by developing a small ReAct agent that can search the web and conduct calculations. This basic example demonstrates core agent ideas. First, establish the necessary project structure and install dependencies.

The following code builds the basic environment settings, loading API credentials from environment variables:

```
# codes/chapter03/01_basic_react_agent.py
import os
from dotenv import load_dotenv

# Load environment variables
load_dotenv()

# Verify API key is available
if not os.environ.get("OPENAI_API_KEY"):
    raise ValueError("OPENAI_API_KEY not found in environment variables")
```

Tip: **Store all API keys in a .env file in your project root. Never commit this file to version control. Add .env to your .gitignore immediately after creating it.**

The following code displays the whole setup for a basic ReAct agent with meteorological capabilities, including LLM initialization, tool loading, and executor configuration:

```
from langchain_openai import ChatOpenAI
from langchain.agents import AgentExecutor, create_react_agent, load_tools
from langchain import hub

# Initialize the LLM
llm = ChatOpenAI(model="gpt-3.5-turbo", temperature=0)

# Load tools - weather API and temperature converter
tools = load_tools(["openweathermap-api", "llm-math"], llm=llm)

# Get the ReAct prompt template from LangChain hub
prompt = hub.pull("hwchase17/react")
```

```
# Create the agent
agent = create_react_agent(llm, tools, prompt)

# Create the agent executor
agent_executor = AgentExecutor(
    agent=agent,
    tools=tools,
    verbose=True,  # Show reasoning steps
    handle_parsing_errors=True  # Gracefully handle LLM output errors
)
```

The definition of an agent executor includes the runtime component that runs the agent's execution loop, including tool invocation, error handling, and iteration limits. The executor coordinates between the agent's decision-making and actual tool execution.

The following code tests the agent with a multi-step weather question that requires both information retrieval and temperature conversion:

```
# Test the agent with a complex weather query
result = agent_executor.invoke({
    "input": "What is the current temperature in Paris? Then convert it to
Fahrenheit."
})

print(f"\nFinal Answer: {result['output']}")
```

Here is the output response:

```
> Entering new AgentExecutor chain...
I need to get the current temperature in Paris first, then convert it to
Fahrenheit.

Action: Weather
Action Input: "get_weather(city='Paris')"
Observation: Temperature in Paris is 10°C, condition: rainy

Thought: Now I need to convert 10°C to Fahrenheit
Action: Temperature Converter
Action Input: celsius_to_fahrenheit(10)
Observation: Answer: 50°F

Thought: I now know the final answer
Final Answer: The current temperature in Paris is 10°C (50°F) with rainy
conditions.
```

The following are a few things to remember:

- `verbose=True` is critical for debugging and understanding agent behavior.
- `temperature=0` ensures deterministic reasoning for agents.
- `handle_parsing_errors=True` prevents crashes from corrupted LLM outputs.
- Tools must be compatible with the agent type you are using.

Let us see what happened step by step:

1. **Initial thought**: The agent identified that it needed two pieces of information.
2. **First action**: Used the search function to find Tokyo's population.
3. **Observation**: Received the search result (14 million).
4. **Second thought**: Recognized that it now needs to make a calculation.
5. **Second action**: Used the calculator tool with the population number.
6. **Final observation**: Received the computation result (2.1 million).
7. **Overall assessment**: Combined both observations into a coherent final answer.

This highlights the key ReAct pattern as interleaving reasoning (thoughts) with actions (tool calls) to solve multi-step problems.

Role of agent executor

By elaborating on the concepts presented above, this section adds more clarity and emphasizes the ways in which each element supports the agent's overall reasoning process. The agent moves from simple pattern matching to deliberate decision-making by combining structured thought generation, tool-based actions, and iterative refinement. This additional context guarantees that readers comprehend the system's step-by-step development and helps them make the connection between the previously described practical implementation and the conceptual framework.

The executor is essentially a while loop that continues until the LLM outputs a final answer or encounters a halting condition (like `max_iterations`). Customizing this loop allows you to include key safety and auditing features.

Customizing agent loop

You can do customization either by extending the `AgentExecutor` class or by wrapping the executor in a custom function that handles pre- and post-processing tasks:

- **Pre-processing**: Intercepting the LLM's suggested action before it is executed. For example, auditing the tool input or validating the arguments against a business rule before the tool (e.g., a database query) executes.

- **Post-processing**: Intercepting the final output before it is provided to the user, perhaps to format it according to user-specific preferences or report the final cost.
- **Human-in-the-loop (HIL)**: HIL is a key safety measure for agents proposing irreversible actions (e.g., deleting a file, commencing a financial transaction). This customization requires the executor to pause the loop and ask for approval.

Stepwise code for a custom HIL executor

To implement HIL, we adapt the main agent loop by validating the proposed action against a list of sensitive tools:

- **Identify sensitive tools**: Mark tools that require human approval.
- **Intercept the action**: Intervene after the LLM creates a tool call but before execution.
- **Request confirmation**: If the tool is sensitive, pause execution and prompt the human.
- **Resume/override**: Continue only if the human authorizes.

The following code exhibits a custom executor that implements HIL approval for sensitive weather data operations:

```
# Conceptual Code Block: Human-in-the-Loop Executor Logic
from langchain.agents import AgentExecutor
from langchain_core.agents import AgentFinish, AgentAction

class HumanInTheLoopExecutor(AgentExecutor):
    """Custom executor that requires human confirmation for sensitive
tools."""

    def _take_next_step(self, name_to_tool_map, color_mapping, inputs,
intermediate_steps):
        # 1. Get the agent's proposed action (Thought + Action)
        output = self.agent.plan(intermediate_steps, **inputs)

        if isinstance(output, AgentAction):
            sensitive_tools = ["update_weather_alert", "broadcast_weather_
warning"]

            # 2. Check if the proposed action is sensitive
            if output.tool in sensitive_tools:
                print(f"\n[WARNING] Agent proposes action: {output.tool} with
args: {output.tool_input}")

                # 3. Request Confirmation
```

```
                confirmation = input(">>> Do you approve this action? (yes/
no): ").lower()

                if confirmation != "yes":
                    # Override the action and feed a rejection observation
back to the LLM
                    rejection_observation = f"Observation: The user rejected
the weather operation {output.tool}. Choose a different approach or provide a
final answer."
                    return [(output, rejection_observation)]

            # 4. If approved or not sensitive, proceed with normal execution
            return super()._take_next_step(name_to_tool_map, color_mapping,
inputs, intermediate_steps)

        # If it's a Final Answer, return it
        return [(output, None)]


# Usage: CustomExecutor(agent=agent_runnable, tools=tools)
```

By customizing the execution loop, you get the power to manage the agent's behavior at the most important points, assuring safety and compliance inside your complex orchestrated system.

Benchmarking and optimization

Benchmarking is the ultimate, non-negotiable step for taking any agent from the prototype stage to a dependable production system. It is the process of quantifying the trade-offs implicit in the reasoning frameworks outlined in the *Implementing advanced agent reasoning frameworks* section.

Final benchmarking comparison

The purpose of this final comparison is to establish which reasoning strategy (ReAct, P&E, or ToT) gives the optimum ratio of accuracy to cost/latency for a certain business job.

A useful benchmark also depends on how the evaluation set is constructed. In practice, the dataset should include representative tasks across easy, medium, and hard difficulty levels, cover both successful and failure-prone scenarios, and preserve a fixed holdout set so framework changes can be compared fairly over time. To improve repeatability, keep prompts, tool versions, model settings, and external dependencies as stable as possible, and run each configuration multiple times to account for nondeterminism in LLM outputs and variable tool latency. A robust methodology then reports not just average accuracy, cost, and latency, but also variance, failure modes, and the exact task mix used for evaluation, so that readers can distinguish genuine framework improvements from benchmark noise or dataset bias.

The following table illustrates the performance characteristics of each reasoning framework across major operational metrics:

Metric	ReAct (dynamic)	Plan-and-Execute (fixed)	Tree-of-thoughts (exploratory)
Speed/latency	Medium/fast (call per step).	Slow (upfront planning phase adds delay).	Slowest (requires multiple parallel LLM calls per decision).
Robustness	Moderate (prone to deviation/loops).	High (fixed plan prevents mid-task derailment).	Highest (self-evaluation/pruning enhances reliability).
Token cost	Moderate (requires N LLM calls for N steps).	High (planner LLM call is verbose; high total tokens).	Very high (token consumption multiplies by the search width).
Best for	Simple, reactive tasks; user-facing chatbots.	Critical, long, sequential tasks (e.g., financial reporting).	Strategic search, multi-hypothesis research (e.g., complex debugging).

Table 3.5: Performance characteristics of reasoning frameworks

Log and table analysis

During development, review the agent logs (the `verbose=True` output) to determine why problems occur. The failure pattern of ReAct and P&E is as follows:

- **ReAct failure pattern**: Typically illustrates the agent being caught in a small loop (e.g., trying the same faulty tool input repeatedly) or diverting from the goal after a perplexing observation. This is characterized by large iteration counts ($N > 6$).
- **P&E failure pattern**: Less common, but it usually occurs during the initial planning process if the LLM misinterprets the purpose. Once the plan is set, the executor is stable unless a tool produces an unexpected, unrecoverable error.

Analyzing the agent's internal scratchpad (the verbose log) is the key to debugging performance and accuracy concerns.

The following table compares two runs of a ReAct agent on identical tasks, highlighting how prompt adherence concerns can contribute to performance degradation:

Run ID	Strategy	Status	Total iterations	Total tokens	Problem spotted
R-401 (Failed)	ReAct	Failed (Max iterations)	7	4,200	Agent repeated *Action: Search(query=A)* three times, ignoring the Observation.
R-402 (Success)	ReAct	Success	4	2,850	Thought process was concise; successful tool call on first attempt.

***Table 3.6**: Comparison of failed vs successful agent runs*

Analysis: Run R-401 was 48% more expensive and failed due to a prompt adherence issue (not correctly processing the observation), indicating the need for better few-shot examples (*Fundamentals of few-shot and chain-of-thought* section) to guide the failure recovery protocol.

Optimizing inference cost and performance efficiency

Agent performance is often governed more by API latency and cost than by the agent's logic itself. Optimization focuses on removing superfluous tokens and intelligently applying models.

Strategic model tiers and model right-sizing

One of the most successful cost-saving solutions is moving away from utilizing the single, most powerful LLM (e.g., GPT-4o) for every step:

- Cascade models implement a dynamic model switching technique where a smaller, faster model (e.g., a fine-tuned GPT-3.5) handles easy stages, and only if the task is judged complex or the fast model fails (by a low-confidence score or mistake), the query is escalated to the bigger, more expensive model.
- Tiered architectures (in P&E) utilize a powerful model (e.g., GPT-4o) exclusively for the strategic planner job, where complicated reasoning is necessary, but utilize a much cheaper model for the frequent calls required by the executor (which simply needs to conduct simple tool mapping).

Prompt and context compression

Since agents iteratively add the thought/action/observation history to the prompt scratchpad, the context window can fill up quickly, leading to high cost and slow performance:

- Prompt compression actively minimizes the size of the input prompt by deleting duplicate instructions, simplifying cumbersome role definitions, and ensuring that few-shot examples are brief.
- Observation summarization before feeding a long observation (e.g., a 100-line database query result) back to the LLM utilizes a dedicated summary chain (from *Chapter 2, Designing Modular and Reusable LangChain Workflows*) to reduce the text into a few key bullet points. This token-aware prompting dramatically reduces the token count of the agent's scratchpad without sacrificing the important factual information needed for the following step.

The other cost control measures are as follows:

- **Token budgeting**: Implement limits on the `max_tokens` option for the LLM's output. For most agent steps, the LLM only needs 200–300 tokens to produce a Thought and an Action. Limiting this minimizes needless verbose output and saves tokens.
- **Cachin**: Implement caching for frequent tool calls (e.g., a simple `get_stock_price` for significant stocks) or for LLM answers to repeated planning inquiries. This reduces excessive API latency and expense for idempotent actions.

Conclusion

This chapter took you from building modular chains to orchestrating real agent intelligence. We broke down how reasoning actually works, showing that the LLM is not just spitting out text but rather actively planning and executing tasks. You learned how to guide the LLM's thinking using CoT and structure its decisions with the ReAct framework. On top of that, you gained the know-how to implement and choose between advanced planning strategies like P&E and ToT. Plus, you picked up critical production skills like benchmarking performance, optimizing costs, and building custom executors with HIL safety features. You are now ready to build agents that are not just capable but durable, efficient, and reliable.

So far, our agents have only worked with text. In the next chapter, we will broaden our scope. You will learn how to build unified pipelines that let your agents see images, listen to audio, and read documents simultaneously for contextual comprehension. We will cover the technical details of loading and syncing different data types, generating embeddings across multiple formats, and aligning time-series information. By the end, you will have built a working multimodal indexer and solved real synchronization challenges, turning abstract concepts into practical, deployable solutions.

CHAPTER 4
Building Multimodal LangChain Pipelines

Introduction

Human discussions, healthcare operations, industrial inspections, and customer support interactions integrate many signal types, including spoken language, images, structured telemetry, and streaming video. Modern foundation models such as GPT-4o, Gemini 1.5 Pro, and Claude 3.5 Sonnet blur the boundaries between modalities, processing not just text but also images, audio, video, and time-series sensor data. LangChain provides consistent abstractions for developing production-grade multimodal pipelines that reason across diverse data formats.

Organizations currently receive measurable value from multimodal agents. A logistics supplier cut incident resolution time by 45% after implementing a LangChain agent that integrates maintenance logs with drone footage. A radiology group feeds ultrasound frames and voice dictation into a LangChain workflow that cuts report turnaround by 38%. A fintech compliance team ingests call-center transcripts, screen captures, and keystroke telemetry to discover policy breaches. Their LangChain methodology maps multimodal data onto unified case files, shortening investigations from 14 days to 4. This chapter demonstrates how to construct these capabilities using replicable patterns matched with the methods outlined in the LangChain manual and established multimodal AI frameworks.

Harrison Chase, the founder of LangChain, said:

> *Multimodal agents only become trustworthy when every modality is observable, testable, and auditable. Treat vision, voice, and sensor data as first-class citizens in your evaluation stack.*

Structure

This chapter covers the following topics:

- Current state of multimodal support in LangChain
- Understanding key concepts

- Understanding and integrating multimodal data
- Preprocessing and chunking media
- Generating and synchronizing multimodal embeddings
- Advanced pipeline orchestration
- Retrieval strategies and agent integration

Objectives

By the end of this chapter, you will understand how LangChain represents multimodal inputs through messages and content blocks, and how to extend RAG pipelines beyond text to include images, audio, and time-series data. You will learn to build ingestion pipelines with modality-specific preprocessing techniques such as OCR, captioning, and transcription; apply chunking strategies that preserve semantic and temporal context across modalities; generate synchronized embeddings with metadata for unified retrieval; orchestrate multimodal workflows using LCEL and production-ready pipeline patterns; and implement a practical multimodal indexer with observability, retries, and incremental indexing.

Current state of multimodal support in LangChain

While LangChain's multimodal capabilities are expanding rapidly, understanding existing support levels helps you make educated design decisions. The following table outlines where multimodal functionality is mature versus emerging:

Component	Input support	Output support	Notes
Chat models	Images, files, audio (provider-dependent).	Limited (audio preview only).	Most mature area.
Embedding models	Text-focused, multimodal emerging.	N/A	External tools needed for image/audio embeddings.
Vector stores	Text embeddings primary.	N/A	Multimodal support evolving.
Tool calls	No raw multimodal in tools.	N/A	Use URL references instead.

Table 4.1: LangChain multimodal support status

Practical takeaway: Use GPT-4o when you need the broadest multimodal coverage in a single model, especially for workflows that combine text, images, audio, and video. Choose Claude 3.5 Sonnet when image understanding and nuanced visual reasoning matter more than broad modality coverage. Use Gemini 1.5 Pro when long-context multimodal reasoning is the priority. For cost-sensitive, self-hosted, or highly customized deployments, open-source multimodal models are often the better fit, though they typically require more engineering effort and orchestration.

Major multimodal foundation models

Different foundation model providers offer varying levels of multimodal support. The following table compares the primary models accessible through LangChain, letting you select the correct model for your individual use case:

Model	Provider	Modalities	LangChain API	Best for
GPT-4o	OpenAI	Text, images, audio, video	`ChatOpenAI(model="gpt-4o")`	Full multimodal workflows.
GPT-4o-mini	OpenAI	Text, images	`ChatOpenAI(model="gpt-4o-mini")`	Cost-effective prototyping.
Claude 3.5 Sonnet	Anthropic	Text, images	`ChatAnthropic(model="claude-3-5-sonnet-20241022")`	Advanced image reasoning.
Claude 3 Opus	Anthropic	Text, images	`ChatAnthropic(model="claude-3-opus-20240229")`	High-accuracy analysis.
Claude 3 Haiku	Anthropic	Text, images	`ChatAnthropic(model="claude-3-haiku-20240307")`	Fast, lightweight tasks.
Whisper v3	OpenAI	Audio-to-text	OpenAI Whisper API	transcription.

***Table 4.2**: Major multimodal models available in LangChain*

The best practice is to start with GPT-4o-mini for cost-effective prototyping, then upgrade to GPT-4o for audio/video or Claude 3.5 Sonnet for greater picture reasoning.

Understanding key concepts

Before building multimodal pipelines, you must understand the fundamental distinctions between processing capabilities and how LangChain structures multimodal data.

Retrieval-augmented generation foundations

In this chapter, RAG matters only to the extent that it changes when the corpus is no longer text-only. In multimodal RAG, the retriever has to ground a query to representations of images, audio, video, tables, and time-series signals on top of prose. That shifts the problem from simple document lookup to cross-modal retrieval, where the system may answer a text question using evidence that originated in a chart, frame, transcript segment, or sensor trace.

The core design questions are therefore different from text-only RAG: how to preprocess each modality into retrievable units, whether to embed everything into a shared semantic space or maintain modality-specific indexes, and how to preserve metadata such as timestamps, page regions, speakers, or frame numbers so retrieved evidence can be reassembled correctly at generation time. LangChain still gives you the familiar indexing and retrieval phases, but the indexing step now includes OCR, captioning, transcription, structural parsing, and embedding alignment instead of plain text chunking alone.

To make the two-stage flow concrete, *Figure 4.1* illustrates the offline indexing phase, where source documents are loaded, chunked, embedded, and stored in a vector database for later retrieval:

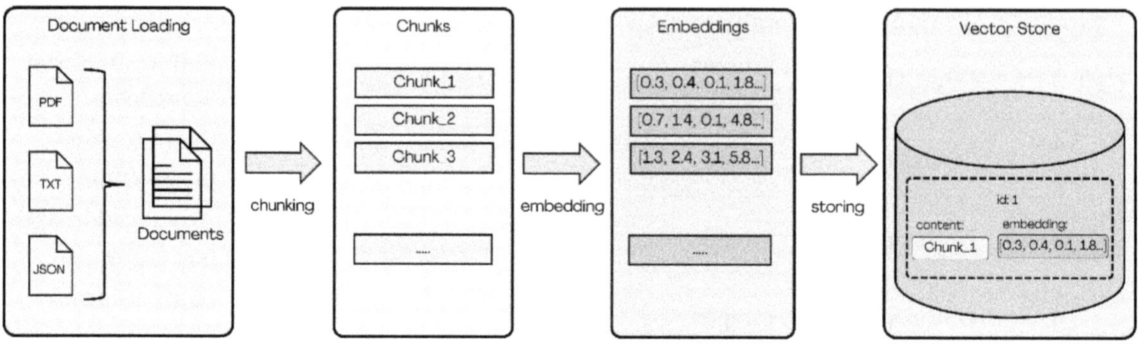

***Figure 4.1**: Indexing phase of RAG workflow*

Once the index is built, *Figure 4.2* shows the runtime retrieval phase, where a user query is embedded, relevant chunks are fetched from the vector store, and the results are added to the prompt to ground the final response.

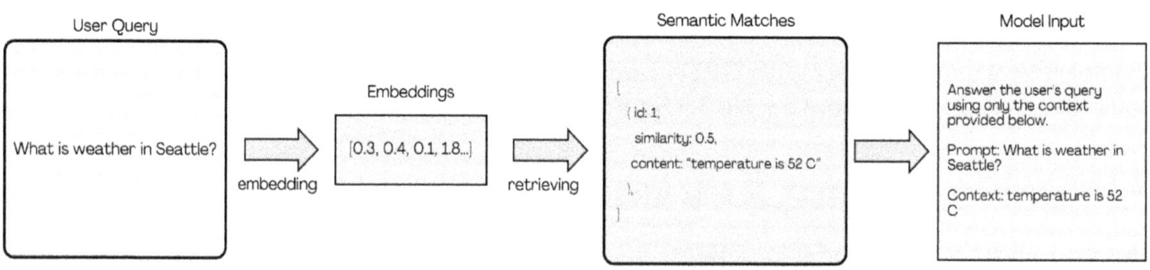

***Figure 4.2**: Retrieval phase of RAG workflow (runtime)*

The RAG workflow consists of two phases with separate procedures at each level. The following table outlines the whole procedure from first document loading through final answer generation:

Phase	Stage	Operations	Purpose
Indexing phase (offline)	Load	Read documents from various sources.	Import raw data into the system.
	Chunk	Split documents into smaller units.	Break content into manageable, semantic segments that fit within LLM context windows.
	Embed	Convert chunks to numerical vectors.	Transform text into dense vectors (768-3072 dimensions) capturing semantic meaning.
	Store	Save vectors in database.	Persist embeddings with metadata for efficient retrieval.
Retrieval phase (runtime)	Query Embedding	Convert user query to vector	Transform natural language question into same vector space as indexed content.
	Retrieve	Search for similar chunks.	Find semantically related content using vector similarity.
	Augment	Add context to prompt.	Combine retrieved chunks with original query.
	Generate	Produce final response.	LLM synthesizes answer using provided context.

***Table 4.3**: RAG workflow phases and operations*

For the rest of this chapter, keep two multimodal extensions in mind:

- **Chunking**: Breaking huge documents into smaller, semantically relevant units. LLMs have context window limits (8K-128K tokens); hence, documents must be separated while keeping semantic coherence. For example, a 50-page guidebook | 200 chunks of ~500 tokens each.
- **Embedding**: Converting text chunks into dense numerical vectors (768-3072 dimensions) that capture semantic meaning. Similar concepts form neighboring vectors in a vector space. For example, *temperature increased rapidly*, and a *sudden thermal spike* would have similar embeddings despite differing languages.

In practice, multimodal RAG usually follows one of two patterns: convert non-text media into high-quality textual surrogates such as captions, OCR output, and transcripts, and index them with text embeddings; or use multimodal encoders that place text and media representations into a shared embedding space for direct cross-modal retrieval. The rest of this chapter focuses on how to make those choices work reliably in LangChain pipelines.

Tip: **RAG is critical when your agent has to reference recent data, proprietary documents, or domain-specific knowledge not contained in the base LLM's training data.**

Understanding messages and content blocks

Messages are the primary unit of context in LangChain. They provide the state of a conversation, carrying the actual payload (message), the role of the sender, and optional metadata like token usage. They represent the input and output of models to reflect the state of a discussion when engaging with an LLM.

Messages are objects that contain the following:

- **Role**: Identifies the message type (e.g., system, user).
- **Content**: Represents the actual substance of communication (like text, photos, audio, documents, etc.).
- **Metadata**: Optional attributes such as response information, message IDs, and token usage.

LangChain provides a uniform message type that works across all model providers, providing consistent behavior independent of the model being called.

The following code demonstrates how to construct and use different message types with a chat model. Notice how each message type serves a distinct purpose in the conversation flow:

```
from langchain.chat_models import init_chat_model
from langchain_core.messages import HumanMessage, AIMessage, SystemMessage

model = init_chat_model("gpt-4")

system_msg = SystemMessage("You are a helpful assistant.")
human_msg = HumanMessage("Hello, how are you?")

# Use with chat models
messages = [system_msg, human_msg]
response = model.invoke(messages)  # Returns AIMessage
```

Message roles and types

LangChain provides a uniform message interface that ensures consistent behavior regardless of the model provider. Every message is assigned a role, which determines the message type:

- **System message**: Tells the model how to behave and offers context for interactions.
- **Human message**: Represents user input and interactions with the model.

- **AI message**: Responses created by the model, including text content, tool calls, and metadata.
- **Tool message**: Represents the results of tool calls.

The following example shows the complete tool calling workflow. The model generates a tool call, the tool executes and returns a result, and the conversation continues with the tool's output:

```
from langchain_core.messages import HumanMessage, AIMessage, ToolMessage

# After a model makes a tool call
# (Here, we demonstrate manually creating the messages for brevity)
ai_message = AIMessage(
    content=[],
    tool_calls=[{
        "name": "get_weather",
        "args": {"location": "San Francisco"},
        "id": "call_123"
    }]
)

# Execute tool and create result message
weather_result = "Sunny, 72°F"
tool_message = ToolMessage(
    content=weather_result,
    tool_call_id="call_123",  # Must match the call ID
    name="get_weather"        # Tool name – required for reliable tool
routing
)

# Continue conversation
messages = [
    HumanMessage("What's the weather in San Francisco?"),
    ai_message,  # Model's tool call
    tool_message,  # Tool execution result
]
response = model.invoke(messages)  # Model processes the result
```

Standardizing multimodal content

While basic prompts can be simple strings, multimodal inputs require a structured approach using content blocks. The **`content`** attribute of a message is loosely typed, supporting lists of objects (like dictionaries) to handle images, audio, and files.

LangChain also offers a **content_blocks** property that provides a type-safe interface for these payloads. This ensures that messages generated from different providers (like OpenAI or Anthropic) can be parsed into a consistent representation.

The following code demonstrates how to construct a multimodal **HumanMessage** using both a text instruction and a weather chart image:

```
from langchain_core.messages import HumanMessage

# Using the provider-native format (OpenAI-style)
weather_message_native = HumanMessage(
    content=[
        {"type": "text", "text": "Analyze the temperature trend in this
chart."},
        {
            "type": "image_url",
            "image_url": {"url": "https://example.com/weather_chart_10am.
jpg"}
        }
    ]
)

# Using LangChain standard content blocks for type safety
weather_message_standard = HumanMessage(
    content_blocks=[
        {"type": "text", "text": "Analyze the temperature trend in this
chart."},
        {"type": "image", "url": "https://example.com/weather_chart_10am.
jpg"}
    ]
)
```

Content block reference

When working with multimodal data, each item in the message content list must adhere to a specific block type. Standard blocks include:

Category	Block type	Use case
Core	`TextContentBlock`	Standard text instructions or logs.
	`ReasoningContentBlock`	Internal model reasoning or *thinking*.

Category	Block type	Use case
Multimodal	`ImageContentBlock`	Visual data from URLs, base64, or file IDs.
	`AudioContentBlock`	Sound files for transcription or analysis.
	`VideoContentBlock`	Video file inputs.
	`FileContentBlock`	Documents like PDFs for visual parsing.

Table 4.4: Standard content block types and typical use cases

Multimodal understanding vs. multimodal generation

Advanced LLM ecosystems separate two complementary features that enable distinct types of applications. Understanding this distinction helps you develop acceptable solutions for your use case:

- **Multimodal understanding**: An AI system's ability to jointly digest inputs from many modalities and provide responses that consider cross-modal context, such as answering a question about an image using accompanying textual metadata.
- **Multimodal generation**: A workflow where a model takes instructions from one modality to synthesize another, for example, generating an image from a textual prompt or synthesizing audio narration from text and reference tone samples.

True multimodal understanding receives heterogeneous inputs concurrently (text, visuals, audio snippets) and reasons about their relationships. By contrast, multimodal generation employs one modality (typically text) to synthesize another (images, audio, video). Production systems orchestrate both to establish feedback loops, such as describe-generate-evaluate cycles.

Tip: **Treat understanding and generation as independent microservices. Even if the same foundation model supports both (for example, GPT-4o), separating concerns enables you to tune performance, caching, and governance for each path.**

Multimodality means working with more than one sort of input data. In practice, this might be anything from mixing text and images in a single input to designing systems that recognize video, audio, or full texts. For AI engineers, this opens up more intuitive and powerful ways to interface with models. Instead of describing an image in words, you can show the visual. Instead of summarizing a video, you can pass the file directly. The model does not just handle data, but it interprets it in its natural form.

This move matters since most real-world data is not just text. Whether you are working on a product recommendation engine, a medical assistant, or a support chatbot, there is value in being able to assess and respond to diverse formats. LangChain is beginning to enable these workflows, and while the tools are still maturing, the ability to plug in multimodal inputs is already affecting how developers think about prompts, context, and retrieval.

Message parts and multimodal prompts

LangChain structures multimodal data through message pieces, also called content blocks. These are typed fragments that mix several modalities inside a single message. Messages expose a **`content`** field that accepts lists of typed descriptors where each block indicates its type (**`text`**, **`image_url`**, **`media`**) and encapsulates the content appropriately. LangChain normalizes these pieces so the same ChatModel call works across GPT-4o, Claude 3.5 Sonnet, and Gemini 1.5 Pro; each portion must include modality-specific metadata like base64 payloads, URLs, or MIME types. Order matters, as models' attention to prior sections when understanding later ones, so position instructions before media content for best outcomes.

Tool use with multimodal data

A crucial constraint to note is that existing chat models cannot receive raw multimodal data directly inside tool calls. This means you cannot give a picture or audio file as a tool parameter. The workaround is to pass a reference instead of raw data, use public **Universal Resource Locators** (**URLs**), file paths, or object storage URIs that the tool may access independently.

The following code displays the correct pattern for tools that work with multimodal data:

```
from langchain_core.tools import tool
from langchain_openai import ChatOpenAI

@tool
def analyze_inspection_photo(image_url: str) -> str:
    """Analyze an inspection photo and return findings.

    Args:
        image_url: Public URL or storage path to the image
    """
    # Tool fetches the image independently
    vision_model = ChatOpenAI(model="gpt-4o")
    result = vision_model.invoke([
        HumanMessage(content=[
            {"type": "text", "text": "Analyze this inspection photo for
defects."},
            {"type": "image_url", "image_url": {"url": image_url}}
        ])
    ])
    return result.content

# Agent calls tool with reference, not raw data
agent.invoke({"input": "Analyze the bridge photo at https://storage.example.
com/bridge-001.jpg"})
```

Best practice: When designing tools that work with multimodal data, always use durable storage URLs. This pattern works with any model that supports tool use and provides flexibility for processing various media types.

Understanding and integrating multimodal data

The basic job of a multimodal agent is to translate various real-world signals into a consistent, numerical structure that an LLM can reason over. This technique needs to standardize three important modalities, namely text, image, and audio, before they can be aligned and indexed.

Defining text, image, and audio modalities

Multimodal AI systems process multiple kinds of data, each with unique properties and processing requirements. Understanding these modalities is key to developing effective pipelines. The following table categorizes the key categories of multimodal data along with their technical challenges:

Modality	Data types	Common formats	Primary use cases	Technical challenge
Text	Documents, logs, reports, structured data	`.txt`, `.md`, `.pdf`, `.json`, `.csv`, `.xml`	Knowledge retrieval, semantic search, context provision.	Managing scale; documents must be broken down without losing semantic integrity.
Image	Photos, diagrams, charts, scans, screenshots	`.jpg`, `.png`, `.tiff`, `.bmp`, `.webp`, `.svg`	Visual inspection, OCR, chart analysis, object detection.	LLMs cannot process pixels directly; requires conversion to textual descriptions via captioning/OCR.
Audio	Speech, ambient sound, sensor acoustics	`.mp3`, `.wav`, `.flac`, `.m4a`, `.ogg`	Transcription, voice commands, acoustic analysis.	Temporal information critical; time and sequence must be preserved during transcription and indexing.
Video	Recordings, streams, surveillance footage	`.mp4`, `.avi`, `.mov`, `.webm`, `.mkv`	Frame extraction, motion analysis, scene understanding.	Most complex; combines visual and audio streams requiring keyframe extraction and separate processing.

Modality	Data types	Common formats	Primary use cases	Technical challenge
Documents	Rich documents with mixed content	`.docx`, `.pptx`, `.xlsx`, PDF with images	Enterprise knowledge management, report analysis.	Requires specialized parsing to extract both text and embedded media.
Sensor Data	Time-series readings, telemetry	`.csv`, `.parquet`, binary streams	IoT monitoring, predictive maintenance.	Temporal alignment critical; must correlate readings across time.

Table 4.5: Comprehensive multimodal data types and characteristics

Tip: **Start with text, image, and audio modalities before attempting video. Video processing can be simplified by treating it as a sequence of images plus an audio track.**

Weather and local media indexer use case

Throughout this chapter, we employ a meteorological and local media indexer as our practical example. This system links events across diverse data sources to answer questions like *What were the visual conditions during the temperature spike?* The following table describes the preprocessing needs for each modality:

Modality	Example data type	Required preprocessing	Indexed output
Text	`sensor_log.txt`	Smart splitting by time/entity.	Chunks of timestamped text.
Image	`rain_chart.png`	OCR and captioning (V-LLM).	Descriptive caption text.
Audio	`wind_audio.mp3`	Transcription (with timestamps).	Transcript text chunks.

Table 4.6: Modality-specific preprocessing requirements

Building unified multimodal ingestion pipelines

The key to a scalable multimodal system is having a consistent flow that every data item follows, regardless of origin. The universal ingestion sequence is load, transform, chunk, embed, store.

We use the runnable protocol and LangChain's loader abstraction to mask the complexities of reading diverse file formats. The result must always be the standard **`Document`** class, which holds content and important metadata.

Working with images

Images can be provided as URLs (remote storage) or base64-encoded local files. URLs reference images via the **image_url** type, but local files require base64 encoding with the data URI format. All providers (OpenAI, Claude, Gemini) provide the same content block pattern through their own **ChatModel** classes. The following code shows both approaches for working with images:

```
from langchain_openai import ChatOpenAI
from langchain_core.messages import HumanMessage
import base64

model = ChatOpenAI(model="gpt-4o")

# Method 1: Using URL (recommended for production)
message_url = HumanMessage(content=[
    {"type": "text", "text": "Describe this image."},
    {"type": "image_url", "image_url": {"url": "https://example.com/photo.
jpg"}}
])
response = model.invoke([message_url])

# Method 2: Using base64 encoding (for local files)
with open("local_image.jpg", "rb") as f:
    image_data = base64.b64encode(f.read()).decode("utf-8")

message_base64 = HumanMessage(content=[
    {"type": "text", "text": "What defects do you see?"},
    {"type": "image_url", "image_url": {"url": f"data:image/
jpeg;base64,{image_data}"}}
])
response = model.invoke([message_base64])
```

Best practice: Use URLs for production systems (S3, Azure Blob) to bypass payload size constraints and allow caching. Use base64 encoding solely for small images or development.

Note: **When encoding images to base64, ensure you read files in binary mode (rb) and properly decode the base64 bytes to a UTF-8 string before creating the data URI.**

Working with audio files

Audio is provided using base64 encoding with the media type, defining the MIME type (**audio/mpeg**, **audio/wav**). After transcription, build a document with metadata including source, modality, and timestamp for proper indexing.

The following code demonstrates audio processing using GPT-4o:

```
from langchain_openai import ChatOpenAI
from langchain_core.messages import HumanMessage
from langchain_core.documents import Document
import base64

# GPT-4o with direct audio input
model = ChatOpenAI(model="gpt-4o-audio-preview")

with open("recording.mp3", "rb") as f:
    audio_data = base64.b64encode(f.read()).decode("utf-8")

message = HumanMessage(content=[
    {"type": "text", "text": "Transcribe this audio."},
    {"type": "media", "mime_type": "audio/mpeg", "data": audio_data}
])
response = model.invoke([message])

# Create Document for indexing
audio_doc = Document(
    page_content=response.content,
    metadata={
        "source": "recording.mp3",
        "modality": "audio",
        "timestamp": "2024-03-15T10:30:00"
    }
)
```

Audio support varies per supplier. GPT-4o supports direct audio input, but Claude 3 models require Whisper transcription first. For operations requiring stronger text reasoning on transcripts, pair Whisper with Claude 3.5 Sonnet.

Tip: **Always retain timestamps in audio metadata. This temporal information is vital for connecting audio material with time-series sensor data or log events.**

Working with video files

Video is transmitted using base64 encoding with the **media** type and **video/mp4** MIME type. GPT-4o enables native video input, but Claude 3 requires removing keyframes and evaluating them as independent images.

The following code demonstrates both URL and base64 approaches for video processing:

```
from langchain_openai import ChatOpenAI
from langchain_core.messages import HumanMessage
```

```
import base64

model = ChatOpenAI(model="gpt-4o")

# Method 1: URL reference (recommended)
message_url = HumanMessage(content=[
    {"type": "text", "text": "Summarize the key events in this video."},
    {"type": "media", "mime_type": "video/mp4", "url": "https://storage.
example.com/inspection.mp4"}
])
response = model.invoke([message_url])

# Method 2: Base64 encoding (small videos only)
with open("short_clip.mp4", "rb") as f:
    video_data = base64.b64encode(f.read()).decode("utf-8")

message_base64 = HumanMessage(content=[
    {"type": "text", "text": "Identify any safety hazards."},
    {"type": "media", "mime_type": "video/mp4", "data": video_data}
])
response = model.invoke([message_base64])
```

For lengthier videos, extract keyframes selectively (0.5-1 FPS) using OpenCV rather than analyzing whole videos. Claude 3.5 Sonnet typically delivers greater per-frame visual reasoning compared to GPT-4o's whole video analysis. Always use URLs pointing to durable storage (S3, Azure Blob) to avoid presigned URL expiration during retries.

Important: **Video files can be very large. Base64 encoding increases size by around 33%. For files over 10MB, always utilize URLs instead of base64 encoding to prevent violating API payload limits.**

Using LangChain document loaders

After understanding how to work with individual modalities, the next step is designing production pipelines that process many files at scale. LangChain provides over 100 document loaders for diverse file formats. The following code demonstrates the main relevant loaders for multimodal RAG:

```
from langchain_community.document_loaders import (
    TextLoader,           # Plain text files
    PyPDFLoader,          # PDF documents
    UnstructuredImageLoader,  # Images with OCR
    CSVLoader,            # Structured data
    JSONLoader,           # JSON documents
```

```
    DirectoryLoader,      # Batch load from directory
)

# Example: Load documents from multiple sources
text_docs = TextLoader("logs/sensor_readings.txt").load()
pdf_docs = PyPDFLoader("reports/maintenance_2024.pdf").load()
image_docs = UnstructuredImageLoader("photos/inspection.jpg").load()
csv_docs = CSVLoader("data/sensor_data.csv").load()
json_docs = JSONLoader("config/metadata.json", jq_schema=".[]", text_
content=False).load()

# Batch load all text files from directory
dir_loader = DirectoryLoader(
    "data/",
    glob="**/*.txt",
    loader_cls=TextLoader
)
all_text_docs = dir_loader.load()

# Each loader returns List[Document] with page_content and metadata
print(f"Loaded {len(text_docs)} text documents")
print(f"First doc metadata: {text_docs[0].metadata}")
```

Important: **Document loaders automatically extract metadata such source file path, page numbers, and creation dates. This metadata is critical for filtering during retrieval.**

Note: **The `UnstructuredImageLoader` requires the unstructured library and optional dependencies for OCR. Install with `pip install "unstructured[all-docs]"` for complete image processing capabilities.**

The following figure demonstrates the whole data flow from multiple sources through preprocessing to a unified vector database:

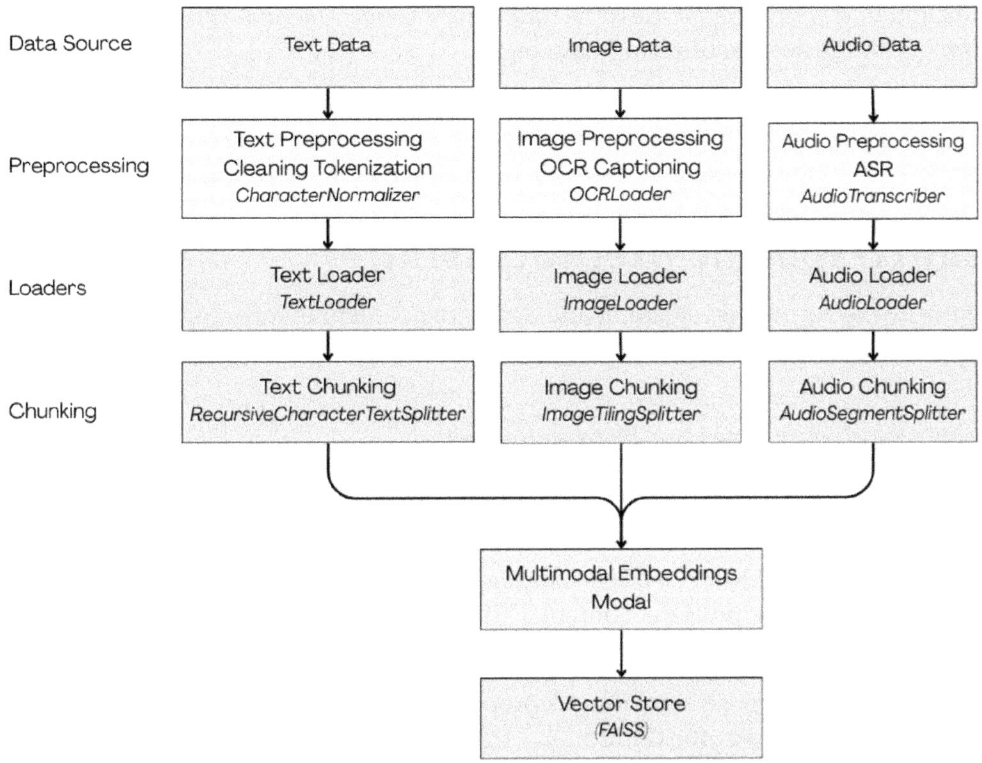

***Figure 4.3**: Complete multimodal ingestion, transformation, and indexing pipeline*

Preprocessing and chunking media

After initial ingestion, raw documents (particularly non-text media) must undergo thorough preprocessing and chunking. These transformations turn different data types into a standardized representation appropriate for AI processing:

- **Preprocessing**: The process of putting raw data into a clean, standardized format. For multimodal systems, this entails transforming images to text via OCR and captioning, transcribing sounds to text, and normalizing metadata like timestamps and encoding.
- **Chunking**: The technique of dividing huge documents into smaller, semantically significant bits. LLMs have context window limits (usually 8K-128K tokens), and documents must be broken into segments that fit inside these constraints while keeping semantic coherence. For example, a 50-page maintenance handbook might be chunked into 200 chunks of around 500 tokens each.
- **Embedding**: The technique of transforming text chunks into dense numerical vectors (usually 768-3072 dimensions). These vectors capture semantic meaning, allowing mathematically equivalent pieces to be positioned close together in vector space. For

example, *temperature increased rapidly*, and a *sudden thermal spike* would have similar embeddings despite differing language.

The whole transformation pipeline follows three stages, namely preprocessing (convert to text) | chunking (split into manageable units) | embedding (convert to vectors) | storing in a vector store. Each stage is critical for establishing effective RAG systems.

Modality-specific preprocessing

Text preprocessing focuses on cleaning and arranging content before chunking. This comprises eliminating extraneous metadata, HTML/Markdown tags, and guaranteeing uniform encoding.

Image preprocessing involves two steps as follows:

- **OCR**: Extracts raw text, numbers, or labels present in the image (data points from a chart, serial numbers from maintenance photos).
- **Captioning (V-LLM)**: A **Vision-Language Model** (V-LLM) creates a natural language summary of the image's content. This caption becomes the main indexed text representing the image.

The following code demonstrates how to preprocess a weather chart using `ChatOpenAI` for captioning and `pytesseract` for OCR:

```
import base64
from langchain_openai import ChatOpenAI
from langchain_core.messages import HumanMessage
from langchain_core.documents import Document
from PIL import Image
import pytesseract

def preprocess_weather_image(image_path: str) -> Document:
    """Extract text via OCR and generate descriptive weather caption."""

    # Step 1: Extract raw data from weather instruments via OCR
    image = Image.open(image_path)
    ocr_text = pytesseract.image_to_string(image)

    # Step 2: Generate visual analysis using gpt-4o
    vision_model = ChatOpenAI(model="gpt-4o")

    with open(image_path, "rb") as f:
        image_data = base64.b64encode(f.read()).decode("utf-8")

    message = HumanMessage(content=[
```

```
        {"type": "text", "text": "Describe the weather conditions and trends
in this image."},
        {"type": "image_url", "image_url": {"url": f"data:image/
jpeg;base64,{image_data}"}}
    ])

    response = vision_model.invoke([message])

    return Document(
        page_content=f"OCR Text: {ocr_text}\nVisual Analysis: {response.
content}",
        metadata={"source": image_path, "modality": "image"}
    )
```

Audio preprocessing converts time-series data into text:

- **Transcription**: Using technologies like OpenAI Whisper to turn spoken audio into text transcripts.
- **Timestamping**: Preserving timestamps and speaker identification (diarization) during transcribing. This metadata is necessary for synchronizing audio content with other time-series data.

The following code demonstrates a transcription workflow for a weather radio report using the OpenAI Whisper API:

```
from openai import OpenAI
from langchain_core.documents import Document

def preprocess_weather_audio(audio_path: str) -> Document:
    """Transcribe weather radio reports into timestamped text documents."""
    client = OpenAI()

    with open(audio_path, "rb") as audio_file:
        transcript = client.audio.transcriptions.create(
            model="whisper-1",
            file=audio_file,
            response_format="verbose_json",
            timestamp_granularities=["segment"]
        )

    # Format segments into a cohesive transcript string with timestamps
    content = "\n".join([f"[{s['start']}s]: {s['text']}" for s in transcript.
segments])
```

```
    return Document(
        page_content=content,
        metadata={"source": audio_path, "modality": "audio", "duration":
transcript.duration}
    )
```

Chunking strategies

After preprocessing, all modalities exist as text documents. The next step is chunking to construct semantically meaningful units that fit into LLM context windows.

For text files, use LangChain's **RecursiveCharacterTextSplitter**:

```
from langchain.text_splitter import RecursiveCharacterTextSplitter

text_splitter = RecursiveCharacterTextSplitter(
    chunk_size=1000,
    chunk_overlap=200,
    separators=["\n\n", "\n", ".", " "]
)
```

Chunking non-text data requires keeping the semantic unit of the source media:

- **Image chunks**: Text from OCR and V-LLM captioning is normally considered as a single, indivisible chunk, as it represents one discrete piece of visual context.
- **Audio chunks**: Transcripts should be chunked depending on speaker turns or time intervals (60-second portions), keeping timestamp metadata for synchronization.

The following function demonstrates semantic text chunking with proper metadata preservation. The splitter uses a hierarchy of separators (paragraphs | sentences | words) to maintain context, while chunk overlap ensures continuity across boundaries:

```
from langchain.text_splitter import RecursiveCharacterTextSplitter
from langchain_core.documents import Document

def chunk_text_document(doc: Document) -> list[Document]:
    """Split text document into semantic chunks."""

    text_splitter = RecursiveCharacterTextSplitter(
        chunk_size=1000,          # Target chunk size in characters
        chunk_overlap=200,        # Overlap to maintain context
        separators=["\n\n", "\n", ".", " "],  # Split hierarchy
        length_function=len
    )
```

```
    chunks = text_splitter.split_documents([doc])

    # Preserve original metadata and add chunk info
    for i, chunk in enumerate(chunks):
        chunk.metadata.update({
            "chunk_id": f"{doc.metadata.get('source', 'unknown')}_chunk_{i}",
            "chunk_index": i,
            "total_chunks": len(chunks)
        })

    return chunks

# Example usage
text_doc = Document(
    page_content="Long sensor log content here...",
    metadata={"source": "sensor_log.txt", "timestamp": "2024-03-15T10:00:00"}
)
text_chunks = chunk_text_document(text_doc)
print(f"Split into {len(text_chunks)} chunks")
```

Generating and synchronizing multimodal embeddings

After preprocessing and chunking, all data (text logs, image captions, audio transcripts) exist as clean text chunks. The next step is generating embeddings. Embeddings serve as the unifying layer, converting text from different modalities into numerical vectors that live in the same semantic space, making them mathematically comparable during retrieval.

Alignment challenge

An embedding is a dense vector representation of a block of data. The closer two vectors are in the vector space, the more semantically connected their underlying text content is.

The key problem in multimodal indexing is alignment. You cannot use a text-only embedding model to embed image captions and expect reliable results:

- **Requirement**: To compare a text query (*What was the temperature anomaly in the chart?*) with an image caption (*A chart showing a sharp drop in barometric pressure...*), we must utilize an embedding model particularly trained to match modalities.
- **Solution**: Use multimodal embedding models [such as **Contrastive Language Image Pretraining** (**CLIP**)-derived models or specific APIs] where the text encoder and the image/vision encoder are trained to generate vectors with the same dimensionality and similar semantic meaning.

The following code illustrates using **OpenAIEmbeddings** to index documents from different weather modalities into a unified **Facebook AI Similarity Search** (**FAISS**) vector store:

```
from langchain_openai import OpenAIEmbeddings
from langchain_community.vectorstores import FAISS

# Initialize the embedding model
embeddings = OpenAIEmbeddings(model="text-embedding-3-small")

# Example collection of preprocessed weather documents
weather_docs = [
    Document(page_content="Sensor: Temp 58°F at 10:15 AM",
metadata={"modality": "text"}),
    Document(page_content="Chart showing a sharp downward temperature spike",
metadata={"modality": "image"}),
    Document(page_content="Radio: 'Sudden cold front moving in'",
metadata={"modality": "audio"})
]

# Create the unified multimodal index
vector_store = FAISS.from_documents(weather_docs, embeddings)

# Test cross-modal retrieval
query = "What evidence is there of a cold front?"
results = vector_store.similarity_search(query, k=3)
```

Metadata and unified context retrieval

Store embeddings in a vector database together with relevant metadata. This metadata permits retrieval based not simply on semantic similarity, but also on temporal (time-based) or categorical filtering.

The following table identifies crucial metadata fields:

Modality source	Essential metadata to store	Retrieval purpose
Audio/log	`timestamp_start`, `speaker_id`	Temporal filtering (e.g., *only show data from 8 AM to 9 AM*).
Image	`source_file`, `ocr_status`	Source filtering (e.g., *only show images*).
Sensor data	`device_id`, `reading_type`	Categorical filtering (e.g., *only retrieve temperature sensor data*).

Table 4.7: *Essential metadata for multimodal vector retrieval*

The synchronized index allows a single text query to launch a thorough, multimodal search over the full data corpus. The following figure visualizes the retrieval process:

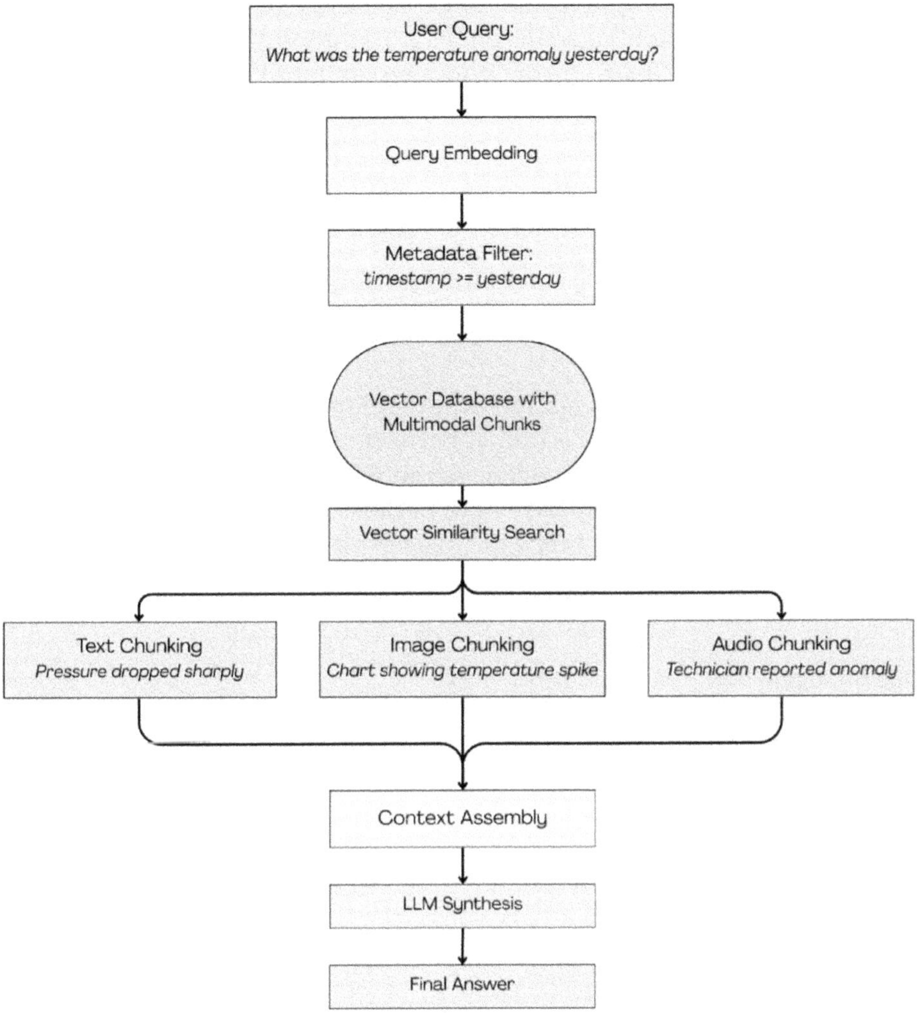

***Figure 4.4**: Multimodal retrieval workflow with metadata filtering and context synthesis*

Advanced pipeline orchestration

Complex multimodal systems need more than working code snippets; they need orchestration patterns that keep heterogeneous processing steps understandable and reliable. In practice, an orchestration layer decides which stages must happen in order, which stages can run concurrently, and where to attach retries, tracing, and human-review checkpoints. LCEL is useful here because it lets you treat each stage as a composable runnable while preserving a clear data flow across modalities.

A simple rule of thumb: use a sequential pipeline when later stages depend on artifacts produced by earlier stages and use a parallel pipeline when branches are independent and mostly I/O-bound. Sequential execution is appropriate when an image report must be produced before summarization, when enrichment depends on OCR or transcription output, or when a human-review gate should only run after scoring and aggregation. Parallel execution is the better choice when text, image, and audio files can be loaded and transformed independently before being merged into a shared index.

Sequential chains for complex workflows

Complex multimodal pipelines can be coordinated using LangChain's sequential chains and LCEL. This approach allows you to chain numerous processes while ensuring observability and error control.

This sequential example has three stages. First, the pipeline performs **vision analysis** to turn the raw image into structured findings. Second, it performs **incident summarization**, combining those findings with operator notes into a concise report. Third, it performs a **severity check** to decide whether the case requires human review. Because each stage depends on the output of the previous one, a sequential chain keeps the logic explicit and easier to debug.

The following code demonstrates a workflow including vision analysis and incident summarization:

```
from langchain_openai import ChatOpenAI
from langchain_core.runnables import RunnableLambda, RunnablePassthrough
from langchain_core.messages import HumanMessage
from langchain_core.prompts import ChatPromptTemplate

vision_model = ChatOpenAI(model="gpt-4o", temperature=0.0)
summarizer = ChatOpenAI(model="gpt-4o", temperature=0.2)

def analyze_image(inputs: dict) -> dict:
    """Analyze image using vision model."""
    prompt = HumanMessage(content=[
        {"type": "text", "text": "Identify defects and severity."},
        {"type": "image_url", "image_url": {"url": inputs["image_url"]}}
    ])
    vision_report = vision_model.invoke([prompt]).content
    return {**inputs, "vision_report": vision_report}

def summarize_incident(inputs: dict) -> dict:
    """Create summary from notes and vision analysis."""
    summary_prompt = ChatPromptTemplate.from_template(
        """Create a concise incident summary.
```

```
        Notes: {notes}
        Vision Findings: {vision_report}

        Summary:"""
    )
    chain = summary_prompt | summarizer
    summary = chain.invoke(inputs).content
    return {**inputs, "summary": summary}

def check_severity(inputs: dict) -> dict:
    """Flag incidents requiring human review."""
    severe_keywords = {"collapse", "critical", "evacuate"}
    requires_review = any(
        word in inputs.get("vision_report", "").lower()
        for word in severe_keywords
    )
    return {**inputs, "requires_human_review": requires_review}

# Chain operations using LCEL
multimodal_workflow = (
    RunnableLambda(analyze_image)
    | RunnableLambda(summarize_incident)
    | RunnableLambda(check_severity)
)

# Execute workflow
result = multimodal_workflow.invoke({
    "image_url": "https://cdn.example.com/bridge-crack.jpg",
    "notes": "Routine bridge inspection"
})

if result["requires_human_review"]:
    print(f"ALERT: Human review required - {result['summary']}")
```

Tip: **Use dictionary passing between chain steps to accumulate state, making interim outcomes available to downstream processes.**

Security consideration: Before activating alerts with image data, apply redaction to sensitive frames. Use image processing libraries to obscure or watermark personally identifiable information.

Incremental indexing and data management

When processing new or updated media files, the pipeline must detect if a document chunk already exists in the vector database and decide whether to update, overwrite, or ignore it.

Every document chunk must be allocated a stable, unique ID, generally a combination of the source file location and the chunk hash/number (e.g., `report_2024.pdf_chunk_005`). This ID is stored in the vector's metadata.

The following table describes document update strategies:

Scenario	Action	Implementation
New document	Insert	Embed the chunk and add the vector and its unique ID metadata using `vectorstore.add_documents(new_docs)`.
Updated document	Overwrite/delete and insert	Retrieve the vector associated with the old ID, delete it from the index, then insert the new vector.
Duplicate document	Ignore	If the unique ID is found in the index, skip the embedding and insertion steps.

***Table 4.8**: Document update strategies for incremental indexing*

Parallel processing with LCEL

LCEL also supports parallel orchestration for stages that do not depend on one another. This pattern is most valuable during ingestion, where text files, images, and audio recordings can often be loaded, transformed, and chunked independently before their outputs are merged. While parallelism improves throughput, it also introduces coordination concerns such as balancing worker counts, preserving consistent metadata, and handling partial failures without losing visibility into which branch failed.

In this parallel example, each branch handles one modality-specific ingestion path: **text processing** loads and chunks textual sources, **image processing** applies OCR and captioning, and **audio processing** performs transcription with timestamps. After those branches complete, the pipeline enters a **merge and indexing** stage that combines all outputs, removes duplicates, and writes the resulting documents to the vector store. This pattern works only because none of the three branches depends on the intermediate results of the others.

The following code exhibits simultaneous processing across modalities:

```
from langchain_core.runnables import RunnableParallel, RunnableLambda
from langchain_chroma import Chroma
from langchain_openai import OpenAIEmbeddings
from langchain_core.documents import Document
```

```
embeddings = OpenAIEmbeddings(model="text-embedding-3-large")
vectorstore = Chroma(collection_name="multimodal_index", embedding_
function=embeddings)

def process_text_files(file_paths: list[str]) -> list[Document]:
    """Load and chunk text documents."""
    # Implementation details...
    return docs

def process_image_files(file_paths: list[str]) -> list[Document]:
    """Extract text via OCR and generate captions."""
    # Implementation details...
    return docs

def process_audio_files(file_paths: list[str]) -> list[Document]:
    """Transcribe audio with timestamps."""
    # Implementation details...
    return docs

def index_multimodal_corpus(text_files, image_files, audio_files):
    """Orchestrate parallel ingestion across all modalities."""
    pipeline = RunnableParallel(
        text=RunnableLambda(lambda _: process_text_files(text_files)),
        images=RunnableLambda(lambda _: process_image_files(image_files)),
        audio=RunnableLambda(lambda _: process_audio_files(audio_files))
    )

    results = pipeline.invoke({})
    all_docs = results["text"] + results["images"] + results["audio"]

    # Batch insert with deduplication
    existing_ids = set(vectorstore.get()["ids"])
    new_docs = [doc for doc in all_docs if doc.metadata.get("unique_id") not
in existing_ids]

    if new_docs:
        vectorstore.add_documents(new_docs)

    return {"total_processed": len(all_docs), "new_indexed": len(new_docs)}
```

Performance note: `RunnableParallel` launches concurrent workers for each modality, cutting overall indexing time from sequential O(n) to parallel **`O(max(text_time, image_time, audio_time))`**.

Error handling and monitoring

Different modalities have different failure characteristics. Vision APIs may throttle under demand, audio transcription can fail on corrupted data, and text processing might meet encoding difficulties.

The following table outlines appropriate retry strategies:

Modality	Common failures	Retry strategy	Fallback behavior
Text	Encoding errors, malformed files.	Immediate retry with alternate encoding.	Skip chunk, log for manual review.
Image	API rate limits, unsupported formats.	Exponential backoff (2s, 4s, 8s).	Cache placeholder caption, reprocess later.
Audio	Transcription timeout, silence detection.	Jittered retry to avoid thundering herd.	Store raw audio reference, mark for retry.

***Table 4.9**: Modality-specific error handling strategies*

Warning: **Never silently skip failed chunks without logging. Missing modalities create blind spots in retrieval that are difficult to diagnose later.**

Add observability with LangSmith using the following code:

```
from langsmith import Client
from langsmith.run_helpers import traceable

@traceable(name="multimodal_indexing", run_type="chain")
def index_with_tracing(text_files, image_files, audio_files):
    """Wrap indexing with LangSmith observability."""
    with Client().tracing_context(tags=["multimodal", "indexing"]):
        return index_multimodal_corpus(text_files, image_files, audio_files)
```

Retrieval strategies and agent integration

With a synchronized multimodal index in place, the final stage is designing a retrieval pipeline that can synthesize answers from multiple sources. This part focuses on developing the RAG chain and integrating it into an autonomous agent.

Building the RAG retrieval chain

A multimodal RAG chain must be able to manage context that includes text logs, visual descriptions, and audio transcripts. The *stuff* documents chain is the simplest, straightforward technique, where all retrieved snippets are concatenated into a single prompt for the LLM.

The retrieval chain is the heart of any RAG system. LangChain provides the `create_retrieval_chain` function to compose retrieval with generation, but for multimodal systems, we require bespoke retrievers that support cross-modal queries.

The following code demonstrates establishing a multimodal RAG chain:

```
from langchain.chains import create_retrieval_chain
from langchain.chains.combine_documents import create_stuff_documents_chain
from langchain_core.prompts import ChatPromptTemplate
from langchain_openai import ChatOpenAI
from langchain_chroma import Chroma

# Initialize components
llm = ChatOpenAI(model="gpt-4o", temperature=0)

# Create prompt template that handles multimodal context
system_prompt = """You are an assistant analyzing multimodal data including
text logs, image descriptions, and audio transcripts. Use the provided
context to answer questions.

Context includes:
- Text documents with timestamps
- Image captions describing visual content
- Audio transcriptions with speaker information

Always cite the source modality and timestamp in your answers.

Context: {context}"""

prompt = ChatPromptTemplate.from_messages([
    ("system", system_prompt),
    ("human", "{input}")
])

vectorstore = Chroma(collection_name="multimodal_corpus")

retriever = vectorstore.as_retriever(
    search_type="similarity",
    search_kwargs={"k": 5}
)

# Combine into RAG chain
question_answer_chain = create_stuff_documents_chain(llm, prompt)
rag_chain = create_retrieval_chain(retriever, question_answer_chain)
```

```
# Execute query
response = rag_chain.invoke({
    "input": "What was the temperature anomaly at 10 AM?"
})
print(response["answer"])
```

Tip: **The `stuff` method in `create_stuff_documents_chain` concatenates all retrieved documents into the prompt. For large contexts, consider `map_reduce` or refine chains.**

The following figure shows how raw multimodal data flows through dedicated preprocessing and embedding pipelines before being unified in a FAISS vector store, enabling cross-modal semantic search that grounds the final ChatOpenAI response:

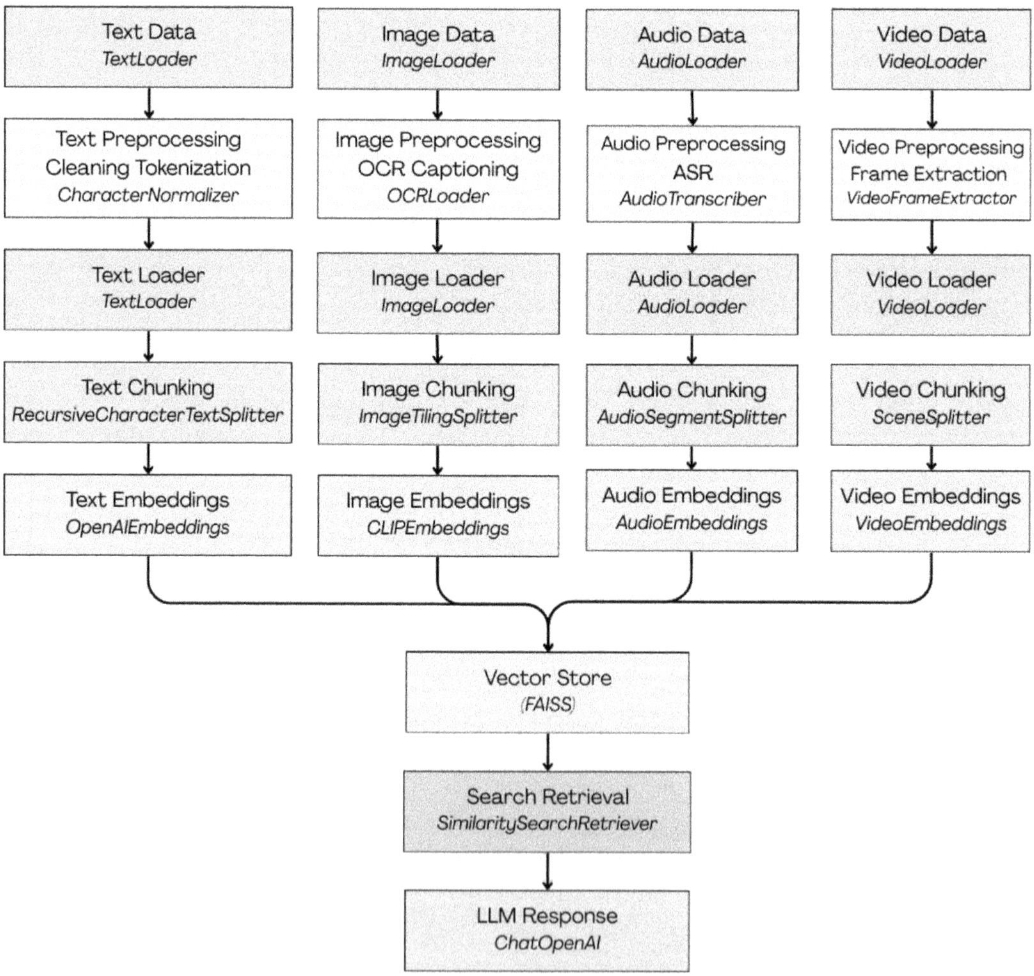

Figure 4.5: *Multimodal agent query execution sequence*

Advanced retrieval techniques

Since the index contains chunks from diverse sources (logs, transcripts, images), simple top-k retrieval is often insufficient. LangChain supports multiple retrieval strategies, as mentioned in the upcoming sections.

Similarity search with metadata filtering:

```
# Filter by temporal and categorical metadata
retriever = vectorstore.as_retriever(
    search_type="similarity",
    search_kwargs={
        "k": 5,
        "filter": {
            "timestamp": {"$gte": "2024-01-15T09:00:00"},
            "modality": {"$in": ["image", "text"]}
        }
    }
)
```

Maximum Marginal Relevance (**MMR**) balances relevance with diversity, preventing redundant results from the same source:

```
retriever = vectorstore.as_retriever(
    search_type="mmr",
    search_kwargs={
        "k": 5,
        "fetch_k": 20,  # Fetch 20 candidates, return 5 diverse ones
        "lambda_mult": 0.5  # Balance between relevance (1.0) and diversity
(0.0)
    }
)
```

For contextual compression, use a compressor to extract only the most relevant parts of retrieved documents:

```
from langchain.retrievers import ContextualCompressionRetriever
from langchain.retrievers.document_compressors import LLMChainExtractor

compressor = LLMChainExtractor.from_llm(llm)
compression_retriever = ContextualCompressionRetriever(
    base_compressor=compressor,
    base_retriever=retriever
)
```

For ensemble retrieval, combine multiple retrieval strategies for robust results:

```
from langchain.retrievers import EnsembleRetriever
from langchain_community.retrievers import BM25Retriever

# Combine dense (vector) and sparse (keyword) retrieval
bm25_retriever = BM25Retriever.from_documents(documents)
ensemble_retriever = EnsembleRetriever(
    retrievers=[vectorstore.as_retriever(), bm25_retriever],
    weights=[0.7, 0.3]  # 70% vector, 30% keyword
)
```

Best practice: Start with a simple similarity search, then add complexity (MMR, compression, ensemble) only if retrieval quality warrants it. Monitor retrieval accuracy with evaluation datasets.

Multimodal RAG agent pipeline

The final goal is to wrap this retrieval logic into a tool that a LangChain agent can call autonomously. This helps the agent to evaluate when it needs to search for weather data versus when it should conduct other actions, like sending an alert, as shown in the following figure:

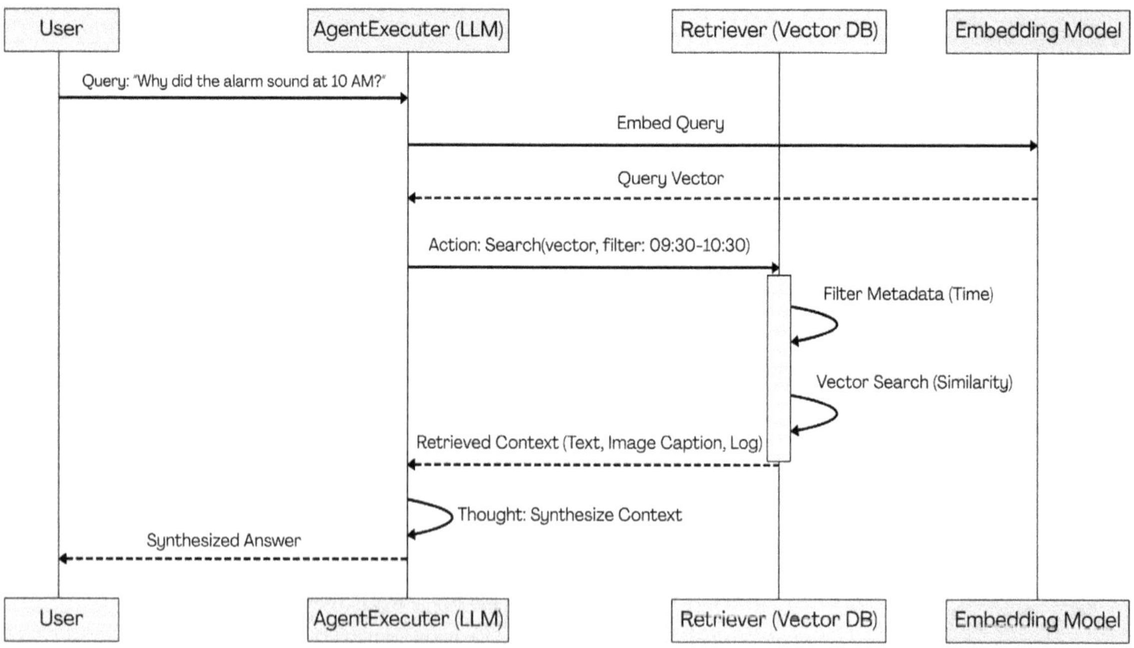

***Figure 4.6**: Time-filtered agentic RAG query flow*

The following code explains how to wrap the multimodal RAG chain into a tool for a tool-calling agent:

```
from langchain.chains import create_retrieval_chain
from langchain.chains.combine_documents import create_stuff_documents_chain
from langchain_core.prompts import ChatPromptTemplate
from langchain_openai import ChatOpenAI, OpenAIEmbeddings
from langchain_chroma import Chroma
from langchain_text_splitters import RecursiveCharacterTextSplitter
from langchain_community.document_loaders import DirectoryLoader, TextLoader

class MultimodalRAG:
    """Complete multimodal RAG system."""

    def __init__(self, collection_name: str = "multimodal_rag"):
        self.llm = ChatOpenAI(model="gpt-4o", temperature=0)
        self.embeddings = OpenAIEmbeddings(model="text-embedding-3-large")
        self.vectorstore = Chroma(
            collection_name=collection_name,
            embedding_function=self.embeddings
        )
        self.text_splitter = RecursiveCharacterTextSplitter(
            chunk_size=1000,
            chunk_overlap=200
        )

    def index_documents(self, directory_path: str):
        """Index documents from directory."""
        # Load documents
        loader = DirectoryLoader(directory_path, glob="**/*.txt", loader_
cls=TextLoader)
        docs = loader.load()

        # Split into chunks
        chunks = self.text_splitter.split_documents(docs)

        # Add to vector store
        self.vectorstore.add_documents(chunks)
        print(f"Indexed {len(chunks)} chunks from {len(docs)} documents")

    def create_rag_chain(self):
        """Create the complete RAG chain."""
        retriever = self.vectorstore.as_retriever(
```

```
            search_type="mmr",
            search_kwargs={"k": 5, "fetch_k": 20}
        )

        system_prompt = """Answer questions using the provided context from
multiple sources.

Context includes text documents, image descriptions, and audio transcripts.
Always cite the source and timestamp when available.

Context: {context}"""

        prompt = ChatPromptTemplate.from_messages([
            ("system", system_prompt),
            ("human", "{input}")
        ])

        qa_chain = create_stuff_documents_chain(self.llm, prompt)
        return create_retrieval_chain(retriever, qa_chain)

    def query(self, question: str) -> dict:
        """Query the RAG system."""
        chain = self.create_rag_chain()
        return chain.invoke({"input": question})

# Usage
rag = MultimodalRAG()
rag.index_documents("data/")
response = rag.query("What was the temperature anomaly at 10 AM?")
print(response["answer"])
```

Evaluating RAG performance

To guarantee the system remains trustworthy, you must measure both retrieval accuracy and generation fidelity. LangSmith provides the tracing infrastructure to monitor these multimodal decisions in real-time:

```
from langsmith import Client
from langchain.smith import RunEvalConfig

# Define evaluation criteria
eval_config = RunEvalConfig(
    evaluators=[
```

```
        "qa",  # Question answering accuracy
        "context_qa",  # Relevance of retrieved context
        "cot_qa",  # Chain-of-thought reasoning
    ]
)

# Create test dataset
test_cases = [
    {
        "input": "What was the temperature at 10 AM?",
        "expected_output": "72°F as recorded by Sensor A"
    },
    {
        "input": "Did any images show structural damage?",
        "expected_output": "Yes, bridge inspection photo showed a crack on
girder section 3"
    }
]

# Run evaluation
client = Client()
results = client.evaluate(
    rag.query,
    data=test_cases,
    evaluators=eval_config.evaluators
)
```

The key metrics are as follows:

- **Retrieval accuracy**: Are relevant documents retrieved? (measure with **precision@k**, **recall@k**)
- **Answer relevance**: Does the answer address the question? (human eval or LLM-as-judge)
- **Modality coverage**: Does the retriever consistently find appropriate images and audio?
- **Temporal accuracy**: Does the LLM appropriately associate events with their timestamps?
- **Faithfulness**: Does the answer hallucinate visual features not present in the image caption?
- **Faithfulness**: Is the answer anchored in the recovered context? (check for hallucinations)
- **Latency**: Time from query to answer (target: <2s for most queries).

Note: **Always maintain a golden dataset of weather queries from validated multimodal sources. Re-run your assessments whenever you adjust your embedding model or vision-prompting method.**

Conclusion

This chapter created the underlying architecture for production-grade multimodal pipelines, moving beyond text-only interfaces to systems that reason across text, image, and audio data. You learned how to normalize disparate data streams through specialized transformations such as OCR for extracting text from documents, vision-language model captioning for images, and transcription for audio inputs. These transformations create a unified context that your agent can work with consistently.

Using LangChain's document loaders and semantic chunking strategies, you built ingestion pipelines that map diverse content types into a shared semantic vector space. The weather and local media indexer project showed you how to synchronize temporal sensor data and streaming sources with static media assets. You created advanced orchestration logic, including metadata filtering, context synthesis, and incremental indexing using FAISS to manage production workloads efficiently. These patterns ensure that your agent can connect events across varied data kinds, giving a coherent and grounded reasoning loop that accounts for what the system sees, hears, and reads.

Now that multimodal data flows have been covered, the next chapter focuses on enhancing your agent's visual perception. You will learn to combine cutting-edge vision models like CLIP and GPT-4V to enable sophisticated visual intelligence. We will advance into high-stakes sectors, creating comprehensive vision-driven infrastructures for medical diagnostics, retail analysis, and industrial inspection.

You will work through real production challenges such as managing high-resolution imagery at scale, controlling latency in real-time visual reasoning, and optimizing API costs without sacrificing performance. By the end of the chapter, your agents will not just process image data, but they will also perceive and reason about the physical world with precision and contextual depth.

CHAPTER 5
Building Vision-enabled Agents with Visual Intelligence

Introduction

Text-only agents can answer inquiries and perform commands, but they cannot see the world around them. This chapter changes your LangChain agents from language processors into visual interpreters capable of evaluating satellite images, reading weather station displays, and collecting data from meteorological charts. You will graduate from basic text-based reasoning to multimodal intelligence that blends language understanding with visual awareness.

The evolution begins with knowing vision-language models and their integration patterns. You will explore how models like OpenAI (**GPT**) 4o and **Contrastive Language-Image Pre-training** (**CLIP**) bridge the gap between pixels and meaning, enabling your agents to describe what they perceive, answer questions about images, and make decisions based on visual input. This foundation extends into practical solutions like **optical character recognition** (**OCR**) for extracting data from weather displays, image classification for identifying weather trends, and video analysis for tracking atmospheric changes over time.

Every notion is based on concrete weather-related applications. You will construct an agent that analyzes satellite weather imagery to identify storm systems, derives temperature values from analog weather station photographs, and processes time-lapse films to discover cloud formation patterns. The chapter culminates in a full workshop where you design a complete vision-enabled weather intelligence system that incorporates picture analysis, data extraction, and decision-making into a unified agent architecture.

Structure

This chapter will cover the following topics:

- Integrating advanced vision models
- Implementing OCR for structured text extraction

- Using external vision APIs for automation
- Building text-to-image and image-to-text systems
- Processing and analyzing video data streams
- Multimodal intelligence in medical case studies
- Designing full vision-driven agent architectures
- Building a vision-enabled weather intelligence system

Objectives

This chapter upgrades LangChain agents from text-only assistants to multimodal systems that can interpret and act on visual inputs. You start with core vision-language concepts and the capabilities of models such as GPT-4o for contextual image reasoning and CLIP for fast cross-modal retrieval and zero-shot classification. Next, you learn practical integration patterns in LangChain, such as accepting images as tool inputs, chaining vision steps with downstream reasoning, and managing multimodal data flow. From there, you build applied skills such as OCR for extracting structured text from weather displays, image classification for categorizing conditions, and object identification for spotting key features in meteorological imagery. The chapter then shifts to production architectures, preprocessing pipelines (resize, normalize, enhance), robust tool wrappers around cloud services (for example, OpenAI Vision), local/open-source alternatives, and error handling strategies. Finally, you extend from single-image analysis to temporal understanding through video workflows (frame extraction, motion/change detection, and temporal reasoning), and you address operational concerns such as cost control, caching, and performance optimization for real-time visual perception.

Integrating advanced vision models

Building a vision-enabled agent requires selecting and combining the correct technologies for the job. Modern **large language models (LLMs)** like GPT-4o offer an all-in-one solution for vision and text reasoning, while specialized models like CLIP excel at specific tasks such as cross-modal retrieval and zero-shot categorization. LangChain provides several interaction points for these capabilities, ranging from direct model invocation to tool-based architectures where vision becomes a modular agent feature.

Core capabilities of vision models

Vision-language models provide numerous fundamental skills that enable intelligent agents to process visual input. Image captioning creates natural language descriptions of visual content, allowing agents to turn images into text that can flow through normal language model pipelines. Visual question answering enables agents to respond to particular queries concerning picture content, such as detecting the temperature indicated on a weather station display.

The following table illustrates the fundamental capabilities of vision-language models and their applications in constructing intelligent agents:

Capability	Description	Weather agent application	Model examples
Image captioning	Generate natural language descriptions	Describe satellite imagery	GPT-4o, BLIP-2
Visual question answering	Answer specific questions about content	Extract instrument readings	GPT-4o, LLaVA
Zero-shot classification	Categorize images without training	Classify weather conditions	CLIP, OpenCLIP
Object detection	Identify and locate specific objects	Detect weather instruments	OWL-ViT, YOLO
OCR	Extract text from images	Read station displays	GPT-4o, Tesseract

***Table 5.1**: Core capabilities of vision-language models*

Analyzing and interpreting images contextually

The most basic way to offer an agent sight is by leveraging a **vision-language model** (**VLM**) like GPT-4o, which takes a picture as part of the **HumanMessage** content block. The key to good analysis is in the prompting, moving from generic explanations to specific, goal-oriented instructions.

The following code demonstrates how to use the **ChatOpenAI** model to analyze a weather chart and extract structured data using **Pydantic**:

```
from langchain_openai import ChatOpenAI
from langchain_core.messages import HumanMessage
from langchain_core.prompts import ChatPromptTemplate
from langchain_core.output_parsers import JsonOutputParser
from pydantic import BaseModel, Field

# Define a structured output schema for the analysis using Pydantic
class WeatherReport(BaseModel):
    """Schema for a structured weather report extracted from an image."""
    highest_temperature_c: float = Field(description="The highest temperature 
observed in Celsius.")
    time_of_spike: str = Field(description="The exact time of the highest 
temperature, e.g., '14:00 UTC'.")
    visual_anomaly: str = Field(description="Any visually notable event, such
```

```
as 'sharp drop in pressure'.")

# Initialize LLM and Parser
vision_model = ChatOpenAI(model="gpt-4o", temperature=0)
parser = JsonOutputParser(pydantic_object=WeatherReport)

# Create a multimodal prompt template
prompt = ChatPromptTemplate.from_messages([
    ("system", (
        "You are an expert weather analyst. Analyze the provided chart and
extract data "
        "following the exact JSON schema provided. Focus only on the
'Temperature' line."
        "\n{format_instructions}\n"
    ).format(format_instructions=parser.get_format_instructions())),
    ("human", [
        {"type": "text", "text": "Extract the highest temperature reading
from this chart."},
        {"type": "image_url", "image_url": {"url": "https://storage.example.
com/weather_chart_jan15.png"}}
    ])
])

# Build the LCEL chain
vision_analysis_chain = prompt | vision_model | parser
```

Building vision-enabled tools

For complicated agents, encapsulating vision models in LangChain tools enables improved modularity. A vision tool accepts picture inputs, interprets them, and returns outputs that other agent components can use for larger reasoning.

The following code explains how to develop a reusable vision analysis tool for weather condition descriptions:

```
from langchain.tools import Tool
from langchain_openai import ChatOpenAI
from langchain_core.messages import HumanMessage

def analyze_weather_image(image_url: str) -> str:
    """Analyze a weather image and return descriptions of current
conditions."""
    vision_llm = ChatOpenAI(model="gpt-4o", max_tokens=300)
```

```
    message = HumanMessage(content=[
        {"type": "text", "text": "Analyze this weather image and describe the
visible features."},
        {"type": "image_url", "image_url": {"url": image_url}}
    ])

    response = vision_llm.invoke([message])
    return response.content

# Create LangChain tool for the agent
weather_vision_tool = Tool(
    name="analyze_weather_image",
    description="Analyze weather images to determine conditions. Input: valid
image URL.",
    func=analyze_weather_image
)
```

Specialized vision models and cross-modal retrieval

Before diving into CLIP's architecture, it helps to first see where specialized cross-modal retrieval models fit relative to general vision-language models. *Table 5.2* provides that framing by highlighting the trade-offs in purpose, input/output behavior, cost, and best-fit use cases. The following table compares the application cases for VLM and specialized (CLIP) models:

Criterion	VLM (GPT-4o)	Specialized (CLIP)
Purpose	Complex reasoning, data extraction	Efficient search, zero-shot classification
Input/output	Text and image text	Image vector; text vector
Cost	Higher, billed per token/segment	Lower, billed per vector after indexing
Best for	Incident root cause analysis	Large-scale image search, pre-screening

***Table 5.2**: Comparison of vision-language models and specialized vision models*

While GPT-4o is effective for contextual reasoning, specialized models like CLIP are needed for efficient, large-scale visual tasks. CLIP establishes a shared embedding environment for both images and text.

The following figure explains how CLIP facilitates cross-modal retrieval by matching text and image encoders into a single semantic vector space:

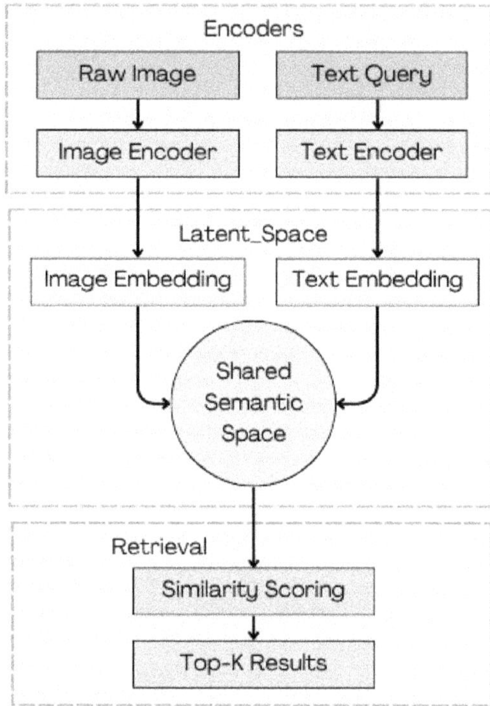

Figure 5.1: *CLIP cross-modal retrieval architecture*

The practical benefit of this architecture resides in its adaptability. You can encode an image once and compare it against endless text descriptions without reprocessing the image, which is substantially faster and cheaper than using a generative VLM for classification.

Handling multiple images for temporal analysis

Many vision tasks require evaluating several images, such as following weather changes over time. LangChain enables multi-image workflows where you include many image references in a single message to help the model discover visual differences.

The following code explains how to compare two weather photos to identify changes in conditions:

```
from langchain_openai import ChatOpenAI
from langchain_core.messages import HumanMessage

def compare_weather_images(before_url: str, after_url: str) -> str:
    """Compare two weather images to identify temporal changes in
conditions."""
    vision_llm = ChatOpenAI(model="gpt-4o", max_tokens=400)

    message = HumanMessage(content=[
```

```
        {"type": "text", "text": "Compare these two weather images. Describe
what has changed."},
        {"type": "image_url", "image_url": {"url": before_url}},
        {"type": "text", "text": "Image 2 (later time):"},
        {"type": "image_url", "image_url": {"url": after_url}}
    ])

    response = vision_llm.invoke([message])
    return response.content
```

Implementing OCR for structured text extraction

OCR is the method of extracting text from images, changing raw pixels into machine-readable letters. While current VLMs can often read text implicitly, a specialist OCR engine is needed for high-fidelity extraction from complex texts, analog gauges, or low-resolution scans where exact character identification is critical.

Combining OCR and VLM in a chain

A popular production pattern is to employ a sophisticated OCR engine, such as Tesseract, for raw text extraction and then feed the text, along with the source image, to a VLM like **gpt-4o-mini**. This *two-pronged* method lets the VLM leverage the visual context to validate and structure the noisy OCR output, dramatically lowering hallucinations that arise when a model tries to read complicated layouts (like tables or forms) without structural grounding.

The following code demonstrates a sequential **LangChain Expression Language** (**LCEL**) chain that orchestrates raw OCR extraction and contextual validation using **Pydantic** and **ChatOpenAI**:

```
import base64
import pytesseract
from PIL import Image
from langchain_openai import ChatOpenAI
from langchain_core.messages import HumanMessage
from langchain_core.runnables import RunnableLambda
from langchain_core.output_parsers import JsonOutputParser
from pydantic import BaseModel, Field

# 1. Define the structured schema for weather data extraction
class WeatherGaugeReading(BaseModel):
    temperature: float = Field(description="The numeric temperature reading")
    unit: str = Field(description="The unit of measurement, e.g., 'C' or
'F'")
```

```
    confidence_score: float = Field(description="Value between 0 and 1
indicating visual clarity")

# 2. Define the OCR step as a RunnableLambda
def perform_ocr(inputs: dict) -> dict:
    """Uses Tesseract to extract raw text from a local file."""
    image_path = inputs["image_path"]
    raw_text = pytesseract.image_to_string(Image.open(image_path)).strip()
    # Pass along the original inputs plus the new OCR result
    return {**inputs, "ocr_output": raw_text}

# 3. Define the VLM validation step as a RunnableLambda
def contextual_validation(inputs: dict) -> dict:
    """Uses VLM to validate OCR output against the actual image context."""
    vision_model = ChatOpenAI(model="gpt-4o-mini", temperature=0)
    parser = JsonOutputParser(pydantic_object=WeatherGaugeReading)

    # Encode local image to base64 for the vision model
    with open(inputs["image_path"], "rb") as f:
        img_b64 = base64.b64encode(f.read()).decode("utf-8")

    message = HumanMessage(content=[
        {"type": "text", "text": f"The OCR engine detected this text:
'{inputs['ocr_output']}'"},
        {"type": "text", "text": "Validate this against the image and format
as JSON: " + parser.get_format_instructions()},
        {"type": "image_url", "image_url": {"url": f"data:image/
jpeg;base64,{img_b64}"}}
    ])

    response = vision_model.invoke([message])
    return parser.parse(response.content)

# 4. Build the unified OCR-VLM chain using LCEL
# We use the pipe operator to connect the OCR function and the validation
logic
ocr_vlm_chain = (
    RunnableLambda(perform_ocr)
    | RunnableLambda(contextual_validation)
)

# Example Execution
# result = ocr_vlm_chain.invoke({"image_path": "weather_gauge_photo.jpg"})
```

LCEL is recommended for OCR operations

OCR workflows are rarely a single model call. In practice, you compose multiple steps, image preprocessing, OCR extraction, post-processing, and VLM-based validation, into one repeatable pipeline. LCEL is a natural fit for this style of orchestration because it makes each stage explicit, testable, and easy to extend as requirements evolve.

Using LCEL for these workflows has significant architectural advantages:

- **Observability**: Each stage in the chain is automatically tracked in LangSmith, letting you to see exactly where the OCR might have failed versus where the LLM committed a validation error.
- **Parallelization**: If you have numerous photos or different OCR engines (e.g., Tesseract and Azure OCR), you can use `RunnableParallel` to execute them concurrently and integrate the results.
- **Type safety**: By utilizing `RunnableLambda` and `Pydantic` schemas, you ensure that the complicated dictionary data sent between the OCR engine and the VLM is consistent and valid.

Tip: **For production environments, install a caching layer before the `contextual_validation` step. If the content hash of the image has already been evaluated, you can forgo the expensive VLM call.**

Using external vision APIs for automation

While local models and conventional LLM vision suites provide excellent general-purpose reasoning, many specialized automation tasks, such as advanced satellite imagery analysis, agricultural monitoring, or high-volume document parsing, benefit from incorporating external, purpose-built vision APIs. By packaging these specialized services as LangChain tools, your agent can delegate high-complexity visual tasks to specialist engines while preserving its own central reasoning logic.

Integrating specialist weather and environmental APIs

Specialized environmental APIs, such as those supplied by satellite data platforms or industrial monitoring services, may include characteristics that general models lack, such as multi-spectral analysis or sub-meter resolution tracking. In a weather-driven agent, these external APIs can be leveraged to automate the detection of localized environmental risks that a normal snapshot might not fully capture.

The following code explains how to develop a LangChain utility that wraps an external vision API for automatic satellite storm detection:

```
from langchain_core.tools import tool
import requests
import os

@tool
def detect_storm_cells(satellite_image_url: str) -> str:
    """
    Calls an external specialized satellite vision API to detect storm cell
coordinates.
    Use this for high-precision environmental automation.
    """
    # Placeholder for an external specialized vision service endpoint
    api_url = "https://api.specialized-weather-vision.com/v1/analyze"
    headers = {"Authorization": f"Bearer {os.getenv('WEATHER_API_KEY')}"}
    payload = {"image_url": satellite_image_url, "task": "storm_detection"}

    response = requests.post(api_url, json=payload, headers=headers)

    if response.status_code == 200:
        data = response.json()
        # Transform API output into a string for agent reasoning
        cells = data.get("detected_cells", [])
        return f"Detected {len(cells)} storm cells. Coordinates: {cells}"
    else:
        return "Error: External vision service unavailable."

# The agent can now use this tool to automate regional safety alerts
```

Orchestrating external vision tools in LCEL

By using LCEL, you may design automated pipelines that combine the broad reasoning of a model like GPT-4o with the precision of an external **application programming interface** (**API**). This hybrid method ensures that the agent handles the broad context while the external API performs the specific *heavy lifting* of visual data extraction.

The following figure depicts the automation cycle where a general vision model activates a specific external API for detailed analysis:

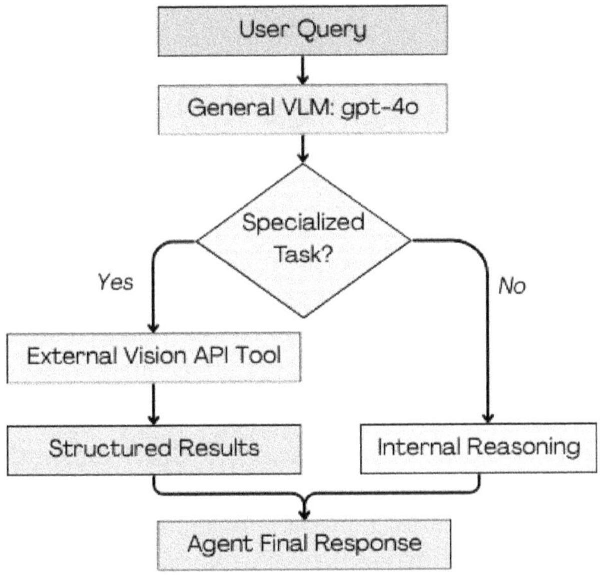

***Figure 5.2**: Automated vision tool orchestration workflow*

Benefits of external API automation

After you wrap a third-party vision service as a LangChain tool, it becomes a first-class step in your agent workflow. The LLM can decide when to call it, LCEL can compose it with preprocessing and post-processing steps, and your application can treat its output as structured evidence rather than an opaque side call. The following benefits explain why this integration pattern is common in production systems.

Relying on specialized external vision APIs for automation gives numerous production-grade advantages:

- **Computational efficiency**: Delegating extensive picture processing to external servers preserves your agent's local memory and computation resources.
- **Domain expertise**: Specialized APIs are generally trained on proprietary datasets (e.g., medical pathology or thermal industrial imaging) that general LLMs have not encountered.
- **Standardized compliance**: Many industrial vision APIs have built-in audit trails and metadata formatting that conform to sector-specific requirements, such as the **Health Insurance Portability and Accountability Act** (**HIPAA**) in healthcare.

Tip: **When automating with external APIs, always incorporate a circuit breaker pattern in your LangChain tool to prevent a failure in the external service from slowing the entire agent's decision loop.**

Building text-to-image and image-to-text systems

A comprehensive vision-enabled agent is rarely limited to passive visual understanding. In real-world systems, agents typically need to shift fluidly between interpretation and creation, transforming images into structured language for reasoning while also generating visuals that transmit decisions, alarms, or insights back to users. This bidirectional feature changes agents from silent observers into active collaborators that can both perceive visual signals and manufacture new visual artifacts on demand.

In practice, image-to-text processes allow agents to extract meaning, metrics, and context from visual inputs, such as charts, dashboards, or photographs, so that visual information can participate in retrieval, validation, and decision-making pipelines. Conversely, text-to-image creation enables agents to externalize reasoning conclusions by providing visual representations, such as alert dashboards, annotated imagery, or quick design prototypes. Together, these capabilities provide a closed feedback loop where agents not only perceive the visual environment but also modify it, providing outputs that are instantaneously consumable by people and downstream systems alike.

Text-to-image visual prototyping

LangChain can integrate image-generating models like **DALL-E** 3 by wrapping them as bespoke tools. This allows the agent to provide a visual output for the user, closing the loop from text analysis to visual synthesis.

The following tool definition explains how to incorporate DALL-E 3 into a LangChain agent to generate weather alert graphics:

```
from langchain_core.tools import tool
from openai import OpenAI

@tool
def generate_weather_graphic(alert_description: str) -> str:
    """Generates a visual image of a weather alert or dashboard."""
    client = OpenAI()
    response = client.images.generate(
        model="dall-e-3",
        prompt=f"Modern weather alert dashboard for: {alert_description}",
        size="1024x1024"
```

```
    )
    return response.data[0].url
```

To build a text-to-image system, LangChain agents use a text prompt to call image generation tools. The general process involves refining a user's initial input into a high-quality prompt before sending it to a generation model like DALL-E 3.

The following figure illustrates the sequence of operations in a standard text-to-image workflow:

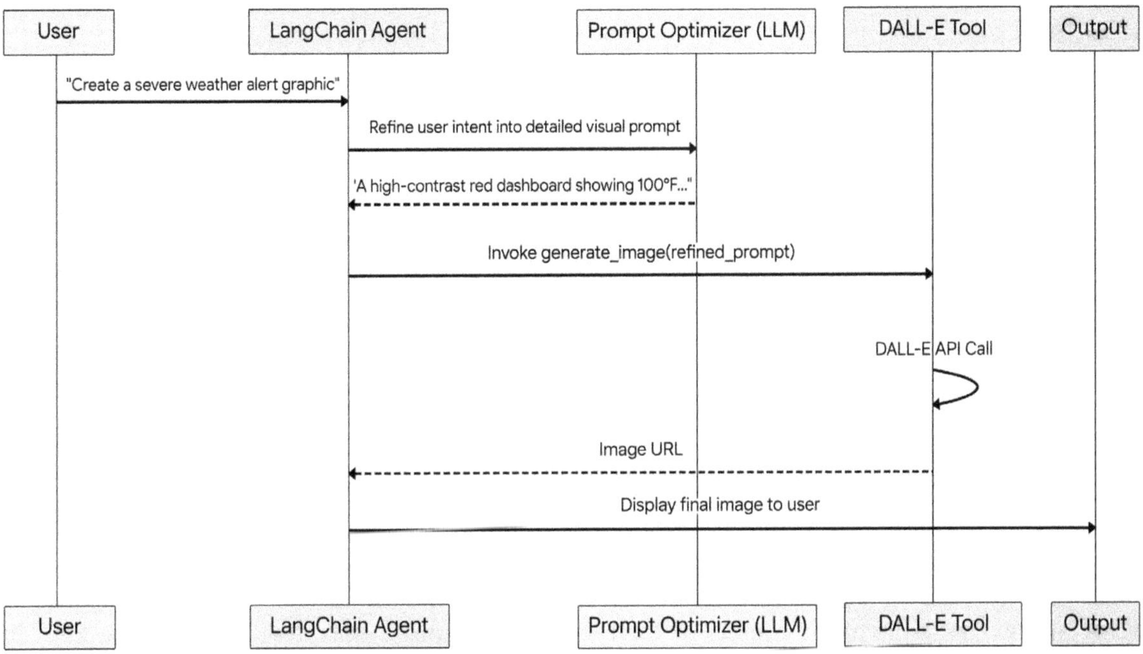

***Figure 5.3**: Text-to-image generation workflow*

Prompt optimization and tool integration

An initial LLM (like **`gpt-4o-mini`**) can act as a *prompt engineer*, expanding a simple query into a rich description that specifies artistic style, palette, and composition. This refined prompt is then passed to a tool that interacts with the generation API.

The following code demonstrates how to define a DALL-E 3 tool and integrate it into a LangChain agent workflow:

```
from langchain_core.tools import tool
from openai import OpenAI as OpenAIClient


@tool
```

```
def generate_weather_alert_image(visual_description: str) -> str:
    """
    Generates a visual image of a weather alert based on a description.
    Input should be a detailed prompt optimized for image generation.
    """
    client = OpenAIClient()

    # Standard visual styles can be appended to ensure consistent UI output
    full_prompt = f"Professional weather dashboard UI, minimalist, {visual_
description}"

    response = client.images.generate(
        model="dall-e-3",
        prompt=full_prompt,
        size="1024x1024",
        quality="standard",
        n=1,
    )

    return response.data[0].url

# The agent can now use this tool during its reasoning process.
# Agent output: "I've generated a prototype alert for the blizzard..."
```

Image-to-text summarization and captioning

Image-to-text systems allow agents to turn visual data into a narrative that may be kept in long-term memory or disseminated in reports. We employ generative models to provide objective, descriptive summaries of visual circumstances.

The following code explains how to establish a captioning chain that translates a weather snapshot into a brief written summary:

```
from langchain_openai import ChatOpenAI
from langchain_core.prompts import ChatPromptTemplate
from langchain_core.runnables import RunnableLambda

vision_model = ChatOpenAI(model="gpt-4o", temperature=0)

# Define the summarization prompt
summarization_prompt = ChatPromptTemplate.from_messages([
    ("system", "You are a weather forensic analyst. Summarize visual
conditions and time-of-day."),
```

```
    ("human", [{"type": "image_url", "image_url": {"url": "{image_url}"}}]),
])

# Create the captioning chain
captioning_chain = (
    summarization_prompt
    | vision_model
    | RunnableLambda(lambda x: x.content)
)
```

Image-to-text systems leverage multimodal models to create textual descriptions, perform OCR, or extract structured data from visual inputs. In LangChain, this involves encoding images [as **Uniform Resource Locator** (**URLs**) or base64] and sending them to a model like **gpt-4o** with a specific instruction.

The following figure shows how images are processed into text context for a **retrieval-augmented generation** (**RAG**) system:

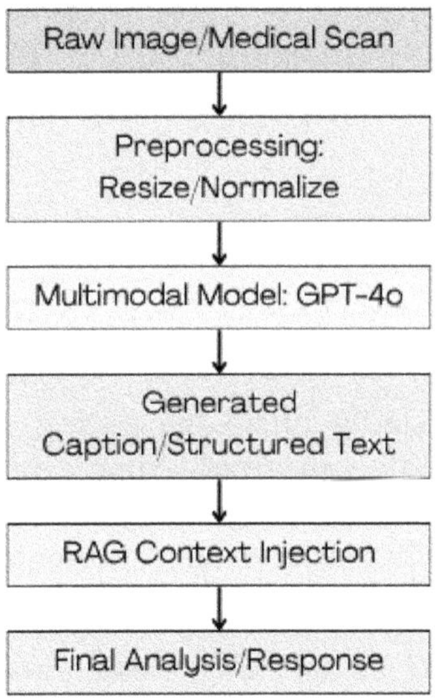

***Figure 5.4**: Image-to-text extraction for context-aware analysis*

Multimodal processing and structured output

Models such as Google Gemini or OpenAI GPT-4o analyze pixels directly to identify objects, read text, or interpret complex data like charts. The resulting text output can be used to formulate a response in a RAG system or extract precise data points like vendor names from invoices or vitals from medical charts.

The following code shows how to use **gpt-4o** to perform complex image-to-text analysis on a weather station display:

```
from langchain_openai import ChatOpenAI
from langchain_core.messages import HumanMessage
import base64

def analyze_instrument_photo(image_path: str):
    """Encodes a local image and extracts textual data via GPT-4o."""
    with open(image_path, "rb") as f:
        img_b64 = base64.b64encode(f.read()).decode("utf-8")

    model = ChatOpenAI(model="gpt-4o")

    # Prompting the model for specific, structured extraction
    message = HumanMessage(content=[
        {"type": "text", "text": "Extract all numerical readings from this
weather gauge as a JSON object."},
        {"type": "image_url", "image_url": {"url": f"data:image/
jpeg;base64,{img_b64}"}}
    ])

    return model.invoke([message]).content
```

Building custom tools for text-to-image generation

LangChain does not natively handle image-generating models (like DALL-E) within a regular **ChatModel** interface since the output is a binary asset or a URL rather than text. The conventional architectural approach is to wrap the generation API inside a LangChain tool. This allows the agent to select whether a visual representation is necessary to augment its textual understanding.

The following code explains how to develop a basic, modular image-generating program suitable for our weather use case:

```
from langchain_openai import ChatOpenAI
from langchain.agents import AgentExecutor, create_tool_calling_agent
from langchain_core.tools import tool
from langchain_core.prompts import ChatPromptTemplate, MessagesPlaceholder
from openai import OpenAI


# 1. Define the core image generation logic as a LangChain tool
@tool
```

```
def generate_weather_visual(prompt_description: str) -> str:
    """
    Generates a visual image of a weather alert or dashboard layout.
    Input should be a detailed description of the weather condition.
    """
    client = OpenAI()

    # We enrich the user's prompt to ensure a consistent dashboard style
    enriched_prompt = (
        f"A professional meteorological dashboard showing: {prompt_
description}. "
        f"High-resolution, digital display style, minimalist weather icons."
    )

    response = client.images.generate(
        model="dall-e-3",
        prompt=enriched_prompt,
        size="1024x1024",
        n=1,
    )
    # Return the URL for the agent to provide to the user
    return response.data[0].url


# 2. Set up the agent to use the tool
llm = ChatOpenAI(model="gpt-4o", temperature=0)
tools = [generate_weather_visual]

prompt = ChatPromptTemplate.from_messages([
    ("system", "You are a weather visualizer. Use the tool to create
alerts."),
    ("human", "{input}"),
    MessagesPlaceholder(variable_name="agent_scratchpad"),
])

# 3. Initialize the agent executor
agent = create_tool_calling_agent(llm, tools, prompt)
agent_executor = AgentExecutor(agent=agent, tools=tools, verbose=True)

# Example Execution
agent_executor.invoke({"input": "Create a visual for a severe blizzard alert
in Chicago."})
```

Benefits of the simplified approach

This simplified version keeps the example focused on modern LangChain patterns and a consistent weather scenario, while removing distractions that are not essential to the core agent workflow. The key improvements in this simplified version include:

- **Focus on current tool-calling patterns**: The example replaces older agent setup approaches with the current **`create_tool_calling_agent`** pattern shown above, which better aligns with modern LangChain tool orchestration.
- **Weather theme consistency**: It replaces generic design-anything prompts with weather visuals to fit the rest of the book.
- **Modular logic**: By isolating the **`@tool`** from the agent initialization, we show the reader how to design reusable components rather than a monolithic script.
- **Removal of UI noise**: Streamlit is fantastic for workshops, but for a technical chapter, it is best to focus on the **`AgentExecutor`** logic and how it parses the DALL-E URL response.

While static image-to-text and text-to-image systems allow agents to see and synthesize periods in time, many real-world monitoring jobs need to understand how these visuals evolve. Moving from a single snapshot of a weather station to a continuous stream of data demands a shift from spatial reasoning to temporal reasoning. The following part discusses how to expand these vision skills into the dimension of time by processing video data streams.

Processing and analyzing video data streams

Video develops visual intelligence from isolated perception into continuous observation across time. Rather than reasoning about a single image, a vision-enabled agent must analyze how scenes evolve, recognizing gradual trends, startling abnormalities, and causal linkages that only become apparent across sequences of frames. This temporal dimension is critical for real-world monitoring systems, including weather surveillance, industrial inspection, and medical imaging, where comprehending change is sometimes more important than understanding any given moment.

Since video is simply a sequence of images synchronized with audio and metadata, naively processing every frame is both computationally demanding and economically prohibitive for **large language models (LLMs)**. Effective video analysis consequently relies on distillation algorithms that preserve the semantic signal while removing redundancy. Techniques such as keyframe extraction, visual change detection, and sliding temporal windows allow agents to focus on the most informative regions of a video stream, avoiding token depletion and high API charges without sacrificing analytical quality.

In this section, you will learn how to equip agents with principled video-processing pipelines that combine conventional computer vision techniques with multimodal reasoning. By carefully sampling frames, synchronizing visual and textual timelines, and building compact temporal contexts, agents have the ability to reason not only about what they perceive but also about how situations originate, evolve, and resolve over time. These foundations enable scalable, production-ready temporal intelligence that interfaces smoothly with LangChain's LCEL operations and agent architectures.

Keyframe extraction and temporal synchronization

For long weather time-lapses, processing every frame is prohibitively expensive. Instead, we use keyframe extraction to identify visually distinct or temporally spaced frames for analysis.

The following figure visualizes the pipeline for transforming raw video files into a searchable multimodal index:

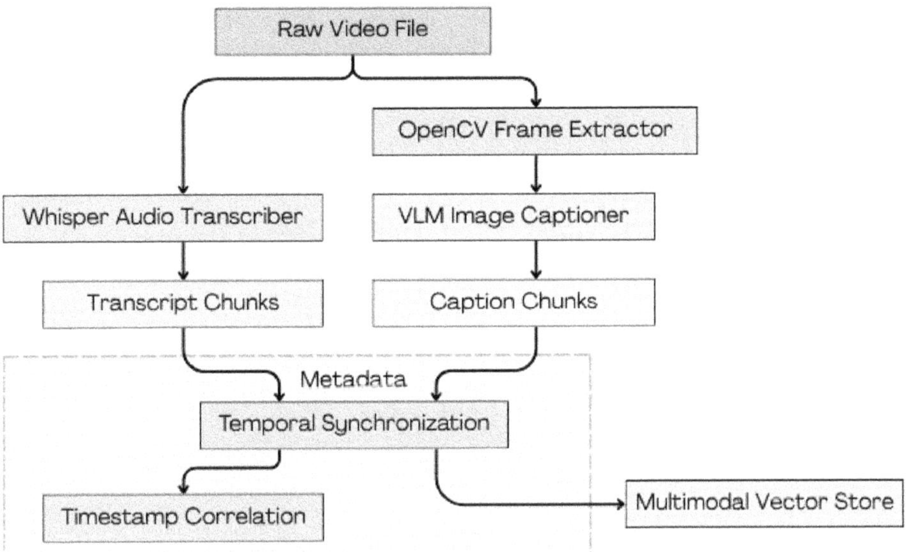

***Figure 5.5**: Pipeline for multimodal video indexing*

A practical way to implement this workflow is to break it into three synchronization steps that keep the visual, audio, and textual signals aligned on the same timeline:

1. **Extract keyframes**: Utilize a library like OpenCV to sample the video at a low rate, such as 0.5 frames per second, or utilize scene-detection algorithms to capture frames only when a substantial visual change happens.
2. **Transcribe audio**: Use a model like Whisper to build a thorough transcript, ensuring that every text segment is accompanied by precise start and end timestamps.
3. **Cross-modal indexing**: Embed the text transcript segments and the keyframe captions into the same vector storage. By including the original timestamp in the metadata of both, the agent can link what was heard with what was seen at any given second.

Analyzing video with multimodal messages

Modern versions like **gpt-4o** permit the incorporation of many images within a single message. This skill lets an agent execute temporal reasoning by monitoring a succession of keyframes simultaneously to spot trends, movements, or anomalies that a single image would miss.

The following code explains how to transmit a sequence of sampled keyframes to an LLM to find structural anomalies in weather monitoring equipment over a video sequence:

```
from langchain_openai import ChatOpenAI
from langchain_core.messages import HumanMessage

def analyze_video_progression(frame_urls: list, prompt_text: str):
    """
    Sends a sequence of keyframes to a VLM for temporal reasoning.
    The model analyzes the images collectively to identify changes over time.
    """
    vision_model = ChatOpenAI(model="gpt-4o", temperature=0)

    # Initialize the content block with the text instruction
    content = [{"type": "text", "text": prompt_text}]

    # Append each keyframe URL to the content list
    for url in frame_urls:
        content.append({
            "type": "image_url",
            "image_url": {"url": url}
        })

    # Invoke the model with the multimodal message
    return vision_model.invoke([HumanMessage(content=content)])

# Example usage for weather infrastructure inspection
# frames = ["https://site.com/frame1.jpg", "https://site.com/frame10.jpg"]
# query = "Identify any signs of blade fatigue or erratic motion between
these frames."
# report = analyze_video_progression(frames, query)
```

Implementing visual change detection

While sampling frames at a set interval [e.g., 1 **frames per second** (**FPS**)] is efficient for short clips, production systems monitoring weather stations for hours require visual change detection to minimize expenses and processing noise. Instead of submitting every extracted frame to a VLM, we employ lightweight computer vision algorithms to identify "interesting" frames where motion or structural changes occur.

The following code explains how to utilize a rudimentary frame-differencing logic to skip duplicate frames before activating a LangChain vision chain:

```
import cv2
from langchain_openai import ChatOpenAI
from langchain_core.runnables import RunnableLambda

vision_model = ChatOpenAI(model="gpt-4o", temperature=0)


def extract_significant_changes(video_path: str, threshold: float = 0.05):
    """
    Analyzes video frames and only returns those with significant visual
changes.
    Prevents redundant VLM calls when weather conditions are static.
    """
    cap = cv2.VideoCapture(video_path)
    significant_frames = []
    ret, prev_frame = cap.read()

    while ret:
        ret, curr_frame = cap.read()
        if not ret:
            break

        # Calculate absolute difference between frames
        diff = cv2.absdiff(curr_frame, prev_frame)
        non_zero_count = cv2.countNonZero(cv2.cvtColor(diff, cv2.COLOR_
BGR2GRAY))

        # If change exceeds threshold (e.g., 5% of pixels), save the frame
        total_pixels = curr_frame.shape[0] * curr_frame.shape[1]
        if non_zero_count / total_pixels > threshold:
            significant_frames.append(curr_frame)
            prev_frame = curr_frame

    cap.release()
    return significant_frames


# Chain this logic as a pre-processor in LCEL
video_analysis_pipeline = RunnableLambda(extract_significant_changes) |
vision_model
```

Temporal reasoning with sliding window context

In long-duration video streams, an agent needs to remember what happened in prior frames to understand the current state. By employing a sliding window technique, we can feed the VLM with a tiny buffer of prior keyframes so it can reason about acceleration, accumulation (like snow build-up), or the direction of an incoming storm front.

The following figure depicts how a sliding window of frames offers temporal context to the agent:

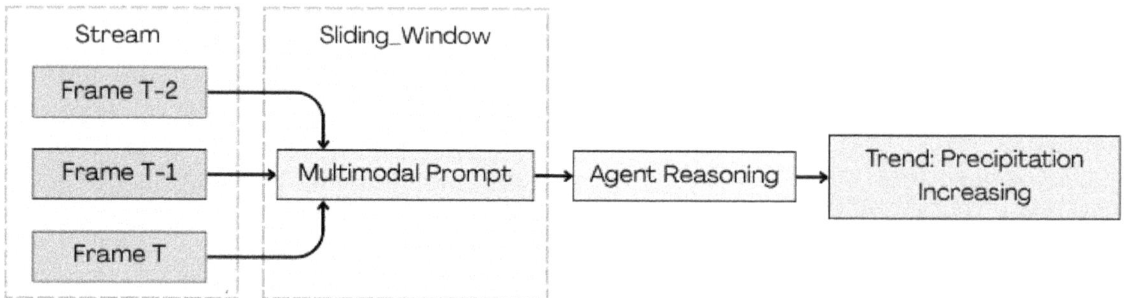

***Figure 5.6**: Sliding window architecture for temporal video reasoning*

Handling high-resolution video through tiling

When analyzing high-resolution video streams (such as 4K drone footage), a single frame may contain too much detail for the VLM to process in one tile. We employ visual tiling, where the agent first looks at a downsampled version of the video to identify a **region of interest** (**ROI**), such as a specific turbine blade, and then requests a high-resolution crop of only that area.

The following table summarizes common video-processing strategies for vision agents and helps you choose an approach based on clip duration, expected scene variability, and the cost or latency constraints of your pipeline:

Strategy	When to use	Cost impact
Fixed sampling	Short, high-action clips	Linear with duration
Change detection	Long-term monitoring (e.g., 24h sky cam)	Significant reduction
Visual tiling	High-precision industrial inspection	Optimized for detail

***Table 5.3**: Video processing strategies for visual agents*

Tip: **When processing video for weather warnings, always synchronize the system clock with the video timestamp in the metadata. This allows the agent to link visual cloud formation with real-time pressure drops in your sensor records.**

Multimodal intelligence in medical case studies

Although this chapter centers on weather intelligence, the same multimodal patterns combining images, text, sensor signals, retrieval, and grounded reasoning also appear in other high-stakes domains. The medical examples in this section help generalize the design lessons, showing how the architectures you have used for weather monitoring transfer to healthcare scenarios where accuracy, traceability, and multimodal fusion are equally important.

Vision models are transforming healthcare and industrial monitoring by breaking down data silos between imaging scans, clinical notes, sensor readings, and inspection reports. Unlike unimodal systems that only look at a single data type, multimodal AI may correlate an X-ray with lab results to increase diagnostic accuracy and provide a more holistic view of patient health.

Triage and specialist medical RAG systems

In pneumonia triage, integrating a chest **computed tomography** (**CT**) scan with oxygen saturation values and clinical nursing notes may lead to more reliable detection than utilizing imaging in isolation. Similarly, advanced research projects like AlzheimerRAG merge biomedical literature with clinical trial photos to deliver evidence-based responses for neurodegenerative illnesses, guaranteeing that every visual discovery is founded in the current scientific research.

The following list shows significant examples where visual intelligence aids medical workflows:

- **Augmented review**: Models emphasize specific spots in a scan, such as a suspected lump or fracture, that correspond to discoveries in the text, decreasing the cognitive strain on radiologists.
- **Longitudinal analysis**: AI systems summarize changes in imaging throughout time, allowing clinicians to follow illness development or evaluate how a patient is reacting to a certain medication.
- **Explainable AI**: Systems like **Preferred Reporting Items for Systematic Reviews and Meta-Analyses** (**PRISM**) employ generative models to create *counterfactual* visuals, graphically demonstrating why an AI made a specific diagnosis by showing how the image would look if the pathology were absent.

Technical framework for medicinal vision agents

Production-grade healthcare systems often adopt an approach called Intermediate Fusion. In this architecture, diverse data modalities, such as **magnetic resonance imaging** (**MRI**) images, blood test results, and **electronic health record** (**EHR**) text, are stored in a single embedding space. This allows the model to make predictions based on the relationship between the various data sources rather than evaluating them separately.

The following table outlines the influence of multimodal AI across numerous medical use cases:

Medical use case	Modal input mix	Impact
Fracture identification	Radiographs and clinical notes.	Detects subtle fractures missed by imaging alone.
Sepsis prediction	Vitals, labs, meds and nursing notes.	Earlier signals for clinical deterioration.
Autism care	Video stream and behavior logs.	Vision-based behavior monitoring without wearables.

Table 5.4: *Multimodal AI impacts in medical imaging and diagnostics*

Designing full vision-driven agent architectures

A production-ready vision agent orchestrates numerous phases, including OCR, VLM reasoning, retrieval, and decision-making. Unlike simple vision API wrappers, comprehensive architectures must handle data intake from numerous sources, preprocessing pipelines, and intelligent tool selection. This section discusses proven architectural patterns and design ideas for constructing strong vision-enabled systems.

As stated earlier in the section, *combining OCR and VLM in a chain*, we utilize the OCR to VLM validation paradigm as a foundational building element for production-grade vision agents. Rather than re-describing the mechanics, this section focuses on how that pattern fits into bigger architectural structures, such as sequential pipelines, parallel processing, and conditional routing, where OCR serves as one component inside a larger decision-making system.

Core architecture patterns for vision agents

Most production vision agents can be described as a small set of repeatable building blocks: ingest the visual input, apply one or more extraction steps (OCR, detection, captioning), validate or enrich the result with a VLM, and then route the output to retrieval or decision logic. The patterns in this section show how to compose these blocks in LangChain so you can choose the simplest architecture that still meets your accuracy, latency, and cost requirements.

Vision agents typically follow one of four main architectural patterns, each optimized for a different trade-off in determinism, concurrency, routing flexibility, or autonomous decision-making. In the examples that follow, pay attention to the situations that favor each pattern, for example, whether you need a fixed OCR-to-validation pipeline, concurrent analysis of the same image, routing by image type, or an agent that decides which tool to call at runtime:

- **Sequential pipeline pattern**: Best for deterministic workflows where each phase depends on the preceding output, such as extracting data from a weather sensor display and then checking it against a threshold.
- **Parallel processing pattern**: Ideal for studying the same image with various models simultaneously, for running OCR for text alongside object detection for identifying weather instruments.
- **Conditional routing pattern**: Used when distinct picture types require specialized processing, such as routing satellite imagery to a storm detector while sending ground-station photos to an OCR pipeline.
- **Agent-driven tool selection pattern**: Best for complicated scenarios where the agent autonomously determines which vision tools to utilize based on a natural language inquiry.

The following code depicts a sequential vision pipeline utilizing LCEL to load, preprocess, and extract data from a weather instrument photo:

```
# Reuses the OCR -> VLM validation pattern introduced in the previous Section
# Note: load_weather_image, normalize_image_size, ocr_text_extraction,
# vlm_context_validation, and format_json_output are illustrative
placeholders.
# Replace each with your domain-specific implementation.
from langchain_core.runnables import RunnableLambda


# Sequential vision pipeline demonstrating deterministic data flow
vision_pipeline = (
    RunnableLambda(load_weather_image)         # Step 1: Load
    | RunnableLambda(normalize_image_size)     # Step 2: Preprocess
    | RunnableLambda(ocr_text_extraction)      # Step 3: OCR
    | RunnableLambda(vlm_context_validation)   # Step 4: Validate
    | RunnableLambda(format_json_output)       # Step 5: Structure
)

# Each step transforms the input and passes it to the next Runnable
result = vision_pipeline.invoke({"image_path": "station_display.jpg"})
```

Design concepts and best practices

Beyond selecting an architecture pattern, the difference between a demo and a production-ready vision agent is usually determined by a handful of engineering decisions: where you validate uncertainty, how you cache expensive calls, how you make runs reproducible, and how you degrade gracefully when images are low quality. The practices in this section provide a pragmatic checklist you can apply to any vision workflow so it remains maintainable as models, tools, and requirements evolve.

Building reliable vision agents demands attention to principles that assure modularity, dependability, and cost-efficiency:

- **Separation of concerns**: Separate picture preprocessing, model invocation, and outcome interpretation into distinct components. This allows you to swap vision models or adjust OCR settings without recreating the complete reasoning algorithm.
- **Graceful deterioration**: Vision models might fail or return low-confidence findings due to inadequate lighting or impediments. Design your architecture to fall back from a costly, high-resolution VLM to a cheaper, faster model (e.g., gpt-4o to gpt-4o-mini) if primary analysis fails.
- **Observability and traceability**: Every vision operation must be logged with specified metadata, including picture hashes, model versions, and confidence scores. This is vital for auditing multimodal judgments in sensitive fields like healthcare or safety-critical weather alerts.
- **Cost-aware processing**: Vision API calls are substantially more expensive than text-only calls. Implement caching with content hashes (SHA-256) to avoid re-processing the same image numerous times.

Industrial inspection agent case study

Consider an agent checking weather station infrastructure using drone imagery. The agent must correlate observable faults, such as a damaged wind turbine blade, with sensor logs revealing inconsistent power output.

The following table outlines the pipeline processes for this synchronized industrial inspection:

Step	Component	Modalities used	Output
Ingestion	`DirectoryLoader`	Image, text log	`List[Document]`
Preprocessing	`OCR_VLM_Chain`	Image text	Document (caption and OCR)
Indexing	`MultimodalIndexer`	Text, image caption	Vector store
Retrieval	Retriever	Text query vector	`List[Context Chunk]`
Synthesis	GPT-4o	Context and agent thought	Final maintenance report

***Table 5.5**: Industrial inspection agent pipeline steps*

The following figure illustrates the agent's runtime flow when a user asks to find the cause of a specific sensor fluctuation:

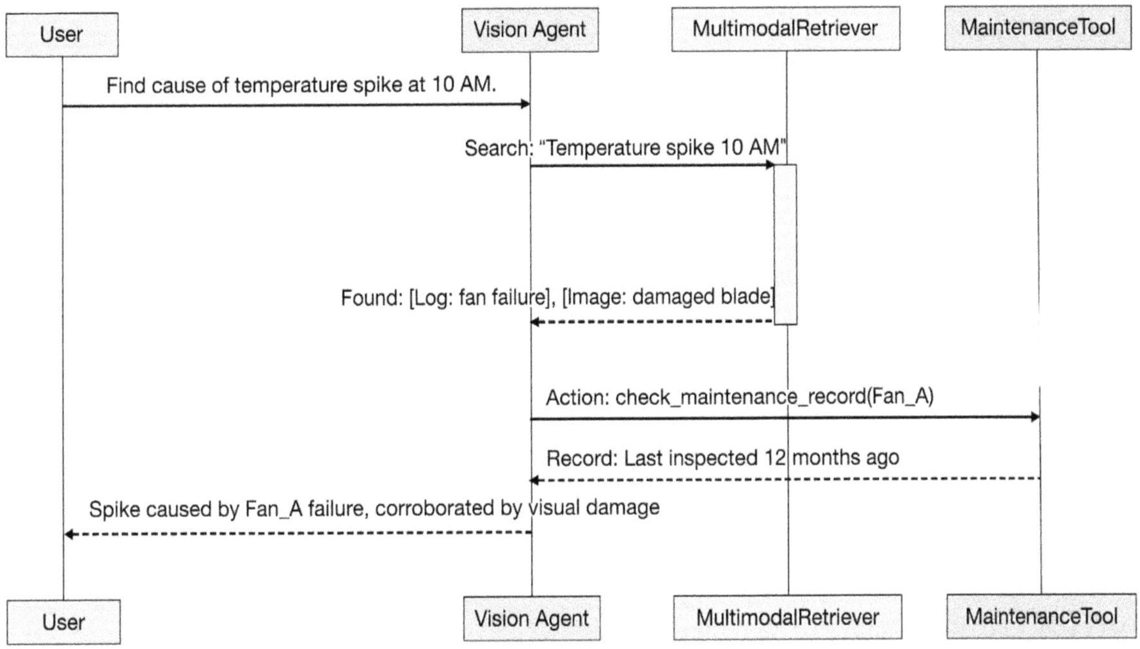

***Figure 5.7**: Agent's runtime flow:*

Architecture template for custom vision agents

In this section, you learned how to translate the earlier design patterns into a reusable blueprint you can apply to any domain. The template that follows breaks a vision agent into stable building blocks, data models for structured outputs, tool wrappers for extraction and generation, and an agent executor that orchestrates calls reliably. Use it as a checklist: define what *good* output looks like, isolate each visual capability behind a tool boundary, and enforce schema-based validation so downstream decision logic stays deterministic, testable, and easy to evolve.

Use this template as a starting point when designing your own vision-enabled agent system. Customize each component based on your specific domain requirements:

```
# Vision Agent Architecture Template
from langchain_openai import ChatOpenAI
from langchain.agents import AgentExecutor, create_tool_calling_agent
from langchain_core.prompts import ChatPromptTemplate, MessagesPlaceholder
from langchain_core.tools import tool
from pydantic import BaseModel, Field
from typing import Any
```

```
# STEP 1: Define Domain-Specific Data Models
class VisionAnalysisResult(BaseModel):
    primary_finding: str = Field(description="Main observation from image")
    confidence_score: float = Field(description="Confidence 0-1")
    requires_action: bool = Field(description="Whether findings require
action")


# STEP 2: Create Specialized Vision Tools
@tool
def analyze_weather_image(image_url: str) -> dict:
    """Analyze weather-related imagery for specific patterns."""
    vision_model = ChatOpenAI(model="gpt-4o", temperature=0)
    # Implementation logic for vision model invocation
    pass


# STEP 3: Assemble Complete Agent
vision_tools = [analyze_weather_image]
llm = ChatOpenAI(model="gpt-4o", temperature=0)

agent_prompt = ChatPromptTemplate.from_messages([
    ("system", "You are a vision-enabled assistant. Use the tools to inspect
images."),
    ("human", "{input}"),
    MessagesPlaceholder(variable_name="agent_scratchpad"),
])

agent = create_tool_calling_agent(llm, vision_tools, agent_prompt)
agent_executor = AgentExecutor(agent=agent, tools=vision_tools, verbose=True)
```

Production problems and optimization

Implementing a vision agent at scale poses special issues regarding data volume, cost, and latency:

- **High-resolution image**: These images handle high-resolution photos (4K plus) that can surpass VLM token limits or lead to exorbitant charges. A typical approach is pre-tiling and patching, when the image is broken into smaller, overlapping patches. The agent only delivers the most relevant patches to the high-end VLM after a fast pre-screening with a lightweight object detection model.

- **Managing vision API costs**: VLM consumption is paid for on image *tiles* or segments. To optimize, implement caching using the content hash. Before accessing a costly API, calculate a SHA-256 hash of the raw image data. If the hash exists in your cache (e.g., Redis), serve the prior analysis instead of reprocessing.
- **Optimizing latency for real-time visual reasoning**: Waiting for VLM analysis in the middle of an agent loop can be slow. Use asynchronous pre-analysis: launch a background job to create captions/OCR as soon as an image is uploaded. By the time the user asks a query, the text-based visual context is already in the vector store for quick retrieval.

Note: **Always record the model name, version, and invocation arguments in metadata. Without these fields, you cannot explain or recreate multimodal judgments during compliance reviews.**

Building a vision-enabled weather intelligence system

This workshop section serves as an architectural walkthrough that brings together the chapter's earlier concepts, OCR, VLM reasoning, and temporal tracking, into a cohesive weather intelligence design. Rather than a full build-along implementation, the following code highlights how the major components fit together so you can adapt the earlier working patterns to your own deployment.

Workshop architecture and data flow

The weather intelligence system is designed to process three independent data streams: satellite imaging for high-level patterns, station pictures for local ground truth, and time-lapse video for trend analysis. The following figure depicts how these components interact to create automatic alerts:

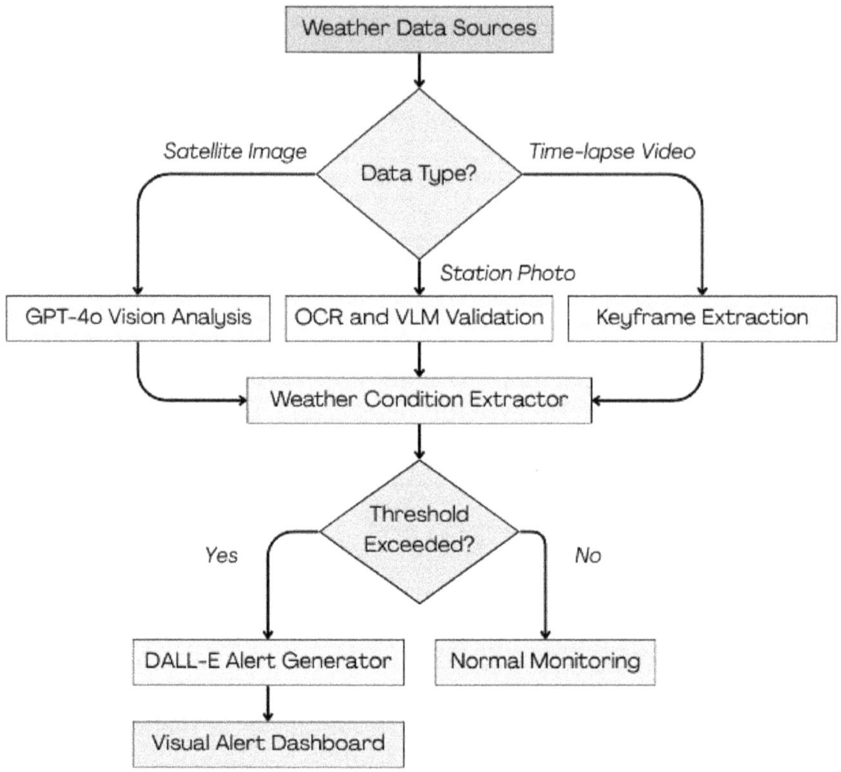

***Figure 5.8**: Complete vision-enabled weather intelligence system architecture*

Implementing the intelligent weather toolkit

This workshop purposefully reuses the OCR to VLM validation procedure established in the section, *Combining OCR and VLM in a chain*, using it in a comprehensive, end-to-end system rather than presenting it as an isolated example. By integrating this previously described pattern into a whole agent architecture, the focus switches from understanding individual processes to seeing how OCR, vision reasoning, retrieval, and alert generation collaborate in a production-ready pipeline.

To develop this system, you must define specialized tools that handle each modality while maintaining a uniform interface for the Agent Executor. The following code creates the core tools for instrument data extraction and automatic alert generation:

```
# Reuses the OCR → VLM validation pattern introduced in Section 5.2.1

from langchain_openai import ChatOpenAI
from langchain_core.tools import tool
from pydantic import BaseModel, Field
```

```
# Define structured schema for deterministic output
class WeatherReading(BaseModel):
    temperature_f: float = Field(description="Temperature in Fahrenheit")
    confidence: str = Field(description="Confidence level: high, medium, or
low")

@tool
def extract_station_display(image_path: str) -> dict:
    """Extract numeric readings from weather station displays using OCR and
VLM."""
    # Logic: Tesseract OCR -> GPT-4o-mini validation -> JSON
    pass

@tool
def create_weather_alert(conditions: str) -> str:
    """Generate visual weather alert dashboard using DALL-E 3."""
    # Logic: Text description -> DALL-E 3 Tool -> Image URL
    pass
```

Tip: **In healthcare or safety-critical weather scenarios, always anchor your model with RAG. Tying discovered visual anomalies to peer-reviewed literature or prior sensor records is crucial for clinical digestibility and minimizing the threat of hallucinations.**

Conclusion

In this chapter, you transformed text-only agents into vision-enabled systems that can interpret images, extract data, and make decisions from visual inputs. You integrated modern vision models such as GPT-4o for contextual reasoning and CLIP for fast cross-modal retrieval, then built reliable OCR pipelines by pairing a dedicated engine (for example, Tesseract) with VLM-based validation to improve accuracy on noisy or complex layouts. You also implemented bidirectional workflows, image-to-text captioning, and text-to-image generation with DALL-E 3 and learned when to delegate specialized tasks to external vision APIs. For time-based scenarios, you introduced video processing techniques such as keyframe extraction, temporal reasoning, and change detection to understand evolving weather conditions. Finally, you brought these capabilities together into production-ready architectures with observability, caching, and repeatable runs, and you saw them applied in an end-to-end weather intelligence workshop.

In the next chapter, you will extend these foundations with human-in-the-loop patterns that add governance, approvals, and auditability to high-stakes agent decisions.

CHAPTER 6
Building Conversational Agents with Voice Intelligence

Introduction

Humans communicate most naturally through speech. Voice carries intent, emphasis, and timing cues that text alone rarely captures, yet many conversational agents still operate mainly through typed prompts. This chapter bridges that gap by showing how to design and implement voice-enabled agents that can listen, understand, and respond with natural speech, turning a traditional chatbot into a more accessible, hands-free interface.

Readers will learn how to assemble an end-to-end audio pipeline and AI workflow, such as capturing microphone input, transcribing it with **speech-to-text** (**STT**), routing the text through an LLM agent with tools, and synthesizing the reply with **text-to-speech** (**TTS**). Along the way, the chapter highlights practical engineering concerns such as streaming for low latency, turn-taking and interruptions, and robust error handling when speech is noisy or incomplete. The concepts are then grounded in a hands-on build of a voice-driven weather assistant that listens, calls a weather tool/API, and speaks responses back to the user in a clear, conversational style. By connecting these pieces, readers will be able to reason about where quality and latency are introduced in the pipeline and how to tune each stage to deliver a smooth, real-time user experience.

Structure

This chapter covers the following topics:

- Mastering speech recognition with Whisper and Azure
- Implementing text-to-speech and speech synthesis
- Building voice-first agent workflows
- Enabling real-time conversational audio pipelines
- Detecting sentiment and emotion from voice

- Supporting multilingual agents with translation models
- Building voice-enabled telemedicine AI assistants

Objectives

This chapter aims to help readers evolve a text-only conversational agent into a responsive, voice-first system. It clarifies the core components of a voice agent, audio capture, speech recognition (STT/ASR), LLM reasoning with tool use, and speech synthesis (TTS), and explains how these parts connect into a reliable end-to-end pipeline for real user interactions.

By the end of the chapter, readers will be able to implement STT using *OpenAI Whisper* and *Azure Speech* and justify a choice between them based on accuracy, latency, deployment constraints, and multilingual needs. Readers will also integrate STT output into a LangChain-powered agent so spoken queries can be handled with the same prompts, tools, and memory patterns used for text chat, and then add TTS using a modern neural voice to control speaking style and assistant persona. Finally, the chapter prepares readers to design real-time interaction by applying streaming patterns, turn-taking and interruption handling, and practical testing practices, culminating in a working voice-enabled weather assistant that listens, calls an external weather API through tools, and speaks responses back to the user.

Mastering speech recognition with Whisper and Azure

Building a voice-enabled agent begins with the ability to accurately transcribe user speech into text. This section integrates two strong speech-to-text engines: OpenAI's Whisper and Microsoft's Azure Speech Service. Both are state-of-the-art, yet each has unique strengths. Whisper is an open-source model that specializes in multilingual transcription and translation, which runs either locally or via OpenAI's cloud **application programming interface** (**API**). Azure Speech is a cloud-based service that delivers real-time streaming, powerful speaker detection, and easy vocabulary customization.

The following table demonstrates the significant capabilities and differences between these two STT frameworks:

Feature	OpenAI Whisper (open-source/API)	Azure Speech Service (cloud API)
Primary use case	Accurate transcription and translation; on-device possible.	Real-time, low-latency conversational AI.
Real-time support	Possible via streaming, but primarily batch-oriented.	Native streaming with ultra-low latency.
Speaker diarization	Requires a separate model or processing.	Built-in speaker identification (multi-speaker).

Feature	OpenAI Whisper (open-source/API)	Azure Speech Service (cloud API)
Customization	Prompting guides style and vocabulary.	Custom models and vocabulary for domain-specific terms.
Language support	Broad multilingual capability (≈100 languages).	100+ languages, with regional dialect options.

***Table 6.1**: Whisper vs. Azure Speech Service comparison*

The OpenAI transcriptions API accepts an audio file as input, along with the desired output file format for the transcription of the audio. All models support the same set of input formats. On the output side, the supported formats are as follows:

- `whisper-1` supports **JavaScript Object Notation** (**JSON**), text, **SubRip Subtitle** (**SRT**), verbose JSON, and **Web Video Text Tracks** (**VTT**) formats.
- `gpt-4o-transcribe` and `gpt-4o-mini-transcribe` support JSON or plain text.
- `gpt-4o-transcribe-diarize` supports JSON, text, and diarized JSON (which adds speaker segments to the response).

A practical rule of thumb is to choose **Whisper** for offline or privacy-sensitive deployments, multilingual transcription or translation, and batch processing where a small delay is acceptable. Choose **Azure Speech** for real-time streaming conversations, speaker-aware scenarios, and enterprise applications that need low latency, built-in customization, and tighter integration with Azure services.

Both can provide near-human-level transcription accuracy under good settings and handle a wide range of languages and dialects. This chapter will use Whisper in the code examples for its versatility (and because an open API is easy to connect with LangChain). However, it is also possible to replace Azure's **Software Development Kit** (**SDK**) or **Representational State Transfer** (**REST**) API for comparable outcomes. Azure's streaming capabilities may be desirable if users want extremely low latency or need to interface with other Azure cloud services.

Implementing a transcription tool with OpenAI Whisper

Once a voice recognition service is selected, users can incorporate it into an agent's toolkit. For the weather assistant, this chapter develops a transcription function that uses OpenAI's Whisper API to convert audio input into text. This function will serve as the agent's *ears*.

The following code shows a rudimentary implementation of a Whisper transcription tool using OpenAI's API via its Python client. In practice, this function would receive recorded audio (for example, from a microphone input) and return the recognized text.

The next snippet illustrates a minimal, end-to-end example of calling OpenAI's Python client to transcribe an audio file, creating a client, opening the audio in binary mode, sending it to the transcription endpoint, and printing the returned text:

```
from openai import OpenAI

client = OpenAI()
audio_file= open("/path/to/file/audio.mp3", "rb")


transcription = client.audio.transcriptions.create(
  model="gpt-4o-transcribe",
  file=audio_file
)

print(transcription.text)
```

Tip: **OpenAI's Whisper API supports several audio formats like Moving Picture Experts Group Audio Layer III (MP3), MPEG-4 Part 14 (MP4), Waveform Audio File Format (WAV), and more. Files must be under 25 MB. For longer recordings, you can chunk the audio and transcribe it in pieces to circumvent size constraints.**

In this code, the `whisper-1` model is chosen for transcription. OpenAI's Whisper returns a text transcript from the audio, managing noise and non-standard speech robustly. The Azure Speech service can be utilized similarly via its SDK or REST API (with a different interface), enabling real-time streaming and additional capabilities, including automated punctuation. Regardless of the service, the goal is the same: quick, accurate transcription of the user's voice so the agent can understand the inquiry.

Advanced transcription features

Whisper offers more than simple transcription. For instance, users can request word-level timestamps or transcribe multi-speaker audio, as follows:

- **Timestamps**: By using the parameter `response_format="verbose_json"` while calling the Whisper API, users can acquire comprehensive timing information for each transcription segment and word. This is useful for synced subtitles or assessing speech speed. The JSON answer provides start and end times for each segment of the text. So, a weather agent may, for example, detect an urgent tone if the user's speech rate is abnormally high.
- **Speaker diarization**: OpenAI provides a model variant (e.g., **`whisper-1`** fine-tuned for diarization) that labels various speakers in the transcript. This is critical for instances

like conference calls or assisting customers, where users need to discern who said what. Azure's service similarly enables speaker identification out of the box, helpful, for instance, in a group chat about the weather where the agent must distinguish between speakers.

The following example demonstrates how to request speaker diarization during transcription, as it sends an audio file to the **gpt-4o-transcribe-diarize** model, optionally provides a known speaker reference to improve labeling, and returns a transcript segmented by speaker so you can process each turn independently:

```
import base64
from openai import OpenAI

client = OpenAI()

def to_data_url(path: str) -> str:
  with open(path, "rb") as fh:
    return "data:audio/wav;base64," + base64.b64encode(fh.read()).
decode("utf-8")

with open("meeting.wav", "rb") as audio_file:
  transcript = client.audio.transcriptions.create(
    model="gpt-4o-transcribe-diarize",
    file=audio_file,
    response_format="diarized_json",
    chunking_strategy="auto",
    extra_body={
      "known_speaker_names": ["agent"],
      "known_speaker_references": [to_data_url("agent.wav")],
    },
  )

for segment in transcript.segments:
  print(segment.speaker, segment.text, segment.start, segment.end)
```

- **Custom vocabulary and biasing**: Both Whisper and Azure provide suggestions or prompts to improve recognition accuracy for domain-specific phrases. In OpenAI's API, users can pass a prompt string with expected context. For example, if there is awareness that the user will ask about the weather, a list of weather-related terms (temperature, precipitation, Celsius, forecast, etc.) can be given as a prompt. This guides the model to favor certain terms and correct spellings.

The following example shows how to improve transcription accuracy for a domain-specific assistant by providing a short context prompt (weather vocabulary and expected terms) to the STT model, helping it correctly recognize ambiguous words such as city names, units, and meteorological phrases:

```
def transcribe_weather_audio(audio_file_path: str) -> str:
    """Transcribe a weather query with context-specific vocabulary
hints."""
    weather_prompt = (
        "This is a weather forecast query. "
        "Common terms include: temperature, precipitation, humidity,
wind, Celsius, forecast."
    )
    with open(audio_file_path, "rb") as audio_file:
        result = client.audio.transcriptions.create(
            model="whisper-1",
            file=audio_file,
            prompt=weather_prompt,
        )
    return result.text
```

Note: **Contextual prompts help the STT model disambiguate similar-sounding phrases or acronyms. By supplying domain-specific vocabulary (city names, meteorological words, etc.), users eliminate errors and ensure crucial terms (like Celsius) are identified correctly.**

Whisper can even translate non-English voice directly to English text (readers will explore multilingual support in depth in the *Supporting multilingual agents with translation models* section, since designing a truly multilingual agent needs more than just transcription). For this chapter, it is enough to note that the Translations API converts supported input audio into English, whereas the **/transcriptions** endpoint preserves the original spoken language. The multilingual workflow and a full Translation API example are covered later in the *Translation API for multilingual support* section.

The next snippet demonstrates how to use the translations endpoint to take non-English speech (for example, German) and return an English translation in one step, which is useful when the downstream agent logic is standardized on English:

```
from openai import OpenAI

client = OpenAI()
audio_file = open("/path/to/file/german.mp3", "rb")

translation = client.audio.translations.create(
  model="whisper-1",
```

```
    file=audio_file,
)

print(translation.text)
```

With speech recognition in place, the agent can now *hear* the user. However, to complete the communication loop, the users also need to give it the ability to *speak*.

Implementing text-to-speech and speech synthesis

Transcribing the user's inquiry is only half the conversation; the agent also needs to talk back to the user. This section will explore the creation of text-to-speech conversion to output natural-sounding audio responses. This capability effectively gives the agent a voice and allows it to talk in a conversational, human-like manner.

End-to-end voice-first architecture

In a typical conversational interface, the agent must manage the transitions between listening, reasoning, and speaking. This cycle is sometimes referred to as a Chained Pipeline (STT | LLM | TTS), where STT is also known as **Automatic Speech Recognition** (**ASR**).

The following figure demonstrates the normal data flow for a conversational AI agent:

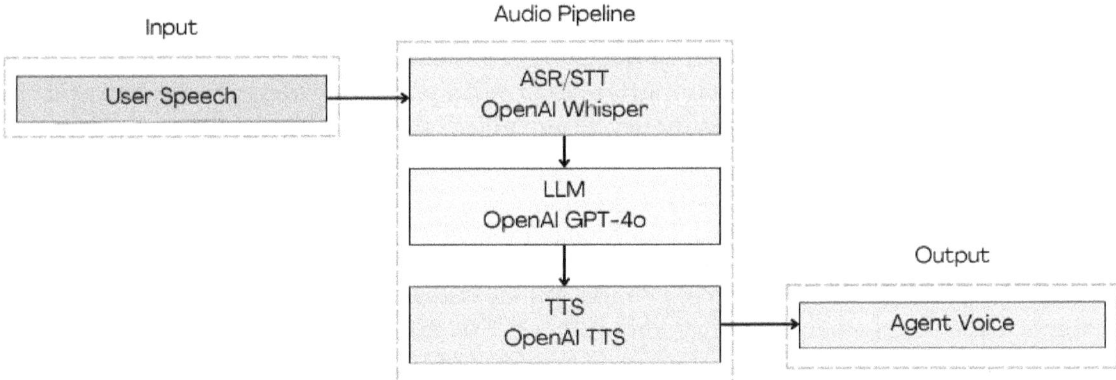

***Figure 6.1**: End-to-end voice agent data flow*

The following are the processing stages:

- **Input capture**: The user's voice is taken via a microphone and preprocessed to remove background noise.
- **STT (ASR)**: The audio signal is translated into a written transcript utilizing models like Whisper.

- **Dialogue management**: A **large language model** (**LLM**) processes the text, maintains the discussion state, and generates a response.
- **TTS (voice synthesis)**: The agent's response is turned back into lifelike spoken audio. Modern TTS services produce remarkably lifelike speech by using powerful neural network models. For the weather agent, users will use OpenAI's new TTS API to synthesize speech from the agent's text output.

The following code explains how to transform a string of text into an audio file:

```
from pathlib import Path
from openai import OpenAI

client = OpenAI()
speech_file_path = Path(__file__).parent / "speech.mp3"

with client.audio.speech.with_streaming_response.create(
  model="gpt-4o-mini-tts",
  voice="nova",
  input="Today is a wonderful day to build something people love!",
  instructions="Speak in a cheerful and positive tone.",
) as response:
  response.stream_to_file(speech_file_path)
```

Note: **OpenAI's TTS service offers multiple built-in voices with distinct characteristics, such as Alloy, Nova, and Shimmer. In the chapter's example Nova was chosen, which has a warm, conversational tone. It is important to experiment with different voices to find the best match for the assistant's personality. Some voices may sound more formal, cheerful, or authoritative, which can influence how users perceive the agent.**

Text-to-speech models

For intelligent real-time applications, use the **`gpt-4o-mini-tts`** model, the newest and most reliable text-to-speech model. Users can prompt the model to control features of speech, including accent, emotional range, intonation, impressions, speed of speech, tone, and whispering.

The additional text-to-speech models are `tts-1` and `tts-1-hd`. The **`tts-1`** model offers lower latency but produces lower audio quality compared to the **`tts-1-hd`** model.

Voice options

The TTS endpoint includes 13 builtin voices to regulate how speech is rendered from text. It is crucial to hear and play with these voices in OpenAI.fm, an interactive demo for exploring the latest text-to-speech model in the OpenAI API. Voices are currently optimized for English and include: `alloy`, `ash`, `ballad`, `coral`, `echo`, `fable`, `nova`, `onyx`, `sage`, `shimmer`, `verse`, `marin`, and `cedar`.

For optimal quality, the use of `marin` or `cedar` is recommended.

Voice availability depends on the model. The `tts-1` and `tts-1-hd` models support a lesser set: alloy, ash, coral, echo, fable, onyx, nova, sage, and shimmer.

If users are using the Realtime API, they should note that the collection of possible voices is slightly different; refer to the Realtime discussions guide for current real-time voices.

Streaming real-time audio

The Speech API provides functionality for real-time audio streaming utilizing chunk transfer encoding. This implies the audio can be played before the entire file is generated and accessible.

The following code demonstrates the stream of spoken audio from input text directly to the speakers:

```
import asyncio

from openai import AsyncOpenAI
from openai.helpers import LocalAudioPlayer

openai = AsyncOpenAI()

async def main() -> None:
  async with openai.audio.speech.with_streaming_response.create(
    model="gpt-4o-mini-tts",
    voice="coral",
    input="Today is a wonderful day to build something people love!",
    instructions="Speak in a cheerful and positive tone.",
    response_format="pcm",
  ) as response:
    await LocalAudioPlayer().play(response)

if __name__ == "__main__":
  asyncio.run(main())
```

For the fastest response times, it is recommended to use `wav` or `pcm` as the response format.

Voice options and alternatives

The OpenAI TTS API supports different languages and accents. It even includes real-time streaming mode (so output audio begins playing before the complete text is transformed). However, numerous additional providers can be utilized for voice synthesis. For example, Microsoft Azure Neural TTS delivers over 400 voices across 140 languages and locales, and Google Cloud TTS provides high-quality WaveNet voices. ElevenLabs specializes in ultra-realistic voices and even permits personalized voice cloning. Each provider has its unique pricing and latency characteristics (e.g., ElevenLabs prioritizes quality over speed, whereas Azure and Google offer a balance of quality, language coverage, and cost). Users can integrate these services via their SDKs or REST APIs in a similar manner.

With the capabilities to both hear and talk, the agent is now equipped for voice contact. The next stage is to combine these components into a fluid dialogue flow, ensuring the agent can understand a transcribed inquiry, discover the solution, and reply audibly.

Building voice-first agent workflows

A conversational voice agent is more than just an STT module flowing into a TTS module. It takes a structured workflow to manage the transitions between hearing, reasoning, and speaking. This section will help in constructing an end-to-end voice agent pipeline and learn about two high-level architectural patterns for voice interactions. Users will then implement their preferred architecture for weather assistance.

Voice agent architecture patterns

Two basic architecture patterns that have arisen for voice agents are **the sandwich architecture** (modular pipeline) and the **speech-to-speech (S2S) end-to-end model**. Each has the following trade-offs:

- **Modular sandwich architecture**: Voice processing is divided into three layers, namely, speech-to-text (input), the language model agent (logic), and text-to-speech (output), assembled in a pipeline. This modular approach provides maximum transparency and control. Users can swap out components (e.g., replace Whisper with a different STT service or alter the TTS voice) without affecting other aspects of the system. Users also get full visibility into each stage for debugging and optimization. The trade-off is latency: each step adds some delay. However, with improvements, such as streaming and concurrency (described later), well-designed pipelines can still reach sub-second response times.
- **End-to-end speech-to-speech model**: A single multimodal model (such as a modified GPT-4 variant that directly takes audio input and makes audio output) can bypass intermediate text. This S2S technique may offer shorter overall latency (fewer processing stages) and more fluid, human-like interactions with continuous tone. The

drawback is limited transparency and flexibility; users are effectively dependent on a single model for everything. Debugging or changing its behavior (e.g., adding new tools or custom logic) is difficult or impossible, as the entire process is a black box.

It is important to note that, for most real-world systems requiring tool integration, memory, or custom logic, a modular pipeline offers greater flexibility and maintainability, despite incurring slightly higher latency. End-to-end speech models can be persuasive when ultra-low latency and genuine prosody are top priorities. However, they compromise the capacity to quickly comprehend or intervene in the reasoning process.

This chapter will follow the **modular sandwich architecture** for the weather helper. This means the agent will handle voice input and output through independent STT and TTS components, with a LangChain-powered reasoning module in between.

The following figure demonstrates the data flow of this pipeline:

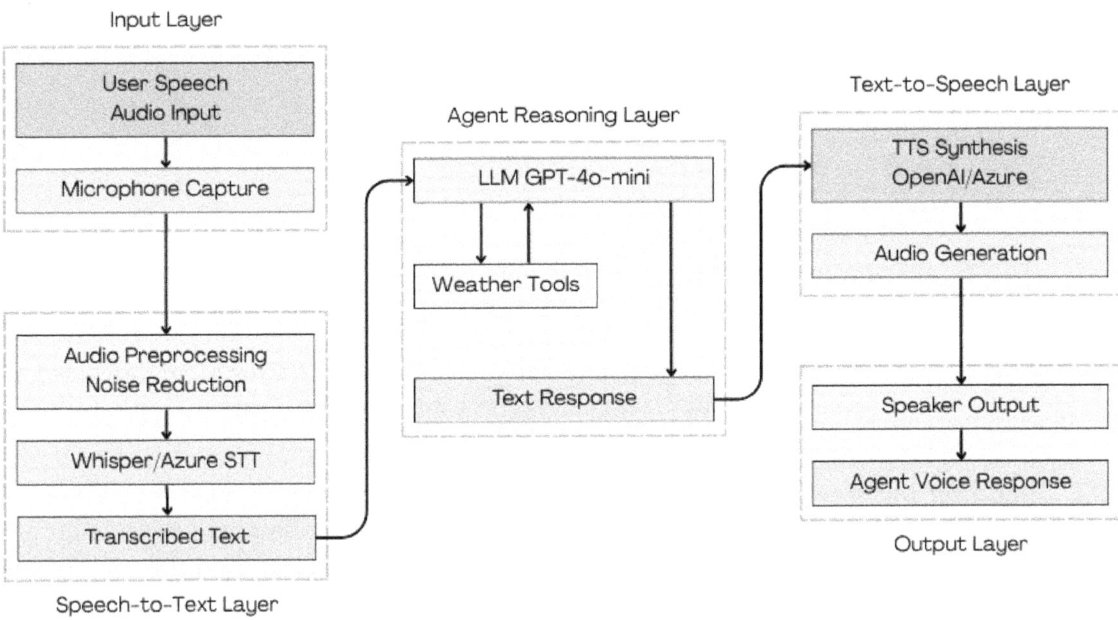

***Figure 6.2**: Voice agent sandwich architecture workflow*

The agent converts user speech to text, processes it through an LLM-based agent with tools, then converts the reply to speech. Each stage is modular and can be independently tuned or replaced.

In the input stage, the user's voice is recorded via a microphone (often with some preprocessing such as noise reduction). The STT component (e.g., Whisper or Azure) converts this audio into text, producing a transcript of the user's query. Next, the core agent reasoning takes place: a language model (such as GPT-4) receives the transcribed text, possibly calls external tools (such as a weather API), and generates a textual answer. Finally, the TTS service synthesizes the answer into spoken audio, which is output to the user.

Equipping the agent with tools and memory

The power of an agent lies in its ability to employ tools to retrieve information. In the weather assistant, users integrate a real-world weather API, such as OpenWeatherMap, to obtain live weather data, transforming the speech-based agent from a prototype into a production-ready system. The following are the steps involved:

1. **Environment setup and imports**: Before developing the agent, users need to set up their environment with the relevant API keys and imports. The following code imports all libraries required for audio processing, agent orchestration, and API communication:

```
import os
import requests
from langchain_core.messages import HumanMessage
from langchain.agents import create_tool_calling_agent, AgentExecutor
from langchain_core.prompts import ChatPromptTemplate,
MessagesPlaceholder
from langchain_openai import ChatOpenAI
from pydantic import BaseModel, Field
from openai import OpenAI as OpenAIClient

# Set up API keys from environment variables
OPENAI_API_KEY = os.getenv("OPENAI_API_KEY")
WEATHER_API_KEY = os.getenv("WEATHER_API_KEY")  # OpenWeatherMap API key
```

   Note: **Ensure the `OPENAI_API_KEY` and `WEATHER_API_KEY` environment variables are set before running the code. Users can receive a free OpenWeatherMap API key at https://openweathermap.org/api.**

2. **Building the weather tool**: Next, it is crucial to construct a **`WeatherTool`** class that connects to a weather API and returns organized weather data in simple language. The following utility explains how to connect external APIs to the LangChain agent workflow:

```
class WeatherTool:
    """Tool for fetching real weather data from OpenWeatherMap API."""

    def get_weather(self, city: str) -> str:
        """
        Get current weather for a specific city using OpenWeatherMap API.
        Args:
            city: Name of the city to get weather for
        Returns:
            A formatted string with weather information
        """
```

```
        url = "https://api.openweathermap.org/data/2.5/weather"
        params = {
            "q": city,
            "appid": WEATHER_API_KEY,
            "units": "metric",  # Use Celsius; change to "imperial" for
Fahrenheit
        }
        try:
            response = requests.get(url, params=params).json()
            # Check if the API returned an error
            if response.get("cod") != 200:
                return f"Sorry, I couldn't find weather information for
{city}."
            # Extract weather details from API response
            description = response["weather"][0]["description"]
            temperature = response["main"]["temp"]
            # Format a natural language response
            return (
                f"The weather in {city} is {description}, "
                f"with a temperature of {temperature}°C."
            )
        except Exception as e:
            return f"Error fetching weather data: {str(e)}"
```

Tip: **In production, users should implement caching for frequent requests (e.g., today's weather for popular cities) to reduce API calls, improve latency, and stay under API rate limits. Consider utilizing Redis or a basic in-memory cache with expiration times.**

3. **Building the LangChain agent**: Now, it is crucial to develop a LangChain agent that uses the weather tool. The following code explains how to establish an agent with GPT-4o-mini as the reasoning engine, equipping it with the weather tool and a conversational persona:

```
# Initialize the weather tool

weather_tool = WeatherTool()

prompt = ChatPromptTemplate.from_messages([
    ("system",
     "You are a helpful voice-based weather assistant. "
     "Use the weather tool to answer weather-related questions. "
     "Keep responses concise and friendly. "
     "Present weather information clearly, as if talking to a friend."),
```

```
        ("human", "{input}"),
        MessagesPlaceholder(variable_name="agent_scratchpad"),
    ])

agent = create_tool_calling_agent(
    llm=ChatOpenAI(model="gpt-4o-mini", temperature=0.7),
    tools=[weather_tool.get_weather],
    prompt=prompt,
)
agent_executor = AgentExecutor(
    agent=agent,
    tools=[weather_tool.get_weather],
    verbose=True,
)
```

It is important to note that the agent's behavior is governed by the system prompt, not hard-coded logic. This modular approach allows the users to alter the agent's personality and response style without affecting the underlying programming.

4. **Agent reasoning function**: To process transcribed user questions and provide responses, users develop a helper function that executes the agent. The following function cleanly isolates input understanding (STT) from reasoning and tool usage:

```
def agent_weather_response(transcript: str) -> str:
    """
    Process a transcribed user query and generate a weather response.
    Args:
        transcript: The transcribed text from user's speech
    Returns:
        The agent's text response about the weather
    """
    result = agent_executor.invoke({"input": transcript})
    return result["output"]
```

5. **Complete voice weather flow**: This step demonstrates how all the components work together in a comprehensive voice-enabled weather interaction. The following orchestration layer links STT, agent reasoning, and TTS into a single workflow:

```
def handle_voice_weather(input_audio_path: str):
    """
    Complete voice weather assistant workflow:
    1. Transcribe user's speech to text (STT)
    2. Process query through agent to get weather info
    3. Synthesize agent's response to speech (TTS)
    Args:
```

```
        input_audio_path: Path to the audio file containing user's
question
    """
    # Step 1: Speech -> Text  (wraps client.audio.transcriptions.create
from earlier)
    transcript = transcribe_audio(input_audio_path)
    print(f"User said: {transcript}")
    # Step 2: Agent reasoning
    response_text = agent_weather_response(transcript)
    print(f"Assistant response: {response_text}")
    # Step 3: Text -> Speech  (wraps client.audio.speech.with_streaming_
response.create from earlier)
    audio_output = speak_text(response_text, "weather_reply.wav")
    print(f"Audio response saved to: {audio_output}")
    return audio_output

# Example usage:
# handle_voice_weather("user_query.wav")
```

In this final implementation, users progressed from simulated data to a genuine weather API integration. The agent can now listen to spoken queries, access the OpenWeatherMap API for real-time weather data, and create natural spoken responses with current weather information.

Handling multi-turn conversations: At this stage, the agent can manage a single inquiry and answer. In real conversations, users often ask follow-up inquiries (for example, *How about tomorrow?* after asking about today's weather). To manage multi-turn discussions, the agent needs to recall what has been stated. LangChain provides memory components (such as `ConversationBufferMemory`) that may be attached to agents to automatically store and prepend the conversation history on each new inquiry. By doing so, the agent can understand that *tomorrow* refers to the same city indicated earlier. Readers will investigate memory systems in depth in *Chapter 7, Developing Context-aware Agents with Persistent Memory*. However, it is essential to know that the speech agent can be enhanced with short-term or long-term memory to ensure it does not forget context between utterances.

Enabling real-time conversational audio pipelines

Thus far, the voice assistant handles audio in a straightforward sequence: record the complete question, transcribe it, generate an answer, and then synthesize the answer to speech. To make the interaction genuinely conversational, users should decrease the time they spend waiting for a response. Humans often expect a reply within a fraction of a second in natural discourse. Studies demonstrate that a total system latency exceeding roughly 500 ms is markedly sluggish or unnatural to consumers. This section will explore how to speed up the agent's pipeline using concurrent streaming. It also explores how to guarantee the agent understands when to start and stop listening using voice activity detection.

Streaming the pipeline for low latency

A naive implementation of the pipeline would process audio and produce a reply in a tight sequence: wait for the user to finish speaking, then transcribe the entire audio, then generate a complete answer, then synthesize the full answer to voice. This strategy is easy but incurs unnecessary delays. It can perform better by streaming data through the pipeline steps in parallel. For instance, as soon as the first few words are transcribed, the language model can start creating a response. As soon as the initial half of the response text is complete, the TTS engine can begin creating audio, even while the latter part of the response is still being written.

The following figure demonstrates a notional streaming pipeline where each component works concurrently on whatever data is available:

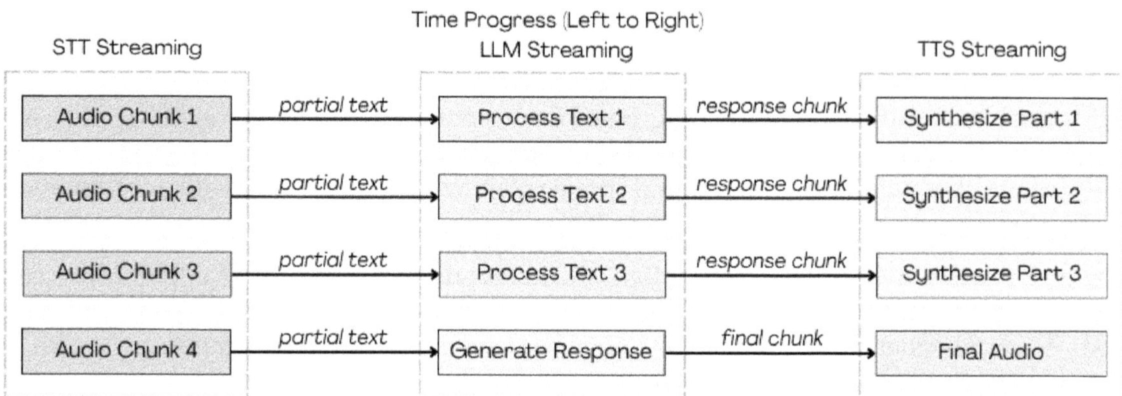

***Figure 6.3**: Streaming pipeline with concurrent processing across stages*

Each component processes data as soon as it becomes available (indicated with dotted arrows). While STT is still transcribing later audio chunks, the LLM can begin processing previously transcribed text, and TTS can start creating audio from the earliest parts of the response. This parallelism reduces total latency compared to waiting for each stage to fully complete before initiating the next.

The following diagram demonstrates the continuous flow of data through the streaming voice pipeline:

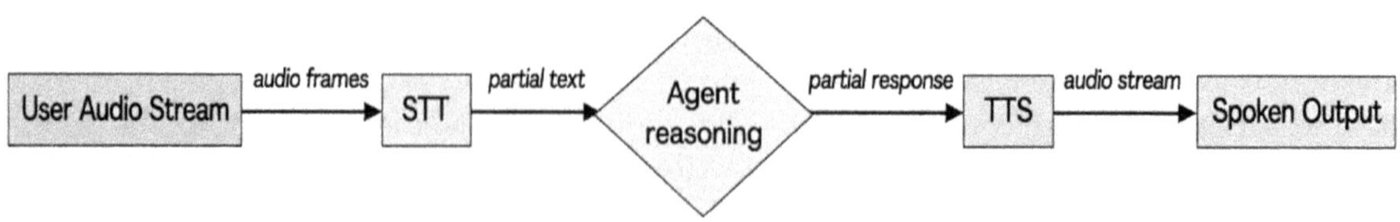

***Figure 6.4**: Streaming voice pipeline showing continuous data flow*

Audio frames from user input are processed by the STT system, which generates partial transcripts for the agent's reasoning layer. The agent creates partial responses that are input into TTS, which produces an audio stream for spoken output. This constant flow minimizes latency.

To estimate where delays occur and how to decrease them, evaluate each stage of the pipeline, as follows:

Pipeline stage	Typical latency impact	Optimization strategies
Network	Signal travel time (tens of ms or more)	Deploy services closer to users to reduce round-trip time (e.g., edge servers, regional data centers).
STT	Audio transcription processing	Use real-time streaming APIs so recognition happens during user speech, not after. Use efficient models or hardware acceleration for faster decoding.
LLM	Response generation time	Use faster (or smaller) models, or stream the model's output tokens as they are generated. Optimize prompts for brevity to reduce required computation.
TTS	Audio synthesis and playback	Use low-latency TTS voices; stream audio output while generating it. Consider trade-offs between voice quality and speed.

***Table 6.2**: Voice pipeline latency factors and fixes*

With these strategies, a well-tuned system can achieve end-to-end response latencies low enough for natural communication. In practice, a user might start hearing the agent's answer even as they finish their question, making the encounter feel fluid and responsive.

Tip: **For production-grade helpers, investigate specialist or faster TTS systems that enable ultra-fast streaming. For example, some providers can begin playing high-quality voice with only \~100 ms of processing latency. Using such services (at a higher cost) can further increase the feeling of immediacy if low response lag is crucial to the application's user experience.**

The following code explains how to implement streaming TTS using OpenAI's official API with the `with_streaming_response` pattern. This solution employs chunk transfer encoding to begin playing audio before the whole file is generated, as follows:

```
from pathlib import Path
from openai import OpenAI


client = OpenAI()


def stream_weather_response(response_text: str, output_path: str = "weather_
```

```
response.wav"):
  """
  Stream TTS audio output to minimize latency.
  Audio begins playing before full synthesis completes.

  Args:
    response_text: The agent's text response to synthesize
    output_path: Path where audio file will be saved
  """
  speech_file_path = Path(output_path)

  # Use streaming response for fastest delivery
  with client.audio.speech.with_streaming_response.create(
    model="gpt-4o-mini-tts",
    voice="coral",
    input=response_text,
    instructions="Speak in a clear, friendly tone suitable for weather
information.",
    response_format="pcm" # PCM format for lowest latency
  ) as response:
    response.stream_to_file(speech_file_path)

  return speech_file_path

# Example: Stream a weather forecast response
weather_info = "The weather in Seattle is partly cloudy with a temperature of
18°C."
audio_file = stream_weather_response(weather_info)
print(f"Streaming audio saved to: {audio_file}")
```

Note: **Using Pulse Code Modulation (PCM) or WAV as the response type provides the shortest response times, as these formats need low processing overhead. The `with_streaming_response` context manager enables chunk transfer encoding, allowing audio playback to begin instantly as data arrives.**

For LLM response streaming, users can generate text responses progressively and feed them to TTS as they become available, as follows:

```
from openai import OpenAI
```

```
client = OpenAI()

def stream_agent_response(user_query: str):
  """
  Stream LLM responses and synthesize audio in real-time.

  Args:
    user_query: The transcribed user question
  """
  # Stream the LLM response
  response_stream = client.chat.completions.create(
    model="gpt-4o-mini",
    messages=[
      {"role": "system", "content": "You are a helpful weather assistant.
Keep responses concise."},
      {"role": "user", "content": user_query}
    ],
    stream=True
  )

  full_response = ""
  for chunk in response_stream:
    if chunk.choices[0].delta.content:
      content = chunk.choices[0].delta.content
      full_response += content
      print(content, end="", flush=True)

  print() # New line after streaming completes

  # Once complete response is available, stream to TTS
  stream_weather_response(full_response, "streaming_weather.wav")

  return full_response

# Example usage
query = "What's the weather like in Portland today?"
stream_agent_response(query)
```

Voice activity detection and end-pointing

Another crucial component of a real-time voice agent is understanding *when to listen and when to talk*. The agent should determine when the user has finished speaking before constructing a response. This is performed by **vocal activity detection** (**VAD**) and end-of-utterance detection. VAD continually examines the incoming audio and decides when there is a long enough gap (quiet) to consider the user's statement complete. Only then should the user stop gathering audio and begin processing the question. If the user is only hesitating mid-sentence, a well-tuned VAD will wait; if the user has genuinely stopped talking, VAD signals the pipeline to continue forward.

Basic VAD algorithms commonly use an audio volume threshold: audio is sent to the STT when volume exceeds a specific level and stops when silence is detected for, say, 500 ms. More advanced VAD uses **machine learning** (**ML**) models (such as the one integrated into the WebRTC library) to better identify speech from background noise. The essential parameter is the period of silence before turning off input (usually 0.5 seconds). Readers would want this threshold long enough that natural pauses do not cause an early cutoff, but short enough that the system replies promptly when the user is genuinely done speaking.

It is important to note that VAD sensitivity dramatically affects user experience. If it is too pushy, the agent may cut the user off mid-sentence; if it is too reluctant, the user will feel a pause after finishing speaking, wondering whether the system will answer. Tuning and testing VAD for the specific use case (and surrounding noise conditions) is critical.

In the weather agent, users could deploy a simple client-side VAD to monitor the microphone input and provide audio frames to the Whisper API only when the user is speaking, then cease after \~0.5 seconds of silence is detected. (Azure's Speech SDK has built-in VAD for its streaming recognizer; with OpenAI's API, users can handle VAD on the client side, for example, using a package like `webrtcvad` in Python to analyze audio frames.)

The following figure depicts how voice input travels through a pipeline with VAD managing the audio stream to the speech recognizer. The agent only captures and transcribes audio while the user is speaking; if silence is detected, the system stops recording and moves on to processing the query:

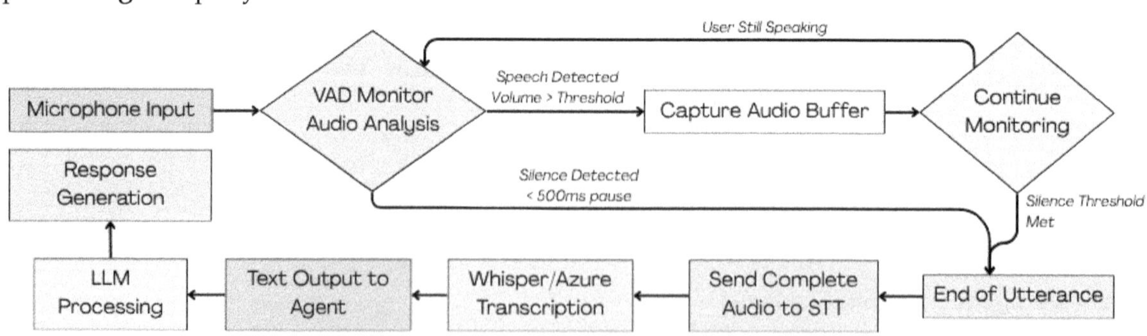

***Figure 6.5**: Voice input pipeline with VAD gating mechanism*

The following code shows a practical implementation of speech activity detection using the `webrtcvad` library:

```
import webrtcvad
import pyaudio
import collections
import sys

class VoiceActivityDetector:
    """Detect when user is speaking and capture complete utterances."""

    def __init__(self, aggressiveness=2, sample_rate=16000):
        """
        Initialize VAD with sensitivity settings.
        Args:
            aggressiveness: 0-3, higher values are more aggressive about
filtering
            sample_rate: Audio sample rate (8000, 16000, 32000, or 48000 Hz)
        """
        self.vad = webrtcvad.Vad(aggressiveness)
        self.sample_rate = sample_rate
        self.frame_duration = 30  # ms per frame
        self.frame_size = int(sample_rate * self.frame_duration / 1000)
        # Buffer to track speech vs silence
        self.ring_buffer = collections.deque(maxlen=10)
        self.triggered = False
        self.voiced_frames = []

    def is_speech(self, audio_frame: bytes) -> bool:
        """Check if audio frame contains speech."""
        return self.vad.is_speech(audio_frame, self.sample_rate)

    def process_audio_stream(self, stream):
        """Process microphone stream and yield complete utterances."""
        num_silence_frames = 0
        silence_threshold = 15  # ~0.5 seconds at 30ms frames
        while True:
            frame = stream.read(self.frame_size)
            is_speech = self.is_speech(frame)
            if not self.triggered:
                # Waiting for speech to start
                self.ring_buffer.append((frame, is_speech))
                num_voiced = len([f for f, speech in self.ring_buffer if
speech])
```

```
                # Trigger when we detect enough speech frames
                if num_voiced > 0.8 * self.ring_buffer.maxlen:
                    self.triggered = True
                    # Include buffered frames
                    self.voiced_frames.extend([f for f, s in self.ring_
buffer])
                    self.ring_buffer.clear()
            else:
                # Currently capturing speech
                self.voiced_frames.append(frame)
                self.ring_buffer.append((frame, is_speech))
                # Count consecutive silence frames
                num_silence_frames = num_silence_frames + 1 if not is_speech
else 0
                # End utterance after prolonged silence
                if num_silence_frames > silence_threshold:
                    # Yield the complete utterance
                    complete_audio = b"".join(self.voiced_frames)
                    yield complete_audio
                    # Reset for next utterance
                    self.triggered = False
                    self.voiced_frames = []
                    num_silence_frames = 0

# Example usage
def capture_utterances():
    """Capture complete user utterances using VAD."""
    audio = pyaudio.PyAudio()
    stream = audio.open(
        format=pyaudio.paInt16,
        channels=1,
        rate=16000,
        input=True,
        frames_per_buffer=480,  # 30ms at 16kHz
    )
    vad = VoiceActivityDetector(aggressiveness=2)
    print("Listening... Speak now!")
    for utterance in vad.process_audio_stream(stream):
        print(f"Captured {len(utterance)} bytes of speech")
        # Send to STT for transcription (transcribe_audio wraps the Whisper
call shown earlier)
        transcript = transcribe_audio(utterance)
        print(f"User said: {transcript}")
```

Voice activity detection examines the input audio and loops (green decision) if the user is speaking. When a period of silence is identified (usually 500ms), the audio stream is transferred to the STT for transcription, and the agent begins processing the text. This guarantees the agent waits for the user to finish before responding, preventing premature cut-offs.

Handling errors and interruptions

Even with a well-designed pipeline, voice interactions can encounter faults or unexpected scenarios. Common issues include background noise or overlapping speech causing transcription mistakes, unfamiliar proper nouns (such as city names) being misrecognized, or the user interrupting the agent's spoken response (known as barge-in). To design a robust helper, users should anticipate and address the following issues:

- **No speech detected or incomprehensible input**: If the STT result is empty or confidence is very low (e.g., it outputs an empty string or just "..."), the agent should respectfully ask the user to repeat the query rather than attempting a potentially wrong answer. For example, it might answer with a brief prompt, *I am sorry, I did not catch that. Could you please repeat your question?* and then re-initiate the listening phase.
- **Background noise or accent issues**: High noise levels or strong accents can lead to transcription mistakes. Both Whisper and Azure have strategies to improve accuracy in tough settings. Azure's Custom Speech allows users to train an acoustic model using domain-specific data (for example, if the users are in a noisy industrial environment). Whisper's resilience and its prompting system can help with accents and rare terminology, but users may still need to address circumstances where the transcript is inaccurate. For crucial applications, giving users visual confirmation (e.g., displaying the transcribed query and letting them amend it) might be helpful, though it goes beyond voice-only interaction.
- **User interrupts the agent (barge-in)**: If the user starts talking while the agent is speaking, the agent should halt its TTS playing and return to listening mode. Many voice assistant frameworks feature built-in barge-in handling. If not, users can implement it by constantly running VAD even during the agent's speech production: if user speech is recognized, instantly cancel the TTS output and switch back to capturing input. The agent could then replan its reaction depending on the new information. This functionality is crucial for natural, turn-by-turn interaction, where users and the agent may occasionally talk over each other.
- **External service failures**: Network difficulties or API errors can occur at any level (STT, LLM, or TTS). A production-grade pipeline should incorporate timeouts and fallback logic. For example, users might retry the transcription once or twice if it fails or utilize a basic offline STT as backup. Similarly, if the weather API is unavailable, the agent may respond with a cached forecast or a graceful error message (e.g., *I am sorry, I am having trouble accessing the latest weather data right now.*). Logging faults and timing data for each stage is critical to monitor performance and continually improve the system.

Note: **Always provide the user with some feedback when an error occurs in a voice conversation. If the agent remains silent after being spoken to, the user may not know whether it ever heard them. The agent should say something like, "Sorry, I am having trouble understanding. Please try again," rather than failing silently. Audio or visual cues (such as a quick chime or an on-screen alert) can also reassure the user that the system is listening or processing, even if it has not generated a full response.**

By anticipating these instances, the voice assistant can manage them elegantly. For instance, if the weather agent's STT misinterprets a city name, it may clarify by asking, *I heard Boston, is that correct?* before presenting the prediction. If the user starts speaking when the agent is mid-response, the replay can be halted to listen. These tactics ensure that errors or interruptions do not derail the conversation, but are treated as just another element of a natural discourse.

Detecting sentiment and emotion from voice

For many applications, understanding how something was expressed might be as crucial as understanding the words. A user's tone of voice can indicate sentiment (whether joyful or annoyed) and emotional state (calm, excited, frustrated, etc.). By arming the agent with a degree of emotional intelligence, users enable compassionate, context-aware answers. This is particularly beneficial in high-stakes industries like healthcare and customer support, where the tone of a conversation is important.

To understand how an AI agent can infer emotion from voice, the key is to extract acoustic elements from the audio data that correlate with human emotion, as follows:

- **Pitch (intonation)**: A higher or wildly changing pitch can imply excitement, surprise, or agitation, whereas a flat, low pitch could reflect sadness or exhaustion.
- **Speaking rate (tempo)**: Fast speech generally conveys hurry or stress; a slow, halting pace could indicate perplexity, indecision, or grief.
- **Volume (intensity)**: Raised volume might express anger or emphasis, whereas a very faint voice might imply fear, shame, or doubt.
- **Voice quality (timbre)**: A shaking or strained voice could indicate strong emotions like wrath or worry; a smooth, warm tone could indicate calmness or happiness.
- **Speech content (words used)**: Emotion recognition is not only about audio. The words themselves and their emotion (positive/negative language, harsh or violent terminology, etc.) provide vital signals when assessed alongside tone.

In practice, specialized ML models (using techniques from speech emotion recognition research) can take raw audio features, such as fundamental frequency (for pitch), energy (for volume), spectral characteristics, and more, and classify the speaker's emotional state (e.g., happy, sad, angry, neutral). For example, a model might learn that a combination of loud volume, high pitch, and quick speaking correlates with *anger*, whereas low volume and sluggish speech connect with *sadness*. Many research datasets and pre-trained models exist for emotion recognition from speech, which users can exploit rather than constructing their own from scratch.

Once an emotion or mood is identified from the user's speech, the agent can adjust its response accordingly. One practical method in a modular system is to inject an extra suggestion to the agent's prompt or conversation memory reflecting the user's emotional state. For example, if the user's tone sounds irritated or furious, it is crucial to add the system message, *The user sounds frustrated, so respond with extra patience and reassurance.* If the user's voice is sorrowful or uncertain, the agent could answer with a more empathic, encouraging tone. The content of the response might also change, as an angry user might receive a fast, concise answer with an apology, if necessary, whereas a puzzled user would get a more extensive explanation. The TTS voice or style can also be adjusted. For instance, adopting a quieter, soothing speech version when the user is agitated.

It is important to note that in healthcare or treatment situations, an emotionally responsive agent is very beneficial. A voice-enabled health assistant might listen not just to a patient's words but also to their tone to detect tension or discomfort. This emotional context allows it to respond with empathy and alters its instructions. For example, if a patient seems concerned about expressing their symptoms, the agent can prioritize a reassuring tone and clear directions, create trust, and help the patient stay calm during a telemedicine session.

For implementing emotion detection, there are various off-the-shelf services and APIs available. For example, Hume AI specializes in vocal emotion identification, whereas Amazon Comprehend and Google Cloud Natural Language API offer sentiment analysis capabilities. These services handle the complexities of feature extraction and categorization, allowing the user to focus on how their agent responds to detected emotions.

The following code provides a simplified approach to emotion-aware responses:

```
def detect_emotion_from_audio(audio_file_path: str) -> str:
    """Return a coarse emotion label for the given audio file.

    Replace this stub with a call to an emotion-recognition service such as
    Hume AI, Amazon Comprehend, or a local model. Should return one of:
    'frustrated', 'sad', 'anxious', 'neutral'.
    """
    return "neutral"


def emotion_aware_weather_agent(audio_file_path: str):
    """Weather agent that adapts responses based on user emotion."""
    from openai import OpenAI
    client = OpenAI()
    # Transcribe with emotion detection (could use external service)
    transcript = client.audio.transcriptions.create(
        model="whisper-1",
        file=open(audio_file_path, "rb"),
    )
```

```
    # Simple text-based sentiment analysis or external emotion API
    emotion = detect_emotion_from_audio(audio_file_path)  # External service
    # Adapt system prompt based on detected emotion
    emotion_prompts = {
        "frustrated": "The user sounds frustrated. Respond calmly with
empathy.",
        "sad": "The user sounds down. Use an encouraging, warm tone.",
        "anxious": "The user sounds worried. Provide clear, reassuring
information.",
        "neutral": "Respond in a helpful, friendly manner.",
    }
    system_message = f"You are a weather assistant. {emotion_prompts.
get(emotion, emotion_prompts['neutral'])}"
    # Get response from agent with emotion context
    response = client.chat.completions.create(
        model="gpt-4o-mini",
        messages=[
            {"role": "system", "content": system_message},
            {"role": "user", "content": transcript.text},
        ],
    )
    # Adjust TTS voice based on emotion
    voice = "shimmer" if emotion in ["sad", "anxious"] else "nova"
    speech_response = client.audio.speech.create(
        model="gpt-4o-mini-tts",
        voice=voice,
        input=response.choices[0].message.content,
    )
    speech_response.stream_to_file("response.mp3")
    return response.choices[0].message.content
```

Tip: **For production emotion detection, consider leveraging specialist services like Amazon Comprehend, Google Cloud Natural Language API, or Hume AI's emotion recognition API rather than constructing one from scratch. These services provide pre-trained algorithms that can recognize emotions from both text and voice with higher accuracy than simple heuristics.**

By making the agent emotion-aware, users create a more engaging, human-like connection. Users generally respond positively when an assistant detects their mood or displeasure. However, be cautious, as misinterpreting emotions might be harmful, so it is wise to create fallbacks. For instance, if the agent is not confident about the user's mood, it may be best to continue with a neutral, helpful tone rather than risk an improper reaction.

Supporting multilingual agents with translation models

So far, the weather helper assumes the user is speaking English. In fact, voice assistants typically need to manage numerous languages or strong accents. Fortunately, both Whisper and Azure Speech support a wide selection of languages. OpenAI's Whisper model can immediately transcribe and translate speech in roughly a hundred languages into English. Microsoft's Azure Speech similarly supports over 100 languages and dialects natively for both recognition and synthesis. This section will explore how to enhance the agent to accommodate multilingual users.

Translation API for multilingual support

The easiest method for a multilingual agent is **auto-detection** and **translation**. OpenAI's Whisper translations API takes audio files of any supported language and transcribes, if necessary, the audio into English. This differs from the transcriptions endpoint in that the result is not in the original input language but is translated to English. The translations endpoint supports just the **`whisper-1`** model.

The following code explains how to convert audio from any language into English text:

```
from openai import OpenAI

client = OpenAI()

def translate_to_english(audio_file_path: str) -> str:
  """Translate speech in any language to English text using Whisper."""
  audio_file = open(audio_file_path, "rb")

  translation = client.audio.translations.create(
    model="whisper-1",
    file=audio_file
  )

  return translation.text

# Example: Translating a German audio query to English text
audio_path = "german_weather.mp3" # contains "Wie ist das Wetter in Seattle
heute?"
english_query = translate_to_english(audio_path)
print(english_query)
# Output: "What's the weather like in Seattle today?"
```

Note: **OpenAI's Whisper translation API currently supports translation into English only. For other target languages, users would need to utilize the transcriptions endpoint to acquire the original text, then use a different translation service to convert to their selected language.**

In this example, the user's German audio question (*Wie ist das Wetter in Seattle heute?*) is transcribed and simultaneously translated to English text utilizing Whisper's translation feature. The representative can now process the query exactly like any other. After the agent generates a response in English, users have two options, like they can either translate the text back into the original language or use a multilingual TTS voice to synthesize the response directly in the user's language. Many modern TTS providers, notably OpenAI and Microsoft Azure, enable multilingual speech synthesis with a single API call by providing the language or voice.

Supported languages

Currently supported languages include Afrikaans, Arabic, Armenian, Azerbaijani, Belarusian, Bosnian, Bulgarian, Catalan, Chinese, Croatian, Czech, Danish, Dutch, English, Estonian, Finnish, French, Galician, German, Greek, Hebrew, Hindi, Hungarian, Icelandic, Indonesian, Italian, Japanese, Kannada, Kazakh, Korean, Latvian, Lithuanian, Macedonian, Malay, Marathi, Maori, Nepali, Norwegian, Persian, Polish, Portuguese, Romanian, Russian, Serbian, Slovak, Slovenian, Spanish, Swahili, Swedish, Tagalog, Tamil, Thai, Turkish, Ukrainian, Urdu, Vietnamese, and Welsh.

The model will yield results for languages not specified above, but the quality will be poorer. For GPT-4o-based models, some **International Organization for Standardization** (**ISO**) 639-1 and 639-3 language codes are supported. For language codes not available, try prompting for specific languages (e.g., *Output in English*).

Tip: **When developing a multilingual agent, ensure that any agent-initiated prompts or clarifications are also translated. For instance, if the agent needs to question "Did I get that right?" to ensure understanding, it should do so in the user's language. Users can either maintain a library of prompt translations or employ real-time translation for such terms.**

Handling multi-language conversations

Designing a completely multilingual agent also requires handling the discussion context across languages. In a multi-turn environment, one user's utterance might be in Spanish and the next in English. Users must determine whether the agent keeps to one language or mimics the user's decision. A typical method is to respond in the language of the user's preceding question. Using Whisper's language identification or Azure's `SpeechRecognizer.recognize_once_async()` language result, users may route the pipeline accordingly (e.g., choose the proper TTS voice or translation direction). The good news is that the fundamental pipeline remains the same, but with an extra translation step when necessary, so the agent's overall design can remain unaltered while serving a larger audience.

Building voice-enabled telemedicine AI assistants

While this chapter has focused on a meteorological agent, the same voice intelligence approaches can alter agents in other fields. One interesting use is a voice-enabled telemedicine assistant, which is an AI bot that interacts with patients via speech to provide medical information, assess symptoms, or offer comforting guidance. This section briefly discusses how the established components can be utilized and what additional issues exist in a healthcare context, as follows:

- **Domain-specific voice recognition and vocabulary**: A medical voice assistant must accurately detect medical language (medications, illnesses, conditions), which may not arise commonly in generic speech data. Using a bespoke vocabulary or language model, fine-tuning is required so that terms such as *ibuprofen* or *hypertension* are transcribed appropriately. Azure Speech lets users add domain-specific terms to its language model, and Whisper can receive context prompts or be fine-tuned with medical recordings for enhanced accuracy.

- **Natural, reassuring speech output**: In telemedicine, the agent's voice needs to express empathy and intelligibility. This can involve choosing a particular TTS voice that sounds peaceful and caring, modifying the speech tempo for clarity, or even dynamically changing tone depending on the interaction. Some TTS systems (like Azure's) allow controlling prosody and style (e.g., a *cheerful* or *empathetic* speaking style), which might enhance patient comfort.

- **Emotion detection for patient state**: As described in the *Supporting multilingual agents with translation models* section, emotion recognition from voice can be a game-changer in healthcare. If a patient sounds anxious or in pain, the agent can reply with greater compassion, simplify its language, or escalate the situation to a human doctor sooner. For example, an upset tone can cause the AI to provide soothing reassurance or urgently encourage seeking emergency assistance. Emotionally aware voice agents listen to vocal parameters, including tone, pitch, speed, and volume, to infer feelings such as tension, sadness, or anxiety. This helps them reply in ways that feel more sympathetic and suitable for patients struggling with health difficulties. In practice, some studies suggest these agents can handle a significant portion of routine appointment calls, which may help reduce wait times. They also indicate that these agents, when coupled with sentiment analysis, can help flag potential mental health concerns earlier than traditional approaches.

- **Multi-language support and accessibility**: Medical assistants must typically serve heterogeneous communities. Multilingual STT and TTS capabilities are crucial so patients can talk in their preferred language and yet be understood. Whisper's translation feature may, for instance, let a doctor who speaks English talk with a patient who speaks Spanish by translating the patient's Spanish speech into English text for the doctor, and then translating the doctor's English response back into Spanish speech. This opens telemedicine to non-English speakers without having a human translator.

- **Privacy and compliance**: Health data is important. Therefore, voice interactions in telemedicine must adhere to privacy standards [such as the **Health Insurance Portability and Accountability Act** (**HIPAA**) in the U.S.]. This may impact technical choices. For example, employing an on-premises or on-device STT model (such as running Whisper locally) to prevent transferring audio to external cloud services, or ensuring any cloud services utilized have suitable encryption and data management standards. In practice, suppliers like Simbo AI stress end-to-end encryption [e.g., 256-bit **Advanced Encryption Standard** (**AES**)] for call records and transcripts, and compliance with health privacy legislation.
- **Integration with medical information and triage logic**: A telemedicine agent would likely employ tools and knowledge sources distinct from a weather agent. For instance, it might integrate with medical databases or symptom-checker APIs instead of a weather API. The LangChain agent might use these tools to answer health questions or organize appointments. The agent's prompt would also be constructed to represent a formal medical assistant persona, presumably with instructions to deliver correct but easy-to-understand explanations and to disclaim that it is not a certified expert.

In summary, a voice-enabled telemedicine assistant leverages the same key construction blocks, robust STT, an LLM-driven reasoning module with tools, TTS output, and an efficient pipeline, but tailors them to the healthcare domain. The focus on empathy and accuracy is much greater: misconceptions or insensitivity can have devastating effects when dealing with someone's health. By combining the techniques from this chapter (and setting the stage for the memory techniques in *Chapter 7, Developing Context-aware Agents with Persistent Memory*), users can create a medical conversational agent that not only informs but also engages and comforts patients, scaling the reach of healthcare professionals and improving patient experiences.

Conclusion

In this chapter, readers evolved a text-based agent into a voice-enabled conversational system. They implemented speech-to-text with Whisper and Azure Speech, added text-to-speech synthesis, and combined them into an end-to-end audio pipeline. Readers also introduced voice activity detection and streaming techniques to keep interactions responsive, along with practical error/interrupt handling for real-world robustness.

With these building blocks, the voice-enabled weather assistant can hold a natural spoken dialogue, listen, use an LLM plus tools to find answers, and speak back clearly. The next chapter details memory, ensuring the agents can retain context across turns and sessions, using approaches such as conversation buffers, summaries, vector stores, and knowledge graphs.

CHAPTER 7
Developing Context-aware Agents with Persistent Memory

Introduction

Imagine an **artificial intelligence** (**AI**) assistant that can recall past context, remember the user's preferences, and modify its responses between sessions. Persistent memory is the source of that ability. Without it, the experience feels disjointed, users repeat themselves, and every conversation resets. Agents that have a well-designed memory layer go beyond simple question answering to become assistants that preserve continuity, customize interactions, and expand on previous conversations.

In this chapter, readers transition from stateless agents to context-aware systems within the LangChain architecture. A wide range of useful memory techniques will be covered, including conversation buffers and sliding windows for recent context, summary memory for condensing lengthy conversations, entity memory for tracking important facts, vector stores for semantic retrieval, and knowledge graphs for capturing more complex relationships. Step by step, readers will apply these strategies, learn when to use each one, and address common production challenges, including memory bloat and token overflow. These concepts are integrated into a hands-on weather assistant that uses adaptive memory to select the most effective storage and retrieval strategy based on the nature of the conversation. The groundwork for creating production-ready agents that can remember, retrieve, and react with significant continuity will be in place by the end of this chapter.

Structure

This chapter covers the following topics:

- Understanding the memory hierarchy
- Implementing conversation buffers for context tracking
- Integrating vector storage for memory retrieval

- Entity memory and knowledge graphs
- Implementing hybrid memory by combining multiple approaches
- Designing adaptive memory systems for intelligent agents

Objectives

This chapter introduces persistent memory and useful patterns for utilizing it in LangChain, thereby transitioning from stateless agents to context-aware systems. The basics of short-term versus long-term memory will be covered, along with the reasons for their importance for meaningful, tailored dialogues. After that, readers will put fundamental strategies such as sliding-window memory and conversation buffers into practice, learning how to maintain recent context while adhering to token limits.

Readers will then investigate compression and structure: knowledge graphs to model relationships that facilitate deeper reasoning, entity memory to record important facts, vector stores to retrieve pertinent history by semantic similarity, and summary memory to preserve the *big picture*. Finally, these strategies will be combined to create hybrid and adaptive memory designs that select the appropriate memory layer according to the content, retrieval requirements, and length of the conversation. To provide more individualized forecasts throughout sessions, the chapter ends with a hands-on weather assistant that retains user preferences and previous requests.

Understanding the memory hierarchy

In the domain of AI agents, memory is not a monolithic storage unit; it is a tiered structure meant to balance speed, cost, and depth of context. Much like a computer uses a hierarchy of L1 cache, **random-access memory** (**RAM**), and hard drives, a context-aware agent uses distinct memory types to handle current conversation flow against long-term factual recall.

Short-term versus long-term memory

Memory is often classified into two basic groups based on its duration and purpose. Short-term memory watches the immediate flow of discourse to resolve local references, while long-term memory allows agents to recall preferences and occurrences from days or weeks past.

The following table compares the two basic dimensions of agent memory:

Dimension	Short-term memory	Long-term memory
Purpose	Maintaining current dialogue flow.	Recalling preferences and past events.
Duration	Single session (volatile).	Multiple sessions (persistent).

Dimension	Short-term memory	Long-term memory
Storage type	RAM / In-memory buffers.	Vector databases / **Structured Query Language** (**SQL**) (MySQL, PostgreSQL) / Graphs.
Retrieval speed	Near-instant.	Dependent on search/indexing.
Scaling	Limited by the **large language model** (**LLM**) context window.	Virtually unlimited.

***Table 7.1**: Comparison of short-term and long-term memory strategies*

Memory architecture patterns

LangChain provides a standard interface for memory that separates storage techniques and retrieval strategies. All memory classes implement common methods: `save_context()` records new interactions, `load_memory_variables()` retrieves appropriate context, and `clear()` restores memory state. This consistent interface allows users to swap memory implementations without modifying agent code.

The memory interface interfaces smoothly with chains and agents using designated memory settings. When users send a memory instance to a chain, LangChain automatically loads relevant context before each LLM call and preserves the resulting interaction thereafter. This automation manages the complexity of context management, allowing users to focus on memory strategy rather than integration mechanics.

The following code displays the main memory interface pattern that all LangChain memory classes follow:

```
from langchain_classic.memory import ConversationBufferMemory
from langchain_openai import ChatOpenAI
from langchain_core.prompts import ChatPromptTemplate, MessagesPlaceholder
from langchain_core.output_parsers import StrOutputParser
from langchain_core.runnables.history import RunnableWithMessageHistory
from langchain_community.chat_message_histories import ChatMessageHistory

# Initialize memory with configuration
memory = ConversationBufferMemory(
  memory_key="chat_history",   # Key for template variable
  return_messages=True,       # Return as message objects
  input_key="input",         # Key for user input
  output_key="output"        # Key for AI response
)

# Save interaction manually
```

```
memory.save_context(
  {"input": "What's the weather forecast for Seattle?"},
  {"output": "The forecast shows rain throughout the week."}
)

# Load memory variables for use in prompts
context = memory.load_memory_variables({})
print(context["chat_history"]) # Access stored messages

# Integrate with chain for automatic context management.
# (ConversationChain is deprecated in LangChain 1.x — replaced by
# RunnableWithMessageHistory wrapping an LCEL chain.)
llm = ChatOpenAI(model="gpt-4o-mini", temperature=0.7)

prompt = ChatPromptTemplate.from_messages([
  ("system", "You are a helpful weather assistant."),
  MessagesPlaceholder(variable_name="chat_history"),
  ("human", "{input}"),
])
chain = prompt | llm | StrOutputParser()

# Per-session history store (swap for Redis/SQL in production)
store: dict[str, ChatMessageHistory] = {}

def get_session_history(session_id: str) -> ChatMessageHistory:
  if session_id not in store:
    store[session_id] = ChatMessageHistory()
  return store[session_id]

conversation = RunnableWithMessageHistory(
  chain,
  get_session_history,
  input_messages_key="input",
  history_messages_key="chat_history",
)

# Memory automatically loads and saves with each interaction
response = conversation.invoke(
  {"input": "Will it be sunny this weekend?"},
  config={"configurable": {"session_id": "user-1"}},
)
```

All LangChain memory classes share a common interface: `save_context()` records interactions, `load_memory_variables()` retrieves context, and `clear()` resets state allowing implementations to be swapped without changing agent code.

Tip: **Enable `verbose=True` in chains to examine exactly when and how memory is loaded and stored during execution. This visibility helps troubleshoot memory-related issues and understand the interaction flow.**

LangChain's memory **application programming interfaces** (**APIs**) are growing rapidly, notably around agent orchestration and persistent stores. While the architectural patterns in this chapter remain stable, readers should confirm class names and constructor signatures against the latest LangChain version.

Token consumption and memory efficiency

Memory systems suffer a fundamental constraint: language models have finite context windows. Every message stored in memory drains tokens from this window, leaving less room for instructions, retrieved information, and created responses. As discussions get longer, naive memory techniques quickly exhaust available context space.

Token consumption varies substantially between memory techniques. Full buffer memory storing 20 message exchanges could use 4,000 tokens, whereas a summary of the same conversation requires only 200 tokens. Window-based techniques restrict token usage by discarding old messages, trading perfect recall for consistent performance. Vector store memory sidesteps token restrictions totally by retrieving only relevant past interactions based on semantic similarity.

Production memory systems must balance opposing objectives: full context retention, token efficiency, retrieval accuracy, and computational cost. Buffer memory delivers flawless recall but scales poorly. Summaries compress effectively but lose details. Vector retrieval is scalable infinitely, but requires an embedding infrastructure. Entity memory collects data effectively but misses conversational nuance. Optimal solutions involve combining multiple tactics and dynamically responding to conversation dynamics.

Performance note: A typical GPT-4 conversation with ten message exchanges consumes approximately 2,000 tokens when using full buffer memory. Summary memory reduces this to 150-300 tokens while keeping 80-90% of critical context. For conversations beyond 20 exchanges, consider hybrid techniques that keep recent messages in full while summarizing previous history.

Memory architecture diagram

A resilient agent utilizes a central *Memory Controller*, *Memory Manager*, or agentic logic to decide the layer of memory to access based on the user's query. Throughout this chapter, Memory Controller, Memory Manager, and Memory Router refer to the same architectural role and are responsible for selecting, orchestrating, and retrieving memory across tiers.

For example, if a user asks, *What did I say earlier?*, the controller may look at the short-term buffer; if the user asks, *What is my home city?*, it starts a long-term vector search.

The following figure demonstrates the whole LangChain memory architecture, showing how different memory types, storage levels, and retrieval mechanisms interact together:

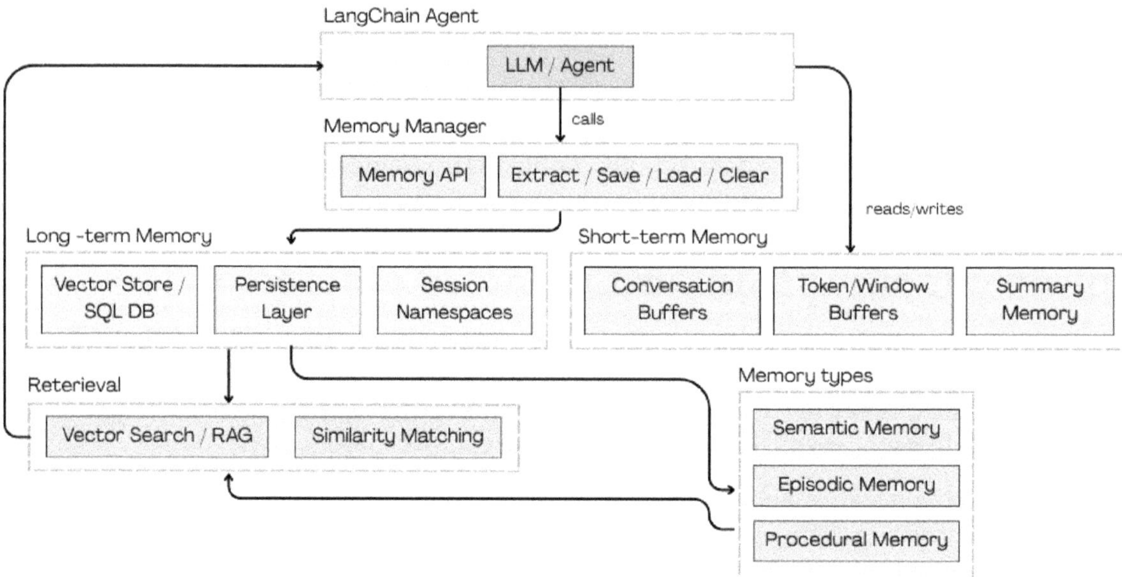

***Figure 7.1**: Complete LangChain memory architecture*

Working of the memory architecture

The figure shows the flow of information through LangChain's memory system, with the following aspects:

- **Agent execution**: The LLM/Agent writes communication history to Short-Term Memory (buffers, windows, summaries).
- **Memory management**: The agent accesses the Memory Manager API to persist or fetch context utilizing load/save/clear operations.
- **Long-term storage**: The memory manager interacts with Long-Term Memory backends (vector databases, SQL databases like PostgreSQL/MySQL/SQLite).
- **Memory categorization**: Information is categorized by Memory Types (semantic facts, episodic events, procedural rules).
- **Retrieval**: Vector search and similarity matching draw relevant long-term memories back into the agent's environment.

This hierarchy ensures that the agent retains a persistent personality and dynamic context without bombarding the LLM with irrelevant info. By storing active session data into long-term storage after a discussion ends, the agent *learns* from every contact.

LangChain memory classes and conceptual types

LangChain provides a rich ecosystem of memory solutions that correspond to varied architectural needs. Understanding both the concrete Python classes users use in code and the conceptual memory types they represent is vital for creating effective agent memory systems.

Memory classes available in LangChain

The following table summarizes the major memory classes provided by LangChain's Python API:

Memory class	Module/purpose
`ConversationBufferMemory`	Simple chat buffer storing full conversation history as text or messages.
`ConversationStringBufferMemory`	Same as above, returns string history.
`ConversationBufferWindowMemory`	Buffer with a sliding window of the most recent *k* interactions.
`ConversationTokenBufferMemory`	Conversation memory is limited by tokens (not turns).
`ConversationSummaryMemory`	Summarizes conversations as they progress.
`ConversationSummaryBufferMemory`	Buffer and summary hybrid.
`VectorStoreRetrieverMemory`	Stores and retrieves memory using a vector database.
`ConversationVectorStoreTokenBufferMemory`	Token-buffered memory backed by a vector store.
`CombinedMemory`	Combines multiple memory modules.
`ReadOnlySharedMemory`	Read-only memory wrapper.
`SimpleMemory`	Basic key/value store memory.
`BaseChatMemory`	Abstract base for chat memory classes.
Entity stores:	
– `ConversationEntityMemory`	Extracts and remembers entities.
– `InMemoryEntityStore`	In-memory backend for entity memory.
– `RedisEntityStore`	Redis-backed entity store.
– `SQLiteEntityStore`	SQLite-backed entity store.
– `UpstashRedisEntityStore`	Upstash Redis entity store.
Service-backed memories:	
– `ZepMemory / ZepCloudMemory`	Persistence via the Zep service.
– `MotorheadMemory`	Backed by Motorhead service.

***Table 7.2**: Major memory classes in LangChain Python API*

Note: **Most of these memory classes are utilized in chains or agents to keep conversational context across calls. Some older classes may be deprecated in recent versions, so always reference the latest LangChain documentation for current best practices.**

Conceptual memory types

Beyond the particular implementations, it is helpful to grasp the conceptual memory types that cognitive science and AI research define. The following notions influence how users construct their agent's memory system:

Conceptual memory type	What it represents
Short-term (thread) memory	Stores conversation history within a single session or thread.
Long-term memory	Persists knowledge across sessions and threads, often stored externally.
Semantic memory	Facts, concepts, and general information about the user or world.
Episodic memory	Experiences or specific interaction events (used for few-shot example prompting).
Procedural memory	Rules or instructions guiding task performance (e.g., system prompts or learned behaviors).

Table 7.3: Conceptual types of memory in AI systems

Tip: **When designing the agent's memory architecture, start by identifying which conceptual types are needed (e.g., I need semantic memory for user preferences and episodic memory for past interactions), then select the appropriate LangChain classes from Table 7.2 to implement them. For example, `VectorStoreRetrieverMemory` works well for semantic memory, while `ConversationEntityMemory` is ideal for tracking specific facts and entities.**

Implementing conversation buffers for context tracking

The most fundamental approach to offer an agent a sense of continuity is through conversation buffers. This strategy requires maintaining a sliding window of the most recent interactions and re-injecting them into the prompt for every new round. Without this method, an agent would interpret every follow-up question as an isolated occurrence, failing to resolve pronouns like *it* or *there*.

Standard conversation buffer memory

In LangChain, the `ConversationBufferMemory` serves as the key mechanism for session-level state management. It keeps a growing list of `HumanMessage` and `AIMessage` objects, ensuring the LLM sees the whole context of the current session.

The following code explains how to initialize a memory-aware weather agent using a standard buffer:

```
from langchain_classic.memory import ConversationBufferMemory
from langchain_openai import ChatOpenAI
from langchain.agents import create_tool_calling_agent, AgentExecutor
from langchain_core.prompts import ChatPromptTemplate, MessagesPlaceholder

# 1. Initialize Memory with a specific key for the prompt
# return_messages=True is essential for ChatModels
memory = ConversationBufferMemory(memory_key="chat_history", return_
messages=True)

# 2. Define a prompt that includes the history placeholder
prompt = ChatPromptTemplate.from_messages([
  ("system", "You are a helpful weather assistant. Use the chat history to
resolve context."),
  MessagesPlaceholder(variable_name="chat_history"), # Memory injected here
  ("human", "{input}"),
  ("placeholder", "{agent_scratchpad}")
])

# 3. Create the agent executor with memory enabled
llm = ChatOpenAI(model="gpt-4o-mini", temperature=0)
agent = create_tool_calling_agent(llm, tools, prompt)
executor = AgentExecutor(agent=agent, tools=tools, memory=memory,
verbose=True)

# 4. Run multi-turn conversation
response1 = executor.invoke({"input": "What is the weather in Seattle?"})
print(response1["output"])
# Output: "The current temperature in Seattle is 62°F with cloudy skies."

response2 = executor.invoke({"input": "Is it going to rain tomorrow?"})
print(response2["output"])
# Output: "Tomorrow in Seattle, there's a 70% chance of rain."
# Note: The agent knows "it" refers to Seattle from the conversation history

# 5. Inspect memory contents
print(memory.load_memory_variables({}))
# Output: {"chat_history": [HumanMessage("What is the weather in Seattle?"),
#               AIMessage("The current temperature..."), ...]}

memory.clear()
```

`ConversationBufferMemory` stores every message in full. Calling `save_context` adds a human/AI pair; `load_memory_variables` returns the full message list.

Managing token limits with sliding windows

While buffers are effective, they create a production challenge: context window overflow. If a conversation continues for dozens of turns, the history will eventually devour the entire token budget, resulting in expensive fees or API problems.

To fix this, users employ a **Sliding Window Buffer** (`ConversationBufferWindowMemory`). This alternative only stores the recent `K` interactions, deleting older messages to make the context size predictable, as follows:

```
from langchain_classic.memory import ConversationBufferWindowMemory

# Keep only the last 5 conversation turns (1 turn = 1 human msg + 1 AI msg)
window_memory = ConversationBufferWindowMemory(
  k=5,
  memory_key="chat_history",
  return_messages=True
)

# Example: Using window memory with an agent
from langchain.agents import AgentExecutor, create_tool_calling_agent
from langchain_core.prompts import ChatPromptTemplate, MessagesPlaceholder

prompt = ChatPromptTemplate.from_messages([
  ("system", "You are a weather assistant. Use chat history for context."),
  MessagesPlaceholder(variable_name="chat_history"),
  ("human", "{input}"),
  ("placeholder", "{agent_scratchpad}")
])

llm = ChatOpenAI(model="gpt-4o-mini", temperature=0)
agent = create_tool_calling_agent(llm, tools, prompt)
executor = AgentExecutor(agent=agent, tools=tools, memory=window_memory)

# Simulate 10 conversation turns
for i in range(10):
  executor.invoke({"input": f"What's the weather on day {i}?"})

# Only the last 5 turns are retained in memory
print(f"Memory contains {len(window_memory.load_memory_variables({})['chat_
```

```
history'])} messages")
# Output: "Memory contains 10 messages" (5 turns × 2 messages per turn)
```

Implementing token-aware buffer management

While window memory provides size restrictions, production systems need exact token count monitoring to prevent context overflow and API problems. The following code exhibits a managed buffer memory class that actively checks token usage and automatically prunes old messages when reaching limits:

```
from langchain_classic.memory import ConversationBufferMemory
from langchain_openai import ChatOpenAI
import tiktoken

class ManagedBufferMemory:
  """Buffer memory with automatic token limit management."""

  def __init__(self, max_tokens=2000, model="gpt-4o-mini"):
    self.memory = ConversationBufferMemory(
      memory_key="chat_history",
      return_messages=True
    )
    self.max_tokens = max_tokens
    self.model = model
    self.encoder = tiktoken.encoding_for_model(model)

  def count_tokens(self):
    """Count total tokens in current memory."""
    messages = self.memory.load_memory_variables({})["chat_history"]
    total_tokens = sum(
      len(self.encoder.encode(str(msg.content)))
      for msg in messages
    )
    return total_tokens

  def save_context(self, inputs, outputs):
    """Save context with token limit enforcement."""
    # Save new interaction
    self.memory.save_context(inputs, outputs)

    # Check token count
    current_tokens = self.count_tokens()
```

```
    # Remove oldest messages if over limit
    while current_tokens > self.max_tokens:
      messages = self.memory.load_memory_variables({})["chat_history"]
      if len(messages) <= 2: # Keep at least one exchange
        break

      # Remove oldest pair (human + AI message)
      messages = messages[2:]

      # Rebuild memory
      self.memory.clear()
      for i in range(0, len(messages), 2):
        if i + 1 < len(messages):
          self.memory.save_context(
            {"input": messages[i].content},
            {"output": messages[i+1].content}
          )

      current_tokens = self.count_tokens()

    return current_tokens

  def get_memory_stats(self):
    """Return memory statistics."""
    messages = self.memory.load_memory_variables({})["chat_history"]
    tokens = self.count_tokens()
    return {
      "message_count": len(messages),
      "token_count": tokens,
      "token_utilization": f"{(tokens / self.max_tokens) * 100:.1f}%",
      "capacity_remaining": self.max_tokens - tokens
    }

# Usage example with weather assistant
managed_memory = ManagedBufferMemory(max_tokens=2000)

# Simulate extended conversation
conversations = [
  ("What's the weather like in Seattle?", "Currently cloudy with light
rain..."),
  ("Will it clear up tomorrow?", "Tomorrow shows partly sunny
conditions..."),
  ("Good for outdoor photography?", "Yes, afternoon light should be
```

```
excellent...")
]

for user_input, ai_response in conversations:
  tokens_used = managed_memory.save_context(
    {"input": user_input},
    {"output": ai_response}
  )
  stats = managed_memory.get_memory_stats()
  print(f"Tokens: {stats['token_count']}/{managed_memory.max_tokens} "
     f"({stats['token_utilization']})")
```

Warning: **Buffer memory without token limitations will eventually cause API problems or quietly truncate history. Always incorporate monitoring and management for production deployments.**

Sequence diagram of buffer state transitions

The following diagram depicts how the buffer memory interacts with the agent and the user during a multi-turn weather query:

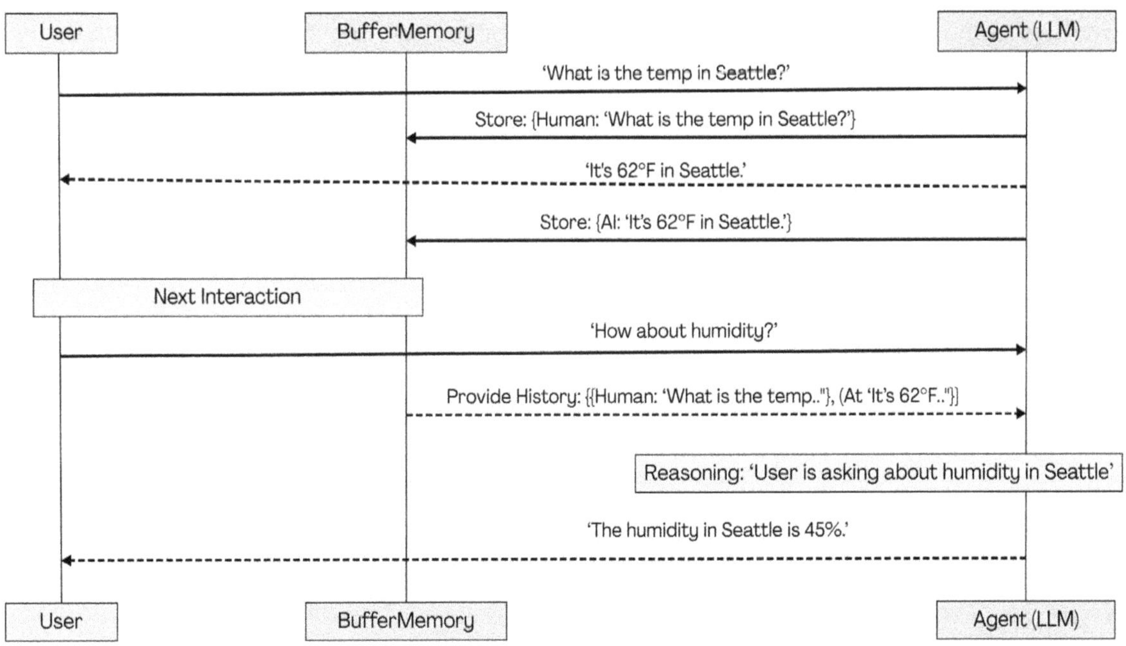

***Figure 7.2**: Conversation buffer state transition flow*

Production considerations for buffers

Table 7.4 summarizes the most common buffer management options and highlights when each one is appropriate, along with the key trade-offs users should expect in real deployments, as follows:

Strategy	Best use case	Trade-off
Full buffer	Short, high-precision tasks.	Expensive; risks token overflow.
Sliding window	Customer support/casual chat.	Agent *forgets* distant details.
Persistent buffer	Multi-day workflows.	Requires external database (Redis/MySQL/PostgreSQL).

***Table 7.4**: Comparison of buffer management strategies*

Persisting buffer memory to SQL databases

For production applications that require long-term memory and durability across sessions, users can integrate SQL databases like MySQL or PostgreSQL. The following code explains how to persist chat history to a PostgreSQL database:

```
from langchain_classic.memory import ConversationBufferMemory
from langchain_community.chat_message_histories import SQLChatMessageHistory
import os

# PostgreSQL connection string
connection_string = "postgresql://user:password@localhost:5432/agent_memory"

# Create SQL-backed message history for a specific session
sql_message_history = SQLChatMessageHistory(
  session_id="user_123_session_1",
  connection_string=connection_string
)

# Create memory using SQL backend
sql_memory = ConversationBufferMemory(
  chat_memory=sql_message_history,
  memory_key="chat_history",
  return_messages=True
)

# Use with agent as before
executor = AgentExecutor(agent=agent, tools=tools, memory=sql_memory)
```

```
# All conversation history is now persisted to PostgreSQL
# Can be retrieved in future sessions using the same session_id
```

Note: **For MySQL, simply change the connection string to `mysql://user:password@localhost:3306/agent_memory`. Both databases provide atomicity, consistency, isolation, durability (ACID) guarantees, ensuring conversation history is never lost even if the application crashes.**

Using SQLite for local development

For local development and testing, SQLite provides a simpler solution that does not involve setting up a database server. The following code demonstrates a complete agent initialization with SQLite-backed memory:

```
from langchain_classic.memory import ConversationBufferMemory
from langchain_community.chat_message_histories import SQLChatMessageHistory
from langchain.agents import create_tool_calling_agent, AgentExecutor
from langchain_core.prompts import ChatPromptTemplate, MessagesPlaceholder
from langchain_openai import ChatOpenAI
import uuid

class WeatherAgentWithMemory:
  def __init__(self, customer_name=None):
    # Generate unique session and customer IDs
    session_id = str(uuid.uuid4())
    customer_id = str(uuid.uuid4()) if not customer_name else None

    # Initialize SQLite-backed chat history
    self.message_history = SQLChatMessageHistory(
      connection='sqlite:///chat_history.db', # File-based SQLite
      session_id=session_id,
      table_name="chat_history"
    )

    # Create memory with SQL backend
    self.memory = ConversationBufferMemory(
      memory_key="chat_history",
      return_messages=True,
      chat_memory=self.message_history
    )

    # Initialize LLM and tools
    self.llm = ChatOpenAI(model="gpt-4o-mini", temperature=0)
    self.tools = [get_weather_forecast] # Your weather tools
```

```
        # Initialize agent with memory.
        # (initialize_agent + AgentType.CONVERSATIONAL_REACT_DESCRIPTION are
        # removed in LangChain 1.x — use create_tool_calling_agent instead.)
        prompt = ChatPromptTemplate.from_messages([
          ("system", "You are a helpful weather assistant. "
                     "Use the chat history to resolve context."),
          MessagesPlaceholder(variable_name="chat_history"),
          ("human", "{input}"),
          MessagesPlaceholder(variable_name="agent_scratchpad"),
        ])
        agent = create_tool_calling_agent(self.llm, self.tools, prompt)
        self.executor = AgentExecutor(
          agent=agent,
          tools=self.tools,
          memory=self.memory,
          verbose=True,
          max_iterations=6,
          handle_parsing_errors=True,
        )

      def chat(self, user_input: str):
        """Process user input and return agent response."""
        return self.executor.invoke({"input": user_input})["output"]

  # Usage example
  agent = WeatherAgentWithMemory(customer_name="Alex")
  response1 = agent.chat("What's the weather in Seattle?")
  response2 = agent.chat("How about tomorrow?") # Remembers Seattle from
  context
```

Note: **For an in-memory SQLite database (useful for testing or temporary sessions), use the connection string `sqlite:///:memory:` instead. Note that in-memory databases are lost when the application closes. Therefore, they are only ideal for ephemeral sessions or unit testing.**

Tip: **SQLite is great for prototyping and single-user applications. When scaling to production with several concurrent users, move to PostgreSQL or MySQL for improved concurrency handling and distributed deployments.**

In production speech agents, combine buffers with speech vocal activity detection (VAD) to guarantee the memory is not filled with background noise or false beginnings.

Intelligent summary memory for compression

While buffer and window memory store message history, they have intrinsic scalability limits. `ConversationSummaryMemory` solves this by utilizing an LLM to progressively summarize talks, reducing extensive dialogues into brief context while maintaining vital information. This strategy drastically reduces token consumption while retaining discourse coherence.

The summarization method operates incrementally: as new messages arrive, the LLM generates a revised summary combining the old summary with the new material. This gradual compression allows agents to keep context from discussions spanning hundreds of exchanges without exceeding token restrictions.

The following code demonstrates building optimized summary memory with a bespoke weather-focused summarization prompt:

```
from langchain_classic.memory import ConversationSummaryMemory
from langchain_openai import ChatOpenAI
from langchain_core.prompts import PromptTemplate

# Define custom summarization prompt for weather context
WEATHER_SUMMARY_PROMPT = PromptTemplate(
  input_variables=["summary", "new_lines"],
  template="""Progressively summarize the conversation about weather
planning.

Current summary:
{summary}

New conversation:
{new_lines}

Updated summary focusing on:
- Specific locations and dates mentioned
- Weather conditions discussed (temperature, precipitation, wind)
- Planning decisions made based on weather
- Concerns or preferences expressed
- Equipment or preparation discussed

Concise updated summary:"""
)

# Initialize LLM with custom summarization
llm = ChatOpenAI(model="gpt-4o-mini", temperature=0)
```

```
# Create memory with custom prompt
optimized_summary_memory = ConversationSummaryMemory(
  llm=llm,
  memory_key="history",
  return_messages=False,
  prompt=WEATHER_SUMMARY_PROMPT # Custom summarization logic
)

# Test summarization quality with weather planning conversation
test_interactions = [
  {
    "input": "I need weather info for a wedding in Portland on June 15th",
    "output": "June in Portland typically sees mild temperatures around 70°F
with occasional rain..."
  },
  {
    "input": "Should I rent a tent for outdoor seating?",
    "output": "Given the 30% rain chance that day, a tent would provide good
insurance..."
  },
  {
    "input": "What about wind for the ceremony?",
    "output": "Wind speeds should be calm, around 5-8 mph, suitable for
outdoor ceremonies..."
  }
]

# Save interactions and observe summarization
for interaction in test_interactions:
  optimized_summary_memory.save_context(
    {"input": interaction["input"]},
    {"output": interaction["output"]}
  )

# Display final summary and metrics
final_summary = optimized_summary_memory.load_memory_variables({})
print("=== Optimized Weather Summary ===")
print(final_summary["history"])
print("\n=== Compression Metrics ===")
print(f"Interactions summarized: {len(test_interactions)}")
original_tokens = sum(len(i['input']) + len(i['output']) for i in test_
interactions) // 4
summary_tokens = len(final_summary['history']) // 4
```

```
print(f"Original tokens: ~{original_tokens}")
print(f"Summary tokens: ~{summary_tokens}")
print(f"Compression ratio: {original_tokens/summary_tokens:.1f}x")
print(f"Key information retained: Location, Date, Weather Factors,
Decisions")
```

Tip: **Create domain-specific summarization prompts that clearly retain essential information kinds. For weather agents, keep locations and dates. For customer support, preserve issue details and resolution processes. For medical consultations, maintain symptoms and recommendations.**

Integrating vector storage for memory retrieval

While buffers and summaries are effective in tracking the immediate flow of a session, they struggle with long-term persistence across numerous days or weeks. When an agent needs to recall a user's specific preference expressed in the past, such as a preferred city or particular medical history, it relies on a vector store to provide long-term, retrieval-based memory.

Semantic retrieval process

Vector store memory works by transforming every past interaction into a numerical vector (embedding) and saving it in a specific database, such as Chroma, Pinecone, or **Facebook AI Similarity Search** (**FAISS**). When a user asks a new query, the agent does a similarity search to locate the most relevant former interactions and injects them into the current prompt.

The following code explains how to create a persistent long-term memory system utilizing Chroma and OpenAI embeddings:

```
from langchain_openai import OpenAIEmbeddings
from langchain_community.vectorstores import Chroma
from langchain_core.documents import Document

# 1. Setup persistent storage on disk
vectorstore = Chroma(
  persist_directory="./memory_db",
  embedding_function=OpenAIEmbeddings()
)

def add_to_long_term_memory(user_input: str, agent_output: str):
  """Encodes and stores a conversation turn as a single memory document."""
  memory_content = f"User: {user_input}\nAssistant: {agent_output}"
  vectorstore.add_documents([Document(page_content=memory_content)])

def retrieve_memories(query: str, k: int = 2):
```

```
    """Retrieves the top K most relevant past interactions based on the
query."""
    docs = vectorstore.similarity_search(query, k=k)
    return [doc.page_content for doc in docs]

# Example: If the user asks "What's the forecast for my home?",
# retrieve_memories("user home location") might return "User Alex lives in
Seattle"
```

When using vector-based memory, getting too many high-similarity results can overwhelm the prompt and introduce inappropriate or outdated context. In production systems, retrieval should be capped (usually k=3–5) and paired with recency or confidence heuristics to prevent semantic drift.

Sequence diagram of conversation state transitions

To reduce context window bloat, agents often follow a *tiered* state transition. Active messages exist in a short-term buffer, and after the session ends or the window is full, they are archived into the vector store for long-term recall.

Figure 7.3 illustrates the typical tiered workflow where recent messages live in short-term memory during the session, then get archived into a vector store so the agent can retrieve them later without inflating the prompt, as follows:

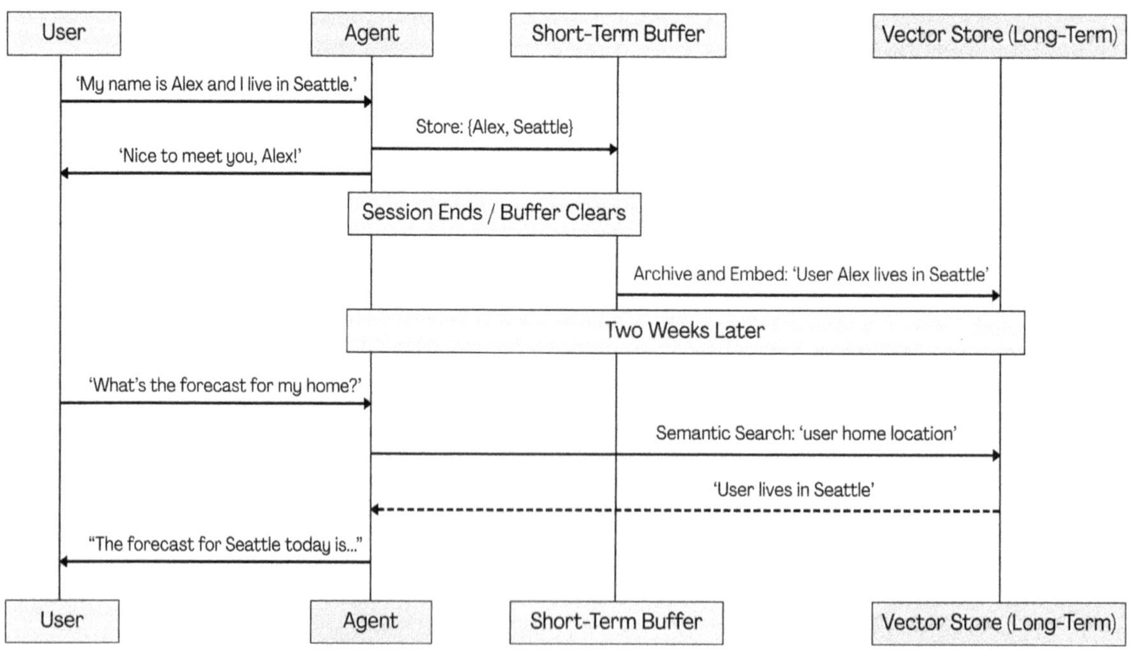

Figure 7.3: *State transition and archival sequence*

Comparison of retrieval-based memory strategies

Before integrating retrievalbased memory in production agents, it is crucial to understand how alternative memory techniques compare in terms of capacity, persistence, and retrieval behavior. While buffer memory excels at maintaining immediate conversational continuity, vector store memory provides scalable, longterm recall based on semantic relevance rather than recency.

The following comparison shows the actual tradeoffs between various approaches and clarifies when each tactic is most effective:

Feature	Buffer memory	Vector store memory
Search method	Chronological (Last N messages).	Semantic (Similarity search).
Capacity	Low (Limited by tokens).	High (Millions of interactions).
Persistence	Volatile (Session-based).	Permanent (Disk-based).
Best for	*It* and *That* references.	*Do you remember when...*

***Table 7.5**: Memory retrieval strategies*

It is important to note that when using vector stores for memory, users must provide metadata filtering. Without filtering for a specific `user_id`, a multi-user agent can mistakenly retrieve one user's sensitive data to answer another user's question.

Entity memory and knowledge graphs

Beyond mere text chunks or summaries, sophisticated agents must comprehend the relationships between the individual people, locations, and objects they encounter. Entity memory and knowledge graphs allow an agent to move beyond *searching for keywords* to *understanding concepts*, generating a more coherent and rational personality.

Applying entity memory for dynamic reference storage

Entity memory focuses on extracting and tracking individual *named entities* from a discussion. Instead of saving an entire paragraph, the agent extracts a table of data that it can update in real-time. In a weather-first environment, this allows the agent to distinguish between *Alex's home* and *Alex's travel destination* without confounding the two locations.

The following table depicts how a weather assistant tracks entities across a multi-turn dialogue:

Entity	Current detail	Contextual note
User	Alex	Prefers hiking on weekends.
Location	Seattle	Primary home; marked as *frequently rainy*.
Location	Portland	Destination for the upcoming Saturday trip.
Preference	Temperature	Uses Celsius for all readings.

***Table 7.6**: Entity memory tracking for a personalized assistant*

Using knowledge graphs to link relationships

While entity memory stores a simple list of facts, a knowledge graph (using technologies like Neo4j or LangChain's `GraphIndex`) stores this information as a web of interconnected nodes and edges. This structure allows the agent to execute graph traversal, enabling intricate reasoning that vector storage cannot simply mimic.

For example, if the agent knows *Diya likes hiking* and *Hiking requires sunshine*, it can proactively warn Diya of rain in Portland without being expressly asked about the hike.

Figure 7.4 shows how a knowledge graph can represent user preferences and locations as connected nodes and relationships, making it easier for an agent to reason over *who likes what* and *where* instead of relying only on keyword matching, as follows:

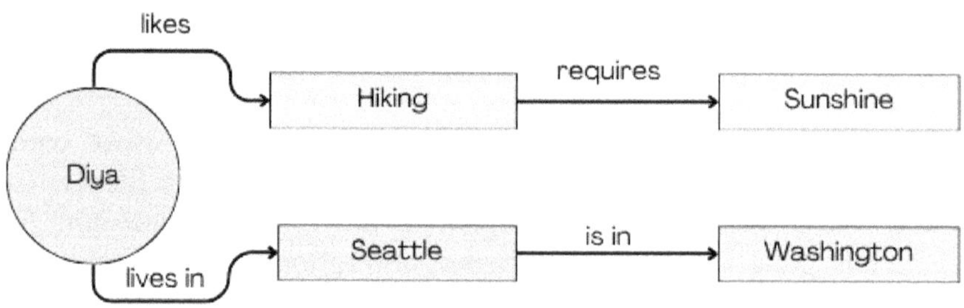

***Figure 7.4**: Knowledge graph visualization of user preferences*

Building conversational knowledge graphs

`ConversationKGMemory` provides a completely different approach by encoding conversation information as a graph of things and relationships. Instead of storing chronological messages or extracting individual data, it develops a network showing how concepts relate. This graph form facilitates complicated reasoning about relationships, multi-hop inferences, and the detection of indirect connections that linear memory overlooks.

Knowledge graphs flourish when interactions contain several interrelated things, where comprehending links counts as much as individual facts. Weather planning conversations automatically develop graphs: locations connect to seasons, seasons relate to activities, activities depend on equipment, producing a web of weather-informed decisions.

The following code demonstrates creating a knowledge graph memory for relationship tracking:

```
# Knowledge graph memory for relationship extraction
from langchain_community.memory.kg import ConversationKGMemory
from langchain_openai import ChatOpenAI
from langchain_core.prompts import ChatPromptTemplate
from langchain_core.output_parsers import StrOutputParser
from langchain_core.runnables import RunnablePassthrough

# Initialize LLM for knowledge extraction
llm = ChatOpenAI(model="gpt-4o-mini", temperature=0)

# Create knowledge graph memory
kg_memory = ConversationKGMemory(
  llm=llm,
  memory_key="knowledge_graph",
  return_messages=False
)

# Build conversation chain.
# (ConversationChain is deprecated in LangChain 1.x — replaced by an LCEL
# chain that injects KG context via RunnablePassthrough.assign and persists
# new turns through kg_memory.save_context.)
prompt = ChatPromptTemplate.from_messages([
  ("system",
   "You are a weather assistant. Use the knowledge graph context below "
   "to reason about relationships between entities.\n"
   "Knowledge graph:\n{knowledge_graph}"),
  ("human", "{input}"),
])

knowledge_agent = (
  RunnablePassthrough.assign(
    knowledge_graph=lambda x: kg_memory.load_memory_variables(
      {"input": x["input"]}
    )["knowledge_graph"]
  )
  | prompt
  | llm
  | StrOutputParser()
```

```
)

# Conversation revealing complex relationships
relationship_conversation = [
  "I am planning outdoor activities in the Pacific Northwest this summer.",
  "I particularly enjoy hiking and photography in alpine environments.",
  "Mount Rainier and the North Cascades are my target destinations.",
  "I prefer June through September for accessibility and weather.",
  "Wildflower blooms peak in July which is perfect for photography.",
  "I will need to prepare for variable mountain weather even in summer."
]

print("=== Knowledge Graph Memory Demonstration ===\n")

for idx, statement in enumerate(relationship_conversation, 1):
  response = knowledge_agent.invoke({"input": statement})
  kg_memory.save_context({"input": statement}, {"output": response})
  print(f"Turn {idx}: {statement}")
  print(f"Response: {response[:100]}...\n")

# Access the knowledge graph
print("=== Extracted Knowledge Graph ===\n")
kg_content = kg_memory.load_memory_variables({})
print(f"Knowledge Graph Structure:\n{kg_content}")
# Manually inspect the graph (if available)
if hasattr(kg_memory, 'kg'):
  print("\nGraph Entities and Relationships:")
  print(f"Entities: {list(kg_memory.kg.get_triples())}")
```

A knowledge graph is a structured representation of knowledge employing entities (nodes) and relationships (edges) that enables semantic reasoning and multi-hop inferences among related concepts.

Implementing entity-aware chains

While entity and knowledgegraph memory contain structured information and relationships, their full value is demonstrated when they are directly linked into conversational workflows. Entityaware chains enable agents to automatically extract, update, and reuse entity information during live interactions, allowing references such as names, places, and preferences to be resolved seamlessly between turns. The following example demonstrates how LangChain's entity memory can be integrated into chains to create agents that reason over structured facts without sacrificing conversational naturalness.

The following code demonstrates how to utilize LangChain's `ConversationEntityMemory` to automatically extract and recall information about certain entities during a weather consultation:

```
from langchain_classic.memory import ConversationEntityMemory
from langchain_openai import ChatOpenAI
from langchain_core.prompts import ChatPromptTemplate
from langchain_core.output_parsers import StrOutputParser
from langchain_core.runnables import RunnablePassthrough

llm = ChatOpenAI(model="gpt-4o-mini", temperature=0)

# Initialize entity memory
# This memory will create a store of facts about entities mentioned in the
chat
memory = ConversationEntityMemory(llm=llm)

# Create a conversation chain with entity awareness.
# (ConversationChain is deprecated; the LCEL chain below injects the entity
# store into the prompt via RunnablePassthrough.assign and persists new
# turns through memory.save_context.)
prompt = ChatPromptTemplate.from_messages([
  ("system",
   "You are a weather assistant. Use the entity context below to answer "
   "questions about people and places mentioned earlier in the
conversation.\n"
   "Entities:\n{entities}"),
  ("human", "{input}"),
])

entity_chain = (
  RunnablePassthrough.assign(
    entities=lambda x: memory.load_memory_variables({"input": x["input"]}).
get("entities", {})
  )
  | prompt
  | llm
  | StrOutputParser()
)

# Interaction 1: "Alex lives in Seattle and loves to hike on weekends."
# Memory result: { "Alex": "lives in Seattle, loves hiking" }
```

```
# Interaction 2: "What is the weather like where Alex lives?"
# The agent retrieves "Seattle" from the Alex entity record automatically.
```

Tip: **Use knowledge graphs when the agent needs to navigate hierarchical or logical relationships (e.g., "If A is part of B, and B is closed, then A is also closed"). For general "vibe" or history recall, Vector Stores remains the relatively cost-effective choice.**

As a rule of thumb, employ entity memory when facts are independent, and escalate to knowledge graphs when links between facts influence reasoning or decisionmaking.

Implementing hybrid memory by combining multiple approaches

In production-grade agents, focusing on a single memory approach generally leads to a *one-dimensional* personality. Hybrid memory architectures combine the strengths of several systems, such as the immediate context of a buffer, the efficiency of summaries, and the depth of a vector store, to create an agent that is both responsive and profoundly knowledgeable.

Designing adaptive memory systems

An adaptive memory system employs a *router* logic to select the memory layer that is most relevant to the current user intent. This ensures the agent does not spend tokens by getting long-term facts when the user is only providing a follow-up comment about the current sentence.

The following table illustrates how a hybrid system categorizes memory types for a weather agent:

Memory tier	Component	Data type	Primary function
Episodic	Conversation buffer	Recent raw messages	Resolving pronouns like *it* or *then*.
Semantic	Vector store	Historical facts	Recalling that the user lives in *Seattle*.
Relational	Knowledge graph	Interconnected nodes	Reasoning that *Seattle* implies *Rain gear*.
Compressed	Summary memory	Narrative overview	Tracking the general *vibe* of a long session.

***Table 7.7**: Hybrid memory tiers for intelligent agents*

Workshop implementing a persistent weather assistant

In this workshop, users will construct a weather assistant that uses **CombinedMemory** to manage both short-term dialogue and long-term user preferences. The agent will remember a user's home city and their choice for metric units across separate sessions.

The following code demonstrates how to organize many memory classes into a single agent using LangChain's `CombinedMemory` utility:

```
from langchain_classic.memory import (
  ConversationBufferMemory,
  ConversationSummaryMemory,
  CombinedMemory
)
from langchain_openai import ChatOpenAI

llm = ChatOpenAI(model="gpt-4o-mini", temperature=0)

# 1. Short-term episodic memory
conv_memory = ConversationBufferMemory(
  memory_key="chat_history_lines",
  input_key="input"
)

# 2. Long-term summary memory
summary_memory = ConversationSummaryMemory(
  llm=llm,
  input_key="input",
  memory_key="conversation_summary"
)

# 3. Combine them into a single memory object
# This allows the prompt to access {chat_history_lines} and {conversation_
summary}
memory = CombinedMemory(memories=[conv_memory, summary_memory])

# 4. Define a prompt that utilizes both tiers
prompt_template = """The following is a friendly conversation.
Summary of distant past: {conversation_summary}
Recent turns: {chat_history_lines}
Human: {input}
AI:"""
```

```
# Now the agent can balance immediate context with the 'big picture'
```

Memory state transition diagram

Managing the lifecycle of a memory, from a live message to an archived vector, is crucial for performance. The following figure is a sequence diagram that visualizes how a *new fact* (the user's residence) is processed and eventually relocated to persistent storage:

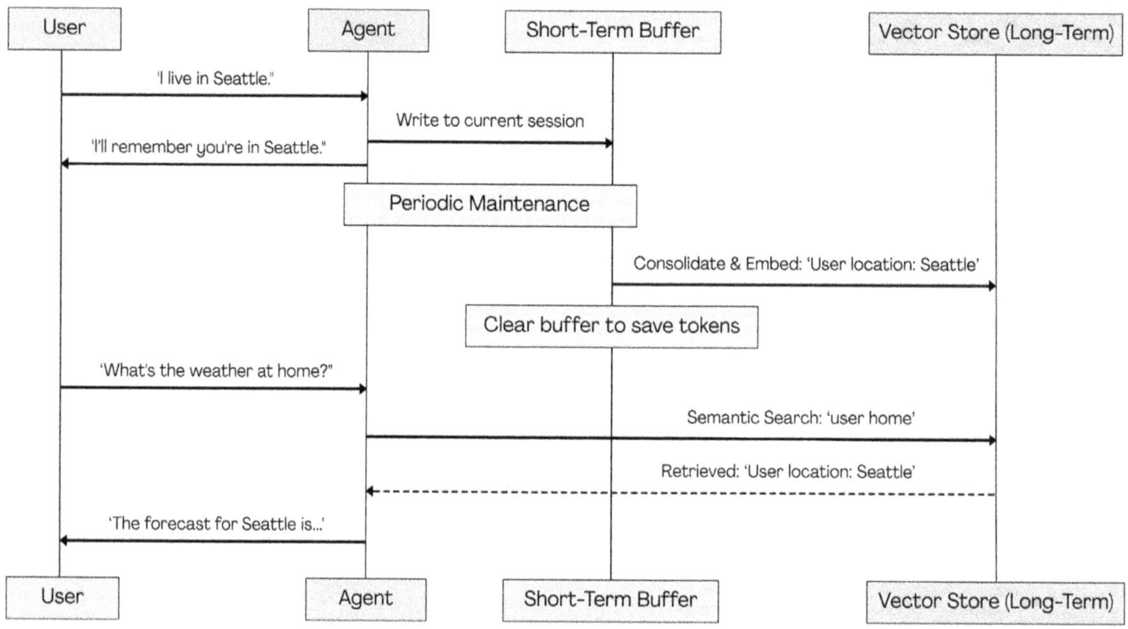

***Figure 7.5**: Hybrid memory lifecycle and retrieval flow*

Figure 7.5 visualizes the end-to-end lifecycle of context in a hybrid memory design, showing how new turns flow through short-term buffers, get summarized or archived for long-term storage, and are later retrieved to enrich future prompts.

Advanced dialog with adaptive memory

Beyond only *storing* data, adaptive memory systems can track sentiment-driven preferences. If the agent's summary memory reveals that the user was frustrated by a previous lengthy technical explanation, the adaptive system can alter the *personality* variable in the prompt to be more succinct and straightforward for future turns.

Tip: **When adopting hybrid memory, always prioritize the conversation buffer for the current prompt. Long-term memories should be considered as contextual hints rather than primary instructions to avoid confusing the LLM if prior material significantly contradicts the current discourse.**

Designing adaptive memory systems for intelligent agents

The most complex memory systems adjust their method based on conversation characteristics. Short interactions employ buffer memory for convenience. Long dialogues transition to summaries. Fact-heavy interactions activate entity extraction. Topic-diverse exchanges employ vector search. This dynamic adaptation optimizes for both performance and context quality.

Implementing adaptive memory selection

Once the necessity for adaptive memory behavior is recognized, the next step is to turn these concepts into real decision logic. Implementing adaptive memory selection needs agents to monitor conversation characteristics, such as length, token usage, entity density, and subject shifts, and dynamically determine the most appropriate memory method at runtime. The following implementation demonstrates how to operationalize this intelligence, enabling agents to easily swap memory approaches while keeping conversational coherence and performance.

We start by initializing the manager with all three memory strategies from the chapter sections 7.2–7.4, alongside tracking counters for conversation analytics:

```
import re
from langchain_openai import ChatOpenAI
from langchain_classic.memory import (
    ConversationBufferMemory,
    ConversationSummaryMemory,
    ConversationEntityMemory
)
from typing import Literal, Dict, Any
import tiktoken

class AdaptiveMemoryManager:
    """Intelligently selects memory strategy based on conversation
characteristics."""

    def __init__(self):
        self.llm = ChatOpenAI(model="gpt-4o-mini", temperature=0)
```

```
        self.encoder = tiktoken.encoding_for_model("gpt-4o-mini")
        self.turn_count = 0
        self.total_tokens = 0
        self.topic_diversity = 0
        self.entity_count = 0
        # Backing state for the two metrics above — kept private so callers
        # interact only with the public counters.
        self._unique_tokens: set[str] = set()
        self._total_tokens_seen = 0

        self.strategies = {
            "buffer": ConversationBufferMemory(return_messages=True),
            "summary": ConversationSummaryMemory(llm=self.llm),
            "entity": ConversationEntityMemory(llm=self.llm)
        }
        self.current_strategy = "buffer"


    @staticmethod
    def _extract_entities(text: str) -> list[str]:
        """Cheap proper-noun heuristic: capitalised words not at sentence
start."""
        return re.findall(r"(?<![.!?]\s)\b[A-Z][a-zA-Z]{2,}\b", text)

    def _update_metrics(self, text: str) -> None:
        """Refresh entity_count and topic_diversity from the latest turn.

        Without this update the entity/diversity branches in
        _select_optimal_strategy would be dead code — the counters would
        stay at their initial values forever and the manager could never
        adapt on those dimensions.
        """
        self.entity_count += len(self._extract_entities(text))
        words = re.findall(r"\b\w+\b", text.lower())
        self._unique_tokens.update(words)
        self._total_tokens_seen += len(words)
        if self._total_tokens_seen:
            self.topic_diversity = len(self._unique_tokens) / self._total_
tokens_seen
```

The core decision logic uses a simple rule-based approach. Short conversations stay with buffer memory; longer ones graduate to summary; entity-heavy conversations switch to entity memory:

```
    def _select_optimal_strategy(self) -> Literal["buffer", "summary",
"entity"]:
        if self.turn_count < 5:
            return "buffer"                          #A
        elif self.total_tokens > 2000:
            return "summary"                          #B
        elif self.entity_count > 10:
            return "entity"                           #C
        elif self.topic_diversity > 0.7:
            return "summary"
        else:
            return "buffer"

#A Short conversations keep full verbatim history
#B Token-heavy conversations compress via summarization
#C Entity-dense conversations track structured knowledge
```

Each time context is saved, the manager counts tokens and checks whether the strategy should change. If the optimal strategy differs from the current one, it triggers a transition:

```
    def save_context(self, inputs: Dict, outputs: Dict):
        self.turn_count += 1
        text = str(inputs) + str(outputs)
        self.total_tokens += len(self.encoder.encode(text))
        self._update_metrics(text)

        self.strategies[self.current_strategy].save_context(inputs, outputs)

        optimal = self._select_optimal_strategy()
        if optimal != self.current_strategy:
            print(f"[Adapting: {self.current_strategy} → {optimal}]")
            self.current_strategy = optimal                #A

    def load_memory_variables(self, inputs: Dict) -> Dict:
        return self.strategies[self.current_strategy].load_memory_
variables(inputs)

#A Production systems would migrate context from the old strategy here
```

Let us demonstrate the adaptive behavior with a conversation that starts short and grows longer, triggering a strategy transition:

```
adaptive_manager = AdaptiveMemoryManager()

conversations = [
    ("What's the weather in Seattle today?", "Currently 55°F and cloudy."),
    ("Will it rain?", "30% chance of light rain this afternoon."),
    ("What about tomorrow?", "Tomorrow looks sunnier, high of 62°F."),
    ("I'm planning a week-long trip. What's the extended forecast?",
     "The 7-day forecast shows sun and clouds, 50-65°F..."),
    ("Should I pack rain gear?", "Definitely. Mid-week shows higher rain
chances..."),
    ("What about wind conditions for sailing?",
     "Wind speeds will be moderate, 10-15 mph, suitable for sailing...")
]

for idx, (user_msg, ai_msg) in enumerate(conversations, 1):
    print(f"Turn {idx} [{adaptive_manager.current_strategy}]: {user_
msg[:50]}")
    adaptive_manager.save_context({"input": user_msg}, {"output": ai_msg})
```

Performance note: Strategy transitions involve computing overhead. Implement hysteresis (delay before switching back) to minimize thrashing between techniques when conversation features change.

Users can also measure the retrieval hit rate, which is the percentage of retrieved memories that meaningfully influence the response.

The following are the things to remember:

- Adaptive memory systems select the best technique based on how the conversation is evolving.
- Common decision signals include turn count, token usage, entity density, and topic diversity.
- When switching strategies, migrate or summarize context so the agent stays coherent across turns.
- Use hysteresis to prevent thrashing (frequent switching) when signals fluctuate near thresholds.
- In production, log strategy choices and outcomes to tune thresholds and catch regressions.

Conclusion

This chapter demonstrated how stateless agents become context-aware systems thanks to LangChain's persistent memory. The memory hierarchy, trade-offs between short- and long-term memory, token constraints, and typical architectural patterns like a memory manager/router were all covered by the readers. They then used useful continuity strategies, such as token-aware pruning, sliding windows, and full buffers, to maintain coherence in conversations while avoiding context overflow. Lastly, readers used progressive summarization and summary memory to condense lengthy histories while maintaining crucial context.

The chapter then used retrieval and structure to expand memory beyond transcripts. Semantic recall from extensive histories was made possible by vector store memory, with a focus on safety and persistence issues like metadata filtering in multi-user systems. Agents can store facts and relationships to support richer reasoning than just linear chat history, as demonstrated by entity memory and knowledge-graph memory. These methods were integrated into hybrid and adaptive memory designs, leading to a workshop that used strategy-selection logic and several memory tiers to create a persistent weather assistant.

Readers expand on this foundation in the next chapter by incorporating emotional intelligence, which includes the ability to recognize sentiment and subtle states, modify tone and verbosity, and apply sympathetic response and escalation patterns for delicate circumstances.

CHAPTER 8
Designing Emotion-aware Agents

Introduction

Emotional intelligence represents the next major advancement in **artificial intelligence** (**AI**) agent design. Traditional agents are great at processing facts and getting things done. Emotion-aware agents, on the other hand, can recognize emotions, sense urgency, and adjust how they talk to people based on how they feel. This ability changes agents from neutral tools into responsive systems that can help when it matters most by reducing frustration, boosting confidence, and providing help.

This chapter covers the technical basics of building agents that understand and respond to human emotions. Readers will build sentiment analysis pipelines, design emotion-aware prompts, and develop adaptive response systems that remain empathetic across a variety of situations. They will learn more than just how to sort emotions into categories. Readers will learn to spot subtle emotional states, plan how to handle crises, and build agents that demonstrate emotional intelligence in real life.

The weather advisory domain is a good place to test skills related to emotional awareness. Users deal with weather systems during stressful times, such as severe storm warnings, travel planning, or anger over inaccurate forecasts. Finally, readers will be able to create production-ready patterns for domains, such as customer service, healthcare support, educational tutoring, and other fields where human emotions are important, by designing agents that can recognize and appropriately respond to different emotional states.

Structure

This chapter covers the following topics:

- Understanding emotional intelligence in AI systems
- Implementing multimodal emotion detection

- Adaptive prompts and empathetic responses
- Simulating real-world emotion detection scenarios
- Implementing crisis management using adaptive logic
- Building an emotion-aware weather agent

Objectives

Readers will learn how to make AI agents that can understand and respond to human emotions with the right amount of empathy and flexibility. The chapter starts with the basics of emotional intelligence, explaining the difference between sentiment analysis and emotion detection and laying the groundwork for affective computing in AI systems.

Then, readers will use LangChain and OpenAI to make real-world sentiment analysis systems that accurately sort emotional states from text input. The chapter covers emotion-aware prompt engineering, teaching readers to create templates that adapt to the mood of the conversation and the person being addressed.

Readers will create algorithms to generate sympathetic responses that maintain the right tone across a wide range of emotional situations, from routine questions to high-stress crises. Crisis management patterns show how to recognize urgent situations, use de-escalation techniques, and escalate when action is needed.

In this chapter, readers will create a full-fledged weather advisory agent that is aware of the user's emotions, adapts its communication, and offers help when the weather is bad. This hands-on project brings together all the chapter's ideas into a working solution that readers can use for customer service, healthcare support, tutoring, and any other area where emotional intelligence is important.

Understanding emotional intelligence in AI systems

Emotional intelligence enables agents to interpret not only what users say, but also how they say it. By understanding emotional cues such as dissatisfaction, worry, or joy, agents may respond with an appropriate tone and tempo, boosting both trust and usability. This transformation transforms agents from simple tools into conversational partners that can de-escalate tension or celebrate accomplishments with the user.

Sentiment vs. emotion classification

A crucial distinction in emotional AI is the contrast between broad sentiment and granular emotion. Sentiment analysis typically classifies information on a one-dimensional scale (positive, negative, or neutral), which is effective for high-level monitoring. Emotion classification, however, distinguishes psychological states such as joy, rage, sadness, and fear, enabling more precise behavioral adjustments.

Emotion-aware systems often incorporate different categorization techniques depending on accuracy goals, latency constraints, and available input modalities. *Table 8.1* compares common sentiment and emotion classification techniques and their practical use cases, as follows:

Method	Capability	Complexity	Primary use case
VADER/TextBlob	Rule-based sentiment scoring	Low	Rapid text sentiment tagging.
Hugging Face Transformers	Multi-class emotion labeling	Medium	Detecting nuanced states like *frustration*.
Multimodal analysis	Acoustic features and text	High	Identifying urgency in a user's voice.
Large language model (LLM) contextual analysis	Zero-shot *vibe* extraction	Low-Med	Summarizing emotional history in memory.

***Table 8.1**: Comparison of emotion and sentiment classification tools*

Implementing basic sentiment analysis

Before building complex emotion-aware systems, it is crucial to start with simple sentiment analysis.

The following code demonstrates using OpenAI for sentiment classification:

```
# Simple sentiment analysis using OpenAI
from dotenv import load_dotenv
from langchain_openai import ChatOpenAI
from langchain_core.prompts import ChatPromptTemplate
from langchain_core.output_parsers import StrOutputParser

load_dotenv()

llm = ChatOpenAI(model="gpt-4o-mini", temperature=0)
parser = StrOutputParser()

def analyze_sentiment(text: str) -> dict:
    """Classify text as positive, negative, or neutral."""
    prompt = ChatPromptTemplate.from_messages([
        ("system",
         "Classify the sentiment as: positive, negative, or neutral. "
```

```
         "Respond with ONLY the classification word."),
        ("human", "{text}"),
    ])
    chain = prompt | llm | parser
    sentiment = chain.invoke({"text": text}).strip().lower()
    return {"text": text, "sentiment": sentiment}


# Example usage
messages = [
  "The forecast was perfect! Saved our event.",
  "Your predictions are completely wrong.",
  "What is the temperature today?"
]

for msg in messages:
  result = analyze_sentiment(msg)
  print(f"{result['text'][:40]}... → {result['sentiment']}")
```

While sentiment ratings provide a valuable starting point, many real-world interactions require a deeper understanding of emotional subtlety. Users may convey displeasure, fear, or disappointment using sophisticated wording that falls outside simple positive or negative categories. To capture these finer emotional signals without training unique models, agents can use fewshot learning with LLMs, enabling domainspecific emotion classification through carefully curated examples.

Building custom emotion classifiers with few-shot learning

While basic sentiment analysis offers positive/negative/neutral classifications, many applications require more nuanced emotion identification (joy, wrath, fear, sadness, anxiety, frustration). Rather than training typical **machine learning** (**ML**) models, which require massive labeled datasets and computational resources, users may use LLMs with few-shot learning to build domain-specific emotion classifiers.

Few-shot learning involves giving an LLM a small number of labeled examples (usually three to ten per emotion class) in the prompt. The model learns the classification pattern from these instances and applies it to fresh text. This approach offers several advantages: no model training required, fast deployment, easy tweaking of emotion categories, and good performance on domain-specific text.

Use few-shot learning to construct domain-specific classifiers without model training, as follows:

```
# Custom emotion classifier with few-shot learning

FEW_SHOT_EXAMPLES = """Examples:
"Forecast perfect! Our wedding was amazing!" → joy
"I'm really worried about the tornado warning" → anxiety
"Your predictions are always completely wrong" → frustration
"Rain again all week? I'm so disappointed" → sadness
"ARE YOU KIDDING ME? THIS IS OUTRAGEOUS!" → anger
"What's the temperature today?" → neutral
"The storm flooding our basement is terrifying" → fear"""


def classify_emotion(text: str) -> dict:
    """Classify emotion and intensity using few-shot examples."""
    prompt = ChatPromptTemplate.from_messages([
        ("system",
         f"{FEW_SHOT_EXAMPLES}\n\n"
         "Classify the emotion and intensity (low/medium/high).\n"
         "Format: emotion,intensity"),
        ("human", "{text}"),
    ])
    chain = prompt | llm | StrOutputParser()
    result = chain.invoke({"text": text}).strip().lower()
    parts = [p.strip() for p in result.split(",")]
    return {
        "text": text,
        "emotion": parts[0] if parts else "neutral",
        "intensity": parts[1] if len(parts) > 1 else "medium",
    }
```

It is important to select a few-shot example that covers the domain's distinctive patterns. Weather messaging demonstrates fear about storms and displeasure about forecasts that deviate from regular customer service.

Detecting emotion alone is insufficient unless those signals actually influence agent behavior. Emotion-aware agents, therefore, introduce emotional intelligence as an architectural layer rather than a post-processing phase. By isolating emotion detection from core thinking, systems reliably modify prompts, tool selection, and response tone based on emotional context while retaining clean design boundaries.

Emotional awareness architecture

In a production LangChain workflow, emotional intelligence works as a middleware *sensor*. Before the main agent reasoning occurs, the system routes the user's input through a classifier to set an emotional context variable. This variable then affects the system prompt or tool-selection logic.

The following figure depicts this *Classify-Adjust-Respond* cycle:

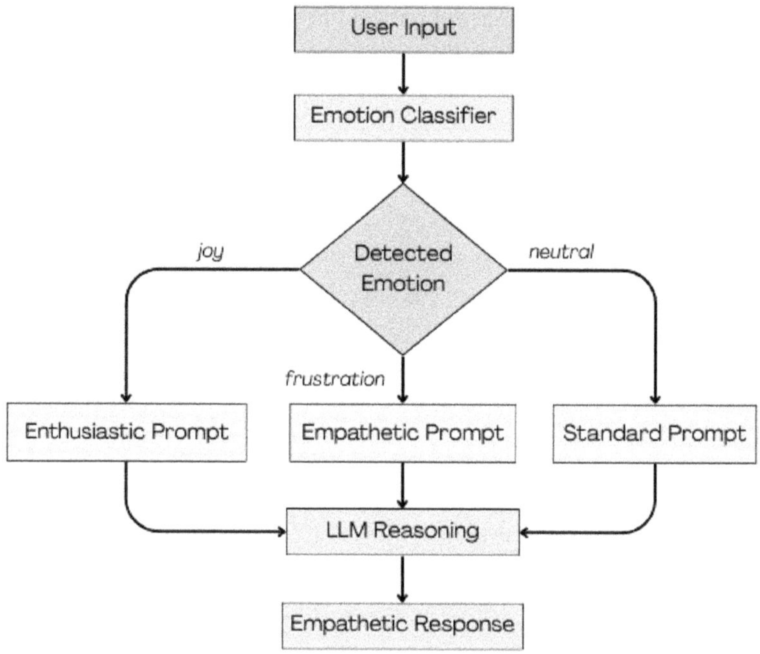

***Figure 8.1**: Adaptive prompt routing based on detected emotion*

With this architecture, the agent can dynamically rotate its personality. For example, a weather agent who is displeased with a rainy forecast can proactively recommend indoor activities instead of just repeating the temperature readings. This technique ensures that the agent's logic remains based in both factual facts and human context.

> Note: **The routing logic in this chapter assumes the LLM returns one of the recognized emotion labels. In production, add an output-validation step that maps unexpected labels to "Neutral" and logs the raw value for monitoring.**

Text alone does not always communicate emotional intensity, urgency, or sincerity. In spoken and voiceenabled interactions, users express emotional cues through fluctuations in pitch, intensity, and speech rhythm that may never surface in written language. Multimodal emotion detection augments textual analysis with audio inputs, allowing agents to more accurately identify highstakes emotional states such as anguish, fright, or enthusiasm.

End-to-end emotion-aware agent pipeline

This section shows the end-to-end control flow that an emotion-aware agent follows on every turn. The user's message enters the pipeline and is evaluated for both *emotion* (what the user is feeling) and *intensity* (how strongly they are expressing it). That structured label is then combined with situational context, including location, prior conversation turns, and active alerts, to decide which response path is safe and appropriate: a standard informational reply, an empathy-adjusted prompt strategy, or a crisis protocol that prioritizes immediate safety actions and escalation. This separation of detection, evaluation, routing, and generation keeps the agent's behavior predictable and testable as users harden it for production.

Understanding how all emotion-aware components interact together is critical for production deployment. The following figure demonstrates the whole processing flow from user input to emotion detection, context evaluation, behavior selection, and response generation:

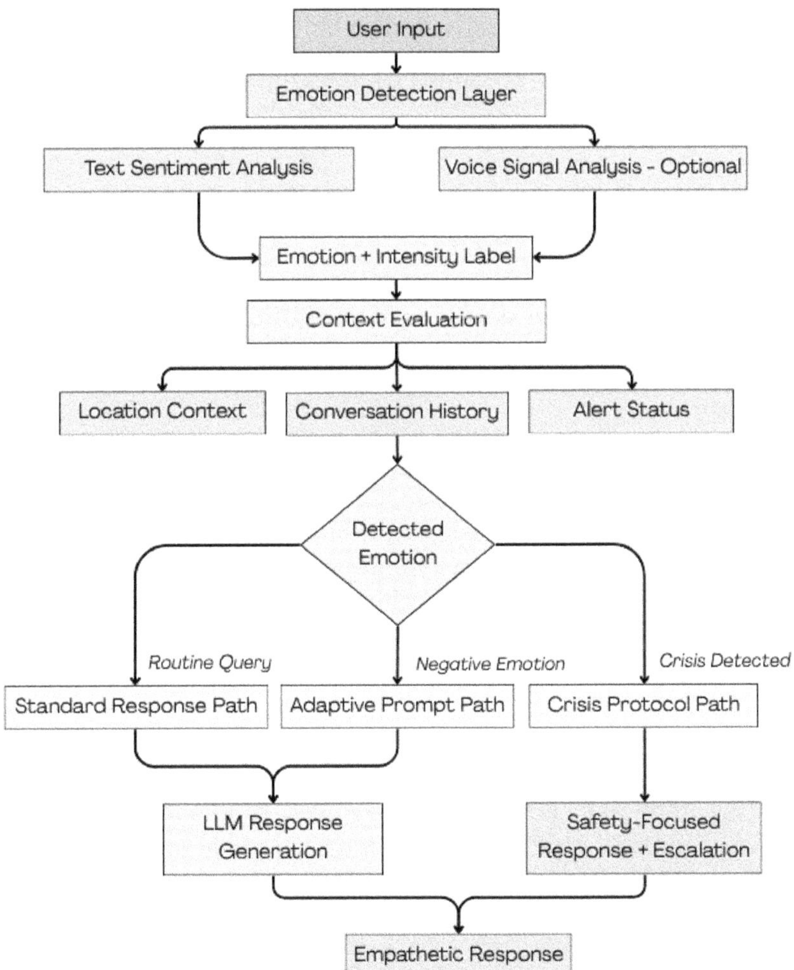

***Figure 8.2**: Complete emotion-aware agent processing pipeline*

This pipeline depicts the decision flow, as follows:

- **Emotion detection layer**: Analyzes user input through text sentiment (always) and speech signals (optional for voice channels).
- **Emotion and intensity label**: Combines detection information into structured emotion classification with intensity (low / medium / high).
- **Context evaluation**: Enriches emotion data with situational information, including user location, conversation history, and active alerts.
- **Behavior selector**: Routes to optimal reaction strategy based on emotion severity and context.
- **Response paths**: Defines the response branch (standard, adaptive prompt, or crisis protocol) based on the selected behavior strategy.
- **Standard**: Neutral emotions receive beneficial, informational answers.
- **Adaptive prompt**: Negative emotions trigger empathy-adjusted prompts.
- **Crisis protocol**: High-intensity distress activates safety protocols and human escalation.
- **Response generation**: LLM generates contextually suitable responses, or a crisis protocol gives urgent safety advice.

Tip: **In production, store emotion detection data with conversation turns to follow the emotional trajectory. Detecting escalation patterns (frustration | rage | crisis) provides preemptive intervention before situations become serious.**

Implementing multimodal emotion detection

Relying primarily on language can mask emotional intensity, urgency, or authenticity. In voiceenabled interactions, users express emotion through pitch, loudness, and rhythm, which are signals that are typically imperceptible in written language. Multimodal emotion detection integrates textual analysis with auditory clues to deliver a more accurate emotional interpretation.

Extracting emotional cues from voice signals

Voice agents interpret emotion by extracting certain acoustic elements from the raw audio data before or during transcription. These elements serve as indicators of the user's psychological state. The elements are as follows:

- **Pitch (fundamental frequency)**: Rising pitch frequently correlates with tension or excitement, whereas a consistent, low pitch may signify sadness or tranquility.

- **Energy and intensity**: Great volume and intensity often convey rage or great urgency, whereas low intensity suggests exhaustion or reluctance.
- **Speech rhythm and tempo**: Rapid speech typically implies tension or haste, while considerable pauses can reflect doubt.

In production systems, emotional information from diverse modalities must be merged into a unified, actionable interpretation. Rather than considering text and speech analysis as distinct outputs, a good empathy engine blends linguistic sentiment with acoustic data to infer the prevalent emotional state. The tool in the following section demonstrates how multimodal signals can be combined into a unified emotion classification technique.

Building a multimodal emotion classifier tool

A production-ready empathy engine utilizes a classifier to integrate text-based sentiment with these acoustic measurements. The following code describes a tool that gets both the transcript and simulated voice data to identify the most likely emotional state:

```
from langchain_core.tools import tool

@tool
def detect_multimodal_emotion(transcript: str, pitch_hz: float, intensity_db:
float) -> str:
  """
  Analyzes transcript content alongside voice metrics to identify emotional
state.
  Use this to inform empathetic reasoning in high-stakes environments.
  """
  # Identify linguistic triggers
  negative_words = ["not", "fail", "error", "terrible", "emergency"]
  has_negative_text = any(word in transcript.lower() for word in negative_
words)

  # Logic: High intensity + negative text signals a state of frustration
  if intensity_db > 75 and has_negative_text:
    return "Frustrated/High Urgency"

  # Logic: High pitch variation without negative triggers signals joy
  elif pitch_hz > 200:
    return "Joy/Excitement"

  else:
    return "Neutral"
```

Technical comparison of modality impact

The following table demonstrates how incorporating speech intelligence enhances the accuracy of emotion recognition compared to text-only systems:

Modality	Key indicators	Strength	Limitation
Text only	Sentiment keywords, punctuation.	High semantic clarity.	Misses sarcasm and tone.
Voice only	Pitch, energy, tempo.	Captures raw urgency.	Misses specific context.
Multimodal	Combined linguistic and acoustic features.	Highest overall accuracy.	Higher computational cost.

***Table 8.2**: Impact of modalities on emotion detection accuracy*

Tip: **In telemedicine or safety-critical weather circumstances, always employ multimodal detection to indicate urgency. A user calmly saying "there is a fire" requires a different response than a person shouting the same words with great vocal power.**

Using LLM-based emotion classification

While external libraries exist for emotion detection, LangChain agents can employ LLMs directly for emotion categorization without any training. This method is particularly helpful for domain-specific cases where users may include relevant examples in the prompt.

The following code demonstrates LLM-based emotion classification with OpenAI:

```
# LLM-based emotion classification using OpenAI
from langchain_openai import ChatOpenAI
from langchain.prompts import ChatPromptTemplate
from langchain_core.output_parsers import StrOutputParser

# Create emotion classification chain
emotion_classifier_prompt = ChatPromptTemplate.from_messages([
  ("system", """Classify the emotion in weather-related user messages.
Output ONLY one word: Joy, Neutral, or Frustrated.

Examples:
- "Perfect weather for my outdoor wedding!" → Joy
- "What is the temperature today?" → Neutral
- "The forecast ruined my weekend plans!" → Frustrated"""),
  ("human", "{text}")
```

```
])

llm = ChatOpenAI(model="gpt-4o-mini", temperature=0)

emotion_classifier = emotion_classifier_prompt | llm | StrOutputParser()

# Classify emotions
test_messages = [
  "This rain completely destroyed my hiking plans",
  "Thanks for the accurate forecast!",
  "Will it rain tomorrow?",
  "Your predictions are always wrong!"
]

print("=== Emotion Classification ===")
for message in test_messages:
  emotion = emotion_classifier.invoke({"text": message})
  print(f"'{message}' → {emotion}")
```

The best practice is to use a few-shot sample in the system prompt to steer the LLM toward consistent classifications. For production, cache results for popular words to save **application programming interface** (**API**) costs and latency.

Real-world emotion detection scenarios

Different domains require different priorities for emotion detection. Healthcare promotes distress detection (using conservative criteria to avoid missing true emergencies), customer support focuses on dissatisfaction and urgency, while weather planning emphasizes displeasure and anxiety about activity disruption.

The following code implements scenario-specific detection with adequate sensitivity:

```
# Scenario-specific emotion detection
def detect_scenario_emotion(text: str, scenario: str) -> dict:
  """Detect emotion with scenario-appropriate thresholds.

  This is a deliberately simple keyword screen — fast, deterministic, and
  useful as a pre-filter. It will miss synonyms, negation, and idiomatic
  variations that show up in real user text. For production, layer this in
  front of the LLM-based classifier (see "Using LLM-based emotion
  classification") and treat the keyword hit as a hint, not a verdict.
```

```
    """
    urgent_words = ["emergency", "urgent", "scared", "danger", "pain"]
    negative_words = ["terrible", "awful", "ruined", "wrong"]

    has_urgent = any(w in text.lower() for w in urgent_words)
    has_negative = any(w in text.lower() for w in negative_words)

    # Healthcare: conservative (favor recall over precision)
    if scenario == "healthcare" and (has_urgent or has_negative):
      return {"emotion": "distress", "urgency": "high", "action": "escalate"}
    # Customer support: balanced detection
    elif scenario == "customer_support" and has_urgent:
      return {"emotion": "frustrated", "urgency": "high", "action":
  "empathize"}
    # Weather: standard detection
    elif has_negative:
      return {"emotion": "disappointed", "urgency": "medium", "action":
  "support"}
    else:
      return {"emotion": "neutral", "urgency": "low", "action": "standard"}

  # Test
  for text, domain in [
    ("Chest pains, I am scared", "healthcare"),
    ("Product does not work!", "customer_support"),
    ("Rain ruined picnic", "weather")
  ]:
    r = detect_scenario_emotion(text, domain)
    print(f"{domain}: {text}\n→ {r['emotion']} | {r['urgency']} urgency |
  {r['action']}\n")
```

Note: **This is a simple keyword-based approach. In production systems, add synonyms, stemming, or an LLM-backed confidence score to reduce missed signals.**

A real-world example is the healthcare systems that adopt conservative criteria (0.4), allowing more false positives to avoid overlooking true concerns. E-commerce employs higher thresholds (0.7+) to avoid over-reacting to casual browsing.

A caution is to never rely solely on computerized emotion recognition for life-critical decisions. Healthcare and crisis scenarios must integrate human-in-the-loop validation, where high-risk emotions prompt rapid human assessment rather than automated responses.

Emotion detection only becomes relevant when it changes how an agent communicates. Once an emotional state has been established, the agent must adjust its tone, pace, and level of explanation to maintain trust and effectiveness. Adaptive prompt engineering is the method by which observed emotions are translated into tangible behavioral changes in the language model's responses.

Adaptive prompts and empathetic responses

Detecting emotion alone has no value unless it changes an agent's action. Once an emotional state is identified, the agent must change its tone, structure, and level of detail to maintain trust and efficacy. **Adaptive prompt engineering** facilitates this transition by altering system instructions dynamically based on observable emotional context.

Designing emotion-aware prompt templates

The most effective technique for implementing empathy in LangChain is the use of dynamic placeholders within the system message. Instead of a static set of instructions, the agent receives a *mood-aware* prompt that enables it to adapt its tone, tempo, and level of detail based on the user's present moods.

The following code explains how to compose a prompt template that dynamically injects emotional guidelines:

```
 Emotion-aware prompt adaptation
EMOTION_GUIDELINES = {
    "Frustrated": "be patient, apologetic, and focus on immediate solutions.
Acknowledge their frustration first.",
    "Joy":        "match their energy with warm, engaging, and enthusiastic
responses.",
    "Neutral":    "maintain a professional, clear, and informative tone.",
    "Anxious":    "provide calm reassurance, emphasize safety, and avoid
alarming language.",
    "Angry":      "stay composed, validate their concern, and offer concrete
next steps.",
    "Sad":        "respond with empathy and compassion, offer gentle
encouragement.",
    "Fear":       "prioritize safety information, speak calmly, and provide
clear steps.",
}

llm_adaptive = ChatOpenAI(model="gpt-4o-mini", temperature=0.3)


def create_emotion_aware_response(user_input: str, detected_emotion: str) ->
str:
```

```
    """Generate a response adapted to the user's detected emotional state."""
    guideline = EMOTION_GUIDELINES.get(detected_emotion, EMOTION_
GUIDELINES["Neutral"])
    prompt = ChatPromptTemplate.from_messages([
        ("system",
         f"You are a helpful weather assistant. The user is feeling
{detected_emotion.lower()}. "
         f"Respond accordingly: {guideline}. Keep responses concise and
empathetic."),
        ("human", "{user_input}"),
    ])
    chain = prompt | llm_adaptive | StrOutputParser()
    return chain.invoke({"user_input": user_input})

# Example usage
user_message = "This rain ruined my outdoor wedding plans!"
emotion = "Frustrated" # Detected via emotion classifier


response = create_emotion_aware_response(user_message, emotion)
print(f"User ({emotion}): {user_message}")
print(f"Agent: {response}")
```

It is important to always acknowledge the user's feelings before proposing solutions. Validation, like *I understand this, is frustrating...* considerably boosts trust.

Context-sensitive prompt adaptation

Beyond emotion, suggestions must adjust to the discussion context, including user history, location, time sensitivity, and past interactions. Context-sensitive prompts combine emotional awareness with situational intelligence to deliver highly tailored responses, as follows:

```
# Context-sensitive prompt system
def create_context_aware_prompt(
    user_input: str,
    emotion: str,
    location: str = "your area",
    severe_alert_active: bool = False,
    previous_query_count: int = 0,
    time_of_day: str = "day",
) -> str:
    """Build a prompt that adapts based on emotion, alert status, and
context."""
    guideline = EMOTION_GUIDELINES.get(emotion, EMOTION_
```

```
GUIDELINES["Neutral"])
    context_notes = []

    if severe_alert_active:
        context_notes.append(
            f"PRIORITY: There is an active severe weather alert for
{location}. "
            "Lead with safety information."
        )
    if previous_query_count > 3:
        context_notes.append("The user has asked multiple questions. Be extra
thorough.")
    if time_of_day == "night" and severe_alert_active:
        context_notes.append("Late-night emergency query. Provide immediate,
clear guidance.")

    context_block = "\n".join(context_notes)
    system_prompt = (
        f"You are a weather assistant for {location}. User emotion:
{emotion}.\n"
        f"Response guidance: {guideline}\n"
        + (f"\nContext notes:\n{context_block}" if context_block else "")
    )

    prompt = ChatPromptTemplate.from_messages([
        ("system", system_prompt),
        ("human", "{user_input}"),
    ])
    return (prompt | llm_adaptive | StrOutputParser()).invoke({"user_input":
user_input})

# Test context-sensitive adaptation
contexts = [
  {
    "location": "Miami",
    "severe_alert_active": True,
    "history": [],
    "time": "night"
  },
  {
    "location": "Seattle",
```

```
        "severe_alert_active": False,
        "history": ["rain query", "umbrella question", "weekend forecast"],
        "time": "day"
    }
]

messages = [
    "Is it safe to stay in my house?",
    "Will it rain this weekend?"
]

for msg, ctx in zip(messages, contexts):
    response = create_context_aware_prompt(msg, "Anxious", ctx)
    print(f"Context: {ctx['location']}, Alert: {ctx['severe_alert_active']}")
    print(f"User: {msg}")
    print(f"Response: {response[:100]}...\n")
```

This context-aware method guarantees responses reflect not only the user's emotional state but also their specific situation, delivering genuinely useful, tailored encounters.

Emotional state alone does not properly explain a user's circumstance. Effective replies must also account for contextual elements such as location, time sensitivity, prior contacts, and environmental risk. By combining emotional awareness with situational information, agents can develop answers that are not only compassionate but also operationally relevant.

Crisis management and de-escalation logic

In high-stakes environments, such as a telemedicine assistant recognizing a medical concern or a weather agent perceiving a life-threatening storm, emotional awareness must trigger specific safety protocols. **Crisis management logic** allows the agent to forsake its typical conversational tools and initiate immediate escalation routes, such as connecting to a human professional or delivering emergency resources.

The sequence diagram depicts the sequence of events when an agent detects an emotional condition that necessitates a crisis pivot, as visualized in the following figure:

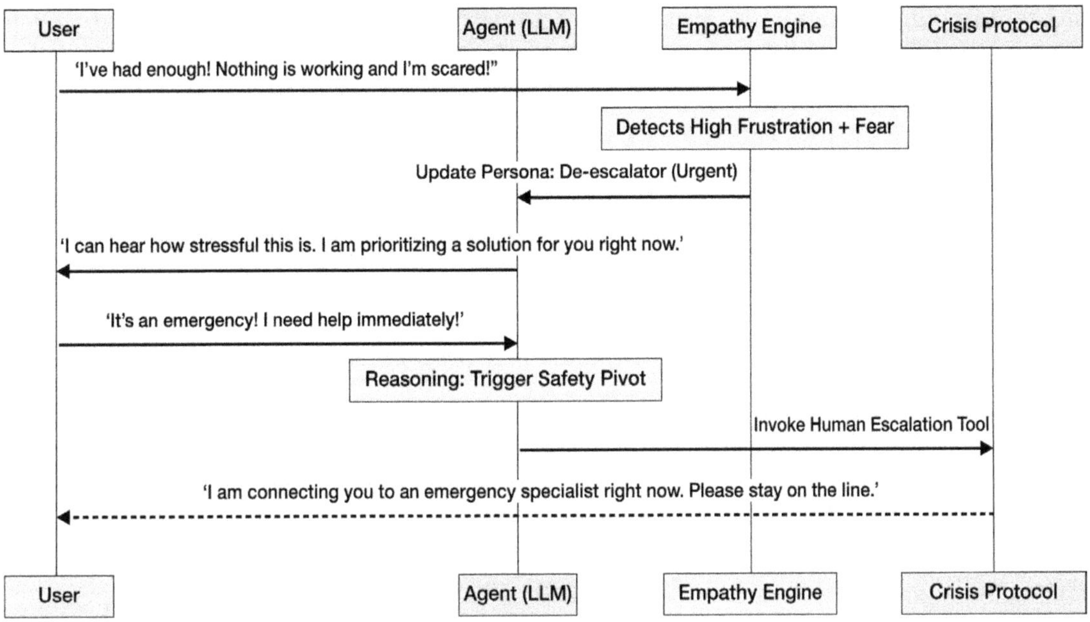

Figure 8.3: *Crisis handling and de-escalation sequence*

Note: **It is because severity is derived from model output text, validate it against the allowed values and use a safe default if the model returns an unexpected label.**

Comparison of response adaptation strategies

Once an agent can recognize emotional signals, the important design question becomes how those signals should shape behavior. Not every emotional shift deserves the same response; some require modest tone adjustments, some demand stringent behavioral limitations, and a few involve abandoning generative reactions entirely in favor of safety-first regulations. The following table is a comparison that demonstrates practical techniques for translating detected emotions into tangible LLM behavior changes, letting users select the best adaptation pattern based on risk level, domain expectations, and user urgency:

Strategy	Trigger mechanism	LLM behavioral shift	Best use case
Persona pivot	Sentiment score shift.	Changes adjectives and tone.	General customer support.
Constraint injection	High frustration detected.	Restricts response length; removes humor.	Professional/technical help.
Crisis bypass	Keywords and high-intensity voice.	Abandons AI generation for scripted safety.	Healthcare and public safety.

Table 8.3: *Strategies for adapting agent responses to user emotion*

When building de-escalation prompts, always advise the LLM to *acknowledge the feeling* before delivering the solution. Validating a user's dissatisfaction (e.g., *I understand this is frustrating...*) considerably enhances trust and minimizes the risk of future escalation.

Designing emotionaware agents requires verifying their behavior across various unpredictable contexts. Controlled simulations make it possible to test how agents respond to emotional variance, mounting urgency, and domainspecific pressures before deployment. The situations in the following section exemplify how emotion detection, intensity estimation, and response adaptation operate together in practice.

Emotion-to-behavior action mapping

The following table provides explicit principles for mapping detected emotions to suitable agent activities. Use this as a guide while designing adaptive response logic, as follows:

Detected emotion	Intensity	Agent behavior	Example response element
Joy	Low–high	Match tone, encourage engagement, and celebrate with the user.	*That is wonderful! The forecast looks perfect for your event.*
Frustration	Low	Acknowledge concern, provide a clear solution.	*I understand your concern. Let me explain...*
Frustration	Medium–high	Acknowledge strongly, simplify response, offer alternatives.	*I hear your frustration. Here is what we can do right now...*
Anxiety	Medium–high	Reassure immediately, emphasize safety, and provide clear action steps.	*Your safety is the priority. Here are the steps to take...*
Fear/distress	High	Activate crisis protocol, provide emergency guidance, and escalate to human.	*Call 911 if in immediate danger. I am connecting you to emergency support.*
Neutral	Any	Standard informative response, maintain a professional tone.	*Here is the forecast for tomorrow...*
Disappointment	Low–medium	Empathize, suggest alternatives or solutions.	*I understand this impacts your plans. Consider these alternatives...*

***Table 8.4**: Emotion-to-behavior mapping for agent response strategy*

The best practice is to default to higher empathy levels when uncertain about emotion intensity. Over-empathizing in response to a neutral query may cause mild difficulty, whereas under-empathizing in situations of genuine pain can permanently break trust.

Simulating real-world emotion detection scenarios

Production emotion-aware agents must handle diverse scenarios across different domains, user states, and crisis levels. This section explores practical scenario simulations that test the agent's emotional intelligence across customer support, healthcare triage, emergency response, and routine interactions. By working through these scenarios, users will develop pattern recognition for emotional cues and build robust response strategies.

Testing emotion detection across scenarios

Real-world emotion detection must handle diverse contexts from routine queries to safety-critical emergencies. The following implementation tests emotion recognition across customer support, safety-critical situations, and varying intensity levels:

```
# Emotion scenario testing across contexts
from langchain_openai import ChatOpenAI
from langchain_core.prompts import ChatPromptTemplate


def analyze_emotion_scenario(message: str, context: str) -> dict:
  """Analyze emotion, intensity, and urgency for a scenario."""
  llm = ChatOpenAI(model="gpt-4o-mini", temperature=0)

  prompt = ChatPromptTemplate.from_messages([
    ("system", "Analyze: emotion (joy/frustration/anxiety/anger/fear), "
         "intensity (low/medium/high), urgency (routine/elevated/urgent). "
         "Format: emotion,intensity,urgency"),
    ("human", "Context: {context}\nMessage: {message}")
  ])

  result = (prompt | llm).invoke({"context": context, "message": message})
  parts = result.content.strip().lower().split(',')

  return {
    "emotion": parts[0],
    "intensity": parts[1].strip() if len(parts) > 1 else "medium",
    "urgency": parts[2].strip() if len(parts) > 2 else "routine"
  }
```

```
# Test across scenario types
scenarios = [
  ("Wedding planning", "I am worried about rain on my wedding day."),
  ("Forecast inaccuracy", "Your forecast was completely wrong yesterday!"),
  ("Tornado warning", "There is a tornado warning! I am alone with my kids!"),
  ("Flash flood", "Water coming into basement! Go upstairs or stay?")
]

print("Emotion Detection Across Scenarios\n" + "=" * 60)

for context, message in scenarios:
  analysis = analyze_emotion_scenario(message, context)
  print(f"\n{context}: \"{message}\"")
  print(f"→ {analysis['emotion']} ({analysis['intensity']} intensity, "
     f"{analysis['urgency']} urgency)")
```

It is crucial to note that safety-critical scenarios (high urgency) must prioritize immediate action guidance over emotional validation. Provide clear safety instructions first, then acknowledge emotions.

Certain emotional signs indicate circumstances in which ordinary conversational etiquette is no longer sufficient. Indicators such as excessive urgency, anxiety, or distress necessitate agents to swing from openended response generation toward safetyfocused protocols. Crisis management logic ensures that emotionaware systems prioritize user protection, clear counsel, and rapid escalation over conversational richness.

Implementing crisis management using adaptive logic

In highstakes contexts, emotionaware agents must prioritize safety over conversational flexibility. Signals such as fear, terror, or acute urgency force the agent to forego normal response generation and trigger established crisis protocols. Effective crisis management logic ensures speedy stabilization, clear guidance, and timely escalation to human assistance when necessary.

An ethical consideration is that emotion detection should aid people rather than manipulate them. High-risk categories must always prioritize safety, transparency, and human escalation over automation.

Integrated crisis detection and response

Crisis management entails spotting danger patterns, producing safety-focused solutions, and escalating as necessary. A two-stage crisis system pairs a fast keyword/caps screen with an LLM-based severity assessment. The screen is cheap and runs first; the LLM call adds nuance and considers active-alert context. Severity values from the model are validated against a known allowlist so unexpected completions cannot silently bypass escalation.

The following short implementation handles all three aspects:

```
# Crisis management system

CRISIS_KEYWORDS = [
    "trapped", "flooding", "flood", "tornado", "hurricane", "evacuate",
    "emergency", "terrified", "danger", "dying", "fire", "collapse",
    "call 911", "help me", "save us",
]
CAPS_THRESHOLD = 0.4
VALID_SEVERITIES = {"low", "medium", "high", "critical"}


def quick_crisis_screen(message: str) -> dict:
    """Fast keyword-based screen before the LLM call."""
    lower = message.lower()
    has_keyword = any(kw in lower for kw in CRISIS_KEYWORDS)
    caps_ratio = sum(1 for c in message if c.isupper()) / max(len(message),
1)
    exclamation_count = message.count("!")

    if has_keyword and (caps_ratio > CAPS_THRESHOLD or exclamation_count >=
3):
        severity_hint = "critical"
    elif has_keyword:
        severity_hint = "high"
    elif caps_ratio > CAPS_THRESHOLD:
        severity_hint = "medium"
    else:
        severity_hint = "low"

    return {
        "has_crisis_keyword": has_keyword,
        "caps_ratio": round(caps_ratio, 2),
        "severity_hint": severity_hint,
    }
```

```
def analyze_crisis(message: str, context: dict | None = None) -> dict:
    """Use LLM to assess crisis severity."""
    ctx = context or {}
    context_line = ""
    if ctx.get("active_severe_alert"):
        context_line = (
            f"Context: Active {ctx.get('alert_type', 'severe weather')} alert
"
            f"in {ctx.get('location', 'the area')}. "
        )

    detect_prompt = ChatPromptTemplate.from_messages([
        ("system",
         "Analyze this message for a crisis situation. "
         "Format: is_crisis(yes/no),severity(low/medium/high/critical)"),
        ("human", f"{context_line}Message: {{msg}}"),
    ])

    raw = (detect_prompt | llm | StrOutputParser()).invoke({"msg": message}).
strip().lower()
    parts = [p.strip() for p in raw.split(",")]
    is_crisis = parts[0] in ("yes", "true", "1")

    # Severity is parsed from free-form model text, so validate it against
the
    # known allowlist before using it as an escalation trigger. Anything we
do
    # not recognise falls back to "low" so an unexpected completion cannot
    # silently push the message into a higher tier.
    raw_severity = parts[1] if len(parts) > 1 else "low"
    severity = raw_severity if raw_severity in VALID_SEVERITIES else "low"

    return {"is_crisis": is_crisis, "severity": severity}
```

It is critical to ensure that crisis systems are designed to fail safely. If unable to identify severity, default to the highest safety protocol and offer emergency contact information (911) rather than underestimating risk.

Having investigated the individual building blocks of emotionaware agents, the next step is to combine them into a coherent, end-to-end system. This course brings together sentiment detection, multimodal analysis, adaptive prompts, and crisis response into a single practical application, illustrating how emotional intelligence operates within a real-world agent workflow.

Building an emotion-aware weather agent

This section incorporates the chapter's basic concepts into a complete, endtoend solution. Users will combine emotion recognition, multimodal analysis, adaptive prompts, and crisis escalation into a single functional agent, demonstrating how emotional intelligence performs within a genuine production workflow.

Workshop architecture and implementation steps

The technology uses a multimodal method that combines text-based sentiment with speech intelligence to produce a comprehensive emotional profile. The workflow follows the following three main phases:

- **Sentiment and urgency check**: The agent evaluates the user's reaction (e.g., disappointment over rain) and identifies vocal intensity to decide if the situation is urgent.
- **Adaptive reasoning and tool selection**: If high frustration is recognized, the agent pivots from presenting raw data to offering compassionate indoor options.
- **Empathetic vocal synthesis**: The response is provided using an expressive **text-to-speech** (**TTS**) voice that reflects the supportive tone set in the prompt.

Building a complete emotion-aware agent

The following code exhibits a complete emotion-aware weather assistant that detects sentiment and changes its responses:

```
# Complete emotion-aware weather assistant
from langchain_openai import ChatOpenAI
from langchain_core.prompts import ChatPromptTemplate
from langchain_core.output_parsers import StrOutputParser

VALID_EMOTIONS = {"Joy", "Neutral", "Frustrated", "Anxious"}


class EmotionAwareWeatherAgent:
  """Weather agent that adapts responses based on detected emotion."""

  def __init__(self):
    self.llm = ChatOpenAI(model="gpt-4o-mini", temperature=0.7)
```

```
        # Emotion detection chain
        self.emotion_detector = self._create_emotion_detector()

        # Response generation with emotion awareness
        self.response_generator = self._create_response_generator()

    def _create_emotion_detector(self):
        """Create emotion classification chain."""
        prompt = ChatPromptTemplate.from_messages([
            ("system", "Classify emotion as: Joy, Neutral, Frustrated, or Anxious.
"
                "Output ONLY the emotion word."),
            ("human", "{text}")
        ])
        return prompt | self.llm | StrOutputParser()

    def _create_response_generator(self):
        """Create emotion-aware response chain."""
        prompt = ChatPromptTemplate.from_messages([
            ("system", """You are a weather assistant. User emotion: {emotion}

Guidelines by emotion:
- Joy: Be warm and enthusiastic
- Neutral: Be professional and informative
- Frustrated: Be apologetic and solution-focused
- Anxious: Be calm, reassuring, and emphasize safety

Provide concise weather information with appropriate tone."""),
            ("human", "{query}")
        ])
        return prompt | self.llm | StrOutputParser()

    @staticmethod
    def _normalize_emotion(raw: str) -> str:
        """Coerce model output to one of VALID_EMOTIONS, defaulting to Neutral.

        The downstream response prompt branches on the emotion label, so a
        trailing space, lowercase variant, or out-of-set completion would
        silently degrade tone. Normalising here keeps the agent's behaviour
        stable even when the classifier wobbles.
        """
        if not raw:
            return "Neutral"
```

```
    first = raw.strip().split()[0].rstrip(".,!").capitalize()
    return first if first in VALID_EMOTIONS else "Neutral"

  def respond(self, user_query: str) -> dict:
    """Process query with emotion awareness."""
    # Detect emotion, then normalise to a known label
    raw_emotion = self.emotion_detector.invoke({"text": user_query})
    emotion = self._normalize_emotion(raw_emotion)

    # Generate emotion-aware response
    response = self.response_generator.invoke({
      "query": user_query,
      "emotion": emotion
    })

    return {
      "query": user_query,
      "detected_emotion": emotion,
      "response": response
    }

# Example usage
agent = EmotionAwareWeatherAgent()

test_queries = [
  "This rain ruined my outdoor wedding plans!",
  "Perfect weather for hiking today!",
  "Is there a tornado warning in my area?",
  "What is the forecast for tomorrow?"
]

print("=== Emotion-Aware Weather Agent ===\n")
for query in test_queries:
  result = agent.respond(query)
  print(f"Query: {result['query']}")
  print(f"Emotion: {result['detected_emotion']}")
  print(f"Response: {result['response']}\n")
  print("-" * 60 + "\n")
```

`EmotionAwareWeatherAgent` chains an emotion-detection LCEL pipeline into a response-generation pipeline. The detected emotion is normalized against an allowlist before being fed into the response prompt, so a trailing space, lowercase variant, or unexpected label cannot derail the guideline lookup.

Evaluating agent empathy and performance

To assure production dependability, the workshop includes a review phase focused on both accuracy and latency, as illustrated in the following table:

Evaluation metric	Goal	Failure mode
Emotion accuracy	>90% match with human labels.	Miscategorizing frustration as neutral.
Response latency	<800ms end-to-end.	High-complexity multimodal analysis.
Empathy score	High user trust rating.	Robotic or tone-deaf responses.

***Table 8.5**: Metrics for emotionally aware agents*

Tip: **Use expressive TTS voices (e.g., OpenAI Nova or ElevenLabs Luna) for compassionate responses. A warm, supporting voice considerably boosts the feeling of empathy compared to typical robotic synthesis.**

Emotion-aware agent architecture

Having implemented the end-to-end weather assistant, it helps to step back and view the solution as a set of cooperating components. A clear architecture makes the design easier to test, extend, and harden for production by separating emotion detection, response adaptation, and safety escalation into well-defined responsibilities.

Figure 8.4 summarizes the weather agent as a small set of roles rather than a single monolithic chain. Incoming user text is first interpreted by the **Emotion Detector**, which produces a structured signal (emotion plus intensity) that the rest of the agent can rely on. **Response Generator** uses that signal to select an appropriate prompt strategy and shape the final answer (tone, brevity, and level of reassurance). When the detected state crosses a safety threshold (for example, high distress combined with urgent situational cues), control is routed to the **Crisis Handler**, which prioritizes prescriptive safety steps and escalation over open-ended generation.

The following diagram demonstrates the major components of an emotion-aware agent and their interactions:

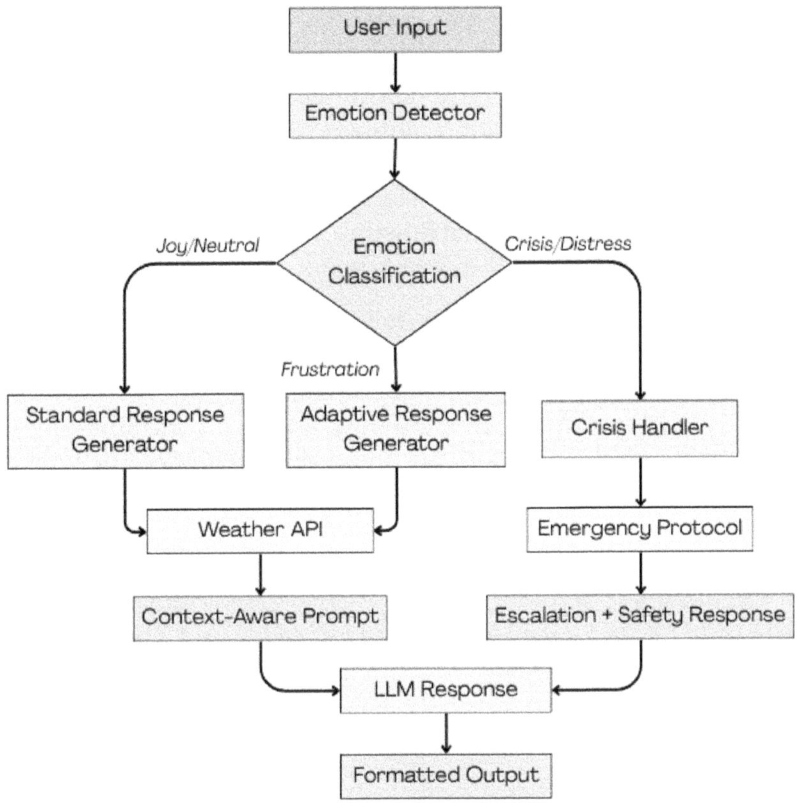

***Figure 8.4**: Emotion-aware agent class structure*

The following are the key components:

- **Emotion Detector**: Analyzes user input for emotional state and intensity.
- **Response Generator**: Adapts tone, detail level, and empathy based on emotion.
- **Crisis Handler**: Activates safety processes and escalation for high-risk circumstances.

Conclusion

This chapter examined how to build AI agents that are aware of emotions and can recognize both basic and more complex feelings. These agents then change their behavior in ways that feel helpful instead of robotic. Readers used text-based sentiment and LLM-driven emotion classification (including few-shot prompting) to identify subtle states such as anxiety, frustration, and distress without the need to train their own models. The chapter then explored how to use adaptive prompt templates and context-aware routing to change the tone, structure, and level of detail based on the user's mood and situation. Readers also learned how to keep track of emotional trajectory across turns to spot escalation early.

Response generation was a big part of the work. This meant recognizing feelings, choosing the right level of empathy, and shifting from *conversation* to *safety-first* when signals indicated high risk. Readers implemented patterns for detecting and escalating crises using multi-factor indicators, including language cues, urgency markers, emotional intensity, and environmental context. Readers also set up fail-safe defaults and ethical guardrails, such as privacy, transparency, and avoiding manipulation. The chapter concluded with a comprehensive emotion-aware weather advisory agent that integrates detection, routing, empathetic response generation, and crisis management within a production-focused architecture.

Readers will use **retrieval-augmented generation** (**RAG**) to add factual grounding in the next chapter. They will build and improve retrieval pipelines (such as vector stores, semantic search, reranking, and context window management), add reliability patterns (such as multi-retriever strategies, routing, fallbacks, and failure handling), and use benchmarking and debugging checklists to assess quality. When readers put these skills together, they get agents who are both emotionally smart and knowledgeable, with knowledge that can be verified.

CHAPTER 9
Building Retrieval-enhanced Agents

Introduction

Every intelligent agent faces one big problem: the information it learns during training becomes outdated as soon as training ends. If users ask a powerful language model about yesterday's weather, last week's climate trends, or their organization's weather archives, it might give them plausible but unverified information. **Retrieval-augmented generation** (**RAG**) addresses this gap by shifting agents from smart guessers into assistants grounded in relevant, verifiable information.

By combining generation with retrieval, RAG connects static model knowledge with dynamic, real-world information. An agent first gets relevant evidence from trusted sources using embeddings, semantic search, and vector databases. Then it uses that evidence to improve the model's response, making it more accurate and up to date.

This chapter will show readers how to build the whole RAG pipeline in LangChain, from loading and chunking documents to embeddings, vector storage, and adding a retriever. Readers will set up retrieval with **Facebook AI Similarity Search** (**FAISS**) and Pinecone, test different retrieval strategies, including similarity search and **Maximal Marginal Relevance** (**MMR**), and use advanced techniques such as query routing, retriever chaining, hybrid search, and fallbacks. Finally, readers will secure the system for production by using token-aware context management, monitoring, and reliability best practices.

Structure

This chapter covers the following topics:

- Principles of retrieval-augmented generation systems
- Setting up and configuring vector databases
- Implementing advanced retrievers and rerankers

- Building semantic search and context retrieval flows
- Managing token limits with smart context windows
- Chaining retrievers and routers for better recall
- Failover logic and production reliability
- Building complete production-ready RAG architectures

Objectives

Using LangChain's RAG components, this chapter shifts agentic intelligence from closed-box reasoning to evidence-based retrieval. Readers will learn how the retrieve-then-generate cycle limits hallucinations by using answers from sources that can be checked. Readers will also map the entire RAG pipeline from ingestion and chunking to embedding, vector storage, retrieval, and prompt assembly.

Readers will also use FAISS (for local prototyping) and Pinecone (for cloud persistence) to build real-world retrieval systems. They will also compare different retriever options, such as similarity search, MMR, parent document retrieval, and contextual compression, to evaluate their effectiveness under token limits. Readers will use advanced patterns, including retriever chaining, query routing, multi-query expansion, and ensembles to make the system more reliable and enhance information retention. The chapter ends with a workshop that creates a production-ready RAG solution for weather data. This includes evaluation metrics, fallbacks from semantic to keyword search, retry logic, and monitoring to ensure the system remains reliable as it grows.

Principles of retrieval-augmented generation systems

Large language models (**LLMs**) are outstanding reasoners, but their internal knowledge is frozen when the training stops. For an agent to serve as a true domain expert, it must be able to provide information, such as real-time weather data, proprietary sensor records, or updated medical guidelines. RAG is an architectural pattern that enhances an LLM by providing it with a relevant context *cheat sheet* before it creates an answer. This approach allows LangChain agents to acquire data beyond their original training data, transforming them from static conversationalists into context-aware knowledge powerhouses.

Table 9.1 maps each major stage of a RAG system to the LangChain component responsible for that step:

Pipeline stage	LangChain component
Ingestion	Document loaders
Chunking	Text splitters

Pipeline stage	LangChain component
Indexing	Vector stores
Retrieval	Retrievers
Reasoning	Chains/agents

Table 9.1: Complete RAG pipeline component mapping

RAG workflow architecture

A conventional LangChain RAG pipeline follows a deterministic set of actions designed to bridge the gap between enormous document libraries and the small context window of an LLM. The process is often separated into two primary phases: **Ingestion**, where documents are prepared for storage, and **Retrieval**, where the agent discovers the most relevant information for a specific query.

The following figure demonstrates the entire RAG loop, demonstrating how data travels from raw loaders into a vector store and subsequently into a grounded response:

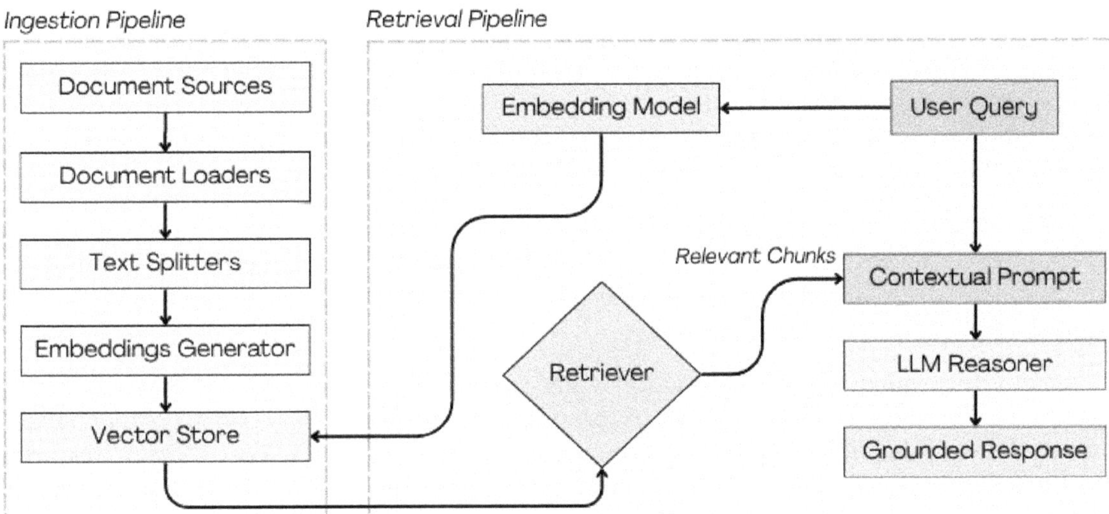

Figure 9.1: LangChain RAG pipeline architecture

RAG is an architecture pattern that enhances language model generation by first retrieving relevant texts from an external knowledge base, then conditioning model outputs on both the original query and retrieved context. This grounds responses on true, up-to-date information beyond the model's training data.

The workflow functions through five important dimensions, as follows:

- **Loading**: Using LangChain's `DocumentLoaders` to ingest raw text from sources, including **Portable Document Format** (**PDF**) files, weather logs, or web pages.

- **Transformation**: Breaking documents into digestible bits with `TextSplitters` so they fit within token restrictions.
- **Embedding**: Converting text chunks into high-dimensional numerical vectors that represent their semantic meaning.
- **Storage**: Persisting these vectors in a dedicated vector storage for quick similarity search.
- **Retrieval**: Searching the store to discover the *Top K* chunks that most closely fit the user's purpose.

Avoiding hallucinations through grounding

LLMs generate text by predicting plausible sequences of words, not by confirming facts against reality. As a result, even wellprompted agents can confidently fake details when a question falls outside their reliable internal knowledge. In highstakes domains, such as weather analysis, healthcare, finance, or enterprise reporting, this behavior is unacceptable. RAG solves this problem by requiring the model to reason from evidence, rather than from probability alone.

Grounding in a RAG system restricts the language model to operate tightly within a recovered evidence set. Before generation begins, the agent receives a curated selection of documents that are semantically aligned with the user's query. These papers constitute an explicit *context boundary*, and the model is taught to answer using only the information contained within it. Any claim the agent makes must be traceable to at least one retrieved source.

From a systems perspective, grounding formalizes a split of tasks that will repeat throughout this chapter: retrievers handle factual recall, while language models focus on reasoning and synthesis. This distinction becomes increasingly significant as retrieval processes grow more complex and involve various data sources.

In a weatherfocused agent, this distinction is very relevant. If a user asks, *What was the highest wind speed recorded in Seattle last February?*, a nongrounded model may construct a believable number. A grounded RAG agent, however, must receive an actual sensor log or historical report. If no such record exists in the knowledge base, the correct response is a clear uncertainty rather than a confident guess.

Effective grounding relies on three reinforcing techniques, as follows:

- Strict prompt limits, such as *Answer only using the provided context* or *If the answer is not contained in the documents, respond with Insufficient data.*
- Lowtemperature generation, which limits creative variance and fosters deterministic usage of retrieved data.
- Source transparency, where retrieved documents are tracked and optionally exposed, enabling audits and user verification.

Grounding also offers measurable quality improvements. Instead of rating responses subjectively, users can measure retrieval fidelity using metrics such as answer-supported-by-context rate, citation coverage, or evidence overlap. These measurements make hallucinations observable, debuggable, and correctable, a key prerequisite for production-grade systems.

Ultimately, anchoring transforms agents from convincing storytellers into trustworthy knowledge helpers. By anchoring every response in recovered data, RAG systems provide answers that are not merely fluent but defensible. This establishes the foundation for dependable, enterpriseready AI.

The following is an expert insight:

One of the most substantial improvements in production RAG systems comes from optimizing retrieval quality rather than increasing model size. In practice, a smaller, faster language model with highly relevant context can outperform a larger model retrieving only marginally relevant documents.

Source: *blog, "Voyage Embeddings in LangChain and ChatLangChain"* **https://www.langchain.com/blog/voyage-embeddings-in-langchain-and-chat-langchain**

Standard RAG interface in LangChain

LangChain provides a single interface that abstracts the intricacies of numerous data sources and vector storage backends. All RAG components follow the same interaction pattern, allowing users to swap a local PDF loader for a cloud-based **Structured Query Language** (**SQL**) database without altering their fundamental retrieval logic.

The following code exhibits the main interface pattern for a retrieval chain, showing how the agent loads context before reasoning:

```
# Standard retrieval interface pattern in LangChain
from langchain_openai import ChatOpenAI
from langchain_core.prompts import ChatPromptTemplate
from langchain_core.runnables import RunnablePassthrough

# 0. The retriever comes from a vector store created in the next section.
#    Shown here for completeness – replace with your real retriever.
# retriever = vectorstore.as_retriever(search_kwargs={"k": 4})

# 1. Define the grounded prompt template
prompt = ChatPromptTemplate.from_template("""
Answer the question based only on the following weather context:
{context}

Question: {question}
""")
```

```
# 2. Initialize the LLM reasoner
llm = ChatOpenAI(model="gpt-4o-mini", temperature=0)

# 3. Compose the RAG chain using LCEL
# RunnablePassthrough allows us to pass the user query to multiple components
rag_chain = (
  {"context": retriever, "question": RunnablePassthrough()}
  | prompt
  | llm
)

# The agent now retrieves weather context automatically before generating an answer
# response = rag_chain.invoke("What was the peak wind speed in Seattle last Tuesday?")
```

Tip: **When developing their first RAG system, users should always utilize `temperature=0` for the LLM reasoner to receive the truest and most predictable grounded responses.**

Vector embeddings and semantic search

Vector embeddings form the mathematical foundation of semantic retrieval. Unlike keyword matching, which requires exact lexical overlap, embeddings capture meaning in a high-dimensional space where semantically similar concepts cluster together regardless of specific word choices.

Modern embedding models convert text into dense vectors, often with dimensions ranging from 384 to 1536. These models are trained on enormous corpora to encode semantic relationships: *temperature forecast* and *thermal prediction* produce similar embeddings despite sharing no words, whereas *bank* in *river bank* versus *savings bank* produce separate embeddings that depend on context.

The following demonstrates basic embedding generation:

```
# Generate embeddings for semantic search
from langchain_openai import OpenAIEmbeddings

embeddings = OpenAIEmbeddings(model="text-embedding-3-small")

# Embed a weather query
query_vector = embeddings.embed_query("What will tomorrow's high temperature be?")
```

```
# Returns: 1536-dimensional vector representing semantic meaning

# Embed multiple documents
weather_docs = [
  "Tomorrow's forecast shows high of 72°F with partly cloudy skies",
  "Historical temperature records for this date average 68°F",
  "Current atmospheric pressure indicates stable weather patterns"
]
doc_vectors = embeddings.embed_documents(weather_docs)
# Returns: List of 1536-dimensional vectors, one per document
```

Semantic search operates through vector similarity calculations. Cosine similarity evaluates the angle between vectors, producing scores from -1 to 1, where higher values indicate stronger semantic alignment. The power of semantic search becomes obvious in practice: a query for *extreme heat conditions* finds documents with *scorching temperatures, heat waves,* and *thermal stress* without explicit keyword matches.

Tip: **Use the same embedding model for both document encoding and query encoding. Mixing models yields incompatible vector spaces where similarity computations become worthless.**

Warning: **Vector similarity alone does not ensure factual significance. A document semantically equivalent to the query could explore relevant concepts without possessing the particular facts needed to answer the inquiry.**

RAG architecture components and data flow

A production RAG system has numerous interconnected components functioning across three core pipelines: intake, retrieval, and creation. Understanding this architecture demonstrates how documents are transformed from raw text into searchable knowledge and how queries are translated into grounded responses.

The following figure displays the entire RAG system architecture:

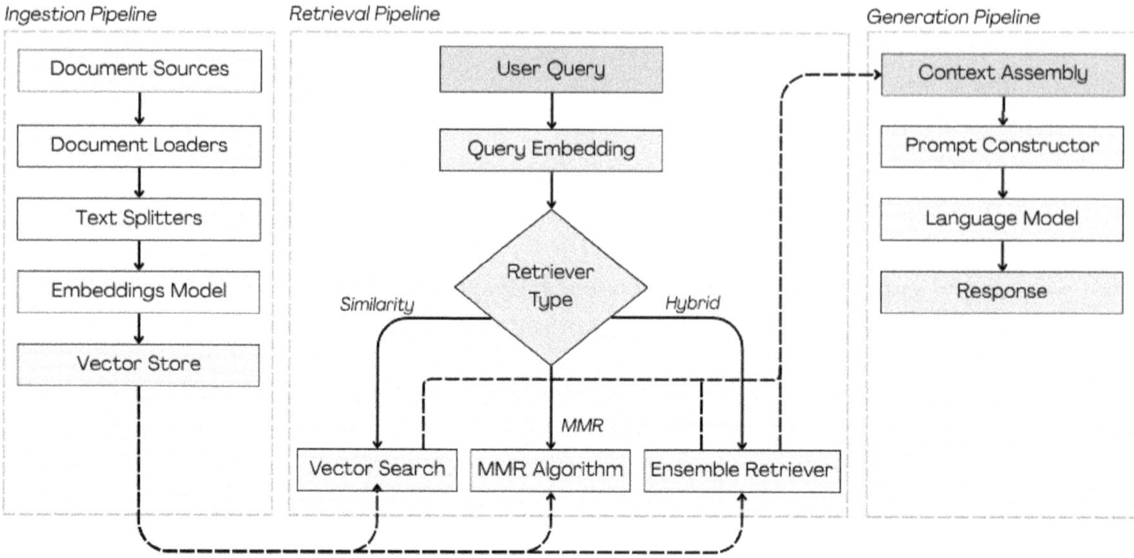

***Figure 9.2**: Complete RAG system architecture*

The intake process transforms raw documents into searchable embeddings. Document loaders handle various sources, including PDFs, web pages, databases, and **application programming interfaces** (**APIs**). Text splitters break documents into sections suitable for embedding and retrieval. The embedding model turns text fragments into vector representations. Vector stores provide indexed storage optimized for similarity search.

The retrieval pipeline evaluates user requests and returns relevant context. Query embedding transforms queries into vectors using the same methodology that encoded documents. Retriever selection guides queries to appropriate search strategies, including similarity search for accuracy, MMR for diversity, or ensemble methods for comprehensive coverage. The generating pipeline assembles retrieved context into useful prompts. Context assembly combines various document chunks with metadata like source and relevance ratings. The prompt constructor arranges inputs to effectively separate retrieved context from user questions. The language model creates responses conditioned on both query and circumstances.

The following figure is a sequence diagram that represents a typical retrieval interaction:

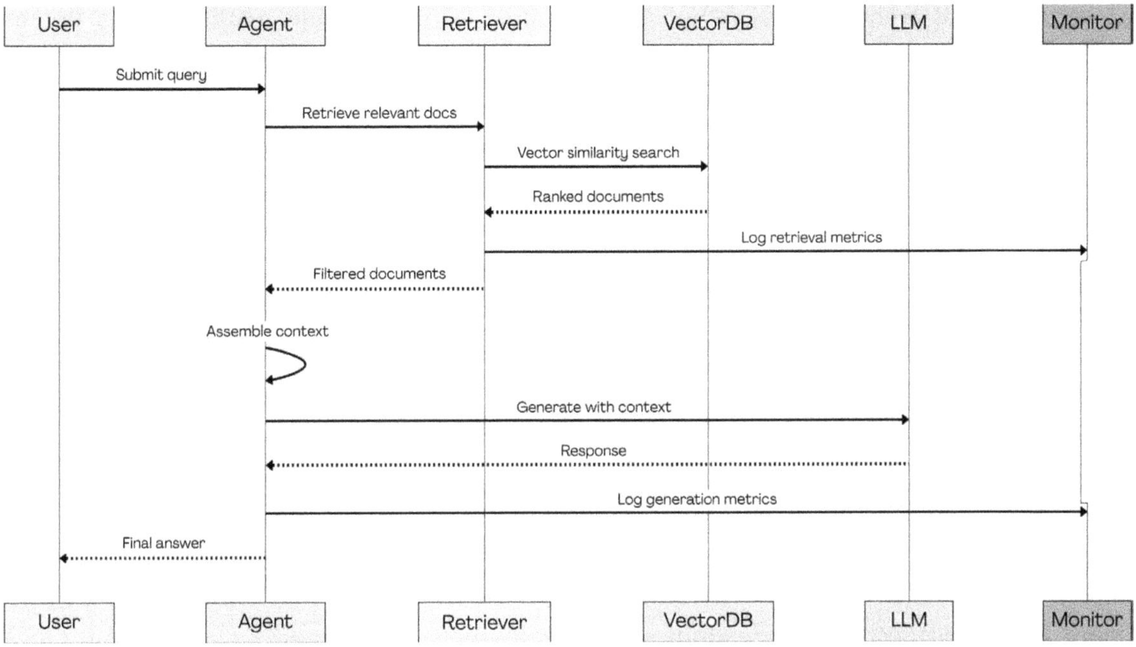

***Figure 9.3**: Sequence diagram for RAG retrieval and generation flow*

Critical optimization points in this flow include embedding caching to avoid duplicate encoding of frequent questions, vector store connection pooling to reduce connection overhead, asynchronous retrieval to parallelize many searches, and streaming replies to reduce perceived latency.

RAG pipeline architecture mapping

To understand how separate retrieval components integrate into a comprehensive RAG system, it is helpful to examine them via a pipeline lens. A production RAG architecture advances through distinct stages, from data ingestion and preparation to retrieval and reasoning, each tied to specific LangChain components. This subsection builds on the earlier orientation table by explaining how those stages connect within the broader RAG lifecycle.

Once the architectural functions of retrieval and reasoning are clearly defined, the next essential decision concerns how factual knowledge is stored and accessible efficiently at scale. This leads directly to the use of vector databases, which provide the foundation for semantic search and high-performance retrieval in RAG systems.

Note: **RAG is not always the best approach. When data is entirely deterministic, firmly structured, and frequently searched (for example, simple create, read, update, delete (CRUD) lookups or fixed business rules), a standard database query or rule engine may outperform RAG in latency, cost, and reliability.**

It is important to profile the RAG pipeline under realistic load to detect bottlenecks before they impede production. Retrieval, embedding creation, and language model inference each dominate in distinct contexts.

Setting up and configuring vector databases

To support semantic search and context-aware retrieval, LangChain agents require a specific storage layer: the vector store. Unlike standard SQL databases that match keywords, vector stores compare high-dimensional numerical representations of data, allowing agents to find information based on meaning rather than exact language. Setting up these databases entails selecting a suitable backend and establishing a robust data intake process.

Comparing various vector store backends

Choosing the best vector store depends on the deployment requirements, ranging from a local prototype to a global corporate scale. LangChain provides a single interface that allows users to transition between different backends with little code changes.

The following table compares the three primary vector storage used for agentic retrieval:

Vector store	Deployment model	Primary advantage	Scaling capability
FAISS	Local library	Optimized for speed; air-gapped systems	Limited by **random-access memory** (**RAM**)
Pinecone	Cloud managed	Enterprise-ready; multi-user isolation	Native auto-scaling
Chroma	Local or hosted	Open-source; easy persistence on disk	Moderate
Qdrant	Local/cloud	Advanced filters, hybrid search	Very good

Table 9.2: Comparison of vector store backends in LangChain

Document loader reference architecture

Document loaders in LangChain standardize the ingestion of data from files, web sources, databases, and APIs into `Document` objects. They extract text, metadata, and structure while abstracting format-specific complexity. Loaders are the first stage in establishing a retrieval pipeline and determine how much semantic context and metadata are reserved.

File-based document loaders

To handle static documents stored in local or versioncontrolled settings, LangChain provides a robust range of filebased document loaders. These loaders abstract formatspecific parsing logic while preserving key structure and metadata, making them well-suited for consuming PDFs, Word documents, **comma-separated values** (**CSV**) files, and other commonly used enterprise artifacts. The following table covers the principal filebased loaders and their common use cases:

Class name	Source type
`TextLoader`	Plain text files
`PDFLoader` / `PyPDFLoader`	PDF documents
`UnstructuredPDFLoader`	Complex or scanned PDFs
`Docx2txtLoader`	Word documents
`UnstructuredWordDocumentLoader`	DOC/DOCX
`CSVLoader`	CSV files
`JSONLoader`	**JavaScript Object Notation** (**JSON**) files
`UnstructuredMarkdownLoader`	Markdown files
`UnstructuredHTMLLoader`	**HyperText Markup Language** (**HTML**) files
`NotebookLoader`	Jupyter notebooks

***Table 9.3**: File-based document loaders in LangChain*

Choosing the right file-based loader in practice

In practice, the choice of loader depends less on the file extension and more on the structure and retrieval goals of the source material. `TextLoader` works well for plain logs, notes, and configuration files where preserving the original line structure matters. `PyPDFLoader` is often the best starting point for digitally generated PDFs because it is lightweight and preserves page-level metadata, while `UnstructuredPDFLoader` is the better choice when PDFs contain complex layouts, scanned pages, or mixed elements such as tables and figures. For structured tabular sources, `CSVLoader` is useful when each row should become a retrievable unit, whereas `JSONLoader` is useful when the input contains nested fields that must be targeted selectively. Similarly, `Docx2txtLoader` is a strong option for simple Word documents, but broader unstructured loaders are more suitable when layout fidelity and embedded elements affect downstream retrieval quality.

For example, a compliance assistant that indexes policy manuals exported as clean PDFs can usually begin with `PyPDFLoader` because page boundaries and source references are more important than visual layout recovery. On the other hand, an invoice-processing or research assistant working with scanned reports would benefit more from `UnstructuredPDFLoader`, since those documents often depend on OCR and layout-aware extraction. Similarily, a telemetry assistant built on sensor exports is better served by `CSVLoader` when each record should be retrieved independently, while a configuration or API knowledge assistant usually gains more value from `JSONLoader` because the retriever can focus on specific keys such as environment, endpoint, or version metadata.

Web and API document loaders

Modern knowledge bases generally rely on regularly updated content published on websites or exposed through APIs. LangChain's web and API loaders enable agents to ingest live or periodically refreshed data, including dynamically generated pages, **Really Simple Syndication** (**RSS**) feeds, and GitHub content. The following table illustrates the most used loaders for webbased and APIdriven sources:

Class name	Source
`WebBaseLoader`	Static web pages
`SitemapLoader`	Sitemap-based crawling
`RecursiveUrlLoader`	Recursive site crawling
`PlaywrightURLLoader`	**JavaScript** (**JS**)-rendered pages
`AsyncHtmlLoader`	Async web scraping
`RSSFeedLoader`	RSS feeds
`GitHubIssuesLoader`	GitHub issues
`GitHubRepoLoader`	GitHub repositories

***Table 9.4**: Web and API document loaders*

Cloud and platform document loaders

In enterprise environments, significant volumes of knowledge are generally kept in cloud platforms and collaborative tools. LangChain's cloud and platform loaders provide native connections to major storage and productivity services, enabling secure, large-scale ingestion of organizational materials. The following table outlines supported loaders for key cloud and productivity platforms:

Class name	Source
`S3DirectoryLoader`	**Amazon Web Services** (**AWS**) **Simple Storage Service** (**S3**)
`GCSDirectoryLoader`	Google Cloud Storage
`AzureBlobStorageContainerLoader`	Azure Blob Storage
`NotionDirectoryLoader`	Notion pages
`GoogleDriveLoader`	Google Drive

***Table 9.5**: Cloud platform document loaders*

Database document loaders

Structured databases typically contain crucial operational and historical information that must be made accessible to retrievalaugmented agents. LangChain's database loaders bridge the gap between structured data storage and semantic retrieval pipelines by turning query results into document representations. The following table describes available database loaders and the data sources they support:

Class name	Source
`SQLDatabaseLoader`	SQL databases
`MongoDBLoader`	MongoDB
`ElasticSearchLoader`	Elasticsearch

Table 9.6*: Database document loaders*

Tip: When creating production RAG systems for weather data, utilize CSVLoader for sensor logs, WebBaseLoader for meteorological bulletins, and S3DirectoryLoader for archival climate records. Always check that the selected loader keeps timestamp metadata, as temporal filtering is crucial for weather applications.

The following code provides a practical example of loading weather data from several source types:

```
from langchain_community.document_loaders import CSVLoader, WebBaseLoader

# Load historical sensor data from CSV
sensor_loader = CSVLoader(
  file_path="weather_sensors_2024.csv",
  csv_args={"delimiter": ",", "fieldnames": ["timestamp", "location", "temp", 
"humidity"]}
)
sensor_docs = sensor_loader.load()

# Load current weather bulletin from web
web_loader = WebBaseLoader("https://weather.gov/seattle/alerts")
alert_docs = web_loader.load()

# Both loaders return Document objects with .page_content and .metadata
```

Implementing document chunking strategies

Before raw text can be incorporated into vectors, it must be broken into digestible parts called chunks. If chunks are too large, they may exceed the model's context window or dilute individual facts; if they are too small, the agent loses the surrounding context needed to reason properly.

Document chunking in LangChain is handled by `TextSplitter` classes, which break big documents into smaller, context-preserving chunks suited for embeddings and retrieval. Different splitters optimize for structure (Markdown, code), semantics (tokens, phrases), or resilience (recursive techniques). Choosing the correct splitter directly affects retrieval accuracy, token efficiency, and answer quality.

The following table provides a complete summary of LangChain's text splitting strategies:

Class name	Purpose	Best use case
`RecursiveCharacterTextSplitter`	Recursively splits using multiple separators.	Default and most robust option.
`CharacterTextSplitter`	Simple fixed character-based splitting.	Small or unstructured text.
`TokenTextSplitter`	Splits by LLM tokens.	Precise token-budget control.
`SentenceTransformersTokenTextSplitter`	Token-aware for sentence-transformer models.	Hugging Face embeddings.
`MarkdownHeaderTextSplitter`	Splits by Markdown headers.	Technical docs, README files.
`MarkdownTextSplitter`	Markdown-aware splitting.	Markdown-heavy content.
`HTMLHeaderTextSplitter`	Splits HTML by headers.	Web pages, scraped HTML.
`HTMLTextSplitter`	Generic HTML parsing.	Raw HTML documents.
`LatexTextSplitter`	Splits LaTeX sections.	Academic or scientific docs.
`PythonCodeTextSplitter`	Code-aware chunking.	Python repositories.
`RecursiveJsonSplitter`	Splits nested JSON structures.	API specs, structured data.

***Table 9.7**: LangChain text splitter classes*

Users use LangChain's `RecursiveCharacterTextSplitter` with a defined overlap to ensure that crucial information, such as a precise temperature reading, is not lost at the split boundaries. The following code explains how to prepare weather sensor logs for a persistent **FAISS** vector store:

```
from langchain_text_splitters import RecursiveCharacterTextSplitter
from langchain_community.vectorstores import FAISS
from langchain_openai import OpenAIEmbeddings

# 1. Define splitting logic with overlapping context
# chunk_size should be balanced for model attention
text_splitter = RecursiveCharacterTextSplitter(
  chunk_size=1000,
  chunk_overlap=100,
  length_function=len,
  add_start_index=True,
)

# 2. Split documents into chunks for the weather agent
# documents = text_splitter.split_documents(raw_weather_docs)

# 3. Embed and store in a local FAISS index
# vector_db = FAISS.from_documents(documents, OpenAIEmbeddings())
```

The commented lines in this example are intentional placeholders for steps that depend on reader-specific inputs, such as a real document collection, embedding credentials, and a local storage path. They are shown to make the full end-to-end workflow visible without requiring readers to run indexing and persistence during the initial explanation. Once readers replace the sample variables with their own document set and environment configuration, they can uncomment these lines to execute the complete chunking and FAISS setup.

Data persistence and local storage

Vector databases are the storage and retrieval backbone of RAG systems. Choosing and configuring the proper solution affects performance, scalability, and operational complexity.

For local development, it is vital to persist the vector index to disk so that the agent does not need to re-embed data every time the script resumes. Persistent storage supports *day-two* processes, such as incrementally adding new weather reports to an existing knowledge base.

FAISS delivers high-performance vector similarity search optimized for both **central processing unit** (**CPU**) and **graphics processing unit** (**GPU**) execution. Developed by Meta AI Research, it thrives in applications demanding low latency, local execution, or bespoke indexing algorithms.

The following exhibits the FAISS setup with document indexing:

```
# Set up FAISS vector store with OpenAI embeddings
from langchain_community.vectorstores import FAISS
from langchain_openai import OpenAIEmbeddings
from langchain_text_splitters import RecursiveCharacterTextSplitter

# Configure text splitting for optimal chunk size
text_splitter = RecursiveCharacterTextSplitter(
  chunk_size=1000, # Characters per chunk
  chunk_overlap=200 # Overlap prevents context loss at boundaries
)

# Split and embed weather documentation
weather_texts = text_splitter.create_documents([
  "Climate data shows average temperatures...",
  "Severe weather patterns indicate...",
  "Historical forecasting accuracy metrics..."
])

# Create FAISS index
embeddings = OpenAIEmbeddings()
vectorstore = FAISS.from_documents(weather_texts, embeddings)

# Persist to disk for reuse
vectorstore.save_local("weather_index")
```

A FAISS index is the simplest local-disk vector store: build it from your chunked documents, call `save_local`, and reload it with `FAISS.load_local` on subsequent runs. No external service is required, which makes it ideal for offline or on-device workloads.

FAISS provides numerous index types tailored for distinct trade-offs. Flat indexes perform exact nearest neighbor search with perfect recall but *O(n)* query time. **Inverted File** (**IVF**) indexes partition the vector space for faster approximate search. **Hierarchical Navigable Small World** (**HNSW**) graphs give good recall-speed trade-offs. **Product Quantization** (**PQ**) compresses vectors for memory efficiency.

Tip: **Start with FAISS flat indexes during development for flawless recall, then transition to IVF or HNSW indexes in production when the dataset grows faster and approximate search is needed.**

For production deployments, FAISS indexes can be memory-mapped for faster loading, stored on high-performance **solid-state drives** (**SSDs**), or replicated across multiple servers for horizontal scaling. GPU acceleration gives 10-100x speedups for large-scale similarity search.

It is important to always utilize a cloud-based store, such as Pinecone, with a namespace while scaling to multi-user situations. This prevents the agent from unintentionally collecting *User A's* private weather history to answer a question from *User B*.

Pinecone for cloud deployments

Pinecone offers fully managed vector databases that handle indexing, scalability, and replication automatically. This reduces operating overhead for production RAG systems that require high availability and worldwide distribution.

The following exhibits Pinecone arrangement for a weather knowledge base:

```
# Configure Pinecone vector store for production
from langchain_community.vectorstores import Pinecone as LangchainPinecone
from pinecone import Pinecone, ServerlessSpec
from langchain_openai import OpenAIEmbeddings
import os

# 1. Initialize Pinecone client
pc = Pinecone(api_key=os.getenv("PINECONE_API_KEY"))

# 2. Create index with specifications
index_name = "weather-knowledge"
if index_name not in pc.list_indexes().names():
  pc.create_index(
    name=index_name,
    dimension=1536, # Matches OpenAI embedding dimensions
    metric="cosine", # Similarity metric
    spec=ServerlessSpec(cloud="aws", region="us-east-1")
  )

# 3. Create LangChain wrapper and add documents
embeddings = OpenAIEmbeddings()
vectorstore = LangchainPinecone.from_documents(
  weather_texts,
  embeddings,
  index_name=index_name
)
```

Pinecone automatically manages index sharding, replication, and load balancing. Metadata filtering provides pre-filtering by source, date, category, or custom fields before semantic search. Namespaces enable logical isolation within a single index for multi-tenant applications.

A security consideration is to store vector database API keys in environment variables or secrets managers. Never commit credentials to source control or embed them in application code.

Implementing advanced retrievers and rerankers

A basic similarity search typically returns a huge amount of *noise*, chunks that are semantically related but do not contain the exact information needed to answer a question. To transform an agent into a knowledge powerhouse, users must develop multi-stage retrieval procedures that filter, rank, and compress information before it reaches the reasoning model. LangChain provides customized retrievers that go beyond simple vector matching to ensure that the highest-quality context is utilized for grounded generation.

Retrievers in LangChain abstract the logic for retrieving relevant documents from a query. They can be vector-based, keyword-based, hybrid, or LLM-powered. Retrievers are interchangeable components that sit between user queries and document storage, offering various retrieval tactics such as semantic search, filtering, reranking, or self-querying.

LangChain retriever architecture reference

Similarity search forms the foundation of semantic retrieval. It discovers documents whose embeddings are geometrically near the query embedding in the vector space. The following is a basic similarity search:

```
# Basic similarity search
from langchain_community.vectorstores import FAISS

# Create retriever from vector store
retriever = vectorstore.as_retriever(
  search_type="similarity",
  search_kwargs={"k": 4} # Return top 4 most similar documents
)

# Execute retrieval
docs = retriever.get_relevant_documents(
  "What causes sudden temperature drops?"
```

```
)

# Each doc contains content and metadata
for doc in docs:
  print(f"Content: {doc.page_content[:100]}...")
  print(f"Source: {doc.metadata.get('source', 'unknown')}")
```

Similarity search works well for factual inquiries where a single document presumably holds the solution. However, it has limits. Results can be highly redundant, returning several chunks from the same document. Similarity does not ensure factual relevance. Semantically similar documents could explore related concepts without answering the precise query.

Core retriever classes

Core retriever classes constitute the backbone of LangChain's retrieval architecture. These retrievers operate directly on vector stores or document hierarchies and are designed to address common retrieval needs, such as semantic similarity, recencyaware access, and hierarchical document reconstruction. The following table covers the key core retrievers and the retrieval mechanisms they implement:

Class name	Retrieval strategy
`VectorStoreRetriever`	Vector similarity search.
`MultiVectorRetriever`	Parent-child chunk retrieval.
`TimeWeightedVectorStoreRetriever`	Recency-aware retrieval.
`ContextualCompressionRetriever`	Compresses results using LLM.
`ParentDocumentRetriever`	Retrieves full parent docs.
`EnsembleRetriever`	Combines multiple retrievers.
`MergerRetriever`	Merges results from sources.

***Table 9.8**: Core retriever classes in LangChain*

Advanced or LLM-based retrievers

While core retrievers rely on deterministic similarity measures, some retrieval difficulties benefit from languagemodel reasoning itself. Advanced or LLM-based retrievers employ an LLM to extend, rewrite, or annotate queries before retrieval, enhancing recall and relevance for ambiguous or complex questions. The following table outlines the advanced retrievers that add LLM reasoning into the retrieval process:

Class name	Description
`SelfQueryRetriever`	LLM generates metadata filters.
`LLMChainRetriever`	Retrieval driven by LLM chains.
`MultiQueryRetriever`	Expands query into variants.
`HypotheticalDocumentEmbedder (HyDE)`	Embeds synthetic answers.
`ScoreThresholdRetriever`	Filters by similarity score.

***Table 9.9**: Advanced or LLM-powered retrievers*

Keyword and traditional search retrievers

Semantic embeddings are useful, but they are not always sufficient, especially when working with specific **identifiers (IDs)**, codes, or narrowly defined terms. Keyword and classical search retrievers augment vectorbased search by utilizing lexical matching techniques such as **Best Matching 25** (**BM25**) and **Term Frequency–Inverse Document Frequency** (**TFIDF**). The following table lists classic retrievers widely employed alongside semantic search in hybrid RAG pipelines:

Class name	Method
`BM25Retriever`	Keyword-based BM25
`TFIDFRetriever`	TF-IDF similarity
`KNNRetriever`	Nearest-neighbor search

***Table 9.10**: Traditional keyword-based retrievers*

Building a multi-stage retrieval flow with rerankers

Production-grade RAG systems often utilize a Contextual Compression retriever to regulate context quality. This includes a two-stage process: first, a base retriever discovers the top 50 probable matches from the vector store; second, a reranker (such as Flashrank or Cohere) re-sorts these results based on exact relevance to the query, selecting only the top five for the final prompt.

The following code explains how to create a reranking layer in LangChain to improve the precision of weather data retrieval:

```
from langchain.retrievers import ContextualCompressionRetriever
from langchain.retrievers.document_compressors import FlashrankRerank

# 1. Initialize a base retriever with high recall
base_retriever = vector_db.as_retriever(search_kwargs={"k": 20})
```

```
# 2. Configure the reranker to optimize for high precision
compressor = FlashrankRerank()
reranking_retriever = ContextualCompressionRetriever(
  base_compressor=compressor,
  base_retriever=base_retriever
)

# 3. The agent now receives a refined subset of weather context
# query = "Identify the highest humidity recorded in Seattle in the last
year."
# relevant_docs = reranking_retriever.invoke(query)
```

Managing token limits with smart context windows

At the retrieval stage, token restrictions impose practical limits on how much context can be passed downstream. Without early control mechanisms such as reranking or compression, excessive or redundant context might obscure the information most necessary for effective reasoning. Users build context-trimming logic using LangChain's built-in capabilities to proactively eliminate the least relevant parts of the recovered text.

Warning: **Always reserve tokens for model output. Filling the entire context window with input prevents the model from generating responses and causes problems.**

The following table describes common ways for managing retrieval context windows:

Strategy	Technical implementation	Impact on the agent
Max marginal relevance	`search_type="mmr"`	Increases the diversity of retrieved facts.
Parent document retrieval	`ParentDocumentRetriever`	Retrieves full paragraphs for better context.
Contextual trimming	`ConversationTokenBufferMemory`	Prevents overflow by counting tokens.

***Table 9.11**: Retrieval optimization strategies for agentic context*

The best practice is to empirically tune chunk size using the actual documents and query patterns. Evaluate retrieval quality at 500-, 1000-, and 1500-character chunks to identify the sweet spot for the domain.

Retrieval state transition flow

To visualize the transition from raw similarity to refined context, the following figure illustrates the multi-hop flow through a reranked pipeline:

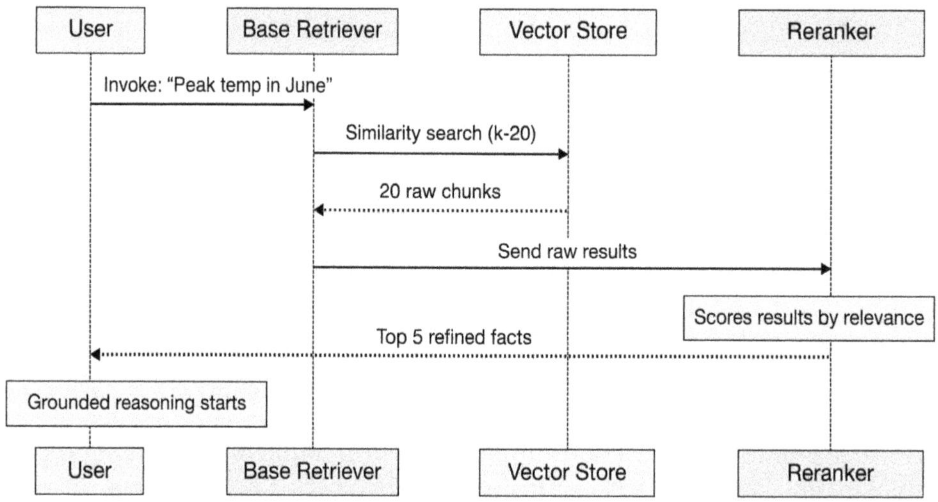

Figure 9.4: *Reranked retrieval sequence for agent context*

Tip: **Use metadata filtering alongside reranking to pre-filter information by location or timestamp. This guarantees the reranker only analyzes documents that belong to the relevant user or time window, dramatically lowering latency and cost.**

Building semantic search and context retrieval flows

Semantic search turns agent retrieval from mere keyword matching into knowledge of intent and context. In a LangChain-powered weather agent, this allows the system to address queries such as *What were the conditions during the historic blizzard?* even if the source documents contain phrases like *extreme precipitation* or *snowstorm*. Building these processes requires a high-fidelity pipeline that travels from user query to high-dimensional vector search.

Semantic search lifecycle

The semantic flow in LangChain involves converting both the knowledge base and the user's active query into the same numerical vector space using an embedding model. By calculating the cosine similarity between these vectors, the agent can identify the most relevant *neighbors* in the document store.

The following code demonstrates a complete semantic retrieval flow for historical climate reports:

```
from langchain_openai import OpenAIEmbeddings
from langchain_community.vectorstores import FAISS
from langchain_core.runnables import RunnablePassthrough
from langchain_core.output_parsers import StrOutputParser

# 1. Initialize embeddings (using text-embedding-3-small for efficiency)
embeddings = OpenAIEmbeddings(model="text-embedding-3-small")

# 2. Connect to the climate vector store
vector_db = FAISS.load_local("climate_history_index", embeddings)
retriever = vector_db.as_retriever(search_kwargs={"k": 3})

# 3. Build the semantic search flow
# The query is passed to both the retriever and the prompt
semantic_chain = (
  {"context": retriever, "question": RunnablePassthrough()}
  | prompt
  | llm
  | StrOutputParser()
)
```

Enhancing search with Maximum Marginal Relevance

A common issue in semantic search is receiving several chunks that contain similar information, which wastes the agent's context window. To remedy this, LangChain gives Maximum Marginal Relevance. MMR balances the similarity to the query with the diversity of the retrieved results, ensuring the agent sees a broad spectrum of data points.

The following table outlines the differences between standard similarity and MMR retrieval:

Search type	Retrieval goal	Best use case
Similarity	Find the most mathematically close matches.	Specific fact extraction (e.g., *What was the temperature?*)
MMR	Find similar but distinct information chunks.	Summarizing broad topics (e.g., *Tell me about the winter season.*)

***Table 9.12**: Comparison of LangChain retrieval search types*

The following code shows how to enable MMR for more diverse weather context retrieval:

```
# MMR retrieval for diverse results
retriever = vectorstore.as_retriever(
  search_type="mmr",
  search_kwargs={
    "k": 4, # Final number of documents to return
    "fetch_k": 20, # Initial candidates to consider
    "lambda_mult": 0.5 # Balance: 0=max diversity, 1=max relevance
  }
)

docs = retriever.get_relevant_documents(
  "How do forecasters predict severe weather?"
)
```

The lambda parameter determines the relevance-diversity trade-off. Values near 1.0 promote relevance, approximating typical similarity search. Values approaching 0.0 maximize diversity, potentially containing less-relevant but complementary information. A value around 0.5 balances the objectives adequately for most applications.

MMR is particularly helpful when documents contain overlapping information, consumers need extensive coverage of a topic, or retrieved context feeds into comprehensive reports rather than targeted questions.

Managing token limits with smart context windows

As retrieval processes get more advanced, token restrictions evolve from an isolated retrieval concern into a systemlevel orchestration challenge. Effective context management today requires coordination among retrieved documents, system commands, conversational history, and response production.

Implementing token-aware context trimming

Counting characters does not guarantee compliance with token limitations, as tokenization is language and model-specific. Token-aware context management counts genuine tokens to prevent context overflow, as follows:

```
# Token-aware text splitting
from langchain_text_splitters import TokenTextSplitter
```

```
token_splitter = TokenTextSplitter(
  chunk_size=500, # Maximum tokens per chunk
  chunk_overlap=50 # Overlap in tokens
)

token_chunks = token_splitter.split_text(weather_doc)


import tiktoken

def trim_context_to_limit(docs, max_tokens=4000, model="gpt-4o-mini"):
  """
  Trims a list of retrieved documents to stay within the model's token
budget.
  """
  encoder = tiktoken.encoding_for_model(model)
  current_tokens = 0
  trimmed_docs = []

  for doc in docs:
    tokens = len(encoder.encode(doc.page_content))
    if current_tokens + tokens <= max_tokens:
      trimmed_docs.append(doc)
      current_tokens += tokens
    else:
      break # Stop adding once the limit is reached

  return trimmed_docs
```

`TokenTextSplitter` defaults to a **`tiktoken`** encoder so chunk sizes are measured in real model tokens rather than characters. Pair it with a `tiktoken`-based trimming function that walks retrieved documents in order and stops once the budget is exhausted.

Production systems must budget tokens among multiple context components. Retrieved papers consume the bulk of the budget. System instructions and reminders require allocation. Conversation history for multi-turn interactions needs space. The response itself requires allocating the output token.

A typical 8,000-token context window would allocate: 1,000 tokens for system instructions and formatting, 5,000 tokens for retrieved documents (four to five chunks at 1,000 tokens each), 1,000 tokens for dialog history, and 1,000 tokens for the model response.

To prevent context window overflow, users must provide proactive trimming logic that examines the total token count before the final LLM call. This requires counting tokens using libraries like `tiktoken` and deleting the least relevant context if the budget is exceeded.

The following code exhibits a *managed* context window that cuts retrieved weather documents to fit a 4,000-token limit:

```
import tiktoken


def trim_context_to_limit(docs, max_tokens=4000, model="gpt-4o-mini"):
  """
  Trims a list of retrieved documents to stay within the model's token
budget.
  """
  encoder = tiktoken.encoding_for_model(model)
  current_tokens = 0
  trimmed_docs = []

  for doc in docs:
    tokens = len(encoder.encode(doc.page_content))
    if current_tokens + tokens <= max_tokens:
      trimmed_docs.append(doc)
      current_tokens += tokens
    else:
      break # Stop adding once the limit is reached

  return trimmed_docs
```

Hierarchical summarization for long documents

When dealing with enormous climate reports that cannot fit in a single prompt, users can employ **hierarchical summarization**. In this method, the agent first summarizes the individual chunks obtained into shorter *gist* versions before integrating them into the final reasoning step. This technique preserves the "essence" of the data while lowering token use by up to 90%.

The following code demonstrates a two-stage summary strategy for huge weather documents:

```
from langchain.chains.summarize import load_summarize_chain
from langchain_openai import ChatOpenAI


# Initialize LLM for summarization
llm = ChatOpenAI(model="gpt-4o-mini", temperature=0)


# Use map_reduce strategy: summarize each chunk, then combine
summarize_chain = load_summarize_chain(
```

```
    llm,
    chain_type="map_reduce" # Alternatives: "stuff", "refine"
)

# Process large climate report in stages
# final_summary = summarize_chain.invoke(large_weather_docs)
```

Chaining retrievers and routers for better recall

Retriever chaining and routing largely address recall and coverage rather than raw accuracy, ensuring that important information is identified before downstream reranking and reasoning refines correctness.

In production weather systems, data is generally dispersed across several formats: historical logs in vector stores, real-time warnings in APIs, and regional policies in structured SQL databases. To achieve high recall, an agent should not rely on a single search strategy; instead, it uses **retriever chaining** and **query routing** to discover the best source for each question.

Routing queries to specialized sources

Query routing functions as a *traffic controller* for the agent's knowledge search. Using an LLM-based router, the agent evaluates the user's intent to determine whether to search a vector database for historical information or use an API for real-time forecasts.

The following figure demonstrates the routing flow for a multi-source weather agent:

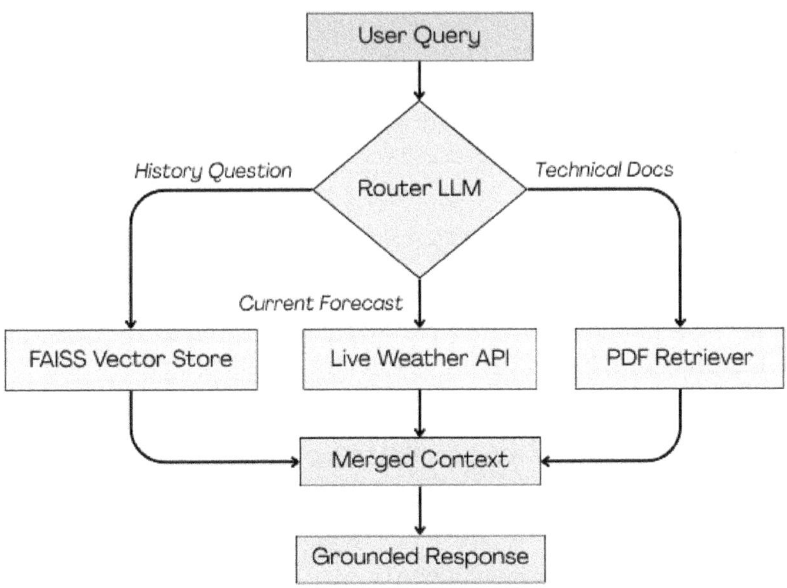

***Figure 9.5**: Multi-source retriever routing architecture*

The following code demonstrates how to implement LLM-based query routing for weather data:

```
from langchain_core.prompts import ChatPromptTemplate
from langchain_openai import ChatOpenAI

# Router prompt to classify query intent
router_prompt = ChatPromptTemplate.from_template("""
Classify this weather query into ONE category: HISTORY, FORECAST, or
DOCUMENTATION.

Query: {query}

Respond with only the category name.
""")

router_llm = ChatOpenAI(model="gpt-4o-mini", temperature=0)
router_chain = router_prompt | router_llm

# Route to appropriate retriever based on classification
# query = "What was the peak temperature last July?"
# route = router_chain.invoke({"query": query}) # Returns "HISTORY"
# Use route to select: vector_store, api_tool, or pdf_retriever
```

A real-world example is the weather forecast services, which maintain different indexes for hourly forecasts (time-series databases), historical averages (vector store), and radar imagery (object storage). Routers direct queries to the appropriate data source based on temporal signals, reducing latency and improving accuracy.

Implementing query expansion for improved recall

Sometimes a user's question is too brief for a similarity search to be helpful. LangChain's `MultiQueryRetriever` stretches a single user query into three to five alternative variations with slightly varied phrasing. By retrieving results for all permutations and integrating them, the agent catches a wider net of important information, considerably increasing retrieval recall.

The following code explains how to use **`MultiQueryRetriever`** to automatically extend weather-related queries:

```
from langchain.retrievers.multi_query import MultiQueryRetriever
from langchain_openai import ChatOpenAI
```

```
# Initialize base retriever
base_retriever = vector_db.as_retriever(search_kwargs={"k": 3})

# Wrap with MultiQueryRetriever for automatic query expansion
multi_query_retriever = MultiQueryRetriever.from_llm(
  retriever=base_retriever,
  llm=ChatOpenAI(model="gpt-4o-mini", temperature=0)
)

# Single query "Seattle storms" becomes multiple variants:
# - "severe weather events in Seattle"
# - "storm history Seattle area"
# - "precipitation extremes Seattle region"
# expanded_docs = multi_query_retriever.invoke("Seattle storms")
```

Tip: **LangChain's `MultiQueryRetriever` generates multiple reformulations of the same question and returns the unique union of retrieved documents, which can improve coverage when vocabulary mismatch would otherwise hide relevant results. It is because this strategy adds extra LLM query-generation and retrieval passes, it can also increase latency, so it is best used when recall matters more than response speed. Source: LangChain reference for `MultiQueryRetriever`.**

RAG chaining methods reference

RAG chaining techniques in LangChain define how retrieved documents are combined with user queries and passed to an LLM. These chains regulate document aggregation, reasoning flow, summarization method, and answer synthesis. Choosing the correct chain affects latency, factual foundation, faithfulness, and scalability of retrieval-augmented systems.

Core RAG document combination chains

To synthesize collected documents into a cohesive solution, LangChain offers numerous main document combination chains. Each strategy regulates how documents are gathered, reasoned about, and summarized before reaching the language model. The following table covers the primary RAG document combination chains, illustrating their behavior and appropriate usage circumstances:

Chain name	Description	Best use case
`StuffDocumentsChain`	Concatenates all documents into a single prompt.	Small document sets
`MapReduceDocumentsChain`	Summarizes docs individually, then combines.	Large document collections
`RefineDocumentsChain`	Iteratively refines an answer per document.	Progressive reasoning
`MapRerankDocumentsChain`	Scores answers and selects the best.	Ranking-based **question answering** (**QA**)
`ReduceDocumentsChain`	Reduces summaries recursively.	Token-limited contexts

***Table 9.13**: Core RAG document combination chains*

High-level RAG question answering chains

While lowlevel document combination chains dictate how context is formed, LangChain also provides higherlevel QA abstractions that cover retrieval, reasoning, and optional citation management. These chains simplify RAG implementation by enabling opinionated, endtoend questionanswering procedures. The following table illustrates the most often used highlevel RAG QA chains and their intended functions:

Chain name	Purpose
`RetrievalQA`	Classic RAG question answering.
`RetrievalQAWithSourcesChain`	QA with citations.
`VectorDBQA`	Legacy vector QA chain.
`ConversationalRetrievalChain`	RAG with chat history.
`ChatVectorDBChain`	Chat-optimized vector QA.

***Table 9.14**: High-level RAG QA chains*

Conversational and memory-aware RAG chains

Many realworld agents function in conversational situations where user queries depend on prior context. To enable multi-turn interactions, LangChain proposes conversational and memory-aware RAG chains that preserve discourse state while executing grounded retrieval. The following table illustrates the chains created specifically for stateful and session-aware retrieval operations:

Chain name	Capability
`ConversationalRetrievalChain`	History-aware retrieval.
`ConversationChain`	Stateful dialogue.
`LLMChain + retriever`	Custom conversational RAG.
`RunnableWithMessageHistory`	Session-aware RAG.

***Table 9.15**: Conversational and memory-aware RAG chains*

Advanced RAG orchestration chains

As retrieval architectures grow more complex, developers often require fine-grained control over execution flow, routing, and coordination across multiple retrievers. LangChain's orchestration chains offer structured, programmable RAG pipelines that go beyond singlestep retrieval. The following table categorizes advanced orchestration chains that support complex, multistage retrieval procedures:

Chain name	Description
`MultiRetrievalQAChain`	Multiple retrievers per query.
`MultiPromptChain`	Prompt routing for RAG.
`RouterChain`	LLM-based routing.
`SequentialChain`	Step-by-step RAG workflows.
`SimpleSequentialChain`	Linear RAG pipelines.

***Table 9.16**: Advanced RAG orchestration chains*

Tip: **For production weather agents, utilize `RetrievalQAWithSourcesChain` to enable citation transparency, allowing users to check which sensor logs or bulletins informed the agent's prediction analysis.**

Retriever chaining

Retriever chains perform consecutive retrieval procedures, where each stage refines or expands the results from preceding stages, as follows:

```
# Multi-hop retrieval chain
from langchain.retrievers import MultiQueryRetriever
from langchain_openai import ChatOpenAI

llm = ChatOpenAI(model="gpt-4o-mini", temperature=0)

# Generates multiple query variations
```

```
multi_query_retriever = MultiQueryRetriever.from_llm(
  retriever=vectorstore.as_retriever(),
  llm=llm
)

# Single user query generates multiple retrieval queries
docs = multi_query_retriever.get_relevant_documents(
  "What weather patterns cause temperature inversions?"
)
```

`MultiQueryRetriever` employs a language model to generate multiple phrasings of the user's question, then retrieves documents for each variation. This handles vocabulary mismatch where users and documents use different terminology for the same topic.

Retriever chains also enable multi-hop reasoning. First, retrieve papers mentioning *temperature inversions*, then retrieve documents linked to those findings by citations or entity references, establishing a knowledge graph traversal through retrieval.

Tip: **Multi-query retrieval improves recall by 15 to 25% for difficult queries but adds delay from LLM-based query expansion. Use for user-facing applications when quality counts more than milliseconds.**

Ensemble retrievers

Ensemble retrievers combine multiple retrieval strategies, merging their results through rank fusion or weighted scoring, as follows:

```
# Ensemble combining semantic and keyword search
from langchain.retrievers import EnsembleRetriever
from langchain_community.retrievers import BM25Retriever

# Semantic retriever
semantic_retriever = vectorstore.as_retriever()

# Keyword retriever
bm25_retriever = BM25Retriever.from_documents(weather_texts)
bm25_retriever.k = 4

# Combine with weighted fusion
ensemble_retriever = EnsembleRetriever(
  retrievers=[semantic_retriever, bm25_retriever],
```

```
  weights=[0.7, 0.3] # 70% semantic, 30% keyword
)

docs = ensemble_retriever.get_relevant_documents(
  "frost point calculation formula"
)
```

Ensemble patterns shine when different retrievers have complementary skills. Semantic search shines at conceptual inquiries. Keyword search (BM25) performs better for accurate terminology, technical IDs, or unusual phrases. Combining both gives robust retrieval across varied query forms.

Reciprocal Rank Fusion (**RRF**) offers an alternative to a weighted combination. It ranks documents based on the reciprocal of their positions in each retriever's results, prioritizing those that appear near the top across multiple rankings.

Router patterns

Routers direct queries to specialized retrievers based on query characteristics, enabling per-domain optimization, as follows:

```
# Route queries to specialized prompts using LCEL RunnableBranch
from langchain_core.prompts import ChatPromptTemplate
from langchain_core.runnables import RunnableBranch
from langchain_core.output_parsers import StrOutputParser
from langchain_openai import ChatOpenAI

llm = ChatOpenAI(model="gpt-4o-mini", temperature=0)

# Define retriever-specific prompts
forecast_prompt = ChatPromptTemplate.from_template(
  "Answer using weather forecast data: {query}"
)
historical_prompt = ChatPromptTemplate.from_template(
  "Answer using historical climate records: {query}"
)

forecast_chain = forecast_prompt | llm | StrOutputParser()
historical_chain = historical_prompt | llm | StrOutputParser()

# Router decides which chain to use based on a predicate over the input.
# Tuples of (predicate, runnable); the trailing runnable is the default.
router = RunnableBranch(
```

```
    (lambda x: "forecast" in x["query"].lower(), forecast_chain),
    historical_chain,
)

# answer = router.invoke({"query": "What is the forecast for Seattle?"})
```

`RunnableBranch` is the LCEL primitive for routing: each branch is a `(predicate, runnable)` tuple, and the first predicate that returns truthy wins. The trailing runnable is the default. This replaces the deprecated `MultiPromptChain` / `LLMRouterChain` stack with a single composable construct.

Routing enables optimization strategies that are unattainable with a unified retrieval approach. Current forecast data lives in a time-series database with temporal indexing. Historical climate data lives in vector stores with semantic search. Meteorological research articles use citation-based retrieval. A router directs *tomorrow's weather* to forecasts, the *warmest decade* to historical data, and *convection models* to research papers.

A real-world example is the weather forecast services that retain distinct indexes for hourly forecasts (time-series database), historical averages (vector store), and radar imagery (object storage). Routers direct queries to the appropriate data source based on temporal signals, reducing latency and improving accuracy.

Search-oriented chains reference

Search chains in LangChain focus on information discovery rather than direct answer synthesis. They enable query rewriting, multi-step exploration, ranking, summarization, and tool-driven search workflows. These chains are commonly used in research assistants, agents, and browsing-based RAG systems.

Web and tool-based search chains

Not all information can be successfully stored or retrieved via vector databases alone. For dynamic or exploratory queries, LangChain enables searchoriented chains that interface with various tools, APIs, and the web. The following table describes the searchfocused chains often used for discovery, study, and tooldriven retrieval scenarios:

Chain name	Function
`WebResearchChain`	Multi-step web research.
`SearchChain`	Generic search execution.
`APIChain`	API-driven search.
`ToolChain`	Tool-orchestrated search.

***Table 9.17**: Web and tool-based search chains*

Query expansion and decomposition chains

When user queries are unclear, underspecified, or multifaceted, a single retrieval pass may fail to acquire all important context. LangChain addresses this difficulty with query expansion and decomposition chains, which reformulate queries into richer or more granular subqueries. The following table demonstrates chains that increase recall and reasoning depth through query modification:

Chain name	Description
`MultiQueryRetriever`	Query diversification.
`HypotheticalDocumentEmbedder (HyDE)`	Synthetic query answers.
`LLMChain` (query rewrite)	Semantic query expansion.
`SelfAskWithSearchChain`	Decomposes complex queries.

***Table 9.18**: Query expansion and decomposition chains*

Ranking and summarization chains

After retrieval, agents typically need to rank, condense, or modify vast amounts of information before generating a final answer. LangChain provides specialized chains for document scoring, ranking, and progressive summarization. The following table outlines chains often used to condense retrieved data into highquality, concise outputs:

Chain name	Purpose
`MapRerankDocumentsChain`	Search result ranking.
`MapReduceDocumentsChain`	Search result summarization.
`RefineDocumentsChain`	Iterative summary improvement.
`ReduceDocumentsChain`	Recursive summarization.

***Table 9.19**: Ranking and summarization chains*

Agent-based search chains

For complex use cases that demand iterative reasoning, planning, and tool usage, LangChain provides agentbased search chains. These chains integrate reasoning loops with tool execution, enabling agents to dynamically select how and where to seek. The following table summarizes agentdriven search chains designed for sophisticated, reasoningheavy discovery tasks:

Chain name	Capability
`ZeroShotAgent`	Search via reasoning.
`ReActChain`	Search and reasoning loop.

Chain name	Capability
`PlanAndExecute`	Planning-based search.
`OpenAIFunctionsAgent`	Tool-driven search.
`StructuredChatAgent`	Schema-guided search.

***Table 9.20**: Agent-based search chains*

RAG versus search chain comparison

Understanding when to use RAG chains versus search chains is crucial for optimal agent design. Although both RAG chains and search chains aim to expose essential information, they serve fundamentally different roles within agent architectures. Understanding when to utilize each method is critical for system design. The following table compares RAG chains and search chains across key architectural dimensions, including determinism, latency, and output structure:

Aspect	RAG chains	Search chains
Goal	Grounded answers	Information discovery
Input	Query and documents	Query and tools
Output	Answer (with sources)	Ranked or summarized results
Determinism	Higher	Lower
Latency	Lower	Higher
Agent use	Optional	Common

***Table 9.21**: RAG versus search chain architecture*

Canonical RAG architecture mapping

To integrate the multiple retrieval components covered throughout this chapter, it is helpful to see them via a single, canonical RAG pipeline. Each LangChain building block translates directly to a specific stage in the retrieval-augmented generation lifecycle, from data ingestion to grounded reasoning. The following table demonstrates a thorough, stage-by-stage mapping of fundamental RAG components used in production-grade systems:

Stage	Component
Load	Document loaders
Split	Text splitters
Embed	Embeddings
Index	Vector stores

Stage	Component
Retrieve	Retrievers
Chain	RAG chain
Reason	LLM/agent

Table 9.22: Canonical RAG architecture component mapping

When creating multi-step weather research agents, users prefer `ConversationalRetrievalChain` to keep context between follow-up inquiries (e.g., *What about yesterday? following What is today's forecast?*). This preserves temporal references and spatial context without requiring the user to repeat information.

Failover logic and production reliability

In a production setting, RAG pipelines are exposed to external failures, such as cloud database outages, API rate restrictions, or network timeouts. A resilient LangChain agent must be architected with failover logic to ensure that if a primary knowledge source becomes unavailable, the system can gracefully downgrade to an alternative source rather than failing the user's request. This section explores how to design resilient retrieval architectures using **LangChain Expression Language** (**LCEL**) and establish troubleshooting procedures for high-availability applications.

Handling RAG pipeline failures with fallbacks

By leveraging the `.with_fallbacks()` method in LCEL, users may build a prioritized list of retrievers. If the primary retriever, typically a high-performance cloud vector store like Pinecone, encounters an error or latency spike, the pipeline immediately switches to a secondary *fallback* retriever, such as a local FAISS index or a simpler keyword-based search.

The following code explains how to create a resilient weather retrieval chain with a local fallback mechanism:

```
# Implementing failover logic for production reliability
from langchain_pinecone import PineconeVectorStore
from langchain_community.vectorstores import FAISS
from langchain_openai import OpenAIEmbeddings

# 1. Initialize primary (cloud) and fallback (local) retrievers.
#    `cloud_vector_store` is the Pinecone instance set up in
#    "Pinecone for cloud deployments" earlier in this chapter:
#    cloud_vector_store = PineconeVectorStore(index_name="weather-knowledge",
#                                             embedding=OpenAIEmbeddings())
primary_retriever = cloud_vector_store.as_retriever()
```

```
# Secondary local store for emergency data access
local_fallback = FAISS.load_local("emergency_weather_index",
OpenAIEmbeddings())
fallback_retriever = local_fallback.as_retriever()

# 2. Define the robust retrieval chain with automatic failover
# If primary fails, the agent seamlessly attempts the fallback
robust_retriever = primary_retriever.with_fallbacks([fallback_retriever])

# 3. Use in a standard RAG chain
# The logic remains the same; the reliability is handled by the component
layer
# response = robust_retriever.invoke("Check for severe storm warnings.")
```

RAG troubleshooting checklist

Reliability also involves proactive monitoring and defined methods for fixing performance concerns. Before deploying an agent to production, utilize the following checklist to detect and prevent common failure modes in the retrieval architecture:

Failure mode	Symptom	Troubleshooting step
Low recall	The agent claims it *does not know,* despite the data being in the store.	Increase the `k` value in search parameters or verify embedding model consistency.
High hallucination	The agent generates incorrect weather data that is not found in the context.	Tighten the system prompt with *strict grounding* instructions (e.g., *only use provided context*).
Context window overflow	API returns *maximum context length exceeded* error.	Reduce document chunk size or implement a reranker to filter context.
High retrieval latency	Semantic search takes longer than two seconds.	Use regional cloud endpoints and implement caching with content hashes.

***Table 9.23**: Production RAG troubleshooting and mitigation guide*

The best practice is to set maximum retry attempts to three to five and cap maximum wait time at 10 to 30 seconds to prevent indefinite hangs while giving acceptable recovery time for transitory difficulties.

Note: **Retrieval latency should be under 100ms for local vector storage and under 300ms for cloud services at p95. Higher latencies suggest index optimization opportunities or infrastructure growth needs.**

Monitoring retrieval quality

Establishing observability within the RAG pipeline is crucial for preserving long-term accuracy. Users should add logging that captures the precise documents retrieved for every user inquiry, allowing them to audit the *chain of evidence* if the agent provides an unacceptable answer.

Tip: **Implement circuit breakers alongside fallbacks to avoid a failing cloud service from repeatedly timing out and slowing down the entire agentic loop. If the primary store fails several times within a short window, the circuit breaker should keep the system on the local backup for a "cool-down" period.**

Building complete production-ready RAG architectures

The preceding sections discussed separate strategies for retrieval quality, orchestration, and resilience. In production systems, these strategies rarely function in isolation. This section consolidates them into a unified checklist for deploying dependable, maintainable RAG systems.

Building a production-ready RAG system pushes beyond the *happy path* of simple **question and answering** (Q&A) to address latency, data freshness, and trust. A world-class weather agent must not only be accurate but also rapid and verified.

Production RAG checklist

Before migrating the agent from a notebook to a user-facing application, it is crucial to ensure the implementation of the following production features:

- **Hybrid search**: Combine vector-based semantic search with BM25 keyword-based search to catch both concepts and exact phrases, such as specific station IDs.
- **Semantic caching**: Store the results of typical searches (e.g., *What is the weather today?*) to minimize expenses and deliver replies in microseconds.
- **Embedding pre-computation**: Index the entire climate library into a vector store before runtime to eliminate the overhead of embedding documents during a live chat.
- **LLM-as-judge verification**: Implement a second LLM layer that validates the agent's answer against the retrieved documents to catch any potential hallucinations before the user sees them.

Tip: In production, remain below 80% of the model's overall token limit. Factual precision generally diminishes as the users approach the hard cap of a context window, so preserving a "safety buffer" enhances overall reliability.

In regulated environments, retrieval filters should impose **role-based access control (RBAC)** at the retriever layer to ensure that only approved documents can enter the model context.

Conclusion

This chapter demonstrated that RAG transforms language models into knowledge-based agents by integrating generation with evidence retrieval. Readers learned the entire RAG architecture, including loading documents, chunking and embedding them, storing and retrieving vectors, and putting together prompts. This way, answers are based on verifiable context instead of model guesswork.

Readers used FAISS for local development and Pinecone for cloud persistence to build practical retrieval stacks. Readers also explored different strategies, including similarity search, Maximum Marginal Relevance, parent document retrieval, contextual compression, and reranking, ensuring the results were more relevant even with token limits. Readers also used token-aware context trimming and summarization patterns to fit high-value evidence into the model's context window without making the response too crowded. Finally, readers put these pieces together with production issues, query routing, and ensembles to improve recall, as well as fallbacks, retries, monitoring, and evaluation to make sure retrieval works well at scale.

In the next chapter, we will go beyond documents and use knowledge networks (knowledge graphs plus vector search) and external APIs for multi-hop reasoning, freshness and versioning, and enterprise controls such as access governance and audit logging.

CHAPTER 10
Fusing Knowledge Networks for Advanced Reasoning

Introduction

Static retrieval has reached its limits. While **retrieval-augmented generation** (**RAG**) enables agents to access discrete documents, real-world decision-making requires an understanding of the relationships among facts across temporal, spatial, and causal dimensions. For example, climate patterns are linked by cause-and-effect relationships, temporal sequences, geographic hierarchies, and physical dependencies, which a semantic search cannot capture completely.

This chapter transforms the agent from a conversational tool to a decision-making system by integrating different knowledge networks into a single hybrid reasoning engine. With graph-based architectures, the agent can perform multi-hop reasoning, meaning it can follow the path from ocean temperature anomalies to atmospheric effects to regional impacts. This approach reveals connections that document retrieval alone cannot capture.

Readers will use knowledge graphs to navigate relationships and perform multi-hop reasoning. They will then integrate these with vector search to construct hybrid retrieval pipelines that achieve high accuracy. They will also connect live search and external **application programming interfaces** (**APIs**) to keep the agent's world model up to date. Readers will use these ideas in weather and climate scenarios that need dispute resolution, version control, and reasoning that can be checked. By the end, readers will have built a Source Fusion Architecture that enables them to make deep discoveries and informed decisions that account for the situation in high-stakes contexts.

Structure

This chapter covers the following topics:

- Integrate reasoning using knowledge graph systems
- Perform relationship traversal and knowledge discovery

- Combine vector and graph-based search methods
- Connect external APIs for real-time insights
- Integrate web search and live data feeds
- Manage knowledge freshness and version control
- Design enterprise-level decision-making AI agents

Objectives

This chapter enhances agentic reasoning by integrating structured and unstructured knowledge. It begins with the fundamentals of knowledge graphs, illustrating how they represent entities and relationships, enable multiple hops, and support reasoning patterns beyond the capabilities of vector search. Readers will employ hybrid retrieval, combining graph traversal with vector similarity. This enables the agent to use both semantic meaning and explicit structure when answering complex questions.

Next, readers will add external APIs, online search, and streaming feeds to the agent so that it can do more than store static data. They also add useful patterns for validation, rate limiting, caching, and error handling. Readers will learn how to deal with conflicting sources by using authority scoring, recency rules, and consensus/weighted approaches. They will also learn how to keep information up to date by using versioning and cache invalidation. By the end of the chapter, readers will have developed an enterprise-ready weather decision support system that combines graphs, vector stores, and real-time data to deliver answers with confidence scores and clear, verifiable evidence trails.

Integrating reasoning using knowledge graph systems

Traditional vector-based RAG treats documents as separate islands of text, which typically fails when queries involve connecting numerous linked facts. To enable complicated reasoning, an agent must grasp the relationships, or *edges*, that connect various pieces of information. By incorporating knowledge graphs, users provide the agent with a *digital map* of reality rather than merely a library of books.

Relationship traversal and knowledge discovery

The power of knowledge graphs resides not in retaining isolated information, but in capturing the complicated network of interactions that connect them. Unlike traditional databases, where information is stored in inflexible tables, or vector stores, where semantic similarity provides the only connection, knowledge graphs depict the real-world structure of how things relate to one another. This structural representation converts basic lookups into intelligent reasoning, enabling agents to uncover insights by following chains of relationships across the knowledge network.

In a knowledge graph, data is represented as a network of **nodes** (entities), **edges** (typed relationships), and properties that capture attributes. This explicit structure allows an agent to reason over links that would otherwise remain implicit in unstructured text. Relationship traversal allows the agent to start at one entity (e.g., *Seattle Sensor*) and uncover associated facts across the network (e.g., *Part of PNW Grid* | *Managed by Central HQ*). This **multi-hop reasoning** is critical for knowledge discovery, enabling the agent to find hidden dependencies that keyword searches would miss.

This explicit encoding of relationships facilitates multi-hop reasoning. Answering the question, *How does ocean temperature affect California drought?* involves traversing: *Ocean Temperature* | *INFLUENCES* | *El Niño/La Niña* | *AFFECTS* | *Jet Stream* | *MODULATES* | *Precipitation Patterns* | *IMPACTS* | *Drought Conditions*. Each hop follows typed relationships that contain semantic meaning lacking in unstructured text.

The following figure depicts how an agent walks a graph to uncover non-obvious connections for an enterprise grid:

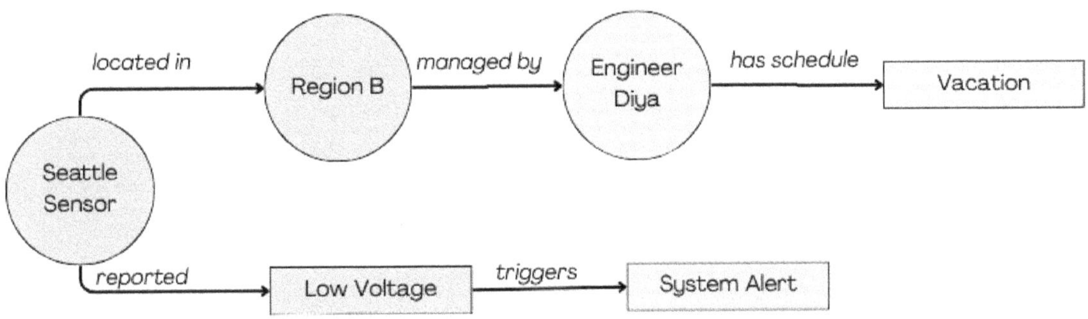

Figure 10.1*: Multi-hop relationship traversal for agentic reasoning*

Tip: **Use descriptive relationship types like `CAUSES`, `INFLUENCES`, and `CORRELATES_WITH` rather than generic `RELATED_TO`. Specific relationship semantics enable more powerful queries and clearer reasoning.**

Implementing GraphRAG with LangChain

Once relationships are formally modeled, the next challenge is making them accessible through natural language. Agents should not require consumers to comprehend graph query languages such as Cypher. This section presents GraphRAG, a paradigm that helps language models automatically transform user intent into structured graph traversals.

Bridging the gap between natural language questions and graph database queries requires sophisticated translation techniques. While graph databases like Neo4j offer extensive querying capabilities through the Cypher language, expecting users or agents to write

Cypher queries directly poses a huge usability hurdle. LangChain addresses this difficulty by providing abstractions that enable language models to dynamically build, execute, and understand graph queries, transforming natural language into structured graph traversals without requiring human query construction.

GraphRAG combines the structured querying power of graph databases with natural language reasoning. LangChain provides abstractions, such as the `GraphCypherQAChain`, which allows a **large language model** (**LLM**) to dynamically build Cypher queries (for Neo4j) from natural language, execute them, and summarize the findings into a human-readable answer.

The following code explains how to initialize a knowledge graph reasoning tool using LangChain and Neo4j:

Note: **If you do not yet have Neo4j running locally, complete the Docker-based setup from the earlier environment/setup section before continuing. Without a running instance, the code below will fail at the first connection step.**

```
from langchain_neo4j import Neo4jGraph, GraphCypherQAChain
from langchain_openai import ChatOpenAI

# Initialize Neo4j connection
graph = Neo4jGraph(url="bolt://localhost:7687", username="neo4j",
password="pwd")

# Build reasoning chain that converts natural language to Cypher
graph_chain = GraphCypherQAChain.from_llm(
  ChatOpenAI(model="gpt-4o-mini", temperature=0),
  graph=graph,
  verbose=True
)

# Query example: "Who manages sensors with low voltage in Region B?"
# Generates: MATCH (s:Sensor)-[:REPORTED]->(:Voltage {status:'low'})
#     WHERE s.region = 'B' MATCH (s)-[:MANAGED_BY]->(e:Engineer) RETURN
e.name
```

The chain converts natural language questions into Cypher queries, runs them against the graph, and synthesizes results into natural language responses. This enables agents to exploit structured graph information without hand-crafted query templates.

Tip: **Enable verbose mode when developing to see the resulting Cypher queries. This helps diagnose mismatched entity names and enhance the graph schema.**

Warning: **LLM-generated Cypher queries can be wrong or inefficient. Always validate created queries in development and add query timeouts to prevent runaway graph traversals in production.**

Creating a weather knowledge graph schema

Before agents can reason over graph structures, users must construct the schema, which serves as the blueprint that describes which entities exist, how they are connected, and what attributes they possess. A well-designed schema represents domain logic: sensors belong to regions, engineers maintain equipment, and warnings are triggered based on data. This underlying structure controls the forms of reasoning the agent can undertake. Poor schema design limits query expressiveness and reasoning depth, while intelligent modeling unlocks powerful multi-hop inference patterns.

The following code demonstrates how to populate a Neo4j knowledge graph with weather monitoring infrastructure:

```
from langchain_neo4j import Neo4jGraph

graph = Neo4jGraph(url="bolt://localhost:7687", username="neo4j",
password="pwd")

# Create sensors, regions, and relationships
schema_queries = [
  "CREATE (s:Sensor {id: 'SEA-001', name: 'Seattle Downtown', type:
'temperature'})",
  "CREATE (r:Region {id: 'PNW', name: 'Pacific Northwest'})",
  "CREATE (e:Engineer {id: 'ENG-001', name: 'Alex Johnson'})",
  "MATCH (s:Sensor {id: 'SEA-001'}), (r:Region {id: 'PNW'}) CREATE (s)-
[:LOCATED_IN]->(r)",
  "MATCH (s:Sensor {id: 'SEA-001'}), (e:Engineer {id: 'ENG-001'}) CREATE (s)-
[:MAINTAINED_BY]->(e)"
]

# Uncomment the loop below to populate the graph against a live Neo4j
instance.
# It is left commented out so importing this module does not mutate the
database.
# for query in schema_queries:
#     graph.query(query)
```

This process constructs nodes representing weather phenomena and relationships that capture causal ties with confidence scores and temporal lags. The graph explicitly contains domain knowledge about how sensors connect to regions and maintenance workers.

Benefits of graph-based reasoning

Understanding when to apply graph-based reasoning over classic vector search entails examining the nature of the questions and the structure of the user's knowledge. Vector embeddings excel at capturing semantic similarity and handling ambiguous conceptual matches, but they struggle with precise factual correlations and logical linkages. Knowledge graphs offer complementary strengths, including explicit encoding of relationships, auditable reasoning paths, and support for complex multi-hop queries. The choice between approaches, or the option to blend them, depends on whether the agent needs to investigate concepts or traverse known relationships.

The following table shows why knowledge graphs are preferable for complicated reasoning tasks compared to standard vector-only systems:

Feature	Vector RAG	GraphRAG
Logic type	Semantic similarity	Explicit relationships
Reasoning	Single-hop/summarization	Multi-hop traversal
Grounding	Text snippets	Verifiable structured facts
Traceability	Probabilistic retrieval	Auditable path of nodes/edges

***Table 10.1**: Comparison of vector and graph reasoning models*

Variable-length path queries might be expensive on large graphs. Always specify reasonable maximum depths and use relationship-type filters to narrow the search space.

Perform relationship traversal and knowledge discovery

In LangChain, relationship traversal is typically implemented by combining a graph connection (such as **Neo4jGraph**) with an LLM-driven query planner (such as **GraphCypherQAChain**). Instead of hard-coding graph queries, you let the chain translate the user's natural-language question into a Cypher query, execute it against the graph, and then summarize the results in a grounded response.

To make traversal reliable, the chain must be constrained by the graph schema (node labels, relationship types, and key properties). In practice, you pass schema context to the prompt (or rely on LangChain's graph helpers to fetch it) and add explicit rules such as allowed relationship types, maximum hop depth, and required filters. These constraints reduce query hallucinations and prevent expensive variable-length traversals:

- A practical way to enable natural-language graph traversal in LangChain is to use **GraphCypherQAChain**, which translates a reader's question into Cypher, executes it against the graph, and returns a grounded result. During development, it is helpful to enable verbose mode so you can inspect the generated Cypher, understand how the chain is interpreting the prompt, and refine both the schema and the instructions when the traversal does not behave as expected.

- Wrap graph access as a **Tool** (or **@tool**) when building an agent so the model can decide when a graph traversal is needed versus vector retrieval or API calls.
- Add guardrails: validate generated Cypher against an allow-list of labels/relationships, enforce hop limits, and apply query timeouts to avoid runaway traversals.
- Return evidence, not just prose: have the graph step return the matched nodes/edges (or a compact path summary) and feed that into the final LLM step so answers remain traceable.

In production LangChain systems, treat traversal as an expensive operation. Configure Neo4j query timeouts, cap result sizes (for example, top N paths), and require deterministic filters (region, status, time window) so the chain does not explore the entire graph. If you are using an agent, also apply tool-level rate limits so repeated calls do not amplify latency or cost.

LangChain works best when the model has a clear view of the graph schema. For Neo4j, you can refresh the schema and pass it into prompts so the LLM generates valid labels, properties, and relationship types. On the output side, format traversal results into an evidence bundle (key entities, relationship paths, timestamps, and confidence/authority fields) and provide that bundle as context to the final generation step. This keeps the answer grounded while still allowing the LLM to explain the reasoning in natural language.

For example, when a user asks, *Why are several Pacific Northwest sensors reporting low voltage today?* a LangChain agent can route the request to a graph tool backed by **GraphCypherQAChain**. The chain generates a constrained Cypher query that starts from the affected sensors, traverses *LOCATEDIN/DEPENDSON/HASALERT*-style relationships, and returns a short path-based evidence set. The final response is then composed from that evidence, allowing the agent to cite the traversal path and timestamps instead of relying on free-form speculation.

Combining vector and graph-based search methods

While knowledge graphs excel at structured associations, vector stores are excellent at capturing semantic similarity and *vibe*. A hybrid reasoning system mixes both to attain the maximum possible recall and precision.

Architecting the hybrid search pipeline

Building a hybrid search engine needs careful orchestration of two fundamentally different retrieval processes. Vector search uses semantic similarity to find documents whose meaning aligns with the query, even when exact terms do not match. Graph search operates on structural relationships, traversing explicit links between items to discover related information. The issue lies in knowing when to apply each strategy, how to execute them quickly, and how to blend their outputs into a coherent context. A well-designed fusion architecture maximizes the strengths of both methods while reducing their unique flaws.

In this architecture, the agent triggers the following two parallel retrieval paths:

- **Semantic path**: Uses a vector store to discover similar conceptual documents.
- **Structural path**: Uses a knowledge graph to uncover specific entity links.

The findings are then fused and reranked, creating a *Source Fusion* context that is both semantically rich and logically sound. Pure graph search finds physically related items but cannot match unstructured semantic material. Pure vector search captures semantic similarities but misses explicit correlations. Hybrid search utilizes both, harnessing complementary qualities.

Source fusion architecture diagram

Visualizing the flow of information through a hybrid search engine highlights the key decision points and integration layers that enable multi-source reasoning. The fusion manager operates as an intelligent router, directing queries to the appropriate knowledge sources based on query attributes. Vector stores handle semantic searches, while knowledge graphs perform relationship traversals. Results from both channels go through a reranking and filtering stage that eliminates duplicates, assesses relevance, and prioritizes authoritative information before providing unified context to the reasoning agent.

The following figure visualizes how a source fusion manager fuses unstructured and structured data into a single unified context for the agent:

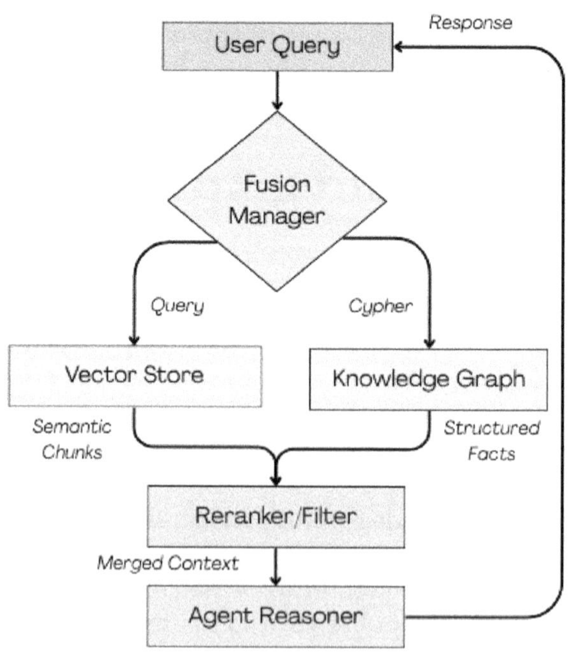

***Figure 10.2**: Source fusion architecture for hybrid reasoning*

Implementing hybrid retrieval with LangChain

With both semantic and structural retrieval channels in place, the agent now requires orchestration logic that can execute them concurrently and blend their outputs into a single reasoning context.

Translating architectural notions into workable code requires constructing retrieval components that can conduct vector searches and graph queries concurrently, then integrate their results intelligently. The implementation must handle edge cases, including empty result sets, query timeouts, and source availability issues. LangChain provides the building blocks for vector store integration and graph chain execution; however, the fusion logic responsible for combining results, resolving conflicts, and displaying coherent context requires bespoke orchestration tailored to the domain-specific requirements.

The following code explains how to develop a production hybrid retrieval system that queries both vector stores and knowledge graphs in parallel:

```
from langchain_community.vectorstores import FAISS
from langchain_neo4j import Neo4jGraph, GraphCypherQAChain
from langchain_openai import ChatOpenAI, OpenAIEmbeddings
from langchain_core.documents import Document

class HybridWeatherRetriever:
  def __init__(self, vector_store, graph, llm):
    self.vector_store = vector_store
    self.graph_chain = GraphCypherQAChain.from_llm(llm, graph=graph)

  def retrieve(self, query: str, k: int = 3) -> list[Document]:
    # Sequential retrieval: vector search runs first, then the graph query.
    # See "Parallel and asynchronous API calls" later in the chapter for an
    # async variant that fans these out concurrently.
    vector_docs = self.vector_store.similarity_search(query, k=k)
    graph_result = self.graph_chain.invoke({"query": query})
    graph_doc = Document(page_content=graph_result["result"],
             metadata={"source": "knowledge_graph"})
    return vector_docs + [graph_doc]

# Usage
retriever = HybridWeatherRetriever(
  FAISS.load_local("weather_index", OpenAIEmbeddings()),
  Neo4jGraph(url="bolt://localhost:7687", username="neo4j", password="pwd"),
  ChatOpenAI(model="gpt-4o-mini", temperature=0)
)
```

`HybridWeatherRetriever` combines two retrieval paths: semantic FAISS vector search for conceptual similarity and a `GraphCypherQAChain` lookup for entity relationships. Both result sets are merged into a single list with source metadata so the downstream RAG chain can cite either type of evidence.

This pattern first detects semantically comparable texts, then runs graph traversal to find associated concepts. The result combines direct semantic matches with structurally related information.

Hybrid retrieval considerably improves accuracy for queries needing both conceptual comprehension (vector) and factual precision (graph). This approach is particularly well-suited for enterprise knowledge that combines unstructured documents and structured relationships.

A best practice is to cache expensive graph traversals keyed by entity sets. Many queries reference the same fundamental entities, enabling significant speed benefits through caching.

Query rewriting for graph optimization

Natural language questions rarely map directly to effective graph database queries. A user inquiring, "Which sensors are broken in the Pacific Northwest?" requires translation into precise Cypher syntax that matches sensor nodes, filters by status, and traverses geographic relationships. Query rewriting acts as an optimization layer, transforming verbose or ambiguous natural language into compact, efficient graph patterns that exploit indexes and minimize traversal depth. This preprocessing step can drastically reduce query execution time while boosting result correctness by clarifying entity types and relationship constraints.

Complex natural language queries typically need transformation into efficient graph traversal patterns. The following code explains how to utilize an LLM to rewrite queries before running them:

```
from langchain_core.prompts import ChatPromptTemplate
from langchain_openai import ChatOpenAI

rewrite_prompt = ChatPromptTemplate.from_template("""
Rewrite to graph traversal pattern:
Query: {query}
Schema: Sensor, Region, Engineer | LOCATED_IN, MAINTAINED_BY
Optimized:
""")

rewrite_chain = rewrite_prompt | ChatOpenAI(model="gpt-4o-mini",
temperature=0)

# "broken sensors in Pacific Northwest" →
```

```
# "MATCH (s:Sensor {status:'broken'})-[:LOCATED_IN]->(:Region {name:'Pacific
Northwest'})"
```

Pattern matching enables sophisticated limitations. Users can filter based on node features, relationship attributes, path length, and structural patterns such as cycles or common neighbors.

Ensemble retrieval with weighted fusion

Once users have obtained findings from both vector and graph sources, the crucial task is to determine the appropriate weighting of their contributions to the final answer. Different query types necessitate different weighting strategies. Research-oriented questions benefit from semantic vector search, whereas compliance queries that require factual precision depend on graph relationship validation. Adaptive weighing goes further, allowing the system to dynamically modify source priority based on query criteria, available data, and historical accuracy patterns. Understanding these tactics enables users to tailor their fusion architecture for individual use cases and domain needs.

The following table provides alternative ways for combining vector and graph results:

Strategy	Description	Weight distribution	Best for
Semantic priority	Favor vector search results	Vector: 0.7, Graph: 0.3	Conceptual queries, research
Structural priority	Favor graph traversal results	Vector: 0.3, Graph: 0.7	Factual queries, compliance
Balanced fusion	Equal weight to both sources	Vector: 0.5, Graph: 0.5	General-purpose queries
Adaptive weighting	LLM decides weights per query	Varies by query intent; the LLM increases graph weight for factual or relationship-heavy queries and vector weight for semantic or exploratory queries, then adjusts using source confidence and result quality.	Complex multi-aspect queries

Table 10.2*: Ensemble retrieval strategies for hybrid search*

Beyond boosting retrieval accuracy, weighted fusion promotes explainability in agent reasoning. By explicitly noting the influence of each source, whether semantic vectors or structural graph traversal, agents can display not only the retrieved facts but also the rationale underlying their prioritization. This transparency is crucial in enterprise environments, where stakeholders may need to understand why a specific response emphasized relational evidence above semantic similarity, or vice versa.

Different solutions suit different scenarios. Semantic priority works when investigating concepts. Structural priority enforces factual precision. Balanced fusion gives general coverage. Adaptive weighting optimizes per-query.

Connecting external APIs for real-time insights

Static databases are outdated the instant they are indexed. For decision-making agents, incorporating real-time data from APIs and live search is crucial for maintaining an accurate world model.

API augmentation of static knowledge

Knowledge graphs and vector stores provide historical context, but the real world evolves continuously. Weather forecasts update hourly, sensor networks feed live readings, and market prices fluctuate by the second. To maintain an accurate world model, agents must tap into external data sources that provide current information unavailable in static databases. API integration bridges the gap between historical knowledge and present reality, enabling agents to enhance graph relationships and vector documents with live data that reflects the current state of the systems they reason about.

Agents utilize specialized tools to retrieve live data, such as current weather, market prices, or sensor statuses, that overwrite or augment historical context. External APIs provide real-time data unavailable in static knowledge repositories.

The following code exhibits a tool configuration that gets real-time system status for fusion with historical records:

```
import os
import requests
from langchain_core.tools import tool

@tool
def get_live_system_status(component_id: str) -> str:
  """
  Fetches real-time status from the monitoring API.
  Use this to verify historical records against live conditions.
  """
  response = requests.get(
    f"https://api.weather-monitoring.com/v1/sensors/{component_id}/status",
    headers={"Authorization": f"Bearer {os.getenv('API_KEY')}"},
    timeout=5
  )

  if response.status_code == 200:
```

```
    data = response.json()
    return f"Live Status for {component_id}: {data['status']} (Updated
{data['last_update']})"
  return f"Error fetching status for {component_id}: {response.status_code}"
```

Production API integration involves comprehensive error handling, timeout configuration, retry logic, and rate limiting to minimize service overload and manage expenses.

A security consideration is to validate API replies and apply timeout limits. External APIs can become attack vectors if not adequately sandboxed. API keys should be stored in environment variables or secrets managers.

Implementing API result caching

External API calls increase latency and expense with every request. A naive approach that retrieves live weather data for every query quickly becomes impractical, as response times degrade with accumulated API latency and consumption costs escalate due to repeated retrieval of the same information. Intelligent caching addresses these difficulties by storing recent API responses and delivering them for subsequent queries within a freshness window. The challenge lies in balancing data staleness and performance, as caching for too long risks serving obsolete information, while caching too briefly yields limited benefits.

To reduce costs and latency, utilize intelligent caching for external API calls, as follows:

```
import time
import requests
from langchain_core.tools import tool

class WeatherAPICache:
  def __init__(self, ttl_seconds: int = 300):
    self.cache = {}
    self.ttl = ttl_seconds

  def get(self, key: str):
    if key in self.cache:
      value, timestamp = self.cache[key]
      if time.time() - timestamp < self.ttl:
        return value
      del self.cache[key]
    return None

  def set(self, key: str, value: str):
    self.cache[key] = (value, time.time())

api_cache = WeatherAPICache(ttl_seconds=300)
```

```
def fetch_live_data(sensor_id: str) -> str:
  """Fetch current sensor status from the upstream monitoring API."""
  response = requests.get(
    f"https://api.weather-monitoring.com/v1/sensors/{sensor_id}/status",
    timeout=5
  )
  response.raise_for_status()
  return response.text

@tool
def get_cached_sensor_status(sensor_id: str) -> str:
  """Return cached sensor status if fresh; otherwise fetch, cache, and
return."""
  cached = api_cache.get(sensor_id)
  if cached is not None:
    return cached
  data = fetch_live_data(sensor_id)
  api_cache.set(sensor_id, data)
  return data
```

Time-based invalidation eliminates cache entries after a set duration. More sophisticated strategies are invalidated based on source update notifications or data change detection.

Note: **For high-frequency requests, caching can substantially reduce API costs and improve response time when many queries repeat within the cache window. The exact benefit depends on factors such as request repetition, cache hit rate, TTL settings, and freshness requirements, so measure these trade-offs in your own workload before setting a caching policy.**

Rate limiting and retry logic

Production API integration extends beyond simple **Hypertext Transfer Protocol (HTTP)** queries to incorporate resilience mechanisms that handle failures gracefully. External services set rate limits to prevent overload, network connections fail intermittently, and transient failures occur without warning. Without sufficient controls, these circumstances cascade into system failures or unforeseen expenses from runaway repeat loops. Rate limiting prevents the agent from exceeding service quotas, while exponential backoff retry logic handles temporary failures by increasing wait times between retries. This approach avoids overwhelming struggling services while eventually surfacing persistent errors that require intervention.

The following code demonstrates production-ready API integration with exponential backoff:

```
import time
import requests
```

```
from tenacity import retry, stop_after_attempt, wait_exponential

class RateLimitedAPIClient:
  def __init__(self, requests_per_minute: int = 60):
    self.rpm = requests_per_minute
    self.request_times = []

  def _check_rate_limit(self):
    now = time.time()
    self.request_times = [t for t in self.request_times if now - t < 60]
    if len(self.request_times) >= self.rpm:
      time.sleep(60 - (now - self.request_times[0]))
    self.request_times.append(now)

  @retry(stop=stop_after_attempt(3), wait=wait_exponential(min=1, max=10))
  def fetch_weather_data(self, location: str) -> dict:
    self._check_rate_limit()
    response = requests.get(f"https://api.weather.com/v1/current/{location}",
timeout=5)
    response.raise_for_status()
    return response.json()
```

Rate limiting prevents service overload, while retry logic with exponential backoff handles transient failures gracefully.

Integrating web search and live data feeds

Sometimes the information the agent requires does not exist in any structured database or API; it is breaking news, a recent policy change, or an emerging pattern that has not yet been fully documented. Web search solves this gap by offering access to the broader internet's constantly evolving information ecosystem. Unlike controlled APIs or curated knowledge graphs, web search offers unstructured, variable-quality results that require filtering and validation. The trade-off is worthwhile when coverage counts more than precision: weather emergencies, breaking climatic events, and recently published research sometimes surface in search results long before being indexed in structured sources.

When internal data is insufficient, agents might use a web search to find up-to-date information. This is necessary for breaking news, recent weather events, or public alerts not yet in the knowledge graph.

The following code demonstrates web search integration with result filtering:

```
from langchain_community.tools import DuckDuckGoSearchRun
from langchain_core.tools import tool, Tool
from datetime import datetime
```

```
# Initialize web search tool
search = DuckDuckGoSearchRun()

@tool
def search_weather_news(query: str, max_results: int = 3) -> str:
  """
  Search the web for recent weather news and alerts.
  Use this when internal data does not cover recent events.
  """
  # Add time context to query
  time_query = f"{query} weather {datetime.now().year}"

  try:
    results = search.run(time_query)
    return f"Web search results for '{query}':\n{results}"
  except Exception as e:
    return f"Search failed: {str(e)}"

# Create tool for agent
web_search_tool = Tool(
  name="WeatherWebSearch",
  func=search_weather_news,
  description="Search the web for current weather news, alerts, and recent
forecasts"
)
```

`DuckDuckGoSearchRun` reaches the open web for current events that are not in the internal knowledge base. The `@tool`-decorated wrapper adds a year token to the query so the model is biased toward recent results.

Web search enables agents to answer inquiries about extremely recent events that have not yet been indexed in knowledge graphs or vector stores.

Tip: **Add temporal context (year, month) into search queries to boost result relevance. Without specific time constraints, web search may deliver outdated content.**

Source authority and trust scoring

Not all data sources warrant equal trust. Internal sensor networks provide ground-truth measurements with millisecond freshness, whereas web search results may contain supposition or outdated information. Establishing clear authority scores for each source type enables conflict resolution algorithms to make rational conclusions when sources dispute. These rankings indicate both inherent dependability (*how reliable is the source?*) and temporal features (*how fresh is the data?*). A well-calibrated authority hierarchy guarantees the agent favors trustworthy, current information over doubtful or stale alternatives when building replies.

The following table outlines how to award authority scores to different data sources:

Source type	Authority score	Freshness	Typical latency	Use case
Internal sensors	0.95	Real-time	<100ms	Ground truth measurements.
Official APIs	0.90	Minutes	200 to 500ms	Government weather data.
Knowledge graph	0.85	Static	<50ms	Historical patterns.
Vector store	0.75	Batch updated	100 to 200ms	Research, documentation.
Web search	0.60	Real-time	1 to 3s	Breaking news, public info.

***Table 10.3**: Source authority scoring for conflict resolution*

Confidence scores incorporate source agreement (*do sources concur?*), source dependability (*how trustworthy are the sources?*), and recency (*how current is the information?*).

Resolving conflicts across multiple sources

Multi-source reasoning inevitably faces contradictions. The knowledge graph might imply a sensor is operational based on yesterday's data, but a live API reports it as unavailable, and online search suggests sporadic failures. Without explicit conflict resolution logic, agents face an impossible choice of selecting a source arbitrarily, presenting contradictory information, or declining to provide an answer. Principled resolution solutions negotiate these problems systematically, applying criteria that account for source authority, information freshness, and majority consensus to determine the most likely accurate response while acknowledging doubt.

When various sources provide conflicting information (e.g., the database says *Active* but the live search indicates *Outage*), the agent must employ a resolution mechanism.

The following table compares resolution strategies:

Strategy	Logic	Use case
Recency bias	Trust the newest data point.	Weather, sensor logs, prices
Authority score	Trust the most reliable source (e.g., API > Search).	Compliance, legal specs
Consensus	Require majority agreement among sources.	Fact-checking, news validation
Weighted	Combine authority and recency scores.	Enterprise decision-making

***Table 10.4**: Conflict resolution strategies for multi-source agents*

The following code implements a conflict resolver that applies these strategies:

```
from dataclasses import dataclass
from datetime import datetime
from collections import Counter

@dataclass
class DataPoint:
  value: str
  source: str
  authority_score: float
  timestamp: datetime

class ConflictResolver:
  def __init__(self, strategy: str = "authority"):
    self.strategy = strategy

  def resolve(self, data_points: list[DataPoint]) -> DataPoint:
    if self.strategy == "recency":
      return max(data_points, key=lambda x: x.timestamp)
    elif self.strategy == "authority":
      return max(data_points, key=lambda x: x.authority_score)
    elif self.strategy == "consensus":
      # Tie-breaking: Counter.most_common() preserves insertion order, so on
a
      # tie the first matching DataPoint in `data_points` wins. If that is not
      # acceptable in your domain, layer authority_score or timestamp on top.
      most_common = Counter(dp.value for dp in data_points).most_common(1)[0]
[0]
      return next(dp for dp in data_points if dp.value == most_common)
    elif self.strategy == "weighted":
      scored = [(dp.authority_score * 0.6 +
           max(0, 1 - (datetime.now() - dp.timestamp).total_seconds() /
86400) * 0.4, dp)
          for dp in data_points]
      return max(scored)[1]
    return data_points[0]

# Usage: resolver = ConflictResolver("weighted")
# Result prioritizes sensor (72°F) over API (71°F) over web (74°F)
```

ConflictResolver reconciles multiple **DataPoint** readings for the same entity using one of four strategies: most-recent, highest-authority, simple consensus, or weighted authority-plus-recency.

Different solutions suit different scenarios. Majority voting works when sources are equally dependable. Weighted averaging adjusts for varied source quality. Recency prioritizes recent information. Source priority imposes domain-specific trust hierarchies.

A best practice is to consistently present confidence scores alongside answers. This enables adequate trust calibration and helps identify instances requiring human judgment.

API authentication and security patterns

Secure API integration extends beyond saving credentials in environment variables. Production systems must support several authentication schemes, including API keys, OAuth tokens, and **JavaScript Object Notation Web Token** (**JWT**)-based authentication, while managing token refresh, credential rotation, and secure storage. Different APIs require different authentication approaches: some use simple header-based keys, others rely on complex OAuth flows with refresh tokens, and government APIs may require certificate-based authentication. A well-designed authentication layer encapsulates these discrepancies while ensuring credentials never leak into logs, error messages, or audit trails.

The following code demonstrates OAuth token refresh with automated retry:

```
import os
import requests
from datetime import datetime, timedelta

class SecureAPIClient:
  def __init__(self):
    self.token_cache = {}
    self.token_expiry = {}

  def get_oauth_token(self, service: str) -> str:
    """Retrieve OAuth token with automatic refresh."""
    if service in self.token_cache:
      if datetime.now() < self.token_expiry.get(service, datetime.min):
        return self.token_cache[service] # Return cached token

    response = requests.post(
      f"https://auth.{service}.com/oauth/token",
      data={"grant_type": "client_credentials",
         "client_id": os.getenv(f"{service.upper()}_CLIENT_ID"),
         "client_secret": os.getenv(f"{service.upper()}_SECRET")},
      timeout=10
    )
    data = response.json()
    self.token_cache[service] = data["access_token"]
    expires_in = data.get("expires_in", 3600)
```

```
        self.token_expiry[service] = datetime.now() + timedelta(seconds=expires_
in - 300)
        return data["access_token"]

    def call_api(self, service: str, endpoint: str, _retried: bool = False) ->
dict:
        """Make authenticated API call with auto-retry on 401.

        The `_retried` flag is a recursion guard: we only retry the call once
after
        refreshing the token. If the refreshed token is also rejected, we stop
        recursing and let `raise_for_status()` surface the 401 to the caller.
        """
        token = self.get_oauth_token(service)
        headers = {"Authorization": f"Bearer {token}"}
        response = requests.get(endpoint, headers=headers, timeout=5)

        if response.status_code == 401 and not _retried: # Token expired — retry
once
            self.token_cache.pop(service, None)
            return self.call_api(service, endpoint, _retried=True)

        response.raise_for_status()
        return response.json()

# Usage
client = SecureAPIClient()
weather_data = client.call_api("weather", "https://api.weather.com/v1/
current")
```

A key security consideration is to never log or return raw authentication credentials. Redact tokens in error messages and audit logs. Implement credential rotation schedules for long-running services.

API response validation and schema enforcement

External APIs do not always return what users expect. Network problems create partial answers, API version changes breach contracts, and upstream defects introduce malformed data. Without validation, these flaws spread throughout the agent's logic, generating hallucinations or faulty conclusions. Response validation serves as a defensive layer by verifying structure, data types, mandatory fields, and value ranges before trusting external input. Schema enforcement with Pydantic models enables compile-time safety and runtime validation, catching errors instantly rather than allowing bad data to infect the knowledge fusion.

The following code demonstrates Pydantic-based API response validation:

```
from pydantic import BaseModel, Field, field_validator
from datetime import datetime

class WeatherReading(BaseModel):
  temperature: float = Field(..., ge=-100, le=150)
  humidity: float = Field(..., ge=0, le=100)
  pressure: float = Field(..., ge=800, le=1100)
  timestamp: datetime
  location: str

  @field_validator('temperature')
  @classmethod
  def validate_temperature(cls, v):
    if abs(v) > 200:
      raise ValueError('Physically impossible temperature')
    return v

def validate_api_response(raw_response: dict) -> WeatherReading | None:
  """Validate API response against schema."""
  try:
    return WeatherReading(**raw_response)
  except Exception as e:
    print(f"Validation failed: {e}")
    return None

# Usage
raw_data = {"temperature": 72.5, "humidity": 65, "pressure": 1013,
      "timestamp": datetime.now(), "location": "Seattle"}
validated = validate_api_response(raw_data)
```

It is important to always validate API responses before incorporating them into agent reasoning. Invalid data can cascade through the system, corrupting decisions and triggering downstream failures.

Parallel and asynchronous API calls

Querying several APIs sequentially builds latency. For example, three 500ms API calls require 1.5 seconds when run serially, but just 500ms when parallelized. For agents asking dozens of sources, this gap influences whether results feel instant or sluggish. Asynchronous API calls using Python's **asyncio** enable parallel execution while avoiding the complexity of threading. The approach is critical for production agents: receive live meteorological data, access backup

APIs, and retrieve historical comparisons simultaneously rather than waiting for each response before starting the next request.

The following code demonstrates concurrent API requests with **asyncio**:

```
import asyncio
import aiohttp

async def fetch_weather(session: aiohttp.ClientSession, source: str,
           location: str) -> dict:
  """Fetch weather data from single source."""
  urls = {
    "primary": f"https://api.weather.com/v1/current/{location}",
    "backup": f"https://api.weatherstack.com/current?location={location}",
    "government": f"https://api.weather.gov/points/{location}"
  }

  try:
    async with session.get(urls[source], timeout=5) as response:
      if response.status == 200:
        data = await response.json()
        return {"source": source, "data": data, "status": "success"}
      return {"source": source, "status": "error"}
  except asyncio.TimeoutError:
    return {"source": source, "status": "timeout"}

async def fetch_all_sources(location: str, sources: list[str]) -> list[dict]:
  """Fetch weather from multiple sources in parallel."""
  async with aiohttp.ClientSession() as session:
    tasks = [fetch_weather(session, source, location) for source in sources]
    return await asyncio.gather(*tasks, return_exceptions=True)

# Usage - queries all sources concurrently
results = asyncio.run(fetch_all_sources("Seattle",
           ["primary", "backup", "government"]))
```

Note: **Parallel API calls can reduce total query time by 60-80% when querying many sources. Use connection pooling and session reuse to minimize overhead.**

Streaming data integration for real-time feeds

Some data sources do not match the request-response pattern; instead, they stream continual updates as conditions change. Weather sensor networks, **Internet of Things** (**IoT**) devices, and event streams push data rather than waiting for polls. Integrating streaming sources needs multiple patterns: maintaining permanent connections, handling reconnection logic, buffering data for batch processing, and managing backpressure when consumers cannot keep up with producers. Streaming integration turns agents from reactive query responders into proactive monitors that recognize patterns and take actions based on current data flows.

The following code demonstrates streaming sensor data with auto-reconnect:

```
import asyncio
import aiohttp
import json
from typing import AsyncIterator

async def stream_sensor_data(sensor_url: str) -> AsyncIterator[dict]:
  """Connect to streaming sensor feed with exponential backoff."""
  retry_delay = 1
  max_retry_delay = 60

  while True:
    try:
      async with aiohttp.ClientSession() as session:
        async with session.get(sensor_url) as response:
          async for line in response.content:

            if line:
              try:
                data = json.loads(line.decode('utf-8'))
                if 'sensor_id' in data and 'temperature' in data:
                  yield data
                  retry_delay = 1 # Reset on success
              except json.JSONDecodeError:
                continue
    except Exception as e:
      print(f"Stream error: {e}. Reconnecting in {retry_delay}s...")
      await asyncio.sleep(retry_delay)
      retry_delay = min(retry_delay * 2, max_retry_delay)

# Usage - process streaming sensor readings
async def process_stream():
  async for reading in stream_sensor_data("https://sensors.weather.com/
stream"):
    print(f"Sensor {reading['sensor_id']}: {reading['temperature']}°F")
    # Update knowledge graph or trigger alerts

# asyncio.run(process_stream())
```

Tip: **Implement circuit breakers for streaming connections. If a stream continually fails, temporarily disable it and fall back to polling or alternative sources.**

API monitoring and observability

Production API integration requires complete monitoring to detect problems, track performance degradation, and manage costs. Without observability, users cannot distinguish between typical changes and emergent problems. Slow API responses may indicate network issues, rate limitation, or upstream service degradation. Monitoring metrics include success rates, latency percentiles, error types, cache hit rates, and cost per query. These insights enable proactive optimization: identifying poorly performing endpoints, adjusting cache TTLs based on actual staleness patterns, and detecting abnormalities before they affect user-facing decisions.

The following code demonstrates API monitoring with health tracking:

```
from dataclasses import dataclass
import time
import requests

@dataclass
class APIMetrics:
  success_count: int = 0
  error_count: int = 0
  total_latency: float = 0.0

  @property
  def success_rate(self) -> float:
    total = self.success_count + self.error_count
    return (self.success_count / total * 100) if total > 0 else 0

  @property
  def avg_latency_ms(self) -> float:
    total = self.success_count + self.error_count
    return (self.total_latency / total * 1000) if total > 0 else 0

class MonitoredAPIClient:
  def __init__(self):
    self.metrics: dict[str, APIMetrics] = {}

  def call_with_monitoring(self, endpoint: str) -> dict:
    """Execute API call with automatic metrics collection."""
    if endpoint not in self.metrics:
      self.metrics[endpoint] = APIMetrics()
```

```
        metric = self.metrics[endpoint]
        start = time.time()

        try:
          response = requests.get(endpoint, timeout=5)
          metric.total_latency += time.time() - start
          response.raise_for_status()
          metric.success_count += 1
          return response.json()
        except Exception:
          metric.total_latency += time.time() - start
          metric.error_count += 1
          raise

      def get_health_report(self) -> str:
        """Generate health report for all monitored APIs."""
        lines = ["=== API Health Report ==="]
        for endpoint, m in self.metrics.items():
          status = "healthy" if m.success_rate > 95 else "degraded"
          lines.append(f"{endpoint}: {status} ({m.success_rate:.1f}% success, "
                f"{m.avg_latency_ms:.0f}ms avg)")
        return "\n".join(lines)

    # Usage
    client = MonitoredAPIClient()
    data = client.call_with_monitoring("https://api.weather.com/current")
    print(client.get_health_report())
```

A best practice is to set up alerting on crucial metrics: success rate below 95%, average latency above 1s, or more than ten failures in five minutes. Proactive monitoring prevents tiny errors from becoming service disruptions.

External APIs, live feeds, and online search help keep an agent aligned with realtime conditions, but they also pose additional challenges related to data longevity, validity periods, and historical traceability. Without clear ways to manage freshness and evolution, agents risk mistaking live updates for obsolete snapshots or presenting superseded information as current fact. To maintain temporal accuracy across fused information sources, agents must reason not only about what is known but also when it was acquired and how long it remains valid. The following section addresses this difficulty by proposing ways to maintain knowledge freshness and version control across multi-source systems.

Managing knowledge freshness and version control

Information has a shelf life. Weather forecasts expire after hours, climate models alter monthly, infrastructure configurations change with deployments, and regulations evolve over the years. An agent working without awareness of temporal validity risks referencing obsolete projections as current predictions, outdated policies as active regulations, or deprecated settings as operational truth. Knowledge freshness management tackles this difficulty by recording when information was acquired, how long it remains valid, and when it should be refreshed or superseded. Temporal reasoning transforms agents from static information retrievers into time-aware systems that discern present facts from historical recordings.

As enterprise knowledge evolves, agents must track which information is current, deprecated, or outdated. Version control for knowledge prevents agents from citing obsolete policies or regulations.

Implementing knowledge versioning

Knowledge graphs must tolerate change without losing historical context. When a sensor's calibration coefficient is updated, the previous value should be preserved, as it reflects true historical knowledge that might explain past readings or inform trend analysis. Version control for knowledge graphs preserves temporal chains, where each fact is tagged with effective dates. This enables agents to query, *What was the calibration on June 15th?* with *What is the current calibration?* This temporal modeling demands careful schema design: version nodes linked to entities, effective date characteristics, and queries that filter by temporal validity.

The following code explains how to version knowledge graph entities:

```
from datetime import datetime
from langchain_neo4j import Neo4jGraph

class VersionedKnowledgeGraph:
  def __init__(self, graph: Neo4jGraph):
    self.graph = graph

  def add_versioned_fact(self, entity_id: str, property: str, value: str,
effective_date: datetime):
    query = """
    MATCH (e:Entity {id: $entity_id})
    CREATE (e)-[:HAS_VERSION]->(v:Version {property: $property, value:
$value,
       effective_from: $effective_date, current: true})
    WITH e MATCH (e)-[:HAS_VERSION]->(old:Version {property: $property,
```

```
current: true})
    WHERE old.effective_from < $effective_date
    SET old.current = false, old.effective_to = $effective_date
    """
    self.graph.query(query, {"entity_id": entity_id, "property": property,
                "value": value, "effective_date": effective_date.isoformat()})

  def get_current_value(self, entity_id: str, property: str):
    result = self.graph.query(
      "MATCH (e:Entity {id: $entity_id})-[:HAS_VERSION]->(v:Version {current:
true}) "
      "WHERE v.property = $property RETURN v.value",
      {"entity_id": entity_id, "property": property}
    )
    return result[0]["value"] if result else None
```

Version timestamps allow agents to distinguish fresh information from older data, which is crucial in time-sensitive areas such as weather forecasting.

It is important to note that different types of information have varying staleness characteristics. Current conditions expire in hours, forecasts in days, and climate trends in years.

Cache invalidation patterns

Caches introduce a basic tension between performance and freshness. Aggressive caching maximizes speed and decreases API fees but risks serving outdated data. Conservative caching preserves freshness but trades off performance improvements. The ideal technique varies by data type: sensor readings change by the second and need short TTLs, whereas historical climatic patterns remain steady for years. Understanding invalidation patterns, including time-based expiration, event-driven updates, and version-based triggers, enables users to customize cache behavior to match the temporal features of each information source.

The following table discusses cache invalidation algorithms for different data types:

Data type	Invalidation strategy	TTL	Trigger
Sensor readings	Time-based	Five minutes	Clock
Weather forecasts	Event-based	One hour	New forecast published
Historical data	Version-based	Indefinite	Data correction
Configuration	Manual	Until cleared	Admin update
API results	Adaptive	1-60 minutes	Response headers

***Table 10.5**: Cache invalidation strategies by data type*

Caching enhances efficiency but requires invalidation procedures to prevent serving stale data. Time-based invalidation eliminates cache entries after a set duration.

Note: **Batch incremental updates hourly or daily rather than processing every new document individually to amortize indexing overhead.**

Designing enterprise decision-making agents

Enterprise implementation involves more than correct answers; it requires transparency, accountability, and verifiability. When an agent suggests evacuating a region based on weather forecasts, stakeholders need to understand whose sources informed the decision, how disagreements were handled, and the confidence level supporting the recommendation. Audit trails become legal mandates, not optional features. Decision-making agents must track every source consulted, every reasoning step made, and every conflict resolved, thereby creating evidence chains that resist scrutiny from compliance officers, domain experts, and regulatory agencies. This level of transparency transforms agents from opaque black boxes into accountable decision-support systems.

Enterprise agents must deliver visible, auditable reasoning chains that business stakeholders can check and trust.

Chain of evidence architecture

Audit logging must capture the entire reasoning process from original inquiry through final response. This details which sources were contacted, what information each source supplied, how conflicting data was addressed, and which authority scores influenced decisions. The sequence of operations counts as much as the data itself. Understanding that the agent searched the knowledge graph before the API and resolved disputes using weighted voting rather than relying on recency bias provides crucial context for validating recommendations. A well-designed evidence chain enables stakeholders to reconstruct the agent's reasoning path step by step, identify potential flaws, and boost confidence in automated choices.

The following figure depicts how an enterprise agent maintains an auditable decision trail:

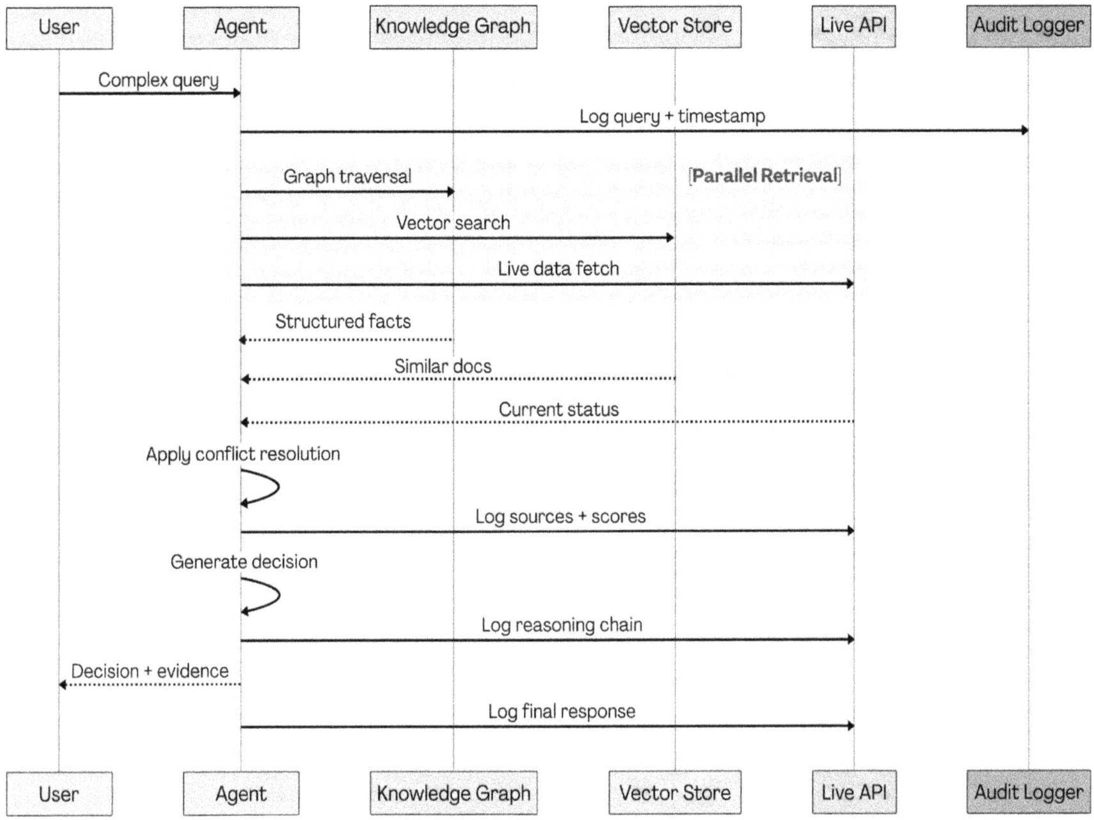

***Figure 10.3**: Enterprise agent decision sequence with audit trail*

The sequence diagram illustrates how complex queries are executed across several sources, how findings are consolidated, disagreements settled, and final answers generated with source credit.

Note: **Emergency management agencies use multi-source weather decision support systems that use APIs for numerical weather models, graphs for historical storm patterns, streams for real-time sensor data, and vector search for meteorological reports to decide whether to evacuate.**

Building the complete fusion agent

To put all the ideas from this chapter together, including graph reasoning, hybrid search, API integration, conflict resolution, and audit logging, users need to design a system in which all the parts function smoothly together. The fusion agent must coordinate multiple concurrent source queries, combine findings from different sources, apply appropriate resolution algorithms, and maintain a complete record of all the evidence. This orchestration layer is the heart of corporate decision support. It turns different sources of information into reliable, unified suggestions. The implementation balances complexity and ease of maintenance, ensuring the system can scale as new sources, resolution methodologies, and compliance needs emerge.

The following code shows a multi-source decision agent that is ready for production:

```
import json
from langchain.agents import AgentExecutor, create_tool_calling_agent
from langchain_core.prompts import ChatPromptTemplate, MessagesPlaceholder
from langchain_core.tools import Tool
from langchain_openai import ChatOpenAI

class EnterpriseDecisionAgent:
  def __init__(self, vector_store, graph, api_client):
    self.vector_store = vector_store
    self.graph = graph
    self.api_client = api_client
    self.evidence_log = []
    self.llm = ChatOpenAI(model="gpt-4o-mini", temperature=0)
    self.tools = self._create_tools()
    self.agent = self._create_agent()

  def _create_tools(self) -> list[Tool]:
    return [
      Tool(name="SearchDocs", func=self._search_documents,
        description="Search vector store for documentation"),
      Tool(name="QueryGraph", func=self._query_graph,
        description="Query knowledge graph for entity relationships"),
      Tool(name="FetchLiveData", func=self._fetch_live_data,
        description="Fetch real-time data from monitoring APIs")
    ]

  def _search_documents(self, query: str) -> str:
    docs = self.vector_store.similarity_search(query, k=3)
    self.evidence_log.append({"type": "vector", "query": query, "count":
len(docs)})
    return "\n".join([doc.page_content for doc in docs])

  def _query_graph(self, query: str) -> str:
    result = self.graph.query(query)
    self.evidence_log.append({"type": "graph", "result_count": len(result)})
    return json.dumps(result)

  def _fetch_live_data(self, endpoint: str) -> str:
```

```
    data = self.api_client.get(endpoint)
    self.evidence_log.append({"type": "api", "endpoint": endpoint})
    return json.dumps(data)

  def _create_agent(self) -> AgentExecutor:
    prompt = ChatPromptTemplate.from_messages([
      ("system", """You are an enterprise decision-making assistant.
      Gather information from all relevant sources. Apply conflict resolution
when sources disagree.
      Cite your sources explicitly. Prioritize internal sensors > official APIs
> documentation > web search."""),
      MessagesPlaceholder(variable_name="chat_history", optional=True),
      ("human", "{input}"),
      MessagesPlaceholder(variable_name="agent_scratchpad")
    ])
    agent = create_tool_calling_agent(self.llm, self.tools, prompt)
    return AgentExecutor(agent=agent, tools=self.tools, verbose=True)

  def decide(self, query: str) -> dict:
    self.evidence_log = []
    result = self.agent.invoke({"input": query})
    return {
      "decision": result["output"],
      "evidence": self.evidence_log,
      "sources_used": list(set(e["type"] for e in self.evidence_log))
    }
```

`EnterpriseDecisionAgent` wires three tools—vector search, graph query, and live API fetch into a single `create_tool_calling_agent` executor. Every tool invocation is appended to an evidence log, giving the final answer a fully traceable audit trail of which sources contributed what.

The system orchestrates numerous knowledge sources, manages disputes, evaluates confidence, and provides clear source attribution.

Enterprise agents need to keep complete audit trails for compliance and troubleshooting. Log every source accessed, dispute resolved, and reasoning step taken.

Conclusion

By integrating knowledge graphs and vector stores, readers have moved beyond basic document retrieval to multi-source reasoning. They built hybrid retrieval pipelines that combine semantic similarity with relationship traversal. They also linked external APIs and live feeds for up-to-date context. They used caching, rate limiting, and conflict resolution so the agent could handle conflicting sources and provide answers that account for the conflict.

It was made possible for businesses to use it by adding verifiable reasoning paths, source attribution, and audit trails that show which tools ran, what data they returned, and how disagreements were settled. The weather decision support workflow shows how to make clear, accountable recommendations that stakeholders can trust once monitoring and governance patterns are in place.

In the next chapter, the readers will apply the concepts in practice. The chapter explores the construction of autonomous agents capable of performing real-world tasks using tool abstraction and function calling. This lets the agent run code, talk to databases, and manage APIs safely, with strict controls on permissions, rate limits, and audit logging.

CHAPTER 11
Creating Autonomous Agents that Perform Real-world Tasks

Introduction

Without tools, agents are confined to thinking and responding. The real change from assistant to autonomous operator occurs when an agent can retrieve live information, query databases, run calculations, and initiate workflows. Even the best model requires a reliable link between natural language intent and actions that can be carried out. This chapter focuses on building that bridge using disciplined tool abstraction and function calling.

With OpenAI's function calling and LangChain's tool ecosystem, readers will learn how agents discover tools, select the appropriate function based on user intent, and turn requests into structured **application programming interface** (**API**) calls and database operations. The discussion then moves from using a single tool to using multiple tools together by breaking down complicated tasks, executing steps in order (or in parallel when appropriate), and integrating the results into clear answers.

The chapter also covers production readiness, including retries with exponential backoff, logging for auditability, and security-first design with sandboxing, access control, and credential management. The chapter concludes with a complete weather intelligence system that retrieves live forecasts, analyzes reports, saves results, and issues actionable alerts.

Structure

This chapter covers the following topics:

- Understanding tool abstraction and function calling
- Building and orchestrating custom toolkits
- Integrating external APIs and databases
- Error handling and retry mechanisms

- Security and sandboxing
- Building a multi-tool weather intelligence system

Objectives

This chapter demonstrates how to build action-capable autonomous agents from start to finish, from choosing the right tools to safely running them in production. The chapter begins with tool abstraction, showing how LangChain standardizes tool interfaces across **Representational State Transfer** (**REST**) APIs, database queries, and code execution. Readers will see why clear schemas matter: they help models recognize the right capability, supply valid arguments, and invoke tools reliably instead of guessing from free-form prompts. OpenAI function calling is then configured, enabling the model to return structured tool invocations instead of free-form text, which allows requests expressed in natural language to be executed reliably.

Next, the chapter covers the construction of cohesive toolkits and orchestration patterns. Agents learn to break down complex requests, select tools using **Reasoning and Acting** (**ReAct**)-style reasoning, and link steps sequentially or execute them concurrently. Readers will use best practices for integration, including retries and timeouts for REST, precise field selection for **Graph Query Language** (**GraphQL**), and parameterized queries to stop **Structured Query Language** (**SQL**) injection. Readers will also keep audit trails by logging every invocation and failure in detail.

Finally, agents are prepared for the real world by adding error classification, exponential backoff, self-correction loops for bad arguments, and security-first sandboxing for any code execution or file access.

Understanding tool abstraction and function calling

The fundamental challenge of autonomous agents lies in translating natural language intent into executable code. When consumers request "*check the weather in Seattle,*" bots must recognize that this requires running a specific function with defined parameters, rather than merely creating conversational text. Tool abstraction offers the standardized interface that makes this possible, defining how language models identify available functions, comprehend their goals, and generate valid invocations. Function calling mechanisms manage the execution flow by parsing model outputs into function calls, executing those functions, and feeding results back for synthesis.

For a **large language model** (**LLM**) to interact with the world, its natural language output must be converted into a format that software can execute. This is achieved by tool abstraction and function calling functioning in concert. Before diving into implementation, it is essential to understand both the structural design of tools and the execution flow at the protocol level.

Anatomy of a LangChain tool

Before agents can invoke tools reliably, they must understand the structural design of the tools. A poorly designed tool can confuse even the most proficient language model, leading to incorrect parameters or inappropriate usage. This section examines the anatomy of a LangChain tool, illustrating how names, descriptions, schemas, and implementations combined enable precise, autonomous action.

Tools represent the connection between plain language intent and programmatic implementation. Unlike simple function calls, where developers hardcode invocations, autonomous agents must identify accessible tools, comprehend their goals, choose when to use them, and create proper arguments based solely on descriptions and schemas. A well-designed tool contains four essential components: a unique name that identifies it unambiguously, a detailed description that explains its purpose and appropriate usage contexts, a typed parameter schema defining required and optional arguments, and the actual implementation function that executes when invoked.

Definition: A tool is a callable component that enables agents to perform tasks beyond text production, including API calls, database searches, file operations, and external service integrations. Tools establish their interface through names, descriptions, and parameter specifications.

Tip: **The description functions as the tool's documentation for the language model. Vague descriptions, such as gets weather, fail to convey crucial information about input formats, output structures, or acceptable usage settings. Effective descriptions clarify what the tool does, which parameters are required, what outputs are returned, and when the tool should be chosen over competing tools.**

For example, the following description:

Fetches current weather conditions for a given location using latitude/longitude coordinates. Returns temperature in Fahrenheit, humidity percentage, and wind speed. Use for real-time weather inquiries, not forecasts.

The following code demonstrates basic tool construction with the decorator approach:

```
from langchain.tools import tool


@tool
def get_current_weather(location: str) -> str:
  """Fetch current weather conditions for a location.


  Args:
    location: City name or coordinates (e.g., 'Seattle', '47.6,-122.3')
```

```
    Returns:
      Temperature, conditions, and humidity as formatted string.
    """
    # Simulated API call
    return f"Current weather in {location}: 72°F, Sunny"
```

Parameter schemas use Pydantic models to establish type restrictions, validation rules, and default values. Strong typing eliminates runtime issues caused by improper arguments, while detailed field names and docstrings encourage the language model to generate accurate parameters. The schema forms part of the tool's signature that the LLM receives, enabling it to produce appropriately organized function calls.

Designing tool schemas for reliable invocation

A strong schema is the most practical way to reduce tool-calling errors because it constrains what the model can legally emit. When a tool is described only in prose, the model must infer argument names, allowed values, and data types. A well-structured schema turns those inferences into explicit contracts. It also improves debugging: when a call fails validation, the error message points to a specific field rather than forcing engineers to interpret an ambiguous prompt or response.

- Prefer **typed enums** over free-form strings for units, modes, and categories (for example, *celsius* or *fahrenheit*).
- Use **required fields** for inputs that are mandatory for execution, and keep optional fields truly optional.
- Add **minimum and maximum constraints** for numeric values (for example, day ranges, thresholds, and pagination limits).
- Specify **formats** for structured strings such as ISO dates, coordinates, or resource identifiers.
- Design arguments to be **stable over time**; avoid names that are likely to change as APIs evolve.
- Model compound inputs as **objects** instead of overloading a single string parameter (for example, a *location* object with *city* and *country*).

The following snippet shows a practical pattern: define a Pydantic model for inputs, validate early, and return a compact, predictable output payload. Even if the tool ultimately calls an external REST endpoint, this validation step keeps invalid requests from leaving the agent boundary.

```
from pydantic import BaseModel, Field
from langchain.tools import tool
```

```
class ForecastInput(BaseModel):
location: str = Field(..., description="City name or coordinates")
days: int = Field(3, ge=1, le=10, description="Number of days to forecast (1-
10)")

@tool
def get_forecast_safe(location: str, days: int = 3) -> str:
"""Get a multi-day forecast with validation and predictable output."""
validated = ForecastInput(location=location, days=days)
# Call external API here using validated.location and validated.days
return f"Forecast(location={validated.location}, days={validated.days})"
```

Output normalization is as important as input validation. If a tool sometimes returns raw JSON, sometimes a sentence, and sometimes an error string, the agent must spend extra tokens interpreting results and the orchestration logic becomes brittle. Prefer returning a consistent structure (for example, a small dictionary rendered as JSON) or a compact, consistently formatted string that downstream steps can parse reliably.

The following table compares typical API types and their corresponding LangChain tool abstractions:

API type	LangChain abstraction	Typical use cases	Key characteristics
REST	`RequestsWrapper`, `APIChain`	Web services, microservices, third-party integrations.	**JavaScript Object Notation** (**JSON**) over **HyperText Transfer Protocol** (**HTTP**), stateless, widely supported.
GraphQL	`BaseGraphQLTool`	Complex data with specific field requirements.	Query flexibility, reduces over-fetching.
SQL	`SQLDatabaseToolkit`	Database queries, analytics, and data retrieval.	Structured queries, transactional integrity.
Google Remote Procedure Call (**gRPC**)	Custom tool with `grpc` client	High-performance service communication.	Binary protocol, strongly typed.
Code execution	`PythonAstREPLTool`	Mathematical modeling, data transformation.	Arbitrary computation, security risks.

***Table 11.1**: API types and tool abstractions*

Tool registration makes functions discoverable to agents. LangChain includes decorators like `@tool` that automatically extract function signatures, translate type hints into schemas, and produce descriptions from docstrings. Manual tool creation enables more control, allowing custom schema definitions, argument validation logic, and error handling that differ from the standard function implementation.

Understanding tool anatomy provides the basis, but tools are ineffective without a mechanism that allows language models to invoke them. OpenAI's function calling API bridges this gap by enabling models to produce structured function calls rather than conversational text.

Beyond structure, tools must be built for trustworthiness. Agents rely exclusively on tool descriptions and schemas to infer purpose, limitations, and safety bounds. Ambiguous descriptions or loosely written parameters increase the danger of wrong invocation, unwanted side effects, or security exposure. Production-grade tools consequently operate as contracts: they must clearly define not only what the tool does, but also what it must never do, the assumptions it relies on, and the guarantees it provides.

Implementing OpenAI function calling

OpenAI's function calling feature transforms language models from text generators into structured decision-making agents. Rather than producing conversational responses, models trained with function calling determine when user queries require external actions and output JSON objects describing which function to invoke with what arguments. This structured output enables reliable programmatic execution: agents can detect function calls, interpret arguments, execute functions, and return results to the model for synthesis.

The function calling flow follows a defined sequence. First, the user provides a query, and the developer provides a list of accessible functions with their schemas. The model analyzes the query against accessible functions and chooses whether to call one, multiple, or none. When functions are invoked, the model outputs JSON containing function names and parameter objects. The application parses this JSON, executes the specified functions, and returns results to the model as *function messages*. The model then integrates these results into its context and produces a natural language response or additional function calls.

The following figure demonstrates the entire tool-calling execution loop:

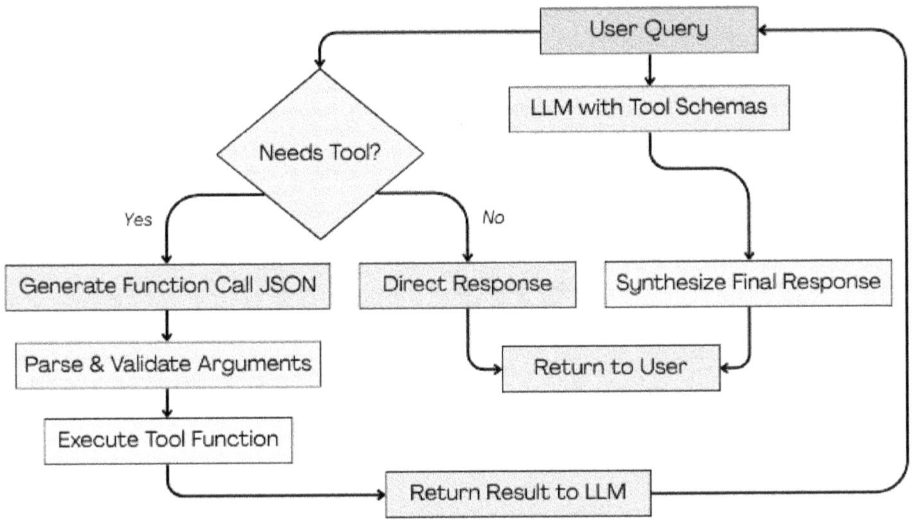

***Figure 11.1**: The autonomous tool-calling execution loop*

The preceding figure depicts how agents assess queries, determine tool requirements, perform functions, and synthesize results into coherent responses with validation at each stage.

Implementing function calling in LangChain requires binding tools to the language model and setting the agent executor to handle tool invocations. The following code demonstrates constructing a weather widget and allowing function calling:

```
from langchain_openai import ChatOpenAI
from langchain.agents import AgentExecutor, create_tool_calling_agent
from langchain_core.prompts import ChatPromptTemplate, MessagesPlaceholder
from langchain_core.tools import tool

@tool
def get_current_weather(location: str, unit: str = "fahrenheit") -> str:
  """Fetches current weather conditions for a specific location.

  Args:
    location: City name or coordinates
    unit: Temperature unit, 'fahrenheit' or 'celsius'
  """
  # Mock implementation – replace with real weather API call
  return f"Temperature: 72°F, Conditions: Sunny, Humidity: 45%"

# Initialize LLM with function calling
llm = ChatOpenAI(model="gpt-4o-mini", temperature=0)
```

```
prompt = ChatPromptTemplate.from_messages([
  ("system", "You are a weather assistant. Use tools when needed."),
  ("human", "{input}"),
  MessagesPlaceholder(variable_name="agent_scratchpad")
])

# Create agent with tool binding
tools = [get_current_weather]
agent = create_tool_calling_agent(llm, tools, prompt)
agent_executor = AgentExecutor(agent=agent, tools=tools, verbose=True)

# Execute query
result = agent_executor.invoke({"input": "What is the weather in Seattle?"})
print(result["output"])
```

The code demonstrates tool building using the `@tool` decorator, which automatically produces schemas from function signatures and docstrings. The agent executor manages orchestration by invoking the LLM, detecting function calls, running tools, and returning results until a final answer is generated.

`create_tool_calling_agent` produces an agent that uses the model's native tool-use API to select and invoke tools. The `AgentExecutor` orchestrates the loop, invoking the LLM, running selected tools, and returning their output back to the model.

> Tip: **Expand tool descriptions beyond a one-line summary. Include when to use the tool, example arguments, and the expected output format so the model can invoke it correctly.**

It is important to note that function calling requires models trained expressly for this feature. OpenAI's GPT-4o, GPT-4o-mini, and GPT-3.5-Turbo allow function calling. Older models or those without fine-tuning will not produce structured function call answers.

With the mechanics of function calling established, agents can move beyond individual tools. Single-function agents tackle specific problems, but real-world activities require coordinating multiple tools, selecting the most appropriate one based on context, and chaining actions where outputs become inputs.

Building and orchestrating custom toolkits

As agents gain increasing autonomy, designers must combine flexibility with determinism. While freeform reasoning permits adaptive behavior, production systems frequently demand predictable execution paths, controlled retries, and reproducible outcomes. Toolkits serve as a stabilizing layer, constraining agent behavior through curated capabilities while still permitting dynamic construction based on intent.

State management, memory, and shared context in toolkits

Toolkits become significantly more useful when tools can share context safely. For example, a weather workflow may look up a location, store canonical coordinates, retrieve a forecast, then set alerts based on that same location. Without shared state, each tool must repeat the same resolution step, increasing latency and the probability of inconsistency. With shared state, the agent can make a single authoritative decision and reuse it throughout the workflow.

However, shared state must be bounded. Production agents should treat state as short-lived and scoped to a single run unless there is an explicit persistence requirement. State should never store secrets or raw credentials, and it should capture only what is required to complete the task: normalized inputs, intermediate results, correlation IDs, and decisions made. The operational pattern is straightforward: define a per-run context, separate transient from persistent data, log every tool call and decision, normalize deterministic steps for reuse, and enforce quotas so one run cannot spiral into runaway cost or latency.

Single-tool invocation marks just the beginning of agent capabilities. Real-world activities seldom map to isolated functions. They require coordinated sequences in which one tool's output becomes another's input, multiple information sources are synthesized, and agents make intelligent decisions about which tools to activate based on context. This section discusses how to arrange tools into cohesive collections, implement the reasoning patterns that enable intelligent tool selection, and optimize execution for performance and reliability.

With individual tools in place, the next challenge is orchestration. Realworld tasks seldom correspond to a single function call; instead, they require coordinated execution across multiple tools, shared state, and intelligent sequencing. This section analyzes how tools evolve from separate capabilities into coherent toolkits that support complex, realworld workflows.

Creating reusable weather toolkits

Building toolkits entails recognizing logical groupings of capabilities that agents typically utilize together. Weather analysis demands current measurements, future predictions, historical comparisons, and alert monitoring. Organizing these tools into a unified toolkit, rather than as isolated functions, ensures consistent interfaces, shared authentication, and coordinated error handling. Each tool focuses on a distinct activity while benefiting from common infrastructure, including API clients, cache layers, and credential management.

The following code exhibits a full weather toolkit with numerous synchronized tools:

```
from langchain.tools import tool
import requests


class WeatherAPIClient:
```

```
    """Shared client for weather API with authentication and caching."""

    def __init__(self, api_key: str):
        self.api_key = api_key
        self.cache = {}

    def get(self, endpoint: str) -> dict:
        if endpoint in self.cache:
            return self.cache[endpoint]
        # Simulated API call
        data = {"temperature": 72, "conditions": "Sunny"}
        self.cache[endpoint] = data
        return data

weather_client = WeatherAPIClient(api_key="your_key")

@tool
def get_current_conditions(location: str) -> str:
    """Get current weather for a location."""
    data = weather_client.get(f"current/{location}")
    return f"Temp: {data['temperature']}°F, {data['conditions']}"

@tool
def get_forecast(location: str, days: int = 3) -> str:
    """Get multi-day forecast."""
    return f"{days}-day forecast for {location}"

@tool
def get_weather_alerts(location: str) -> str:
    """Check for active weather alerts."""
    return f"No active alerts for {location}"

# Bundle into toolkit
weather_toolkit = [get_current_conditions, get_forecast, get_weather_alerts]
```

The `WeatherAPIClient` instance is module-level, so all three tools share the same cache and credentials, avoiding repeated initialization on every call. Bundling the tools into a `weather_` `toolkit` list makes them a single object that any agent can consume, and the toolkit can grow without touching the agent code that uses it.

> Tip: **Share expensive resources like API clients, database connections, and caches across toolkit tools. Initialize once and reference in tool implementations rather than adding per-call overhead.**

Building integrated toolkits overcomes the organizational difficulty, but agents still require intelligence to select which tool to invoke, whether to chain several tools, and how to synthesize outcomes. This is where ReAct thinking transforms sets of tools into orchestrated workflows.

Tool selection logic and ReAct reasoning

As toolkits grow, autonomous agents must decide not only how to execute tools, but whether any tool is needed, which of several applicable tools is most appropriate, and when to chain tools versus respond directly. ReAct provides this decision-making layer by interleaving reasoning about the current state with tool-based actions in a controlled, auditable manner.

The reasoning phase checks available tools against query requirements. For *What is the weather in Seattle?*, the agent knows weather data is needed and identifies `get_current_conditions` as relevant. For *Compare Seattle's current weather to last year*, the agent must chain multiple tools, synthesizing results from both.

The following figure demonstrates the entire ReAct decision cycle for a multi-tool task:

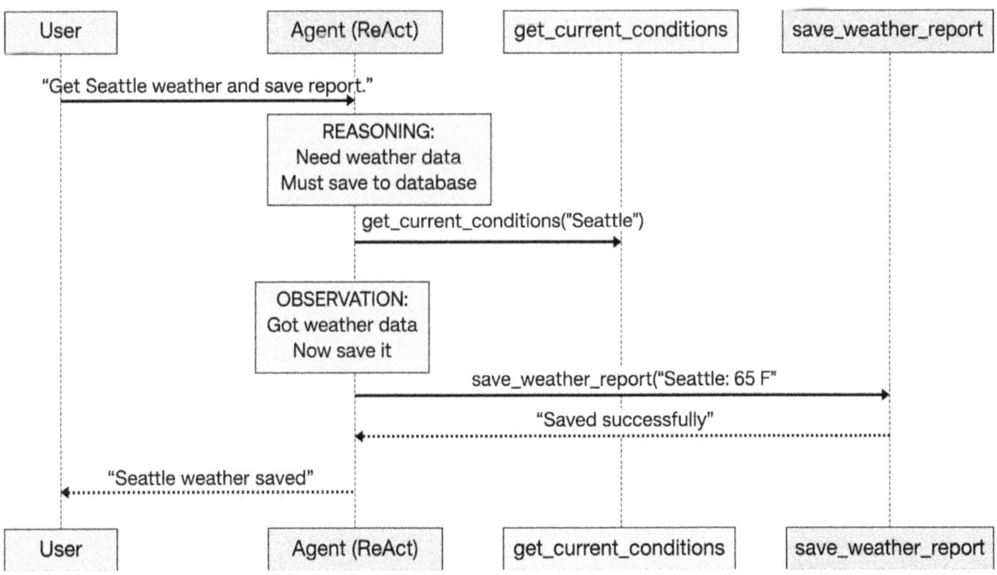

***Figure 11.2**: Multi-tool ReAct workflow with reasoning steps*

Implementing ReAct demands prompt engineering that supports precise reasoning. The following code demonstrates configuring an agent for successful ReAct behavior:

```
from langchain_openai import ChatOpenAI
from langchain.agents import AgentExecutor, create_openai_functions_agent
from langchain_core.prompts import ChatPromptTemplate, MessagesPlaceholder

prompt = ChatPromptTemplate.from_messages([
  ("system", """You are a weather assistant with access to tools.

For each query:
1. REASON about needed information and tools
2. ACT by calling appropriate tool(s)
3. OBSERVE results
4. DETERMINE if more steps needed

Available tools:
- get_current_conditions: Current weather
- get_forecast: Future predictions
- get_weather_alerts: Active warnings"""),
  ("human", "{input}"),
  MessagesPlaceholder(variable_name="agent_scratchpad")
])

llm = ChatOpenAI(model="gpt-4o-mini", temperature=0)
agent = create_openai_functions_agent(llm, weather_toolkit, prompt)
agent_executor = AgentExecutor(
  agent=agent,
  tools=weather_toolkit,
  verbose=True,
  max_iterations=5,
  handle_parsing_errors=True
)

result = agent_executor.invoke({
  "input": "Check Seattle weather and any storm alerts"
})
```

The setting specifies `max_iterations` to prevent runaway loops and `handle_parsing_errors` to recover from faulty calls.

It is important to set `max_iterations` on agent executors to prevent infinite loops. Without limitations, agents locked in reasoning loops can exhaust API quotas or time out user requests.

ReAct reasoning enables intelligent tool selection, but sequential execution produces performance limitations. When actions are independent (for example, fetching the weather for three places), parallel processing greatly reduces total latency.

Parallel tool execution for performance optimization

Sequential tool execution accumulates latency: for example, three 200ms API requests take 600ms serially but only 200ms when run in parallel, provided the operations are independent. LangChain provides simultaneous tool execution when the model generates several function calls in a single response.

The following code demonstrates configuring simultaneous tool execution:

```
from langchain_openai import ChatOpenAI

# Enable parallel tool calling
llm = ChatOpenAI(
  model="gpt-4o-mini",
  temperature=0,
  model_kwargs={"parallel_tool_calls": True}
)

agent = create_openai_functions_agent(llm, weather_toolkit, prompt)
agent_executor = AgentExecutor(
  agent=agent,
  tools=weather_toolkit,
  verbose=True
)

# Query benefiting from parallelization
result = agent_executor.invoke({
  "input": "Check weather in Seattle, Portland, and Vancouver simultaneously"
})
```

Note: **Parallel tool execution can significantly reduce total workflow time for independent tasks and is often worth enabling in production when latency matters. However, use it only for independent operations; dependent tool chains should remain sequential to preserve data consistency and reasoning integrity.**

Orchestration patterns provide the basis for coordinating tools, but most real-world agents must interact with external systems that use diverse communication protocols. REST, GraphQL, and database integrations each introduce unique challenges related to authentication, error handling, and data security.

Integrating external APIs and databases

Agents operating in production must interact with multiple services using different protocols. REST APIs dominate web service interactions, GraphQL enables precise, field-level querying for sophisticated data demands, and databases provide the persistence layer for audit trails and state management. Each protocol requires specific implementation patterns for authentication, error management, and data validation.

Authentication, secret management, and rate limiting

Most integration failures in production are not caused by code syntax errors, but by operational realities: expired tokens, mis-scoped permissions, and throttling. Autonomous agents amplify these issues because they can invoke tools frequently and under unpredictable user demand. A production design must therefore treat authentication and rate limiting as first-class concerns, not as afterthoughts.

Tools should never accept secrets as normal user-supplied parameters. Instead, retrieve credentials from a secure store at runtime, inject them into the client layer, and redact them from logs. When possible, use short-lived tokens and managed identities so that the blast radius of leakage is limited. If a tool detects an authentication failure, it should return a structured error indicating whether the fault is retriable (for example, token refresh) or terminal (for example, permission denied). In practice, production agents should rely on managed identities or service principals instead of embedded API keys, request only the minimum scoped permissions each tool needs, and centralize token refresh in a shared client rather than duplicating it across tools. They should also treat rate limits as part of the contract by handling HTTP 429 responses with exponential backoff and jitter, capping outbound calls per run, and returning machine-readable errors that include the error type, whether the failure is retryable, and any recommended wait time.

This section provides production-grade integrations that address real-world challenges such as network timeouts, rate limitations, expired authentication, and faulty responses. Starting with REST as the foundation, best practices include implementing security methods to prevent SQL injection, designing retry logic to recover from temporary failures, and organizing queries to retrieve only the necessary data.

REST API integration with retry logic

REST APIs are the backbone of most web service integrations. Production solutions feature authentication, retry logic, and timeout handling for reliability.

The following code demonstrates REST API integration with exception handling:

```
import requests
import time
from langchain.tools import tool


@tool
def query_weather_api(location: str) -> str:
  """Query weather API with automatic retry."""
  max_retries = 3
  for attempt in range(max_retries):
    try:
      response = requests.get(
        f"https://api.weather.gov/points/{location}",
        timeout=5
      )
      response.raise_for_status()
      return f"Weather data: {response.json()}"
    except requests.RequestException as e:
      if attempt < max_retries - 1:
        time.sleep(2 ** attempt) # Exponential backoff
        continue
      return f"API error after {max_retries} attempts: {e}"
```

Production API integrations incorporate retry logic with exponential backoff and timeout management to ensure reliability even when external services are unstable.

While REST APIs manage external communication, databases provide the key persistence layer where agents store results, keep audit trails, and access past data. Database security becomes crucial when agents generate queries dynamically.

Secure database operations

Database tools require careful security implementation to prevent SQL injection and unauthorized access. Parameterized searches ensure user inputs are regarded as data, not executable code.

The following code illustrates secure database integration:

```
import sqlite3
from langchain.tools import tool

@tool
def add_weather_alert(location: str, threshold: float) -> str:
  """Store weather alert preference in database."""
  conn = sqlite3.connect("weather_alerts.db")
  cursor = conn.cursor()

  # Parameterized query prevents SQL injection
  cursor.execute(
    "INSERT INTO alerts (location, threshold) VALUES (?, ?)",
    (location, threshold)
  )
  conn.commit()
  conn.close()

  return f"Alert set for {location} at {threshold}°F"
```

A key security consideration is to always use parameterized queries or **object-relational mapping (ORM)** frameworks for database operations, as string formatting with user input creates SQL injection vulnerabilities.

Database operations provide durability, while GraphQL presents a powerful alternative to REST for complex data requirements. Rather than relying on multiple REST APIs that may return superfluous fields, GraphQL enables precise field selection within a single query.

In regulated environments, database access for agents should be restricted using role-based credentials and continuously audited.

GraphQL API integration

Together, REST, databases, and GraphQL provide complementary integration patterns, ranging from broad interoperability to precise data access, enabling agents to communicate efficiently with diverse organizational systems.

GraphQL allows exact data retrieval, reducing the over-fetching that often occurs with REST APIs by requesting only the specific fields needed.

The following code demonstrates GraphQL integration:

```
import requests
from langchain_core.tools import tool

@tool
def query_weather_graphql(location: str) -> str:
  """Query weather via GraphQL for precise data."""
  query = """
  query($location: String!) {
    weather(location: $location) {
      temperature
      conditions
    }
  }
  """

  try:
    response = requests.post(
      "https://api.weather.com/graphql",
      json={"query": query, "variables": {"location": location}},
      timeout=5
    )
    response.raise_for_status()
    payload = response.json()
  except requests.RequestException as e:
    return f"GraphQL request failed for {location}: {e}"
  except ValueError:
    return f"GraphQL response for {location} was not valid JSON."

  # GraphQL returns errors in a top-level 'errors' field, not via HTTP status
  if payload.get("errors"):
    return f"GraphQL errors for {location}: {payload['errors']}"

  weather = (payload.get("data") or {}).get("weather")
  if not weather:
    return f"No weather data returned for {location}."

  return f"Weather: {weather}"
```

GraphQL lets the tool fetch only `temperature` and `conditions` instead of the full weather payload that a REST endpoint typically returns. Smaller responses keep the agent's context window leaner and reduce token-billed cost, useful when many tool calls compound into a long conversation. The error-handling block covers the four failure modes a production GraphQL tool must anticipate: network errors (`RequestException`), non-2xx HTTP responses (`raise_for_status`), malformed JSON (`ValueError`), and GraphQL-level errors that arrive with a 200 status but populate the top-level `errors` field instead of `data`.

GraphQL provides query flexibility and saves data transport by retrieving only the essential fields.

With integration patterns for REST, databases, and GraphQL in place, the next essential consideration is reliability. External systems can fail unpredictably: networks may time out, services may return rate limit errors, and authentication tokens can expire. Production agents require sophisticated error handling that can distinguish between transient failures and persistent faults.

Error handling and retry mechanisms

As agents move from controlled demos to production workflows, reliability becomes as important as capability. Every external call, tool invocation, and generated argument can fail in different ways, so autonomous systems need a disciplined strategy for detecting failures, deciding which ones are safe to retry, and stopping immediately when security or data integrity is at risk.

Putting it all together with an end-to-end agent workflow

This section ties the chapter concepts together using a compact but realistic scenario: a user asks an agent to evaluate the upcoming weather for a trip, save a summary, and configure alerts if conditions cross a threshold. Even though the example uses weather, the same design applies to enterprise automation workflows such as filing tickets, scheduling jobs, and generating reports.

1. **Normalize inputs**: Resolve destination to a canonical form (city + coordinates) and store it in run state.
2. **Select tools**: Choose forecast and alerts tools based on the user intent and required outputs.
3. **Validate arguments**: Enforce schema constraints (for example, days range, units enum, threshold bounds) before any outbound calls.
4. **Execute tools**: Call external APIs with retry + backoff, and store results in the run context with correlation IDs.

5. **Persist outcomes**: Write only the required artifacts (summary record, alert configuration) via explicit database tools.
6. **Explain and audit**: Return a human-readable answer, while logs capture tool choices, latencies, and failures for traceability.

When these elements are combined, an agent becomes more than a prompt-driven chatbot. It becomes an operational system: inputs are validated, actions are controlled, failures are managed, and results are auditable. This is the practical foundation for autonomous agents that can perform real-world tasks without sacrificing reliability or security.

In autonomous systems, errors are not merely exceptions to ignore; they are signals the system must learn from. Network timeouts, faulty inputs, and partial service failures are unavoidable at scale. Effective agents consider recoverable failures as feedback, transitory faults as retriable conditions, and security violations as hard stop events. Clearly defining these characteristics distinguishes robust agents from brittle prototypes.

Integrations and orchestration alone do not ensure reliability. In production, agents must anticipate failures, including network interruptions, faulty inputs, and authentication issues, and respond appropriately. This section provides structured error handling strategies that transform weak workflows into resilient autonomous systems.

Production agents require robust error handling to identify temporary failures versus persistent faults and to implement suitable recovery procedures. For example, a network timeout during a weather API call requires retry logic with backoff delays, whereas an authentication failure necessitates immediate termination to prevent unauthorized access. Invalid tool parameters induce self-correction, sending error messages back to the language model for regeneration.

The key to production reliability lies in identifying faults accurately and implementing the appropriate recovery method for each category. This section provides a comprehensive error handling architecture that enables agents to withstand real-world failures.

Error classification and handling strategies

Not all errors are equal. A temporary network timeout differs fundamentally from an authentication failure. The following table categorizes common error types and their relevant handling strategies:

Error type	Strategy	Handling behavior
Transient (429, 503)	Retry with backoff	Wait and try again up to three times.
Invalid Args (400)	Self-correction	Feed error back to LLM to fix arguments.
Auth/Security (403)	Fail fast	Raise an exception; stop the agent immediately.

***Table 11.2**: Error handling and retry strategies*

In production contexts, error handling must be observable. Every retry, failure categorization, and failfast decision should be reported with adequate context for auditing and debugging. Structured logs, correlation **identifiers (IDs)** for each agent run, and toollevel metrics enable teams to trace autonomous executions and pinpoint systemic errors without manual reproduction.

Effective error handling identifies errors by type and applies appropriate recovery strategies, retrying temporary failures, feeding validation errors back for self-correction, and failing fast on security violations.

Once errors are categorized, implementing exponential backoff provides an appropriate retry mechanism for transitory failures. This strategy prevents overwhelming already-stressed services while offering appropriate recovery time.

Implementing exponential backoff

The following code demonstrates exponential backoff for transitory failures:

```
import time
import requests
from langchain_core.tools import tool

@tool
def resilient_api_call(endpoint: str) -> str:
  """API call with exponential backoff retry."""
  max_retries = 3
  base_delay = 1

  for attempt in range(max_retries):
    try:
      response = requests.get(endpoint, timeout=5)
      response.raise_for_status()
      return response.json()
    except requests.RequestException as e:
      if attempt < max_retries - 1:
        delay = base_delay * (2 ** attempt)
        time.sleep(delay)
      else:
        raise Exception(f"Failed after {max_retries} attempts: {e}")
```

Unlike the earlier REST tool, this version *raises* on the final failure rather than returning an error string. Pick the style that fits your error-handling strategy: return a string when you want graceful degradation inside the agent loop, raise an exception when an outer caller needs the failure to propagate as a hard stop.

Exponential backoff increases the delay between retries, reducing the risk of overwhelming failed services while allowing recovery from temporary difficulties.

While error handling addresses operational reliability, security issues require a higher level of protection. When agents execute code, access file systems, or run shell commands, even sophisticated error handling cannot prevent malicious exploitation. Sandboxing provides the necessary isolation layer to contain the dangerous operations.

Security and sandboxing

Code execution tools provide great power but also create substantial security issues. Allowing agents to run Python code, execute shell commands, or modify files exposes the system to malicious prompts, injection attacks, and unforeseen effects. A seemingly innocent *calculate statistics on weather data* request could escalate to disk access or network scanning if not properly confined.

Sandboxing provides a crucial separation layer by executing agent-generated code within constrained environments with limited disk access, regulated network connectivity, and resource restrictions. Docker containers, virtual machines, and remote execution services like E2B or Modal offer varied trade-offs among security, performance, and operational complexity.

Secure sandboxing workflow

Code execution must occur in confined contexts where filesystem access is limited, network connectivity is regulated, and resource usage is monitored.

The following figure depicts the secure execution path:

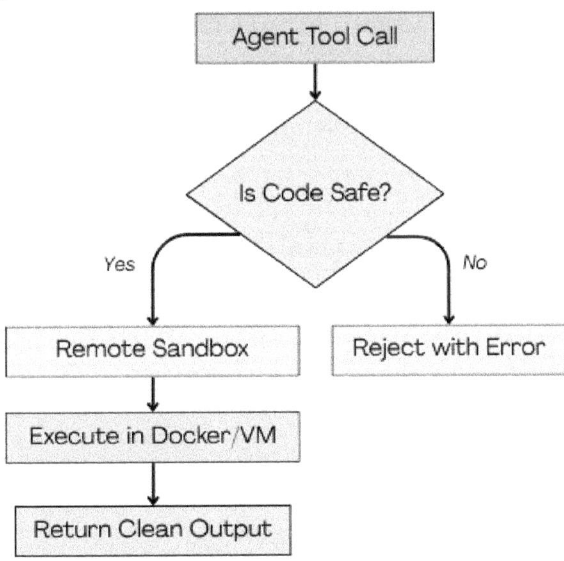

Figure 11.3: *Secure sandboxing workflow*

A key security consideration is to never execute agent-generated code directly on production systems. Always use Docker containers, virtual machines, or remote execution services (E2B, Modal) that provide isolation, resource limitations, and automatic cleanup.

With tool abstraction, orchestration patterns, API integration, error handling, and security measures all defined, readers are ready to synthesize these principles into a fully functional system. The following tutorial demonstrates how to construct an end-to-end weather intelligence agent that coordinates multiple technologies to fulfill real-world objectives.

Sandboxing is not a onetime setting but a continual risk surface. As agents acquire access to powerful tools and external systems, sandbox policies must advance alongside threat models. Continuous assessment of allowable system calls, dependency access, and network egress guarantees that expanding agent capabilities do not accidentally increase the attack surface.

Building a multi-tool weather intelligence system

Having examined individual features in isolation, this workshop demonstrates how all essential concepts, including tool abstraction, orchestration, error management, and security, integrate into a single, productionoriented solution.

This workshop demonstrates the construction of a complete system in which an agent orchestrates multiple tools to fetch weather data, analyze conditions, and store outcomes. The solution incorporates everything covered previously: tool building with unambiguous schemas, ReAct reasoning for intelligent orchestration, database integration for persistence, and conditional logic for alert production.

The weather intelligence system accepts natural language requests, such as "Get *Seattle* weather, save the report, and send an alert if the temperature exceeds 85°F," and autonomously breaks them down into individual tool calls. It executes operations in the correct sequence and synthesizes the findings. This represents the minimal viable implementation for production-ready autonomous agents.

Complete multi-tool implementation

A complete agent combines database persistence, alert notifications, and weather queries under a single `AgentExecutor`. The system prompt instructs the agent to chain tools—fetch conditions, check thresholds, send alerts, and save reports in the correct order without any extra orchestration code.

The following code creates a complete weather intelligence system:

```
import sqlite3
from langchain_openai import ChatOpenAI
from langchain.agents import AgentExecutor, create_tool_calling_agent
```

```
from langchain_core.prompts import ChatPromptTemplate, MessagesPlaceholder
from langchain_core.tools import tool

DB_PATH = "weather.db"

def _init_db() -> None:
  """Create the reports table once at startup – not on every insert."""
  conn = sqlite3.connect(DB_PATH)
  conn.execute(
    "CREATE TABLE IF NOT EXISTS reports (location TEXT, report TEXT)"
  )
  conn.commit()
  conn.close()

_init_db()  # run once at module load

# Database tool
@tool
def save_weather_report(location: str, report: str) -> str:
  """Save weather report to database."""
  conn = sqlite3.connect(DB_PATH)
  conn.execute(
    "INSERT INTO reports VALUES (?, ?)", (location, report)
  )
  conn.commit()
  conn.close()
  return "Report saved successfully"

# Weather tool
@tool
def get_weather_conditions(location: str) -> str:
  """Get current weather conditions."""
  # Mock implementation – replace with real weather API call
  return f"Weather in {location}: 72°F, Sunny, Humidity: 45%"

# Alert tool
@tool
def send_weather_alert(message: str) -> str:
  """Send a weather alert notification.

  PRODUCTION NOTE: this is a placeholder that writes to stdout for
  demonstration only. Before deploying, replace the body with a real
  notification channel – for example, an SMS via Twilio, an email via
```

```
    Amazon SES, or a webhook to PagerDuty / Slack.
    """
    # Placeholder — NOT a production alert channel
    print(f"ALERT: {message}")
    return "Alert sent successfully"

# Configure agent
tools = [get_weather_conditions, save_weather_report, send_weather_alert]
llm = ChatOpenAI(model="gpt-4o-mini", temperature=0)

prompt = ChatPromptTemplate.from_messages([
  ("system", "You are a weather automation assistant. Use tools to complete
tasks."),
  ("human", "{input}"),
  MessagesPlaceholder(variable_name="agent_scratchpad")
])

agent = create_tool_calling_agent(llm, tools, prompt)
agent_executor = AgentExecutor(agent=agent, tools=tools, verbose=True)

# Execute multi-tool workflow
result = agent_executor.invoke({
  "input": "Get Seattle weather, save the report, and send alert if
temperature exceeds 85°F"
})
print(result["output"])
```

Three tools, one prompt, one executor and the agent autonomously chains them in the right order: fetch conditions, evaluate the threshold, send the alert, save the report. Adding a fourth capability (say, an SMS gateway or a forecast lookup) means writing one more `@tool` function and appending it to the `tools` list; the orchestration code stays unchanged. Two production-readiness details are worth highlighting: schema setup runs once via `_init_db()` at module load rather than on every insert (which would race under concurrency), and `send_weather_alert` is explicitly a placeholder, its docstring marks the boundary where a real notification channel (Twilio, SES, PagerDuty, Slack) must be wired in before deployment.

This system demonstrates synchronized execution of multiple tools, including data retrieval, database persistence, and conditional message delivery. The workshop provides a framework that readers can build with new tools, more sophisticated error handling, and stronger security mechanisms as production requirements evolve.

This architecture serves as a reusable foundation for any domain where agents must observe, reason, act, and safely persist outcomes.

While this workshop illustrates key architectural principles, production deployments often enhance this design with centralized configuration, secrets management, access rules, and environment isolation. The purpose of this workshop is not to deliver a final product, but to provide a composable blueprint that teams can change, harden, and scale according to their operational requirements.

Conclusion

In this chapter, readers advance their agents from passive conversationalists to autonomous operators capable of performing real-world tasks. Readers established a reliable bridge from natural language intent to executable operations through tool abstraction and OpenAI function calling. This enables agents to discover available tools, understand clear schemas, create valid arguments, and call external capabilities without relying on brittle, hardcoded logic.

Readers also learned how to assemble capabilities into coherent toolkits, applying ReAct-style reasoning to plan them out, linking steps and executing them in parallel when the tasks are independent. These workflows were made production-ready through retries with exponential backoff, self-correction loops for invalid tool arguments, structured logging for auditability, and security-first practices such as sandboxing, access control, and careful credential handling.

Next, readers will extend these single-agent patterns to multi-agent systems that collaborate and specialize to accomplish complex, multi-step goals. The next chapter introduces planner-executor architectures and other planning frameworks that break down large goals into smaller, manageable tasks. It also demonstrates the use of metrics such as completion, correctness, and efficiency to evaluate system performance. Readers will also explore techniques for scaling and resilience, including caching, quotas, and graceful degradation, ensuring that multi-agent automation remains reliable even under high task loads.

CHAPTER 12
Planning, Collaboration, and Evaluating Autonomous Agents

Introduction

The previous chapters laid the groundwork for agency by exploring voice, memory, reasoning, and tool execution. However, true autonomy needs higher-level coordination. Systems need to plan, act, observe results, and make changes without needing constant human guidance. This chapter integrates all those parts by demonstrating how architectures can turn reactive assistants into proactive problem-solvers in complex real-world situations.

The planner-executor pattern is detailed in the chapter. In this pattern, a planning agent breaks down multi-step goals into structured plans, and executor agents carry them out. By separating strategy from action, readers can create modular designs and ensure they can recover quickly when conditions change. Next, readers will move from single-agent orchestration to multi-agent orchestration, where a supervisor and shared state enable specialists to collaborate, enhancing system scalability and resilience. Finally, readers will learn why quantitative evaluation is so important for production: it helps readers set success metrics and check the efficiency, reliability, cost, and quality of the output.

Structure

This chapter covers the following topics:

- Understanding autonomous artificial intelligence agents
- Understanding planner-executor architecture design principles
- Building planner agents with autonomous self-correction
- Orchestrating multi-agent collaboration
- Evaluating agent performance with measurable metrics
- Building a multi-agent weather event response system

Objectives

This chapter moves from examining the actions of individual agents to designing autonomous systems that operate end-to-end. Readers will create planner-executor architectures that transform complex goals into structured task graphs, allowing agents to think before acting and recover when plans encounter problems. Readers will use patterns inspired by specific versions of **Baby Artificial General Intelligence** (**BabyAGI**) and **Autonomous Generative Pre-trained Transformer** (**AutoGPT**), while acknowledging that both projects evolve rapidly and their implementations can change significantly over time. The focus is therefore on the durable planning concepts these systems illustrate, such as tracking remaining work, incorporating feedback from tools, and adjusting or retrying tasks as needed.

Agents will gain greater freedom by working collaboratively, with a supervisor coordinating specialists, a shared state, and reliable context handoffs to maintain consistency and traceability. Readers will also define measurable success criteria, including reasoning accuracy, tool reliability, efficiency, hallucination rates, cost, and end-to-end latency. Readers will then use automated evaluation to strengthen systems for production.

The chapter concludes with a capstone project: a multi-agent weather event response system that monitors alerts, integrates historical context into decisions, plans around limited resources, and tests behavior to ensure correctness.

Understanding autonomous artificial intelligence agents

Before creating planners and collaborative systems, users must explicitly define what autonomy implies in practice and how it differs from typical LLM-based applications. Before exploring advanced planning and collaboration patterns, it is necessary to understand what makes an **artificial intelligence** (**AI**) agent truly autonomous and why autonomy constitutes a major departure from traditional **large language model** (**LLM**) interactions. This foundational understanding will guide the architectural decisions throughout this chapter.

Defining artificial intelligence agents

An AI agent is an autonomous system that can sense its environment, make decisions, and perform actions to achieve certain goals. Unlike traditional LLM encounters, which are single-turn question-answer exchanges, agents function across several dimensions of capability. They can plan multi-step approaches to complicated issues by reducing high-level objectives into executable task sequences. They perform actions using external tools, extending their capabilities beyond text generation to include **application programming interface** (**API**) calls, database searches, file operations, and real-world integrations. Agents evaluate their performance and adapt strategies based on execution results, implementing self-correction when errors occur or situations change. They preserve context throughout many interactions through persistent memory systems, enabling continuity and learning from earlier experiences. Finally, agents can collaborate with other specialized agents, dispersing difficult workloads across teams with specific expertise.

Tip: **Consider agents as digital assistants that can take real actions, rather than merely providing information. A typical LLM might report the weather forecast, whereas an autonomous agent can review the forecast, identify severe weather hazards, coordinate emergency response teams, and monitor execution progress without requiring human participation at each step.**

Importance of autonomy

Autonomy is the defining trait that separates reactive chatbots from proactive problem-solvers. Traditional LLM applications often require humans to choreograph every step: a user asks a question, receives an answer, interprets it, decides the next action, and manually executes that action before asking another question. This kind of human-in-the-loop workflow can create bottlenecks in scenarios that demand speed, scale, or continuous operation. However, that does not mean human checkpoints are inherently undesirable. In many production systems, human review is an intentional design choice for safety, compliance, quality control, or high-stakes decisions. Autonomous agents reduce unnecessary manual coordination where appropriate, while still supporting escalation and approval points when human judgment adds value. They perceive objectives, plan execution methods, carry out activities, monitor results, and adapt when reality deviates from expectations without requiring humans to direct each intermediate step.

The importance of autonomy becomes obvious in production operations that require ongoing monitoring and fast coordination. Consider a manufacturing operations coordinator overseeing equipment health across multiple facilities. A classic LLM-based system would require a human operator to monitor alerts, manually review maintenance logs for context, consult separate inventory and scheduling systems for parts and technician availability, and synthesize all this information before making decisions. An autonomous agent can execute these steps independently, correlate signals across systems, recommend the next action within seconds, and escalate only when human approval is necessary. Autonomy converts agents from tools that aid humans into systems that function alongside humans, handling routine complexity while elevating only extraordinary cases that demand human judgment.

Building blocks of autonomy

Autonomy arises from the integration of the following four basic capabilities developed throughout this book:

- Planning and decomposition enable agents to break complex goals into manageable subtasks. The planner-executor design separates strategic thinking from tactical execution, allowing agents to think before acting rather than reacting impulsively to each new input.

- Tool execution provides the means to act on judgments. Agents equipped with tools can access databases, use external APIs, make computations, and alter real-world systems based on their reasoning.
- Memory and context management give agents continuity across encounters. Persistent memory systems ensure agents remember past decisions, learn from failures, and maintain a cohesive long-term strategy rather than treating each interaction as isolated.
- Self-correction and adaptability allow agents to recover from errors. By monitoring execution results and feeding failures back into the planning loop, agents iterate toward successful outputs without human involvement.

The patterns implemented in this chapter, including BabyAGI task prioritization, AutoGPT self-correction loops, multi-agent collaboration with context handoffs, and quantitative evaluation frameworks, establish the architectural foundations for genuine autonomy. Each pattern tackles a unique aspect of autonomous operation, and together they enable systems to address open-ended issues with minimal human assistance.

It is important to note that autonomy does not mean removing humans from the loop entirely. Production autonomous agents should implement escalation protocols where they recognize circumstances beyond their competence and require human judgment. The idea is to automate routine complexity while keeping human oversight for high-stakes judgments.

Understanding planner-executor architecture design principles

Most realworld problems are too complex to solve with a single zeroshot approach. A planner-executor architecture separates high-level planning from low-level execution, replicating the human cognitive process of creating a to-do list before beginning a task. This separation enables agents to deliberate strategically before responding, change plans based on observations, and optimize for purposes beyond immediate responses.

Task decomposition and execution planning

In production-grade planner-executor systems, decomposition is not just a one-time step. Planners often re-decompose goals after each tool call to reflect new constraints, partial results, and updated priorities. This keeps the plan aligned with reality and prevents long, brittle reasoning chains.

The core of a planner agent is decomposition. When presented with a complex prompt, the planner identifies necessary subtasks, determines their dependencies, and produces a structured execution plan. This prevents the agent from becoming overwhelmed by a single long reasoning chain, while enabling recovery from errors and adaptation to changing conditions.

The following code exhibits a complete planner agent using LangChain's `AgentExecutor`:

```
from langchain_openai import ChatOpenAI
from langchain.agents import create_react_agent, AgentExecutor
from langchain_core.prompts import PromptTemplate
from langchain_core.tools import tool

# Define tools for weather planning
@tool
def get_weather_forecast(location: str, days: int) -> str:
    """Get multi-day weather forecast for a location."""
    return f"Forecast for {location} over {days} days: Clear skies, 65-75°F"

@tool
def check_trail_conditions(trail_name: str) -> str:
    """Check current trail conditions and accessibility."""
    return f"Trail {trail_name}: Open, moderate difficulty, dry conditions"

@tool
def get_equipment_checklist(activity: str, days: int) -> str:
    """Get recommended equipment for outdoor activity."""
    return f"Equipment for {days}-day {activity}: tent, sleeping bag, first
aid, food"

# Create planner agent with ReAct reasoning
llm = ChatOpenAI(model="gpt-4o-mini", temperature=0)
planner_prompt = PromptTemplate.from_template("""
You are a planning agent that decomposes complex goals into steps.
Answer the following question by planning and using available tools.

Available tools: {tools}
Tool names: {tool_names}

Question: {input}
Thought: {agent_scratchpad}
Final Answer:
""")

tools = [get_weather_forecast, check_trail_conditions, get_equipment_
checklist]
agent = create_react_agent(llm, tools, planner_prompt)

# AgentExecutor runs the planner-executor loop.
```

```
# max_iterations is set to 8 to give the planner enough headroom for a multi-tool
# decomposition (3 tools + plan synthesis can take 4+ Thought/Action/Observation cycles).
agent_executor = AgentExecutor(
    agent=agent,
    tools=tools,
    verbose=True,
    max_iterations=8,
)

# Execute the planning task
result = agent_executor.invoke({
    "input": "Plan a 3-day hiking trip to Mount Rainier"
})
print(f"Final Plan: {result['output']}")
```

The `AgentExecutor` automatically manages the planner-executor loop: the agent plans which tool to call next, executes it, observes the result, and continues planning until the goal is achieved. This separation allows planning logic to evolve separately from execution capabilities, while the executor addresses the operational concerns of tool invocation, error management, and iteration bounds.

With decomposition as the planner's key task, the next decision is how to create planners that reason transparently throughout development yet stay reliable in production.

Choosing agent creation approaches for planners

With task decomposition established as the planner's fundamental role, the next design decision is selecting an agent creation approach that balances transparency during development with reliability in production. Understanding these approaches helps users select the correct foundation for the planner-executor systems. The two basic strategies applicable for autonomous planners are `create_react_agent` for transparent reasoning and `create_tool_calling_agent` for production reliability.

The `create_react_agent` approach uses text-based reasoning, in which the agent openly writes down its thought process in a Thought-Action-Observation cycle. This makes the planning process more apparent, which is essential when troubleshooting complex decomposition logic or understanding why an agent chose a particular task sequence. However, this transparency can introduce parsing issues when the LLM does not format its responses correctly. In BabyAGI-style planners, where evaluating task prioritization decisions is critical, the detailed reasoning trail provided by **Reasoning and Acting** (**ReAct**) agents often outweighs occasional parsing issues.

In contrast, `create_tool_calling_agent` uses the LLM's native function-calling capabilities to launch tools using structured **JavaScript Object Notation** (**JSON**) rather than relying on text parsing. This approach is substantially more dependable in production since it minimizes parsing errors and decreases hallucinations. The agent's reasoning happens inside rather than being exposed as text, which makes it faster and more token-efficient but less transparent. When creating production planner-executor systems that must run autonomously without human troubleshooting, tool-calling agents provide the stability required for enterprise deployment.

The following table compares agent development approaches for planner systems:

Approach	Reasoning style	Reliability	Transparency	Best use case
`create_react_agent`	Explicit text-based thoughts	Medium (parsing errors possible)	High (visible reasoning)	Research, debugging, BabyAGI experiments
`create_tool_calling_agent`	Implicit function calls	High (structured JSON)	Low (hidden reasoning)	Production planners, AutoGPT systems
`initialize_agent`	Template-based (legacy)	Medium	Medium	Quick prototypes, learning

***Table 12.1**: Agent creation approaches for planner systems*

A best practice is to start development with `create_react_agent` to discover how the planner decomposes tasks and prioritizes actions. Once the logic stabilizes, migrate to `create_tool_calling_agent` for production deployment to achieve reliability and performance benefits.

For developers using LangChain's old `initialize_agent` API, the framework provides many predefined agent types accessible via the `AgentType` enumeration. While current LangChain versions suggest the explicit construction techniques shown previously, understanding these agent kinds remains essential for working with existing codebases and legacy systems.

The following list summarizes the classic agent kinds and their characteristics:

- **ZERO_SHOT_REACT_DESCRIPTION**: Uses ReAct, works with tool descriptions, is memory friendly, and is the default choice for reasoning plus tools.
- **CONVERSATIONAL_REACT_DESCRIPTION**: Uses ReAct with chat memory, works with tool descriptions, is memory friendly, and is best for chatbots with memory.
- **CHAT_ZERO_SHOT_REACT_DESCRIPTION**: Uses chat-optimized ReAct, works with tool descriptions, is memory friendly, and is best for chat models such as GPT-4 and GPT-4o.
- **STRUCTURED_CHAT_ZERO_SHOT_REACT_DESCRIPTION**: Uses ReAct with JSON schema, works with structured tools, is memory friendly, and is best for APIs and predictable outputs.

- **OPENAI_FUNCTIONS**: Uses native function calling, works with JSON functions, is memory friendly, and is best for reliable production agents in legacy systems.
- **SELF_ASK_WITH_SEARCH**: Uses self-ask decomposition, works with search tools, has limited memory friendliness, and is best for multi-step factual queries.
- **REACT_DOCSTORE**: Uses ReAct with document lookup, works with **`docstore`** tools, has limited memory friendliness, and is best for QA over indexed documents.

The most relevant agent types for planner systems are `ZERO_SHOT_REACT_DESCRIPTION` for simple reasoning tasks and `CONVERSATIONAL_REACT_DESCRIPTION` when planners must retain discussion history across multiple interactions. The `OPENAI_FUNCTIONS` type has been superseded by `create_tool_calling_agent` but continues to be used in older systems. For new planner-executor implementations, choose the explicit creation methods (`create_react_agent` or `create_tool_calling_agent`) over `initialize_agent` with agent types, as they allow better control over prompts and behavior.

The following table compares single-agent reasoning against planner-executor architecture across major operational dimensions:

Feature	Single agent (ReAct)	Planner-executor
Logic type	Linear, step-by-step reasoning	Hierarchical, strategic planning
Complexity	Best for simple, few-turn tasks	Best for complex, multi-day workflows
Recovery	Hard to backtrack after errors	Can re-plan or skip failed sub-tasks
Token usage	Lower per interaction	Higher (requires initial planning call)

Table 12.2: Comparison of agentic reasoning patterns

Planner-executor architecture is a design pattern that separates strategic planning from tactical execution. Planner agents break down goals and create action sequences, while executor agents carry out these actions using the available tools and capabilities.

Architecting the planner-executor loop

A sophisticated planning loop involves a planner that defines the task list, an executor that performs individual stages, and a reviewer that modifies the plan based on the results.

The following figure demonstrates the entire planner-executor flow:

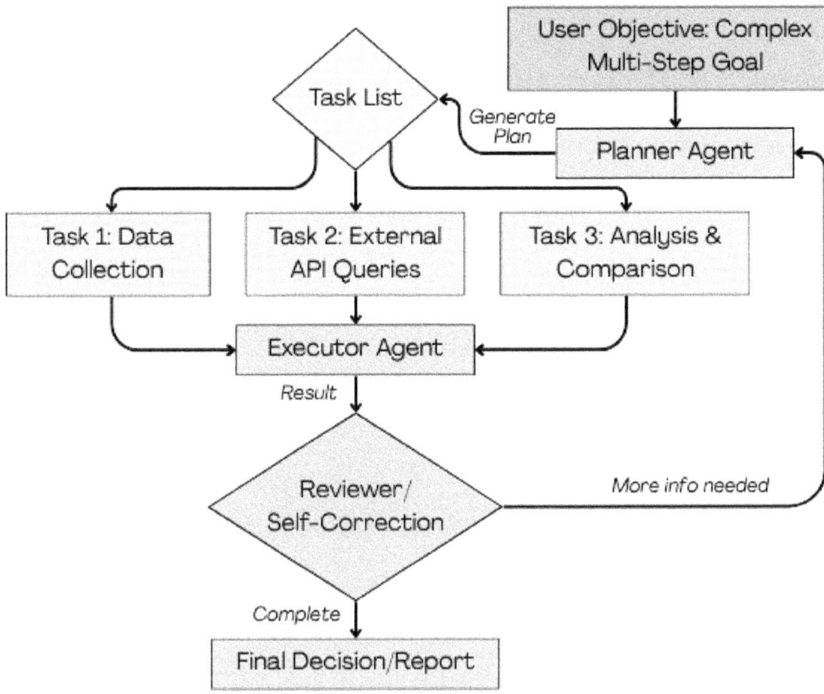

Figure 12.1: *The planner-executor task decomposition flow*

The planner decomposes high-level objectives into parallelizable subtasks, executor agents carry out specific operations using available tools, and a reviewer analyzes outcomes to trigger either completion or re-planning. This architecture offers error recovery, adaptive processes, and hierarchical issue decomposition.

A best practice is to start with coarse-grained decomposition, identifying major stages, then recursively break down complex subtasks. This hierarchical technique manages complexity while keeping clarity regarding the ultimate objective structure.

With the architectural framework set, readers are ready to develop actual planner agents that independently break down tasks, execute plans, and repair errors. Patterns like BabyAGI and AutoGPT demonstrate how agents can keep task lists and dynamically re-prioritize based on findings.

Building planner agents with autonomous self-correction

Planner agents go beyond simple tool activation by keeping dynamic task lists that grow throughout operation. Rather than responding reactively to individual impulses, planners anticipate future steps, develop execution roadmaps, and continuously alter plans as realworld conditions invalidate prior assumptions.

Implementing BabyAGI task prioritization patterns

BabyAGI established the concept of an agent that develops, prioritizes, and executes tasks in a loop. The agent maintains three important components: a task list, an execution outcome history, and a prioritization algorithm that reorders tasks depending on completed activity.

The following code demonstrates constructing a BabyAGI-style planner with dynamic task prioritization:

```
from langchain_openai import ChatOpenAI
from langchain_core.prompts import ChatPromptTemplate


class DynamicTaskPlanner:
    """BabyAGI-style planner with autonomous task management.

    Modeled on the original BabyAGI pattern (yoheinakajima/babyagi, 2023).
The
    upstream project has evolved considerably since then; this class captures
    the *pattern* (decompose → prioritize → re-rank against completed work)
    rather than tracking any specific upstream release.
    """

    def __init__(self):
        self.llm = ChatOpenAI(model="gpt-4o-mini", temperature=0)
        self.task_list: list[dict] = []
        self.completed_tasks: list[dict] = []

    def create_tasks(self, objective: str) -> list[dict]:
        """Decompose objective into prioritized tasks."""
        prompt = ChatPromptTemplate.from_messages([
            ("system", "Break objectives into numbered steps."),
            ("human", "Objective: {objective}"),
        ])
        result = self.llm.invoke(prompt.format_messages(objective=objective))
        return self._parse_tasks(result.content)

    def prioritize_tasks(self) -> list[dict]:
        """Reorder tasks based on completed work."""
        if not self.completed_tasks:
            return self.task_list
```

```
        # Only the last 3 completed tasks are kept as context to bound token
use;
        # increase the slice if your task list is long and history is
important.
        prompt = ChatPromptTemplate.from_messages([
            ("system", "You reorder a task list based on recently completed
work."),
            ("human", "Remaining: {remaining}\nRecently completed:
{completed}"),
        ])
        result = self.llm.invoke(prompt.format_messages(
            remaining=self.task_list,
            completed=self.completed_tasks[-3:],
        ))
        return self._parse_tasks(result.content)

    def _parse_tasks(self, content: str) -> list[dict]:
        return [{"description": line.strip(), "status": "pending"}
                for line in content.split("\n") if line.strip()]


# Usage example
planner = DynamicTaskPlanner()
planner.task_list = planner.create_tasks("Analyze Q4 sales and generate
forecast")

# Expected planner.task_list (illustrative — exact wording varies by run):
# [
#   {"description": "1. Gather Q4 sales records from the data warehouse",
"status": "pending"},
#   {"description": "2. Compute revenue, units, and growth vs. Q3",
"status": "pending"},
#   {"description": "3. Segment by product line and region",
"status": "pending"},
#   {"description": "4. Fit a forecast model on the last 8 quarters",
"status": "pending"},
#   {"description": "5. Summarize findings and projected Q1 numbers",
"status": "pending"},
# ]
```

BabyAGI's primary innovation is storing task state between iterations and dynamically re-prioritizing based on execution results. As activities finish, the planner assesses their outputs and reorders remaining work to take the most promising path toward the aim. This permits autonomous adaptation when the agent identifies new subtasks or abandons unproductive approaches without human intervention.

Tip: Store completed task outcomes in vector memory so the planner can recover important historical context when re-prioritizing. This reduces unnecessary work and increases decision quality.

AutoGPT execution loops with self-correction

AutoGPT expanded on BabyAGI by introducing self-correction, the capability to recognize when a task has failed, and either retry with modifications or move on to alternative ways. This requires monitoring tool outputs and relaying faults back to the planning loop.

The following code exhibits self-correction logic for external API data retrieval:

```
from langchain_core.tools import tool
from langchain_openai import ChatOpenAI
import requests


@tool
def fetch_external_data(endpoint: str, params: dict) -> str:
    """Fetch data from external API."""
    try:
        response = requests.get(endpoint, params=params, timeout=5)
        response.raise_for_status()
        return f"Data retrieved: {response.json()}"
    except requests.RequestException as e:
        return f"ERROR: {str(e)}"


class SelfCorrectingExecutor:
    """Executor with retry and correction logic.

    Modeled on the original AutoGPT pattern (Significant-Gravitas/AutoGPT,
2023).
    The upstream project has evolved significantly since then; this class
    captures the *pattern* (execute → detect failure → ask LLM for correction
→

    retry/skip) rather than mirroring any specific upstream release.
    """

    def __init__(self, max_retries: int = 3):
```

```
        self.llm = ChatOpenAI(model="gpt-4o-mini", temperature=0)
        self.max_retries = max_retries

    def execute_with_correction(self, task: dict, tools: list) -> dict:
        """Execute task with automatic error recovery."""
        for attempt in range(self.max_retries):
            result = self._execute_task(task, tools)

            # Error detection uses the explicit "ERROR:" prefix produced by
            # fetch_external_data above. Plain substring matching ("ERROR" in
            # result) is too loose – it would treat any output mentioning the
            # word as a failure. Tools called here must follow the same
convention.
            if not result.startswith("ERROR:"):
                return {"status": "success", "result": result}

            # Ask LLM for correction strategy
            correction = self._get_correction(task, result)

            if correction["action"] == "skip":
                return {"status": "skipped", "reason": correction["reason"]}

            task = correction["modified_task"]

        return {"status": "failed", "error": result}

    def _execute_task(self, task: dict, tools: list) -> str:
        """Invoke the tool named by task['tool'] with task['params']."""
        tool_name = task.get("tool")
        params = task.get("params", {})
        for t in tools:
            if t.name == tool_name:
                return t.invoke(params)
        return f"ERROR: tool '{tool_name}' not found"

    def _get_correction(self, task: dict, error: str) -> dict:
        """Ask the LLM how to recover from the error (modify, skip, or
fail)."""
        prompt = (
            f"Task: {task}\nError: {error}\n"
            'Reply JSON: {"action": "modify"|"skip", '
            '"modified_task": <new task dict>, "reason": <short reason>}'
        )
```

```
        # Caller is expected to parse JSON; minimal stub returns a skip
directive.
        return {"action": "skip", "reason": error, "modified_task": task}
```

Self-correction converts brittle execution into resilient processes that respond to API failures, incorrect inputs, and unexpected conditions without human intervention.

It is important to set maximum retry limits to prevent infinite loops. After three failed correction efforts, escalate to human review or skip to the next task rather than stopping the entire workflow.

While self-correction addresses task-level failures, real-world systems must also adapt to changes in the environment, data, and system restrictions.

Automated response strategies for dynamic scenarios

Checklist for making dynamic response strategies: set clear rules for what counts as a "change" (data drift, tool failure, new constraint, new objective), find it with clear signals (timeouts, validation failures, freshness checks, budget monitors), and pick a response policy (retry, switch tools, re-plan, defer, escalate). To make sure your code is strong, keep retry logic and planning logic separate, set limits on how many times you can try something, and save intermediate outputs so that a re-plan can pick up where it left off at the last safe checkpoint.

While self-correction addresses task-level mistakes, production planners must also adapt to broader environmental changes, such as shifting data, unavailable tools, or emerging objectives. Automated response strategies enable agents to change plans without starting from scratch.

The following table categorizes frequent dynamic circumstances and their automatic reaction patterns:

Scenario type	Detection method	Response strategy	Example
Data invalidation	Compare new versus cached results	Re-execute dependent tasks	Source data updated, dependent analysis obsolete
Tool failure	Monitor error rates	Switch to the backup tool or skip	Primary API is down; use the fallback service
Priority shift	External trigger/ alert	Re-prioritize the task list	Urgent notification triggers immediate action
Resource constraint	Monitor token/cost budgets	Simplify the plan or defer tasks	Approaching the API rate limit, reduce calls
Goal completion	Validate success criteria	Terminate early	All objectives were met before the full plan

***Table 12.3**: Automated response strategies for dynamic scenarios*

Implementing these solutions involves monitoring system state and trigger conditions, then activating the appropriate reaction handler when thresholds are surpassed.

Note: **It is important to cache intermediate results so that when plans change, users can resume from the last valid state rather than re-executing finished activities. In practice, this can substantially reduce latency and API costs in dynamic settings, especially when workflows frequently re-plan or reuse expensive tool outputs.**

With planning and self-correction established, readers are ready to move beyond single-agent systems. Multi-agent collaboration allows specialization, ensuring that tasks can be addressed even when no single agent possesses all the essential knowledge and tools.

Orchestrating multi-agent collaboration

Some objectives require multiple areas of expertise that exceed the capabilities of a single generalpurpose agent. In these cases, multiagent collaboration enables systems to distribute responsibilities across specialized agents, coordinating their efforts while minimizing contention, redundancy, and hallucinations.

Supervisor pattern for agent coordination

In the supervisor pattern, a **supervisor agent** is the coordinating agent responsible for routing work to the right specialists, maintaining the shared state, and combining partial outputs into a final result. It matters because multi-agent systems become difficult to control when every agent communicates with every other agent directly. By giving one agent responsibility for task assignment, sequencing, escalation, and synthesis, the system gains clearer coordination, lower redundancy, and more predictable behavior. In the example below, the supervisor is the coordinating layer that decides when to invoke each specialist agent and how to merge their outputs into a coherent response, even though the code first introduces the specialist agents themselves before showing fuller orchestration in the later capstone system.

The following code explains how to define specialized agents inside a collaborative team:

```
from langchain_openai import ChatOpenAI
from langchain.agents import create_tool_calling_agent, AgentExecutor
from langchain_core.prompts import ChatPromptTemplate
from langchain_core.tools import tool

# Initialize specialized LLM
llm = ChatOpenAI(model="gpt-4o-mini", temperature=0)


# Stub specialist tools so the agents below are runnable
@tool
```

```
def query_database(query: str) -> str:
    """Run a read-only SQL query against the analytics warehouse."""
    return f"rows: [{{'metric': 'revenue', 'value': 1234567}}]  -- query:
{query}"


@tool
def run_optimization(problem: str) -> str:
    """Solve a small optimization problem and return the chosen plan."""
    return f"optimal plan for: {problem}"


# Define specialist agent personas
data_analyst_prompt = ChatPromptTemplate.from_messages([
    ("system", "You are a data analysis specialist. Extract insights from
datasets."),
    ("human", "{input}"),
    ("placeholder", "{agent_scratchpad}"),
])

optimization_prompt = ChatPromptTemplate.from_messages([
    ("system", "You are an optimization specialist. Find efficient
solutions."),
    ("human", "{input}"),
    ("placeholder", "{agent_scratchpad}"),
])

# Create specialized agents with focused tool sets
analyst = create_tool_calling_agent(llm, [query_database], data_analyst_
prompt)
analyst_executor = AgentExecutor(agent=analyst, tools=[query_database],
verbose=False)

optimizer = create_tool_calling_agent(llm, [run_optimization], optimization_
prompt)
optimizer_executor = AgentExecutor(agent=optimizer, tools=[run_optimization],
verbose=False)


# Supervisor agent: routes each request to the appropriate specialist
@tool
def delegate_to_analyst(task: str) -> str:
    """Delegate a data analysis task to the analyst specialist."""
```

```
    return analyst_executor.invoke({"input": task})["output"]


@tool
def delegate_to_optimizer(task: str) -> str:
    """Delegate an optimization task to the optimizer specialist."""
    return optimizer_executor.invoke({"input": task})["output"]


supervisor_prompt = ChatPromptTemplate.from_messages([
    ("system",
     "You are a supervisor that coordinates specialist agents. "
     "Use delegate_to_analyst for data questions and delegate_to_optimizer "
     "for optimization questions."),
    ("human", "{input}"),
    ("placeholder", "{agent_scratchpad}"),
])

supervisor_tools = [delegate_to_analyst, delegate_to_optimizer]
supervisor = create_tool_calling_agent(llm, supervisor_tools, supervisor_
prompt)
supervisor_executor = AgentExecutor(agent=supervisor, tools=supervisor_tools,
verbose=False)
```

The supervisor pattern's power lies in specialization. Instead of training a single agent to handle all parts of a difficult problem, users distribute duties among experts. A data analyst focuses entirely on extracting insights, an optimizer emphasizes efficiency, and a coordinator synthesizes their findings. This division of labor lowers hallucinations, enhances accuracy, and facilitates concurrent execution of independent subtasks.

Handling context handoffs in complicated workflows

A context handoff in a multi-agent system is the organized set of data that one agent (or step) sends to the next. Do not think of handoffs as conversation history; think of them as clear artifacts. A good handoff usually includes the goal and scope, the decisions that have been made so far, the outputs (or references) of the tools, the assumptions, the constraints (time, cost, and rate limits), and the next step. When you can, put this information in a shared state, like a LangGraph state object or a shared memory store, so that specialists can read the same source of truth and not get off track. Add guardrails like schema validation for handoff payloads, provenance tags for each data item, and rules for resolving conflicts when specialists disagree to cut down on compounding errors.

Context handoffs and state management

The biggest issue in teamwork is ensuring Agent B knows what Agent A just did. Frameworks such as LangGraph, which is designed for graph-based agent orchestration with shared state, or other shared memory systems, can retain a global state that all agents can read and update.

The following figure depicts multi-agent context handoffs:

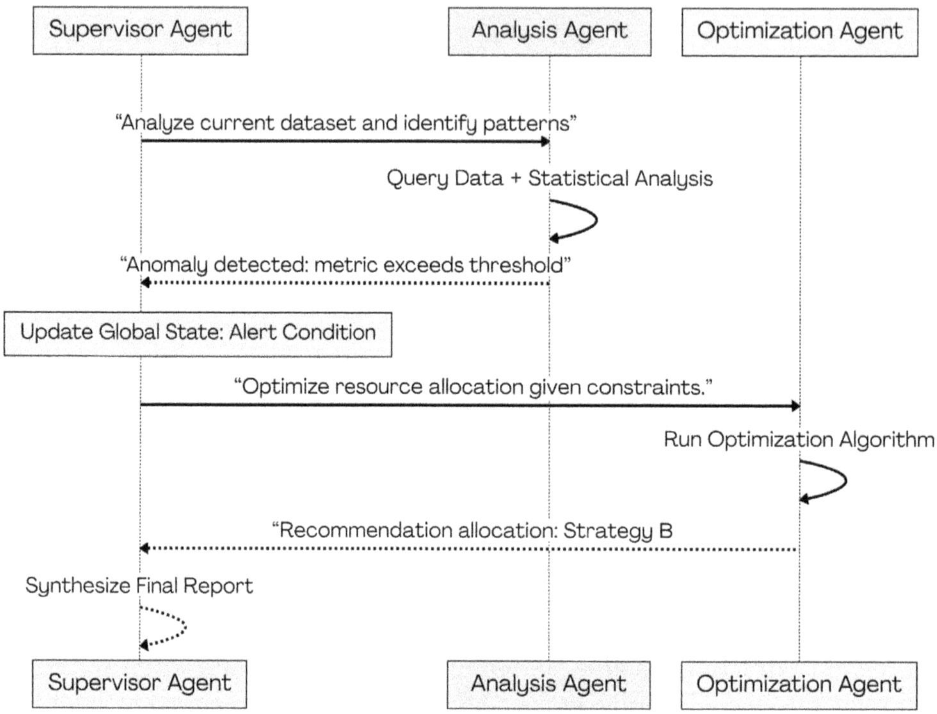

***Figure 12.2**: Sequence diagram for multi-agent context handoffs*

Context handoffs are the communication backbone of multi-agent systems. The supervisor distributes focused tasks to specialists, each agent executes using its domain expertise and specialized tools, outcomes flow back through shared global state, and the supervisor synthesizes outputs into coherent judgments. Effective handoffs require well-defined task limits, detailed state updates that track data provenance, and mechanisms to resolve conflicts when agents provide contradictory recommendations.

Note: **Include provenance metadata in context handoffs indicating which agents produced which data. This facilitates debugging and enables agents to weigh information depending on source reliability.**

With multi-agent orchestration operational, the crucial difficulty becomes monitoring whether the autonomous system truly functions reliably. Production deployment requires a quantitative evaluation to verify that performance satisfies criteria.

Evaluating agent performance with measurable metrics

After agents can plan, correct themselves, and collaborate through shared state, the next question is whether they perform well enough to trust in production. This section connects the orchestration patterns from the previous section to the measurement practices needed for deployment. Instead of treating evaluation as a final checkbox, readers will define measurable criteria that reveal whether the agent is reasoning correctly, using tools reliably, coordinating efficiently, controlling cost, and recovering from failures.

Capstone evaluation, optimization, and deployment

The capstone project should be treated as a mini production rollout. Start by defining an **evaluation set** of representative scenarios (happy paths, edge cases, tool failures, and ambiguous requests), then establish **baselines** (for example, a single-agent ReAct implementation) so improvements are measurable. Run the agent end-to-end across the evaluation set and record metrics such as success rate, retries, and re-plans per task, average tool calls per run, latency, and cost. Use these results to identify the bottleneck layer (planner, executor/tooling, or coordination) and iterate on one change at a time.

Before deployment, define **acceptance thresholds** (for example, minimum success rate, maximum hallucination rate, maximum average cost per run, and a strict upper bound on retries). Add **runtime guardrails**: timeouts for each tool, global budgets (tokens/cost), safe defaults and fallbacks when tools fail, and explicit **human escalation** rules for high-stakes decisions. Finally, implement monitoring for regressions (metric drift, increased failure rate, rising costs) and keep a simple rollback plan so the system can be disabled or downgraded if reliability drops.

Evaluation metrics for planning and collaboration

Beyond single-agent correctness, autonomous systems should be evaluated on **planning quality** and **collaboration quality**. Useful planning metrics include plan validity (percentage of steps that are executable), re-plan rate (how often the planner must revise), dependency correctness (whether prerequisites were met), and recovery efficiency (steps/time to recover after a failure). For multi-agent collaboration, measure coordination overhead (messages/turns between agents), handoff completeness (required fields present in the handoff payload), contradiction rate (frequency of conflicting specialist outputs), and traceability (whether outputs can be linked back to sources and tool calls). These metrics make it easier to identify whether issues come from the planner, the executor/tool layer, or the coordination layer.

Deploying an autonomous agent without quantitative evaluation entails significant operational risk. Beyond subjective judgments, production systems require objective metrics that evaluate reasoning quality, execution accuracy, efficiency, and dependability at scale.

Defining agent success criteria

Evaluating an agent includes measuring both its reasoning accuracy and its execution success across various dimensions. The following table defines production-grade metrics that quantify agent performance:

Metric category	Specific metric	Description
Reasoning	Answer correctness	Does the final answer match the ground truth?
Execution	Tool call accuracy	Did the agent provide correct arguments to the tool?
Efficiency	Step count	How many turns did the planner take to solve the task?
Reliability	Hallucination rate	How often did the agent cite data not in context?
Cost	Token cost per run	What is the total token or model cost required to complete one end-to-end task?
Performance	Latency (end-to-end)	Total time from user input to final result.

***Table 12.4**: Production agent evaluation metrics*

These measurements provide baseline performance visibility, showing whether agents achieve objectives reliably while maintaining efficiency and cost-effectiveness.

Implementing automated testing frameworks

Beyond specifying metrics, users require automated testing that confirms agent behavior before deployment. Testing frameworks test agents against known situations and compare outputs to expected results, discovering regressions early.

The following code provides an evaluation system for autonomous agents:

```
from langchain_openai import ChatOpenAI
from langchain_core.prompts import ChatPromptTemplate
from langchain_core.output_parsers import JsonOutputParser


class AgentEvaluationFramework:
    """Automated testing for autonomous agents."""

    def __init__(self):
        self.qa_evaluator = self._build_evaluator()
```

```
        self.test_cases: list[dict] = []

    def _build_evaluator(self):
        """Build a small LCEL evaluator chain that returns {score,
reasoning}."""
        prompt = ChatPromptTemplate.from_messages([
            ("system",
             "You are evaluating whether an AI assistant's answer correctly
addresses the question. "
             "Compare the actual answer to the reference answer.\n"
             'Respond with ONLY a JSON object: {"score": <0.0 to 1.0>,
"reasoning": "<brief reason>"}'),
            ("human", "Question: {query}\nReference answer: {reference}\
nActual answer: {prediction}"),
        ])
        return prompt | ChatOpenAI(model="gpt-4o-mini", temperature=0) |
JsonOutputParser()

    def add_test_case(self, input: str, expected_output: str):
        """Register a test scenario."""
        self.test_cases.append({
            "input": input,
            "expected": expected_output,
        })

    def evaluate_agent(self, agent_executor) -> dict:
        """Run all tests and compute metrics."""
        results = []
        for case in self.test_cases:
            result = agent_executor.invoke({"input": case["input"]})

            # Evaluate correctness
            score = self.qa_evaluator.invoke({
                "query": case["input"],
                "reference": case["expected"],
                "prediction": result["output"],
            })
            results.append({
                "case": case["input"],
                "passed": float(score.get("score", 0)) > 0.8,
                "score": float(score.get("score", 0)),
            })
        return self._compute_aggregate_metrics(results)
```

```
    def _compute_aggregate_metrics(self, results):
        """Calculate overall performance."""
        total = len(results)
        passed = sum(1 for r in results if r["passed"])
        return {
            "accuracy": passed / total,
            "total_tests": total,
            "passed": passed,
            "failed": total - passed,
        }


# Usage example
evaluator = AgentEvaluationFramework()
evaluator.add_test_case(
    input="Analyze sales data and identify top performers",
    expected_output="Top 3 products by revenue identified",
)
```

Automated evaluation provides confidence that updates do not disrupt current functionality and that agents meet performance standards before production deployment.

Tip: **Build a regression test suite with at least 20 to 30 varied scenarios addressing edge cases, including API failures, unclear inputs, and multi-step reasoning chains. Run this suite on every code modification.**

Production hardening checklist

Before the agent goes online, it must pass a safety and stability check. Use the following checklist to guarantee the system is resilient to real-world edge cases:

- **Error handling**: Implement try/except blocks around every tool call to prevent crashes.
- **Token safeguards**: Use summarizing or cutting to guarantee memory does not hit context restrictions.
- **Security**: Ensure all code execution happens in a secure, sandboxed environment.
- **Traceability**: Log all intermediate reasoning steps for auditing and debugging.
- **Rate limiting**: Handle API 429 errors with exponential backoff retries.

With assessment frameworks and production standards established, readers are ready to integrate all these concepts into a comprehensive autonomous system that displays enterprise-grade capabilities.

Building a multi-agent weather event response system

This workshop integrates every concept from the book into a comprehensive autonomous weather emergency coordinator. The system displays planner-executor architecture, multi-agent collaboration with specialized roles, self-correction logic, and quantitative evaluation, all the pieces required for production deployment.

System architecture and agent roles

The weather event response system coordinates three specialized agents: a Monitor agent that detects severe weather alerts, an Analyst agent that gets historical climate data for context, and a Coordinator agent that formulates emergency action plans. A Supervisor agent orchestrates their collaboration and maintains a shared state.

The following figure displays the entire multi-agent architecture:

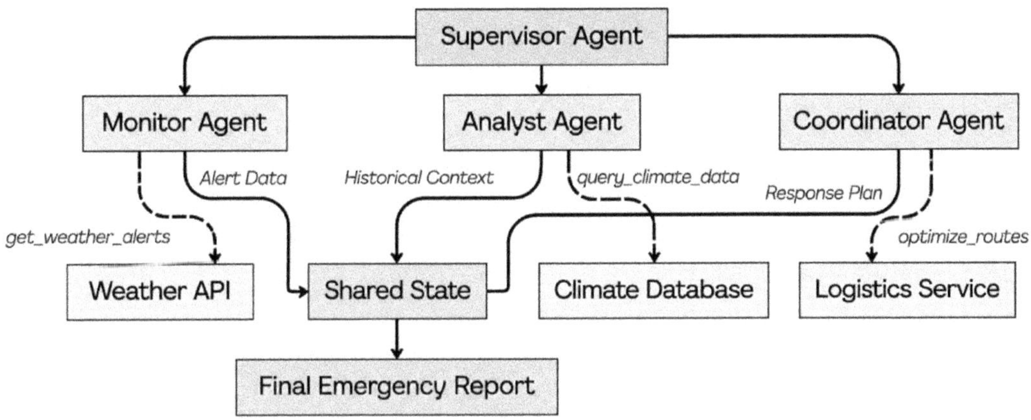

***Figure 12.3**: Multi-agent weather response system architecture*

Each agent functions independently with specific expertise, communicating through a shared state controlled by the supervisor.

Complete implementation with evaluation

The following code offers the entire multi-agent weather response system:

```
from langchain_openai import ChatOpenAI
from langchain.agents import AgentExecutor, create_openai_functions_agent
from langchain_core.prompts import ChatPromptTemplate, MessagesPlaceholder
from langchain.tools import tool
from typing import Dict, List
```

```python
@tool
def get_weather_alerts(region: str) -> str:
  """Fetch severe weather alerts."""
  return f"SEVERE: Storm warning for {region}, 4hr validity"

@tool
def query_climate_data(region: str) -> str:
  """Retrieve climate patterns."""
  return f"{region}: 12 storms/year average (5yr history)"

@tool
def optimize_routes(location: str) -> str:
  """Calculate evacuation routes."""
  return f"Route: Highway 5, avoid downtown {location}"

class WeatherResponseSystem:
  """Multi-agent weather emergency coordinator."""

  def __init__(self):
    self.llm = ChatOpenAI(model="gpt-4o-mini", temperature=0)
    self.shared_state: Dict = {}
    self.agents = self._create_agents()

  def _create_agents(self) -> Dict:
    agents = {}
    configs = [
      ("monitor", [get_weather_alerts], "Monitor severe weather alerts."),
      ("analyst", [query_climate_data], "Analyze historical patterns."),
      ("coordinator", [optimize_routes], "Create response plans.")
    ]
    for name, tools, msg in configs:
      prompt = ChatPromptTemplate.from_messages([
        ("system", msg), ("human", "{input}"),
        MessagesPlaceholder(variable_name="agent_scratchpad")
      ])
      agent = create_openai_functions_agent(self.llm, tools, prompt)
```

```
        agents[name] = AgentExecutor(agent=agent, tools=tools, verbose=False)
      return agents

    def coordinate_response(self, region: str) -> str:
      """Orchestrate multi-agent response."""
      self.shared_state["alert"] = self.agents["monitor"].invoke(
        {"input": f"Check {region}"})["output"]
      self.shared_state["context"] = self.agents["analyst"].invoke(
        {"input": f"History for {region}"})["output"]
      self.shared_state["plan"] = self.agents["coordinator"].invoke(
        {"input": f"Plan for {region}"})["output"]

      return f"REPORT\nAlert: {self.shared_state['alert']}\nContext: {self.
shared_state['context']}\nPlan: {self.shared_state['plan']}"

# Deploy
system = WeatherResponseSystem()
print(system.coordinate_response("Seattle"))
```

This entire system illustrates planner-executor principles, multi-agent orchestration, shared state management, and specialized tool execution functioning in harmony.

In production, it is essential to implement error handling for each agent invocation, create retry logic for failed tool calls, and persist all intermediate results in memory to support debugging and compliance.

Evaluating the capstone system

The final phase is testing whether the autonomous system meets production requirements. Using the evaluation framework from the *Implementing automated testing frameworks* section, users validate performance against quantitative criteria.

The following code demonstrates evaluating the weather response system:

```
class CapstoneEvaluator:
    """Evaluate multi-agent weather system."""

    def __init__(self):
        self.framework = AgentEvaluationFramework()

    def evaluate_system(self, system: WeatherResponseSystem):
        """Run comprehensive evaluation suite."""
```

```
        test_scenarios = [
            {"region": "Seattle",   "expected": "emergency plan"},
            {"region": "Portland",  "expected": "evacuation routes"},
            {"region": "Vancouver", "expected": "resource allocation"},
        ]

        results = []
        for scenario in test_scenarios:
            result = system.coordinate_response(scenario["region"])
            score = self.framework.qa_evaluator.invoke({
                "query": f"Coordinate response for {scenario['region']}",
                "reference": scenario["expected"],
                "prediction": result,
            })
            passed = float(score.get("score", 0)) > 0.8
            results.append({
                "scenario": scenario["region"],
                "score": float(score.get("score", 0)),
                "passed": passed,
            })

        accuracy = sum(r["passed"] for r in results) / len(results)
        return {"accuracy": accuracy, "results": results}


evaluator = CapstoneEvaluator()
metrics = evaluator.evaluate_system(system)
print(f"System Accuracy: {metrics['accuracy']:.1%}")
```

Quantitative evaluation ensures the autonomous system runs reliably and fulfills the performance levels required for production deployment.

Conclusion

Readers have completed a comprehensive journey from core LangChain concepts to production-grade autonomous agent systems. This final chapter tied together every thread woven throughout the book, transforming individual capabilities into unified intelligent systems that operate with minimal human interaction. Readers began by studying what makes agents genuinely autonomous, including the ability to sense environments, develop multi-step methods, execute actions through tools, reflect on performance, and communicate with other agents. These defining traits distinguish reactive chatbots from proactive problem-solvers capable of managing complex, time-sensitive challenges independently.

The planner-executor architecture was developed as the core design pattern enabling autonomous operation. Readers mastered task decomposition techniques that break complex objectives into structured execution plans, learned to choose between create_react_agent for transparent debugging and create_tool_calling_agent for production reliability, and implemented the AgentExecutor loop to handle planning, execution, observation, and re-planning automatically. The comparison of classic AgentType options provided historical context while guiding readers toward present best practices. This architectural basis ensures the agents can think intelligently before acting, recover gracefully from errors, and alter plans when reality deviates from expectations.

Building on this foundation, readers created sophisticated autonomous patterns inspired by BabyAGI and AutoGPT. The BabyAGI task prioritizing system demonstrated how agents maintain dynamic task lists that evolve based on completed work, continuously re-evaluating priorities to pursue the most promising paths toward objectives. AutoGPT's self-correction techniques illustrated how agents can monitor tool outputs, detect problems, and either retry with improvements or skip to alternative approaches, transforming brittle execution into resilient processes. These automated response solutions allow agents to handle data invalidation, tool failures, priority adjustments, and resource limits without restarting from scratch. Collectively, these patterns enable agents to operate autonomously over extended periods, adapt to changing environments, and recover from unexpected occurrences.

Multi-agent orchestration extends the capabilities beyond what single agents can accomplish. The supervisor pattern divides complex tasks among specialized agents, each with focused expertise and specific tools, while coordinators synthesize their outputs into cohesive choices. Readers created context handoff mechanisms to ensure information flows appropriately between agents, learned to manage shared global state accessible to all team members, and established provenance tracking for debugging and credibility assessment. The weather event response capstone combined these principles into a production system, coordinating monitor, analyzer, and coordinator agents to detect alarms, obtain historical context, and autonomously develop emergency plans. This demonstrated how multi-agent collaboration uses specialized knowledge while avoiding the hallucinations and errors common in generalist agents.

Finally, readers progressed from qualitative assessment to quantitative evaluation, developing the measurements and frameworks required for production deployment. Production-grade success criteria measure reasoning accuracy, tool execution correctness, efficiency, hallucination rates, and end-to-end latency. Automated testing frameworks check agent behavior against known scenarios before deployment, finding regressions early and creating trust in system reliability. Production hardening checklists enable thorough error handling, token management, security sandboxing, audit logging, and rate limiting. The comprehensive evaluation framework for the capstone system revealed that autonomous agents may meet the performance thresholds required for real-world deployment, transforming experimental prototypes into enterprise-grade solutions.

The features studied in this chapter, including planner–executor architectures, autonomous task management, selfcorrection loops, multiagent orchestration, and quantitative evaluation, form the key primitives of the agentic era. As readers continue working with LangChain, these concepts will enable them to create systems that act purposefully, collaborate effectively, and operate dependably in realworld contexts. The agents constructed next will not only respond to instructions; they will plan, adapt, and execute with the rigor of a human team.

Path ahead

This book has provided the framework for constructing the next generation of intelligent software. Readers have learned to equip the agents with ears to listen through speech intelligence, a memory to learn from persistent context, and hands to act through autonomous tool execution.

The area of AI agents is evolving at an unparalleled rate. The patterns learned here, including LCEL, ReAct, GraphRAG, and multi-agent orchestration, serve as the fundamental building blocks of the agentic era. As readers move forward, continue to experiment with different models, investigate future multimodal capabilities, and always prioritize the safety and dependability of the systems being built. The journey with LangChain is only beginning; the agents that readers design today will shape how humans engage with technology in the future.

To access the entire source code, annotated notebooks, and capstone projects for these chapters, visit the official LangChain AI GitHub organization at **https://github.com/langchain-ai**. This organization provides the foundational framework and numerous dedicated repositories for autonomous agents and advanced reasoning patterns.

Essential GitHub repositories for this book

For the implementations discussed in *Chapter 11, Creating Autonomous Agents that Perform Real-World Tasks*, and *Chapter 12, Planning, Collaboration, and Evaluating Autonomous Agents*, the following repositories provide the foundational code and capstone blueprints:

- **LangChain Core** (**https://github.com/langchain-ai/langchain**): The primary platform for reliable agents. It contains the standard interfaces for tool calling, function definitions, and the AgentExecutor logic used in *Chapter 11, Creating Autonomous Agents that Perform Real-World Tasks*.

- **LangGraph** (**https://github.com/langchain-ai/langgraph**): This repository is critical for the capstone in *Chapter 12, Planning, Collaboration, and Evaluating Autonomous Agents*. It provides the low-level orchestration framework for building plan-and-execute agents and multi-agent teams.

- **DeepAgents** (**https://github.com/langchain-ai/deepagents**): A specialized agent harness built on LangChain and LangGraph. These agents are equipped with planning tools and can create subagents as needed.

- **NirDiamant GenAI Agents (https://github.com/NirDiamant/GenAI_Agents)**: A comprehensive community repository that provides tutorials for many specific agents, including memory-enhanced conversational agents.

Using the code samples

Readers can use the code samples as follows:

- **Clone the repository**: Use git clone to pull the project templates to the local machine.
- **Environment setup**: Each project includes a requirements.txt or pyproject.toml file. Use pip install to set up the environment.
- **API configuration**: Rename .env.example files to .env and add the OpenAI or Anthropic API keys.
- **Run annotated notebooks**: Most capstone projects are provided as Jupyter Notebooks (.ipynb), enabling users to step through the planning and execution logic interactively.

To continue learning and observing these systems in action, readers can explore the DeepAgents repository. It provides Docker Compose files to help set up secure, sandboxed environments for the autonomous agents.

Index

A

B

C

V

W

Z

www.ingramcontent.com/pod-product-compliance
Ingram Content Group UK Ltd.
Pitfield, Milton Keynes, MK11 3LW, UK
UKHW051117290926
15471UKWH00010B/1724

9 789378 544200